City of God

THE ANTHROPOLOGY OF CHRISTIANITY

Edited by Joel Robbins

City of God

CHRISTIAN CITIZENSHIP IN POSTWAR GUATEMALA

Kevin Lewis O'Neill

UNIVERSITY OF CALIFORNIA PRESS

BERKELEY LOS ANGELES LONDON

Dec 2009 hardback

University of California Press, one of the most
distinguished university presses in the United States,
enriches lives around the world by advancing scholarship
in the humanities, social sciences, and natural sciences. Its
activities are supported by the UC Press Foundation and
by philanthropic contributions from individuals and
institutions. For more information, visit
www.ucpress.edu.

University of California Press
Berkeley and Los Angeles, California

University of California Press, Ltd.
London, England

Library of Congress Cataloging-in-Publication Data

O'Neill, Kevin Lewis, 1977–.
    City of God : Christian citizenship in postwar
Guatemala / Kevin Lewis O'Neill.
        p.   cm.   (The anthropology of Christianity ; 7)
    Includes bibliographical references and index.
    ISBN 978-0-520-26062-7 (cloth : alk. paper)
    ISBN 978-0-520-26063-4 (pbk. : alk. paper)

    1. Evangelistic work—Guatemala—Guatemala.
2. Evangelistic work—Pentecostal churches.
3. Pentecostal churches—Missions—Guatemala—
Guatemala.   4. Christianity and politics—Guatemala—
Guatemala.   5. Guatemala (Guatemala)—Religion
I. Title.

BV3777.G9O54   2010
289.9'40972811—dc22   2009009152

Manufactured in the United States of America

18   17   16   15   14   13   12   11   10
10   9   8   7   6   5   4   3   2   1

This book is printed on Natures Book, which contains
30% post-consumer waste and meets the minimum
requirements of ANSI/NISO Z39.48–1992 (R 1997)
(*Permanence of Paper*).

CONTENTS

ACKNOWLEDGMENTS

This book has been made possible by the enormous emotional and spiritual generosity of the El Shaddai community. Though there are hundreds of congregants who found their way into the pages of this book, I will thank only two by name—the others must remain anonymous. The first is Dr. Harold Caballeros, a true scholar and political mind, for allowing me into his congregation. The second is Pastor Juan Carlos Abril, for helping me navigate the mega-church's dizzying complexity. Both church leaders did not need to open their community to the ethnographic gaze, but they did—and did so with the utmost confidence in me.

I am also grateful to the financial generosity of several institutions that allowed my research to progress in a timely fashion over the years: the Wenner-Gren Foundation, the Ford Foundation, the Stanford University Department of Cultural and Social Anthropology, the Stanford University School of Humanities and Sciences, Harvard Divinity School, the Harvard University Center for the Study of World Religions, the Harvard University David Rockefeller Center for Latin American Studies, Indiana University's Department of Religious Studies, the Indiana University American Studies Program, and the Indiana University New Frontiers in the Arts and Humanities Program.

The scholars who (knowingly or unknowingly) pointed me not only toward scholarship but also toward this particular study are numerous and begin with my undergraduate advisers at Fordham University. Special thanks go to Mark Massa, Thomas Kopfensteiner, and Susan Simonaitis, as well as to Luz Lenis. At Harvard University, Elisabeth Schüssler and Steven Caton both directed me toward cultural and social anthropology, and visiting professors Enrique Dussel and Merold Westphal reminded me that anthropology and philosophy are inseparable.

My conversation partners at Stanford University stoked my research. Most immediately, I thank my cohort. We have often been called "the monster cohort" because of the unusually large number of admits our year, but I often think that the "monstrous" dimension that we all share has much more to do with a commitment to bold anthropological analysis than mere numbers. Many thanks to Tania Ahmad, Stacey Camp, Mun Young Cho, Rachel Derkits, Oded Korczyn, Serena Love, Ramah McKay, Zhanara Nauruzbayeva, Erica Williams, and Thet Win. Others at Stanford who challenged me along the way in seminar settings or during informal conversations include Aaron Shaw, Austin Zeiderman, Nikhil Anand, Hannah Appel, Elif Babul, Robert Samet, Rania al Sweis, and Tomas Matza. I always found the Stanford Department of Cultural and Social Anthropology to be an exciting place, and, in many ways, these people made it so for me. At the same time, I would be remiss not to give a special thanks to Shelly Coughlin and Ellen Christensen, who genuinely made the department a home not just for me but for every student in the department.

I also benefited from a cluster of colleagues whom I came to know over the years—at conferences, in seminars, or while in the field. In the states, they include Ed Gallagher, Ludger Viefhues-Bailey, William Garriott, Peter Benson, Kedron Thomas, and Alex Hinton. In Guatemala, Didier Boremanse, Marco Tulio Martínez, Dennis Leder, Andrés Cifuentes, Rodrigo Véliz, Gustavo Solórzano, Estela Morales, Pedro Luis Avendaño Arenales, and Carolyn Baisi helped me immensely. My students at Universidad Rafael Landívar and Universidad del Valle also provided me with support and friendship. I am grateful to my students at Universidad del Valle for reading early drafts of my introduction, chapter 1, and chapter 3. Those students are María José Aldana, María Goubaud, Aida Bocock, María José Pérez , Luisa Fernanda, Bianca Espinoza, Rodrigo Véliz, Gaby Canek, Alessia Kossmehl Bolten, Beberly Leon, and Francisco Javier Martínez Melgar. Of this group, I am especially appreciative for those who helped me in the field: Rodrigo, Andrés, Javier, and Gaby, as well as Lucía Jiménez during the spring of 2008.

I presented portions of this book at a range of venues and I am indebted to the questions and comments I received at each presentation. I presented early drafts of chapters at Hamilton College's Department of Sociology, the Villanova University Department of Political Science, Indiana University at Bloomington's Department of Religious Studies, the University of Toronto Department of Religious Studies, the University of California at San Diego's Department of Anthropology, the annual meetings of the American Anthropological Association, the American Academy of Religion, the Midwest Political Science Association, and the American Ethnological Society, and graduate student conferences at Stanford University, Harvard University, Fordham University, and the New School for Social Research. Those who read one or more chapters, in some form, at some point, include Archana Sridhar, Bruce O'Neill, Aaron Shaw, Austin Zeiderman, Tomas Matza, Erica Williams, Mun Young Cho, Kathryn Lofton, and Natalia Roudakova. I am especially grateful to Natalia's students at the University of California, San Diego, where she taught (and had her students respond to) earlier versions of the introduction, chapter 3, and the conclusion.

New colleagues and students at Indiana University at Bloomington provided this book with important insights at some of the most critical moments. The Department of Religious Studies, especially the 2007 fall colloquium at which I presented an earlier version of chapter 2, inspired me to make the chapter something entirely different. The American Studies Program, directed by Matthew Guterl, provided a world of support and conversation. Kathryn Lofton provided an unbridled sense of excitement for the project as a whole and read several chapters and conference papers. Students in my courses "Christianity and Democracy" and "Religion and Violence" at Indiana University also read versions of chapters 1, 3, 4, and 6. Thank you.

It seems almost impossible to express just how grateful I am to my committee members, who consistently challenged me to clarify and extend my analysis. If scholarship follows the apprenticeship model of old, I am grateful for having studied under James Ferguson—a generous and true scholar whose ethics and analytical clarity are stunning. I am certain that this book would have been something less without his guidance, and my proficiency as a scholar would have been something entirely different. Thank you. I am also thankful to Liisa Malkki for my e-mail correspondence with her while in the field. Her notes always seemed to come at a moment when the extraordinary was becoming ordinary, reminding me that everything can be seen anew from a different perspective. My work with Carol A. Smith provided me with priceless area studies support as well as a conversation partner about the state of Guatemala. Her sincere commitment to the country as well as to Latin America has always reminded me that one can never really leave Guatemala; it always seems to call one back. Finally, the first graduate course I ever took at Harvard was entitled "Theories of Religion: From Max Mueller to Catherine Bell," and it was with great persistence that I finally convinced Catherine Bell to sit on my committee. Her insights were invaluable and often delivered in spite of extraordinary obstacles. Her generosity and kindness astound me, and her early passing saddens me deeply. A great mind and a gifted mentor: I will always miss her.

Joel Robbins, series editor, deserves a great deal of credit for believing in this book as well as stewarding its production with a strong sense of professionalism and intellectual pride not just in the series but also in my work. I would also like to thank the University of California Press for selecting such capable and thoughtful readers. For me, it was an absolute pleasure to receive comments from readers who clearly engaged with my manuscript openly but also critically, producing suggestions and observations that helped clarify my arguments and advance the manuscript toward publication. The manuscript is a decidedly stronger contribution because of this process. I also wish to thank Stan Holwitz of the University of California Press for his support and wisdom during the process, and Nick Arrivo for his patience and professionalism during production. Caroline Knapp of the University of California Press also deserves a great deal of credit for managing this book's production. Ann Twombly also provided an impressive copyedit at an important stage of production and so did Shruti Krishnan of Indiana University.

My in-laws, Mojundar and Usha Sridhar, also deserve thanks for their unrelenting support for a career that is not the most intuitive at times. My parents, Bruce and Mary O'Neill, also warrant great recognition and thanks for their patience and support during my graduate career and for their boundless enthusiasm. I would also like to give my brother, Bruce, special thanks—for providing an anthropologically informed sounding board for this study, a close read of every page printed here, and true friendship. At the same time, Bruce was one of those few people who listened to the unedited griping of an ethnographer in the field. I look forward to repaying the debt and to seeing his work unfold in what promises to be exciting ways.

Finally, I wish to thank, as well as to dedicate, my research and this book to my wife, Archana Sridhar, who has been not only supportive of my research but also genuinely curious about what I study, asking critical question upon critical question. Archana has read and edited every single page of this manuscript several times, and she has also influenced its very content—pushing me to be clear, concise, and creative. Her own research on tax reform in Guatemala as a U.S. student Fulbright scholar overlapped with my time in the field, which provided me with valuable State Department resources as well as the comfort of having my partner in the field with me. Life in Guatemala was not easy, but it was good, and we will always have that.

PREFACE

"Excuse me?" I asked the question with some surprise. Caught off-guard, I could feel my face turning pink and my hairline beginning to sweat. Carlota, a *pastora* and the woman leading this particular "cell," or Christian support group, asked again, "Kevin, why don't you give the closing prayer tonight?" As all eyes turned to the once-silent observer and now-awkward participant, I scrambled to think of what I could possibly say that might be salient to the group of ten neo-Pentecostals huddled around a Guatemala City kitchen table, and yet would acknowledge that we do not share a common theology. Trying desperately to synthesize the material I had heard over the last few hours as well as the reams of sermons, interviews, prayers, radio broadcasts, and cassette recordings that I had combed through up to that point, I squeaked out a spiritually tone-deaf prayer that left the group dissatisfied with both quality and quantity. Carlota was not happy. As she sighed, I fished a tissue from my back pocket to mop my brow. "Kevin, I know you have a plan. You're investigating how the mega-churches are changing the culture of Guatemala." Carlota's understanding of my research project was reassuring, but her tone was not. As she spoke to the group, her eyes lingered on me from time to time for effect. She encouraged us to be engaged in our prayer lives—unlike how I had performed—and to feel the weight of what the cell was trying to do:

to *save* Guatemala. She ended her meditation with a reminder that could also be read as a mandate: "We have a lot of work to do."

Based on nearly two years of fieldwork, this book assesses ethnographically this kind of work and the moral responsibility that it ascribes to neo-Pentecostals in postwar Guatemala City.[1] Of particular interest is how this effort at saving Guatemala takes place not only at the intersection of neo-Pentecostal Christianity and efforts at democratization, but also in the name of Christian citizenship. I develop the term *Christian citizenship* as an observable category throughout this book, but it is important to note as early as possible that my informants also use the phrase to describe their Christian efforts in behalf of Guatemala. The term (*el ciudadano cristiano*) is both an analytical and a folk category.[2] Neo-Pentecostals such as Carlota work feverishly to combat the problems of postwar Guatemala City, of which there are many, not simply as citizens motivated by their Christianity but also as citizens who consciously work *through* their Christianity. As this book details, a growing number of Guatemalans define and perform their citizenship through neo-Pentecostal practices. They pray for reduced levels of crime; they fast for less political corruption; and they sermonize on the service of self to the nation. My botched efforts at prayer frustrated Carlota not just because I proved to her (yet again) to be either an unwilling participant or a totally inept Christian, but also because I flubbed an opportunity to do something for Guatemala. With so much work to do, every little prayer counts.

The idea of neo-Pentecostals enacting their citizenship through Christian practices is, to be sure, unexpected, even disorienting, but I am confident that this book makes the case that Christian citizenship is an ethnographic fact—is something lived by millions of believers in and beyond Guatemala City. Significant for these preliminary comments, however, is the fact that Christian citizenship was an unanticipated object of study for me. This book emerges from the rather common ethnographic experience of having expected to find one thing while in the field but in the end having come across something entirely different. The rub was that government documents and civil society position papers prepared me to accept as fact the idea that Guatemalans are incredibly inactive citizens: low voter turnout, record levels of tax evasion, and sluggish volunteerism.[3] Well after the signing of the 1996 Peace Accords, which formally ended Central America's longest and bloodiest civil war, I came to Guatemala certain that inactive citizenship further complicated otherwise anemic efforts at democratization—and that new forms of Christianity, such as neo-Pentecostalism, with its otherworldly concerns, dabbled at the margins of postwar politics.

As it turned out, only half of my preconceptions were true, which is, of course, the enduring power of ethnographic analysis: the ability to upset common assumptions through an extended engagement. What was true, and sadly remains true, is that citizenship in Guatemala is half-made at best. The introduction to this book and subsequent chapters will recount how Guatemala's incredible ethnolinguistic diversity combines with violent histories of colonialism, liberalism, genocide, and now postwar efforts at economic restructuring in ways that make a shared sense of national belonging and responsibility a continued (and deeply painful) project for all. At its most basic, this book narrates valiant but otherwise inchoate efforts at making citizenship amid stunningly difficult conditions.[4]

What was not true, what I never could have expected, was the unavoidable observation that neo-Pentecostals do not "dabble at the margins" of democracy; nor are they inactive. Neo-Pentecostalism represents one of Guatemala's most sophisticated efforts at making citizenship in postwar Guatemala. Mega-churches, for example, have placed themselves at the very heart of Guatemalan democratization in ways that go well beyond electoral politics.[5] These churches provide an increasing number of Guatemalans with an ethics of personhood that contributes to the formation of Christian citizenship as a way of life. Moreover, my research made me confront something that only extended ethnographic research can substantiate: some of postwar Guatemala's most active citizens, for better or for worse, are neo-Pentecostals. Carlota's cell group is just the tip of a confessional iceberg that comprises Sunday services, reflection groups, praise and healing sessions, prayer and fast campaigns, journal entries, moral manuals, and testimonies that expose the shadowy corners of the broken and fallen self. In short, I simply cannot imagine more active citizens than those I came to know during my time in Guatemala. Neo-Pentecostals are the self-regulating subjects that postwar Guatemala has long sought, which is a statement that I make with a sense of both respect and suspicion.

My ambivalence aside, at least for now, one exciting part of this research is its ability to account for what Christians really *do* as citizens of a burgeoning democracy. The focus here is not on what Christians say they do, and not on what pastors tell Christians to do (or not to do), but rather on what Christian citizens actually do daily for both Christ and country. The focus throughout this book is on action. This is significant at the most empirical level because social scientists actually know very little about what Christians do as citizens beyond anecdotal examples of believers running for office and statistically constructed composite characters that vote one way instead of another.[6] This, again, is the gift of ethnography; though slow and, at times, frustratingly plodding, the method brings to clearer relief the sometimes fuzzy conclusions made from the archives, statistical analyses, or more comparative projects.

The problem, however, is that many are sure to be surprised to learn what neo-Pentecostals do as Christian citizens in postwar Guatemala City. Neo-Pentecostal formations of Christian citizenship result in practices and performances that are far afield from what the political scientist would recognize as active citizenship. Christian citizens cultivate candidates for elected office, and they also discuss how Christians should vote; but they do so only a fraction of the time. I would estimate that less than 1 percent of my own audio archives contain formal interviews, informal conversations, and public sermons that address these more expected examples of citizenship participation. Christian citizens in Guatemala, I found, are more likely to pray for Guatemala than pay their taxes; they tend to speak in tongues for the soul of the nation rather than vote in general elections; and they more often than not organize prayer campaigns to fight crime rather than organize their communities against the same threat. This is all to say that a study of neo-Pentecostal voting tendencies in Guatemala would be interesting and, I think, valuable; but, from an ethnographic perspective, it would also be an exercise in underreporting to an almost perverted extent.[7] Christian citizens do a great deal, but they do things that ultimately frustrate Western, ostensibly secular, and deeply liberal expectations of what it means to participate as a citizen of an emerging democracy. I reflect on this kind of disappointment in this book's conclusion—not to make the otherwise flat critique that Christian citizens are somehow disappointing (because, in the end, they really are not), but rather to suggest that citizenship itself proves (time and time again) to be a complete disappointment.

The ultimate charge, then, is for this book to make the difficult (but surely not impossible) case that neo-Pentecostals are actually doing things as Christian citizens—that their efforts at prayer, fasting, and exorcisms have an effect not just on the individual but also on Guatemalan society and its struggling democracy. As the book makes clear, the argument will not be that prayer works in some theological sense, but rather that prayer (along with a litany of other Christian practices) is a potent kind of cultural work that produces a sense of self, which believers learn to govern for the sake of Guatemala as Christian citizens. Yet the challenge of this entire project (again) is to demonstrate how and why this cultural work matters to postwar Guatemala as well as to those concerned with religion's continued entanglement with politics; it is a challenge that in many ways begins with putting into context what was at stake in my failed attempt at prayer, as well as what Carlota did next.

Before dismissing the cell for the evening, Carlota asked if we could all pray for my research. As awkward became uncomfortable, I soon found that several cell members were laying their hands on me, praying that my research would not just go smoothly but be inspired. In this moment I asked myself what I expect all ethnographers must ask themselves from time to time while in the field: "What am I doing here?" Yet at that very moment I realized that my question is the same one that neo-Pentecostals ask themselves daily. Believers, this book demonstrates, are taught how to keep their thoughts, actions, habits, and character aimed at a goal that is clearly outlined during Sunday morning sermons. As the pastor of a prominent neo-Pentecostal mega-church announced: "We understand [God's] cultural mandate as the construction of a city, as the construction of a society. What city? The city of God."[8] Making the city of God begins in gaping church structures as well as in small group settings; making Guatemala anew begins with individual believers taking on the responsibility to govern themselves for the greater glory of God and Guatemala. Saving Guatemala, building the city of God brick by brick, starts with taking up what I describe in the introduction as the weight of Christian citizenship.

THE FIELDWORK

This is an ethnography rather than a formal history or a comparative project, which means (at least for this study) an emphasis on the everyday—on daily lives and activities, practices and performances, opinions and emotions. Almost nothing I observed proved irrelevant. Included within this study's critical frame, for example, are the faithful who would prostrate themselves to oversized maps of the world, howling to Christ for the soul of their nation; women who would roll their eyes as their husbands outlined a kind of domestic politics that seemed to make them insignificant; and children who generally seemed unfazed at the idea that the devil haunts Guatemala City and that it would one day be their responsibility to fight him. It is a robust approach that I cultivated across four social fields.[9] The first was Guatemala City's neo-Pentecostal mega-churches. Sunday services, weekly healing and prayer sessions, and an assortment of other church activities allowed me to observe the bustle of these well-organized but otherwise overworked hotbeds of activity, as well as to understand how mega-churches indoctrinate their congregants as Christian citizens. El Shaddai, one of Guatemala City's most prominent mega-churches, served as my primary site, which I complemented with a sustained research interest in other mega-churches.[10]

El Shaddai begins with grandeur; it is a worldwide congregation with 12,000 members in the capital city alone, and its central church holds up to 6,000 participants. Shaped more like a soccer stadium than a house of worship, the structure is equipped with movie theater–quality seats and top-of-the-line audio and video equipment. And more than eighty El Shaddai–incorporated satellite churches dot the Guatemalan countryside, from Chiquimula to Chimaltenango, as well as the Americas, from Bogotá to Boston, all connected via the Internet and radio stations. Weekly services use contemporary Christian music to excite large crowds, which guides the participants through emotional peaks and valleys. Upbeat songs electrify the congregation; sad melodies slow the pace of the service, bringing many to tears. The main church structure also houses a small café, a twenty-four-hour ATM and a bookstore with thousands of taped sermons for sale as well as Spanish translations of well-known titles by pastors around the world. As an almost comical gesture to scale, a swimming pool serves as the church's baptismal well.

Historically upper middle class and nonindigenous, or *ladino/a,* the El Shaddai congregation embodies what critics have come to call the Gospel of health and wealth.[11] The church's emphasis on healings and material prosperity through living a good Christian life mixes with a deeply nationalized rhetoric of salvation that ultimately generates a peculiar sense of Christian citizenship. I write that the El Shaddai congregation has been "historically upper middle class and . . . *ladino/a*" because the church, like so many of Guatemala City's mega-churches, is quickly becoming an ecclesiastical representation of its country's diversity. Seen as sites of inspiration and upward mobility as well as salvation and sanctification, mega-churches attract those with money, but they also draw men and women, young and old, who seek a better life. Within the El Shaddai congregation are, to be sure, hardworking ladino/a professionals trying to maintain a comfortable lifestyle amid a troubled postwar economy. But the church also ministers to poor indigenous families who attend the main church in Guatemala City as well as much smaller El Shaddai churches in the rural interior. Given that many of El Shaddai's satellite churches in the United States minister to undocumented Guatemalans, the congregation's actual demographic composition often can be disguised by the mega-church's surface appearance. Its congregants appear sophisticated, skilled, and solvent at first glance, but the life stories of those who attend—those who sometimes participate the most enthusiastically as Christian citizens—reveal worlds that are far less privileged than the one implied by the church's sleek veneer.

Driving this appearance as well as its mission is Dr. Harold Caballeros, El Shaddai's founding pastor. Since 1983 Dr. Caballeros has cultivated the El Shaddai church, from a few family members to a multinational neo-Pentecostal empire. Along the way he has developed his proficiency in two registers: neo-Pentecostal theology and international affairs. He was trained as a lawyer at the notoriously conservative Guatemalan Universidad Francisco Marroquín, and his résumé is impressive by any standard. Dr. Caballeros holds a doctorate in theology from a North American seminary and a masters degree from the Fletcher School of Law and Diplomacy of Tufts University. He also completed postgraduate work at Harvard University's Weatherhead Center for International Affairs. Frequently quoted by the Guatemalan press, Dr. Caballeros has also been mentioned in articles in the *Wall Street Journal* and the *Economist* for his very public role in advocating neo-Pentecostalism as a vehicle for development.[12] His own campaign for presidency in 2007 not only developed his political persona but also overlapped with my own time in the field, bringing to relief for me what congregants actually do as Christian citizens in a democratizing context.

The second social field was El Shaddai's weekly cells, such as Carlota's. Comprising between five and sixteen congregants, these cells meet weekly in informal settings (homes and eateries, for example) and provide opportunities for believers to reflect on their place in this world as well as the next. If my fieldwork in mega-churches allowed me to approximate the sometimes oceanic dimensions of these ecclesiastical structures, then my work in cells enabled me to glimpse the emotional texture of how individuals wrestle with questions of morality and belonging. During my time in Guatemala I visited dozens of cells but attended four regularly, each for at least eight months. There were more than five hundred in the capital city alone, and I chose these four cells carefully, making sure that they contrasted in regard to gender, class, and ethnicity. The contrast among them proved productive, allowing me to understand the cellular production of Christian citizenship across a range of social milieus.[13]

One cell gathered each week in Zone 2, a solidly middle-class section of Guatemala City. This group of middle-aged ladina women provided me with a perspective not just on motherhood and proper social etiquette but also on the place of women in the neo-Pentecostal imagination. The wisdom I gained from this cell can be felt in several of the following chapters. Another cell, made up of young, indigenous men and women, met in a depressed section of the otherwise middle-class Zone 5. As several of the cell members negotiated family structures that stretched well beyond the Guatemalan-Mexican border and into the migrant labor pools of central California, my time with these believers further contextualized the promise of upward mobility and citizenship participation that mega-churches provide the faithful. A third cell congregated in Zone 11, an upper-middle-class residential area. This cell was exclusively ladino/a and organized for married couples; its members held prominent roles in the church community and felt at liberty to speak authoritatively about the church's place in Guatemalan politics and culture. The fourth and final cell gathered once a week in Guatemala City's business district, Zone 10, where we met after-hours in a dentist's office. There, young professionals convened from across the city to discuss how their futures were interrelated with Guatemala's. Taken together, these cells provided me with thousands of hours of informal conversations about faith and the formation of Christian citizenship as well as hundreds more hours of discussion of the miscellaneous happenings that constitute any given life. In a sense, cells allowed me to observe how Guatemalans of faith make their citizenship through their Christianity in the most mundane ways.

The third field was textual. Neo-Pentecostal mega-churches communicate their vision of Christian citizenship through a plethora of media outlets: audio- and videocassettes, popular music, Internet sites, and radio and television programming, for example. The church's stunning level of production makes Susan Harding's observations about Jerry Falwell's ministry eerily appropriate to the Guatemalan context. Like Falwell's ministry, El Shaddai proved to be "a factory of words, a veritable Bible-based language industry . . . [and], in effect, a hive of workshops, of sites of cultural production, that smelted, shaped, packaged, and distributed myriad fundamentalist rhetorics and narratives" (2000, 15). It was often Harding's industrial metaphors that resonated with me most; El Shaddai's audio and video team (AV), for example, records every public sermon. Impressive about this practice is not just the growing archive that this compulsion generates, but also the fact that the AV team duplicates each sermon hundreds of times only moments after each sermon has been delivered. Their rush provides excited churchgoers with the opportunity to purchase a cassette copy of that day's talk. Remarkable, for me, was to sit with these machines at the tail end of Sunday service and listen to the whiz of the equipment, the hum of cassettes being made dozens at a time. In these moments of mechanical reproduction, I often thought about Harding's language of "smelting" and "shaping" and how it once seemed hyperbolic, bloated to make a much simpler point, only to appear later to undersell the materiality of this production, the blunt physicality of tape rubbing against plastic at unimaginable speeds, all for the sake of evangelization.

This kind of mass production is significant because Guatemalan nationalism has historically been interrelated with Roman Catholicism—with public sermons and processions that formed a sense of Guatemalan identity alongside the Church. Ever since the early nineteenth century, the Roman Catholic Church has played a significant role in the formation of Guatemala as a modern nation-state through theologies that positioned the country as a chosen nation.[14] Mega-churches' textual production of Christian citizenship, however, marks the emergence of a new vocabulary for national belonging. It is a narrative worth listening to, but given the vast amount of materials available, I could never have digested the entire archive. Instead, I allowed the most powerful and popular texts to find me by way of key informants ("You just need to read this book!" "This cassette changed my life." "Have you used this moral manual yet?"). From this still-impressive amount of material I then selected a sample of cassettes and books for intensive analysis, allowing my informants to influence my reading.[15]

The fourth field sought contrast. I interviewed Catholic clergy, civil society leaders, political party representatives, government workers, and Maya activists. Catholic clergy provided my research with a critical assessment of mega-churches from a competing religious perspective. Political party representatives, civil society leaders, and government workers allowed me to judge the similarities and differences that exist between neo-Pentecostal constructions of citizenship and mainstream political formations of postwar Guatemalan citizenship. At the same time, Maya activists offered my study a different language for political engagement that was based on ethnic differences rather than a single "brotherhood in Christ." Beyond these formal attempts at collecting contrasting perspectives, I also absorbed unsolicited opinions and, at times, diatribes from acquaintances, friends, colleagues, fellow commuters, members of smaller Pentecostal churches, and taxi drivers. These residents of Guatemala City spoke about mega-churches and their credibility—or lack thereof—as religious and politically influential institutions.

CONTRIBUTION

This book is first and foremost a study of neo-Pentecostal formations of Christian citizenship in postwar Guatemala City and the kind of responsibilities that such an identity prompts Guatemalans to shoulder; yet several other intellectual concerns have guided this project. The first is the study of citizenship and my continued surprise that this growing field has not yet addressed the issue of Christianity in any significant way. In fact, for a field whose continual points of departure have been such Christian themes as "belonging," "responsibility," and "stewardship," and whose current conceptual framing gives priority to transnational processes and globalization's cultural complexities, astoundingly little has been written in citizenship studies about Christianity.[16] This is particularly surprising given that the problem of citizenship has been present from the very beginning of Christianity and that citizenship has forever existed as an aspect of the religion's cultural content.[17] As I detail in the introduction, some of Christianity's most foundational thinkers have written at great length about citizenship's theological problems and possibilities, and Western thought's most canonical intellectuals have grappled with Christianity and citizenship's fretted relationship. This analytical oversight is also astonishing since democracy, or at least the rhetoric of democracy, continues to gain momentum alongside the evangelization of non-Western locales the world over. Guatemala is just one example among many. This book, in response, demonstrates how scholars of citizenship might begin to think about Christianity and, more important, about the formation of Christian citizenship not just in Guatemala but throughout Latin America, Asia, and Africa, as well as the United States.

The second concern is the anthropology of Christianity. Although studies of Christianity are scattered throughout the anthropological literature, there is only now a growing sense among the authors of a shared intellectual purpose. That is, no scholarly community has developed fully around the anthropology of Christianity that is comparable to the one that has emerged in the case of the anthropology of Islam. Establishing such a community is essential as anthropologists struggle to make sense of this worldwide awakening. This book joins a growing number of works in the formation of, to use Joel Robbins's words, an anthropology of Christianity *for itself* rather than *in itself* (Robbins 2003).[18] The anthropology of Christianity *in itself* refers simply to any anthropological study in which Christianity is taken as an object of analysis, whereas an anthropology of Christianity *for itself* refers to a more self-conscious enterprise, one in which "people working in different geographic areas publish in the same fora, read one another's work, recognize the relevance of that work for their own projects, and seek to develop a set of shared questions to be examined comparatively" (Robbins 2003, 192). Christian citizenship is one such theme that invites comparison. Citizenship exists as a part of Christianity's theological and cultural heritage, but what it means to be a citizen continues to change in and beyond Christian communities. Thus, examining formations of Christian citizenship opens avenues of research that advance the kind of comparative approach advocated by an anthropology of Christianity *for itself.*

The third consideration is the anthropology of Guatemala City. Recent years have witnessed a growing interest in the ethnographic analysis of urban Latin America and postwar Guatemala. Yet these two lines of scholarship have been kept separate, which has resulted in a dearth of research on Guatemala City itself. The ethnographic attention given to Latin American cities arises in part from the region's rapid urbanization over the last three decades. An estimated 80 percent of Latin America's population now lives in urban areas (UNFPA 1999). At the same time, studies of postwar Guatemala build on a century's worth of ethnographic material as well as an astute awareness of the country's civil war. The problem, however, is that there still does not exist enough social scientific information to compare Guatemala City with cities similar in size (Gellert 1995, xi). Some notable efforts to correct this inadequacy include the work of Bryan Roberts (1973), Deborah Levenson-Estrada (1994), Santiago Bastos (2000), Manuela Camus (2002), and Thomas Offit (2008). This book joins the work of these scholars in making clear that Guatemala City is an especially productive site for ethnographic investigation while also highlighting the fact that the theorization of the city remains troublingly incomplete. One of this book's more ambitious projects is to make Guatemala City relevant not simply to other scholars of Guatemala but also those working in other parts of Latin America and beyond.

The fourth concern is religious studies' continued rapprochement with the work of Michel Foucault. Though Foucault's concepts, such as power and discourse, have been eagerly employed over the last twenty years by scholars of Christianity with a fervor that at times approaches hagiography, the vast majority of this scholarship has drawn on Foucault's earlier work, namely *The Order of Things* (1971), *The Birth of the Clinic* (1973), and *Discipline and Punish* (1977). Though those can be productive, this study initiates a more robust examination of Foucault's later work, especially the concept of governmentality and its relationship to the pastoral (Foucault 1991). This analytical turn toward questions of governmentality explains not only my analysis but also my citational practices. I draw heavily from two seminal volumes, *The Foucault Effect: Studies in Governmentality* (Burchell et al. 1991) and *Foucault and Political Reason: Liberalism, Neo-Liberalism, and Rationalities of Government* (Barry et al. 1996), as well as from the work of Nikolas Rose (1990, 1996a, 1996b, 2007), Peter Miller (1990), Pat O'Malley (1992, 1996, 2004), Mariana Valverde (1998), Barbara Cruikshank (1999), and Patrick Joyce (2003). Because of the study of religion's growing interest in qualitative research methods, the hope is that scholars of Christianity will continue to find increasing opportunities to lend a critical eye to "the humble and mundane mechanisms by which authorities seek to instantiate government" (Rose and Miller 1992, 183). When they do, scholars of Christianity will find that the pastoral as a mode of governance is alive and well today within the very religious fields in which the pastoral itself originated.

The fifth concern is the anthropology of neoliberalism. Though the relationship between economic restructuring and democracy continues to receive increased attention, neo-Pentecostal Christianity's worldwide development has not yet been connected fully to the culture of free trade, privatization, and decentralization in a sustained way. A separate, book-length study is needed on how neo-Pentecostal Christianity provides a cultural register for the kind of individual responsibility that structural adjustment seems to demand, but this book provides scholars of neoliberalism with opportunities to find points of critical correlation between the anthropology of Christianity and the anthropology of neoliberalism—to understand how faith mingles with the retreat of state services and a marked decline in protections from market fluctuations, structural inequalities, crime, and violence.

THE BOOK

The organization of this book reflects these concerns. The introduction presents the book's major arguments and theoretical commitments while also delivering a number of preliminary remarks about Christianity, nationalism, democracy, and citizenship in and beyond postwar

Guatemala. Chapter 1 is an exercise in contrast and context. It notes that Guatemala has experienced a tremendous degree of change over the last thirty years and that a range of civil society organizations now promote citizenship as a means to manage transitional times. By presenting portraits of three citizenship campaigns (one from the municipal government, one from a secular civil society organization, and one from a neo-Pentecostal mega-church), the chapter demonstrates how the promise of citizenship in postwar Guatemala promotes a kind of participation that places the responsibility for developing the nation on the individual shoulders of each citizen.

Chapters 2–5 explore different modes of Christian citizenship, each playing on more traditional forms of participation to make the overall argument that Christian citizens are active in postwar politics but in ways that make strange conventional conceptions of political involvement. Chapter 2 addresses the practice of community policing and how this otherwise mainstream form of citizenship participation takes place in church-organized support groups rather than in the streets. Within these intimate spaces of belonging, believers learn how their thoughts and attitudes exist as interrelated with the fate of their nation and, thus, how to police their interior worlds for the sake of postwar Guatemala. Chapter 3 speaks to democracy's long-held tradition of the citizen-soldier: the idea that if citizens want the rights and liberties that come with living in a free society, they must also share the duties of defending that society. Neo-Pentecostals routinely defend postwar Guatemala but do so through the practice of spiritual warfare—a biblical metaphor for the Christian life that has since lost its moorings. As Christian citizen-soldiers, neo-Pentecostals understand themselves as fighting Satan every day in their prayer lives for the soul of Guatemala City. "The founding fathers" as a democratic cliché drives chapter 4. With an eye to gender and kinship, the chapter notes that Guatemalan neo-Pentecostals understand the father, not the mother, as responsible for transmitting moral values to their children, which places the moral responsibility on fathers to make Christian citizens for a new generation. Chapter 5 explores the politics of volunteerism by way of El Shaddai's philanthropic wing, Manos de Amor, or Hands of Love. This organization provides social services to indigenous communities throughout the Guatemalan highlands, but not in the capital. In an ethnically diverse capital city, where much of the population lives in poverty, it is not clear why one needs to leave the city to do this kind of work. The chapter examines the decision to help "there" rather than "here," tracing the church's moral construction of indigenousness and poverty alongside its conceptualization of city as opposed to country.

Chapter 6 glimpses the international dimensions of the neo-Pentecostal mega-church, exploring how El Shaddai's construction of Guatemala as a city of God involves a larger vision of world change. Complemented by fieldwork in Chicago, the chapter focuses on an ethnographic account of El Shaddai's 2006 World Evangelical Council—a weeklong series of meetings that brought church leadership from around the world to Guatemala City to speak on the state of neo-Pentecostal Christianity. The conclusion, "Disappointment," reflects on the promise of citizenship in and beyond post-war Guatemala, with particular interest in citizens' tendency to disappoint—to leave Western, secular critics scratching their heads and wondering why citizens can never seem to get it right. In response, this book flips this critique: the conclusion maintains an enduring sense of disappointment but shifts such affect away from citizens and toward citizenship.

ARE YOU A CHRISTIAN?

Anthropologists of Christianity quickly realize how often they must give an account of themselves—both to colleagues and to informants. Openness to this confessional practice, at least with fellow anthropologists, certainly builds from the discipline's own literary turn and its now commonplace move to disclose one's own place in one's own study.[19] Yet the anthropological study of Christianity is particularly beguiling, demanding from the anthropologist something a little more testimonial. As I mention often in passing, not in this book but among peers, and with much more flippancy than grumpiness, no one ever asks my colleagues who study poverty whether they are poor, though I am asked often, and with much seriousness, to outline the bounds of my faith. My informants, with possibly more understandable need to know where I stand, follow suit, asking me often: Are you a Christian? The question, answered repeatedly by anthropologists of Christianity in the conference setting and in the field, is worth some reflection.

Epistemologically, this curiosity has much to do with Christianity itself and how the religion upsets a long-held anthropological dichotomy between the familiar and the strange (Garriott and O'Neill 2008). The anthropologist of religion's usual tack, Clifford Geertz argues, is to begin with "our own, more or less unexamined, everyday sense" of religion and then to contrast the familiar with the strange, finding along the way a "family-resemblance" between our conception of religion and "those whose life-ways we are trying to portray" (2005, 5). Yet Christianity troubles this project since Christians are neither familiar nor strange to the Western anthropologist. Joel Robbins writes, "Neither real others nor real comrades, Christians wherever they are found make anthropologists recoil by unsettling the fundamental schemes by which the discipline organizes the world into the familiar and the foreign" (2003, 197). In a similar vein, noting Susan Harding's (1991) characterization of Christians as "repugnant cultural others," Fenella Cannell (with echoes of Hegel) addresses Christianity as "the impossible religion," explaining that Christianity "has seemed at once the most tediously familiar and the most threatening of the religious traditions for a social science" (2006, 30). Webb Keane similarly announces that "Christianity . . . lurks as the suppressed core of much of what goes under the name Western culture" (2006, 308). The very nature of Christianity can make difficult (maybe even sloppy) the ethnographic project because of its frustrating familiarity. Cannell writes, "Despite the existence of distinguished ethnographies on Christian areas there has been a tendency to avoid or under-theorize the subject of Christianity or to assume that its meanings are 'obvious' because they are part of the culture from which anthropologists themselves are largely drawn" (2005, 340). Likewise, Matthew Engelke, during a thoughtful analysis of Christian belief and method, writes on the problematic role of Christianity in the history of anthropological thought. Dealing specifically with the work of Victor Turner and E. E. Evans-Pritchard (both converts to Roman Catholicism), Engelke states: "But when we read [the work of Turner and Evans-Pritchard] we should take note of the moments when they slipped out of a clearly professional frame and treated such considerations as a mixture of personal and intellectual challenges—when [Christian] belief, in other words, became method" (2002, 6). Engelke spots a guiding epistemological anxiety; it is, simply put, that anthropologists can be too familiar with Christianity and that Christianity is too much a part of Western formations of the secular (Asad 2003). The ultimate concern is that anthropologists of Christianity will treat belief as method, that they will leave assumptions unquestioned and lines of analysis unexplored.

The practice of fieldwork, at least in my own experience, often displaces this anthropological anxiety with the Christian's own interest in the quality of the anthropologist's faith. My informants would speculate aloud: If Christian, then *how* Christian is he? If not Christian, then how can we convert him? The questions invoke Keane's observation that "most Christians surely claim at least some kind of commonality with other Christians, even if only far enough to assert that others have got it wrong and should know better" (2007, 40). This Christian tendency to assert that "others have got it wrong" and that others "should know better" is alive and well within the Guatemalan context. One recent dissertation for a doctorate of ministry from Southeastern Baptist Theological Seminary in the United States demonstrates this debate to a somewhat amusing extent.

In his opening chapter, Roger W. Grossmann explains that "Guatemala has enjoyed an explosive numerical growth of evangelicals since the early 1960s," but that "polling data" do "not explain the nature and health of the church" (2002, 1–2). The Church, Grossman later announces, is unhealthy. In a subsection entitled "Crisis: Most Guatemalan Evangelicals Are Not Christian," Grossmann writes that "based upon statistical analysis . . . 36.3% of evangelicals have excellent Bible doctrine, 8.7% of evangelicals have good Bible doctrine, 38.1% of evangelicals have poor Bible doctrine, 16.9% of evangelicals have non-Christian doctrine" (2002, 182). Grossmann concludes: "In the race to evangelize and bring more into the fold, the Guatemalan church has done a poor job of producing disciples of Christ, not to mention making real Christians" (2002, 185). There are Christians in Guatemala, Grossman essentially argues, but the quality of the Christianity is not what people once thought.

Ethnographically, the distinctions made among Guatemalan Christian communities are as dismissive as Grossman's narrative but much less dependent on statistical work. There exists a constant debate about who is (and who is not) a Christian that naturally envelops the anthropologist. As I quickly learned during the course of my fieldwork, one is either a Christian (*cristiano*) or a Roman Catholic (*católico*) in Guatemala, and by *Christian* one usually means charismatic or Pentecostal Protestant. This initially created problems, or at the very least misunderstandings, given that I would answer "yes" when asked if I was a Christian. During those first forays into this project, I would answer "yes" in something of a North American demographic sense—in a way that communicated (apparently only to me) that I am a Christian, but that my wife is Hindu and that I have friends who are Jewish. It was a "world religions" approach that failed to recognize nuance. These were the missteps of a novice ethnographer, given that I am not so much *cristiano* as *católico* (but only in a cultural sense).[20]

Anthropologists of Christianity often find themselves at the intersection of two anxieties. The colleague, in the professional setting, tends to wonder whether the anthropologist is faithful (and how such faith might obscure his or her findings), while the informant wonders if the anthropologist is Christian (and whether he or she is Christian enough). It is actually amid this anxiety that I can say in no uncertain terms that my own informants worked hard to convert me, joking with me on occasion about my "pagan" (i.e., Roman Catholic) childhood. These efforts at conversion took the form of long conversations about the state of my soul as well as my family; awkward interventions that included numerous offers of impromptu baptisms in nearby showers and utility buckets; and gentle encouragements to welcome the Holy Spirit into my heart at every turn during my research stay. I politely declined each offer, hoping that my unwillingness to convert would not create a distance between me and my informants. To my surprise, the opposite occurred—the more I politely declined offers of salvation, the more engaged my informants became in my research. They wondered how someone could ask such probing questions about neo-Pentecostal Christianity and spend so much time at the church if he was not actually on the verge of conversion. My research, then, may have appeared as flirting with faith; but, to their credit, my informants' logic of conversion holds that only God knows the time of salvation, and that salvation is always a possibility—even for the most skeptical. To this, my informants and I could only smile at each other and say, "Not yet," or "Not today." It is an ambivalent answer that surely satisfies neither the Christian nor the anthropologist.

City of God

An Introduction

But our citizenship is in heaven, And it is from there that we are
expecting a Savior, the Lord Jesus Christ.

PHILIPPIANS 3:20

[Christians] pass their time upon the earth, but they have their
citizenship in heaven.

EPISTLE TO DIOGNETUS

I COULD MAKE OUT JULIO's skeleton. His ocular cavities were slightly
more pronounced than usual and his cheekbones were no longer padded
by fat. Julio was literally starving. The emptiness of his belly mixed with
fatigue and weakness to produce a rather dramatic sight that did not distract me from the interview so much as color his comments to me. Dressed
well, with a tie and pressed shirt, Julio would lean in toward me when
making his bigger claims about personal renewal, about the power of Jesus
Christ to restore Guatemala—to bring peace and prosperity to this long-
tortured country—and about the individual responsibility that each
Guatemalan has to his or her nation. That we spoke together in a busy
Guatemala City eatery made Julio's active decision not to eat—to mind-
fully fast from food altogether—an ever more conspicuous topic of conversation. The question, although asked many times before, was
unavoidable: Why aren't you eating today? Growing more distracted by
the food shuttling past us—the smell of chicken, tortillas, and beans teasing him—Julio regained focus. Passion won out over low blood sugar.
Julio explained, sitting up in his chair, that he was undergoing another fast
for the very same reason he prayed in tongues nightly, anointed strangers

with oil on crowded city buses (often without their knowledge and consent), and constantly turned inward to monitor his own feelings and attitudes. He did all this, he explained, to save Guatemala: "It's through prayer and fasting that we'll be victorious . . . because the Bible tells us that [prayer and fasting] brought victory in all the great battles. Right? The walls of Jericho fell because of prayer, fasting, and praise." Through hunger, Julio chipped at some of Guatemala City's thicker walls.

A middle-class neo-Pentecostal, Julio made these comments not only in the middle of a bustling (and increasingly lawless) postwar Central American city but also during an election year. As Julio's stomach growled for both Christ and country, dozens of presidential hopefuls jockeyed for position on the evening news, at political rallies, and on city billboards. Under the public spotlight, candidates gave speeches and made promises— to reduce urban violence, eliminate political corruption, and unite a postwar country. They rolled up their sleeves, capitalized on photo opportunities with indigenous farmers, and shook hands, vowing to lead Guatemala to its rightful place as a politically stable country in the global free market.[1] Yet, amid this low-budget carnival, Julio's stomach (and millions of similar stomachs) continued to rumble—not because they did not have enough food, although malnutrition is itself a critically important issue in many parts of Guatemala, but because they believed that their faithful fasts would result in the very promises that the candidates held forth: security, stability, and strength. While candidates talked and talked and talked, Julio told me, he and millions of neo-Pentecostals like him were taking action. They were fasting, praying, exorcizing demons, examining their consciences—engaging in a range of monastic practices—to make Guatemala the kind of nation that God demanded. In fact, to make Guatemala a chosen nation, Julio and his colleagues in Christ knew with absolute certainty that Christian leadership alone would never be enough to make Guatemala anew; Christian *citizenship*—the kind of Christian citizenship made and performed through fasts, prayers, and acts of self-governance—would be the key to national salvation.

Given neo-Pentecostal Christianity's continued and often peculiar rapprochement with democracy at the level of citizenship in places like postwar Guatemala, this book deliberately turns away from the loud drumbeat of electoral politics to focus on the low hum of Christian citizenship, especially the mundane practices that Bible-believing Guatemalans pursue every day in the name of Christ and for the sake of Guatemala. This is not, then, a study of Christian leadership or even Christian politics per se, but a study of Christian citizenship. It is an ethnography of a prominent neo-Pentecostal mega-church, and of the faithful who work tirelessly to carve out for themselves (and for their nation) what it means to live a good Christian life in a complicated world. At the same time, it is also, necessarily, a study of the city in which this moral drama takes place—the increasingly poor, multiethnic, and exceedingly dangerous *zonas* of postwar Guatemala City. And, finally, at its most theoretical, this book is an extended argument about the relationship between Christianity and citizenship. Although civil society theorists have long argued that Christian churches are voluntary organizations where congregants learn to be citizens, that argument places Christianity on the periphery of democracy (and democratization processes) through an ethnographically untenable divide between the private (i.e., the Christian) and the public (i.e., the citizen). This book demonstrates that Christian churches, especially neo-Pentecostal mega-churches, do not simply deliver life lessons to congregants on how to act as citizens in the public sphere—by voting or protesting, for example. These churches also provide a morality with which congregants constitute themselves as citizens (and perform their citizenship) through Christian practices, such as prayer, fasting, and examinations of conscience (K. O'Neill 2009).[2] Julio made his fast as a Christian citizen in order to change Guatemala. They are efforts that make Christianity neither incidental nor somehow prior to citizenship. In cities such as postwar Guatemala City, Christianity has become central to citizenship's very construction, practice, and performance.

The central claim here is that neo-Pentecostal Christians in Guatemala City perform their citizenship through Christian practices and that these Christian practices make neo-Pentecostal Guatemalans into citizens.[3] Another brief example illustrates what this means. Following a weeklong fast, which included nightly prayer and praise sessions, hundreds of youths gathered in a mega-church parking lot. They divided into four groups and then caravanned to Guatemala City's four cardinal points. Synchronizing their efforts via cell phones, those in the north, south, east, and west clamored for Guatemala for over an hour, dirtying their pants by kneeling in the streets. They stomped for salvation and raised their arms to the heavens. Most spoke in tongues, but the ones who did not focused their prayers toward very concrete problems, such as urban violence, the national economy, and divorce. They prayed. They wept. They exhausted themselves in behalf of Guatemala. And, when it was all over, they returned to the mega-church for a two-hour Sunday service. There the congregation greeted them like soldiers returning from battle. Chapter 3 makes the argument that in many ways they were.

The guiding assumption is that actively praying for the soul of Guatemala is an act of Christian citizenship, and that these acts have observable consequences. Praying for safer streets and fasting for a better economy, for example, are not futile exercises; prayer is a kind of cultural work that does something in and to the world: "Prayer is not an innocent social or psychological activity," Robert Orsi explains. "It is always situated in specific and discrepant environments of power, and it derives its meanings, implications, and consequences in relation to these configurations. Indeed praying is one of the most implicating social historical practices because it is in and through prayer that the self comes into intimate and extended contact with the contradictions and constraints of the social world" (1996, 186). Acts of Christian citizenship are relational practices (and relation-making activities) that carry effects.

Two of the most precarious effects, pursued throughout this book, are the following. First, Christian practices performed in behalf of Guatemala place the moral responsibility for societal problems, such as unsafe streets and a faltering economy, onto the shoulders of the believer. This moral ownership ultimately privatizes, or better yet internalizes, Guatemala's economic and political ills and, in the process, releases the nation-state, multinational corporations, and organized crime from being held accountable for, among many other things, unsafe streets and a faltering economy. In Guatemala City, through a neo-Pentecostal rationality, the public becomes private and the private becomes political. Second, the practice of Christian citizenship further instantiates what Julia Paley has called the "paradox of participation"—albeit through a decidedly Christian register. Christian citizenship provides an increasing number of Guatemalans with a deep sense of meaning while also limiting the avenues through which they can act (Paley 2001, 146). The more Christian citizens fast for Guatemala or weep at each of Guatemala City's four cardinal points, the less energy and interest (as well as time) they have to participate in more traditional modes of citizenship, such as community organizing and voter registration campaigns. The promise of Christian citizenship generates a whirl of activity that limits what the faithful can do as citizens of Guatemala; this effect does not depoliticize neo-Pentecostals so much as repoliticize them.[4]

Neo-Pentecostal mega-churches sit at the very center of this repoliticization. These churches not only exhibit incredible levels of organization but also make it clear that believers have the moral responsibility to save Guatemala—to be good Christian citizens. The following quote from Dr. Harold Caballeros provides an evocative but not uncommon example: "In reality, [Christianity] is the only real option to unite our country in the future. The only option for a united Guatemalan identity. There is no other. Multicultural. Pan-cultural. Multi-everything. No. Where are we as a nation? Where we are is looking for a united, singular vision of a Guatemalan nation. We have no other options . . . without a doubt. . . . We have the key in our hands. We have an obligation to produce this transformation of Guatemala into a Christian nation."[5] Every Christian has the unending responsibility to unify as well as purify the nation.

Setting aside Dr. Caballeros's problematic flattening of postwar ethnic identity, at least for now, it is important to note that making good on one's moral obligation to transform Guatemala starts with the believer's own heart and mind; it is a neo-Pentecostal rationality based on a causal logic where the thoughts and feelings of an individual form his or her actions, and these actions eventually congeal into habits, molding character and, ultimately, the nation. The rationality not only links individual states of mind with the nation-state but also makes Christian practices, such as fasts, prayers, and examinations of conscience, very real acts of citizenship. And these acts of Christian citizenship make neo-Pentecostals morally responsible for the successes (and failures) played out in the streets of Guatemala City. One congregant, for example, made it eminently clear that the stakes are not just high but also strikingly concrete: "Are we [saving Guatemala]? A guy got shot in the face four times this morning just over there [pointing to a street corner]. There's so much work for us Christians to do! There is so much spiritual warfare to wage!"[6]

To approximate the feel of this moral ownership, I develop the metaphor of *weight* throughout this book, relying on the experience of something pressing down on someone to communicate the felt reality of responsibility. It is the brute-ness of Christian citizenship that the metaphor glimpses. Yet moral weight, in this context, should not be confused with guilt. The two terms differ at the levels of temporality and scope, at least. Guilt is lament for what one should (or should not) have done in the past, whereas weight refers to the shouldering of a burden in the present moment in behalf of the future. The moral weight assessed ethnographically throughout this book is always forward looking, whereas guilt dwells in the past. In regard to scope, moral weight here is also lonely—radically individual—and at the same time (and with no sense of contradiction) collective: I—not we—am supporting the weight for us—not just me and not just you. The Christian citizen struggles all alone in Guatemala City but in behalf of Guatemala. Milan Kundera, building on Friedrich Nietzsche's theory of the eternal recurrence, philosophizes on the unbearable lightness (and weightiness) of being: "If every second of our lives recurs an infinite number of times, we are nailed to eternity as Jesus Christ was nailed to the cross. It is a terrifying prospect. In the world of eternal return the weight of unbearable responsibility lies on every move we make. That is why Nietzsche called the idea of eternal return the heaviest of burdens (*das schwerste Gewicht*)" ([1984] 2004, 5). Christian citizenship, as the heaviest of burdens, is an unbearable responsibility in Guatemala City, but one that neo-Pentecostals shoulder constantly. The weight of Christian citizenship nails congregants to the cross again and again.[7]

This book therefore examines neo-Pentecostal formations of Christian citizenship in postwar Guatemala City and the moral weight that Christian citizenship places on the believer. Christianity is not distinct from citizenship; it is, rather, the very rationality that provides many neo-Pentecostal Guatemalans with their sense of citizenship—with the felt reality of belonging to a nation, of being responsible for that nation, and of having the means to act in behalf of that nation. Before I go any further, however, a number of introductory remarks are in order about the relationships that exist among Christianity, nationalism, democracy, and citizenship in and beyond postwar Guatemala.

CHRISTIANITY AND NATIONALISM

The nation has long been one of Christianity's more peculiar concerns. Julio, for example, struggles as a Christian citizen not only *of* Guatemala but also *for* Guatemala—rather than for God, for those who happen to live in what is today known as Guatemala, or for humanity writ large. His nation is his focus. Given that Guatemala as a modern nation-state is not even two hundred years old and that the country's borders have never truly been established, not even to this day,[8] it seems counterintuitive that a Christian God, however that Christian God may be imagined, would look down from heaven and make distinctions between Guatemalans and, say, Salvadorans or Mexicans. Yet Julio insists that God does, and, more important, Julio lives his life in a way that takes these divine distinctions seriously. Though chapter 6 addresses this international imagination in greater depth, it is nonetheless important to note why "the nation" is so prominent throughout not only this book but also the lives of Christian citizens—why the nation exists as a biblical unit of salvation as well as a Christian vehicle for belonging.

The immediate answer is biblical. The Hebrew Scriptures, through the creation narrative, announce that God made humanity in God's own likeness, and, thus, there is only one race—the human race (Genesis 1:27). Everyone is equal. Yet difference is not the same thing as inequality, the Scriptures attest. Noah and the Great Flood (Genesis 6–9) fractured humanity into different nations—each with its own land, culture, and ethnic identity (Genesis 10:5, 20, 31). The story of the Great Flood, in fact, is the first scriptural reference to the nation: "These are the families of Noah's sons, according to their genealogies, in their nations; and from these the nations spread abroad on the earth after the flood" (Genesis 10:32). The Tower of Babel, at the center of the biblical tale in which God continues to divide the human race with different languages, further concretizes national differences (Genesis 11:1–9); yet a covenantal imagination ultimately elects ancient Israel as God's chosen nation, providing biblical fodder for so many future nations, both modern and otherwise, to read themselves (by way of analogy) as also God's chosen people. Abraham's covenant with God, which promises him a city "whose architect and builder is God" (Hebrews 11:10), becomes expanded by a divine promise made to Moses: "I will walk among you, and will be your God, and you shall be my people" (Leviticus 26:12). Following David, forming a new covenant, the Gospels note that God sent Jesus Christ to the nation of Israel as opposed to any other: "I was sent only to the lost sheep of the house of Israel" (Matthew 15:25). This promise has since been co-opted by sixteenth-century New England Puritans, African-born slaves in the Americas, nineteenth-century South Africans, and, most important for this book, Guatemalans over the last three centuries.[9]

In the mid-nineteenth century, as Guatemala struggled to form what Benedict Anderson would call an "imagined community" (1991), the Roman Catholic Church, through sermons and processions but also amid great political and ethnic strife, announced that Guatemala was God's chosen nation. Bishop Juan José de Aycinena, on September 15, 1863, preached on Guatemala's independence from Spain: "What more could a nation desire than what this magnificent promise offers? God is no less just nor liberal with us than for the Hebrew nation who served as an example of what the Christian church had to become. . . . Behold the reason why our republic, being a Catholic congregation, has the right to appropriate the divine promise, and if we fulfill the divine condition—and time will tell—God will not change the rules: He will reward the good and punish the evildoers" (Sullivan-González 1998, 2). This religious discourse evoked as well as evolved an understanding of Guatemala not just as a nation but also as one chosen by God to be extraordinary—to strive above and beyond all other nations. The narrative has stood the test of time.

By the twentieth century, as Guatemala's Roman Catholic population melted into something far more charismatic, the country's covenantal focus theologized on Guatemala's privileged relationship not only with God but, also with Israel. Guatemala, following the Second World War, cast the deciding United Nations vote to make Israel a sovereign nation-state. This decision, the faithful attest in excited tones, has since placed the Central American country in good favor with God. Marta Pilon de Pacheco, a neo-Pentecostal author and Guatemala City resident, writes: "After they had suffered for so long and endured tragedies such as the Holocaust ordered by Hitler, wherein more than 6 million Jews were killed, Israel was born once again on May 14, 1948 by a vote of the United Nations. Why am I telling you this? Because it was Guatemala's vote that made possible the rebirth of the blessed nation of Israel. We know with certainty that Guatemala's political vote in favor of God's land and people was God's spiritual vote in favor of Guatemala's land and people."[10] This covenantal language forms, even forges, a sense of responsibility and belonging to the nation. It allows for slippages to occur between a biblical sense of the nation (i.e., tribes and ethnicities) and the modern nation-state—geopolitical entities with sovereign territories. The idea of a covenant between God and Guatemala, moreover, prompts neo-Pentecostal Christianity in and beyond Guatemala to mesh comfortably with efforts at democratization—with the writing of constitutions, the implementation of free and fair elections, the consolidation of a civil society as well as the construction of a national identity. The El Shaddai Ministries of Guatemala City are testament enough. The unfamiliar might ask Julio in all sincerity how God could make distinctions between nations and prefer one over another, but Julio would most likely respond with equal sincerity: How could God not? God has chosen one nation over all others since the time of creation.

NEO-PENTECOSTALISM AND DEMOCRACY

The growth of Protestant Christianity and the worldwide spread of democratic systems have only made Julio's worldview more vivid. An estimated 800 million people, or 13 percent of the world's population, are Protestant, and the majority of these believers reside in the "global south," marking a major shift over the last one hundred years.[11] In 1900 an overwhelming 81 percent of all Protestants were Caucasian, whereas by 2005 this number had dropped to 43 percent as Protestant Christianity continued to spread beyond the Western world. In 1900, 2 percent of Africans and Latin Americans and only .5 percent of Asians were Protestant. By 2000 the percentages had risen to 27 percent of Africans, 17 percent of Latin Americans, and 5 percent of Asians. In these three continents together, Protestantism went from just 1.5 percent of the population in 1900 to 16.5 percent in 2000. This is more than a 1,000 percent increase (Shah 2004, 118).

The most dramatic Protestant growth emerges in Pentecostal, charismatic, and neo-Pentecostal churches. All three are characterized by personal conversion, evangelization, belief in the Bible's authority, and the understanding that Jesus Christ's crucifixion was a sacrifice made in behalf of humanity's fallen nature (Bebbington 1989).[12] Pentecostalism, the first of the three movements, arose in the early 1900s through a series of revivals in Kansas, Texas, and California and places great emphasis on the so-called Gifts of the Holy Spirit: speaking in tongues, or glossolalia, healing, prophecy, spiritual discernment, and miracles. News reports of Pentecostalism's fiery, even contagious, style of worship propelled the movement across North America. A 1906 *Los Angeles Times* article describes the Azusa Street Revival: "Colored people and a sprinkling of whites compose the congregation, and night is made hideous in the neighborhood by the howlings of the worshippers who spend hours swaying forth and back in a nerve-racking attitude of prayer and supplication."[13] At a pitch sometimes best described as "howling," Pentecostalism has since expanded throughout the world, the movement yielding converts at such an impressive clip that many suggest that Pentecostalism may soon overtake the Roman Catholic Church as Latin America's largest Christian presence.[14]

Traditional Pentecostalism of the twentieth century eventually gave birth to charismatic Christianity—the movement's second wave—which began in the 1950s and includes self-conscious efforts to renew historic churches, such as the Roman Catholic Church, through an emphasis on the Gifts of the Holy Spirit (Csordas 1994). Yet it is neo-Pentecostalism, a much more recent development that takes place in largely independent churches, that has set postwar Guatemala aflame. Understanding neo-Pentecostalism begins with the movement's ministerial focus. These independent, nondenominational churches emphasize their responsibility to usher in the kingdom of God today instead of waiting for Jesus Christ's second coming. The time to act is now. This kind of Christian participation means subscribing to an apocryphal narrative that announces the Church's responsibility to save nations from the power of Satan through the saving grace of Jesus Christ. Neo-Pentecostalism also involves an active demonological imagination that understands the world as constantly under attack by fallen angels. In the Guatemalan context, neo-Pentecostals also stress a personal relationship with God through worship services defined by song, testimony, healings, and speaking in tongues. And though traditional Pentecostalism has been historically popular among Guatemala's poorer communities (both urban and rural) and has been relatively conservative in behavior and dress (e.g., no dancing, no makeup, no revealing clothes), neo-Pentecostalism, in contrast, tends to thrive in the capital city and is popular among middle- and upper-middle-class professionals—as well as those who long to be upwardly mobile. As I mentioned in the preface, neo-Pentecostalism has also been historically ladino/a, but today is increasingly indigenous as mega-churches broaden their ministerial scope. Guatemalan neo-Pentecostalism also tends to maintain strong ecclesiastical relationships with congregations in the United States as well as those in Africa and Asia. Mega-churches in Guatemala, for example, tend to have North American–trained pastors as well as satellite churches throughout the United States; they also worship in large auditoriums modeled after mega-church structures in the American South.

Three more characteristics define neo-Pentecostalism in Guatemala. First, the congregations tend to be media-savvy, airing sophisticated Internet, television, and radio programming. El Shaddai, for example, owns clusters of radio towers throughout the country and stewards a Web site with an online archive of sermons as well as live broadcasts of Sunday services. Second, neo-Pentecostals tend to be politically active, focusing on the moral dimensions of Guatemala's well-being—crime, divorce, and corruption. The Church's emphasis, once again, is on saving the nation. The third characteristic is an interest in material prosperity, the idea that God wants people to be financially successful. In Guatemala, for example, informants commonly explained to me that the Roman Catholic Church's preferential option for the poor, one of liberation theology's tenets, misses the biblical fact that Jesus himself was a hardworking and upwardly mobile professional, that he was a carpenter, making good money, and enjoying a relatively high social status.[15] Why would God prefer the poor, or even poverty, when God himself was (and continues to be) of particular means?

Neo-Pentecostalism's flexible, nondenominational take on Christianity has become tremendously popular. From 1970 to 1997 the number of nondenominational Christians throughout the world rose from 167 million to 533 million (Barrett and Johnson 2004). Interestingly, though, this worldwide spike in religious affiliation tends to take hold in postcolonial regions and often alongside dramatic efforts at political reform (Marostica 1998). Democracy, or at least the rhetoric of democracy, continues to gain momentum in conjunction with evangelization in non-Western locales the world over. From 1972 to 1997 the number of electoral democracies jumped from 52 to 118, as democracy was introduced to such neo-Pentecostal hotbeds as South Korea, South Africa, and Brazil (Freedom House 2008). The democratization of Latin America over the last twenty-five years, moreover, has been especially pronounced. Today most Latin American countries fulfill the basic requirements of a democratic regime, whereas only three fulfilled the same requirements twenty-five years ago (UNDP 2004b).

Democracy, of course, is not something that one country has and another has not. Democracy is not something that one can measure with much ease or clarity; as Alexis de Tocqueville made eminently clear more than a century and a half ago, democracy is not so much a substance as a sensibility (Knott 2004). Democracy as a mode of government, whereby citizens freely elect decision makers in open, fair elections, raises many questions, and in Latin America the quality and consistency of democracy are constant sources of debate. Democracy's unevenness has led to what Julia Paley, reporting from the Chilean context, calls *democracia con apellidos*— democracy with last names: *democracia restringida* (restricted democracy), *democracia cupular* (elite democracy), *democracia lite* (low-fat democracy), and *democracia entre comillas* (democracy in quotation marks) (2001, 3). The qualifiers, in all their cynicism and wryness, give us a glimpse of just how unfinished democracy can appear to Latin Americans.

Postwar Guatemala mirrors this hybridity while also offering a dramatic example of democracy's entanglement with neo-Pentecostal Christianity. Since 1981 Guatemala's slow transition from military rule to a formal democracy has coincided with the rapid evangelization of a once overwhelmingly Roman Catholic population. In the early 1970s more than 90 percent of Guatemalans were Roman Catholic. Now Guatemala is as much as 60 percent Pentecostal or charismatic Christian (Pew 2006). In terms of percentage, Guatemala is also the most Protestant country in Latin America and has had two Protestant presidents over the last twenty-five years. There have been, and continue to be, acute points of contact between democracy and Protestantism in Guatemala.[16] In 1982, for example, a coup d'état resulted in Efraín Ríos Montt, a Protestant military leader, becoming president of the republic. On the night of the coup he addressed the nation on television, declaring, "I am trusting my Lord and King, that He shall guide me because only He gives and takes away authority" (Garrard-Burnett 1998, 138). Montt is largely recognized as the architect of Guatemala's genocide and has been indicted by international tribunals for crimes against humanity; the Christian dimensions of his governance are well documented and rooted in a religious conversion that took place in one of Guatemala City's mega-churches, Verbo (Stoll 1990, 187–190; Steigenga 1999). Montt's Christian approach to public office (his presidency lasted less than two years) included codes of conduct for government workers that were rooted in biblical principles (*no robo, no miento, no abuso*—I do not rob, I do not lie, I do not cheat), weekly radio addresses to the country that eventually became known among Guatemalans as Montt's sermons, and close ties to the United States' growing Moral Majority, which included a guest appearance on the conservative U.S. Christian television show *The 700 Club* (Garrard-Burnett 1998). Amid a sustained, as well as manufactured, fear of communism, Montt became Guatemala's Christian soldier; he dressed in battle fatigues and answered to the title of El General, and his scorched-earth policies (known colloquially as his "beans and bombs campaign") quickly defined his tenure as president. Sobering statistics eventually made the international community take notice. According to an Amnesty International report published in 1982, Montt's first year in office resulted in the violent murder of an estimated 100,000 indigenous Guatemalans and peasant farmers as well as the displacement of more than 100,000 Guatemalans from their homes (Amnesty International 1982). Moral righteousness mixed with radical violence to define Guatemala's first Protestant president until, in August 1983, a military coup overthrew Montt.

Almost a decade later, in 1991, Guatemala held a relatively fair and open presidential election. The neo-Pentecostal candidate, Jorge Serrano, ran against Montt, who, in spite of his history, remains active in Guatemalan politics to this day. A convert since 1977 and a member of Elim, the politically moderate Serrano won with a campaign that emphasized the importance of the family, free-market economics, social programs, lawfulness, and respect for God-given human rights (Hallum 2002). Although Guatemalans, both Protestant and Roman Catholic, certainly did not vote in droves, the 1991 elections signaled the growing political involvement of neo-Pentecostals—urban, upwardly mobile, nondenominational

Christians. Winning the election with 67 percent of the vote, Serrano became the first elected Protestant president in Latin America (Freston 2001, 275). Upwardly mobile voting blocs saw themselves as well their future in Serrano until he attempted to dissolve the Congress and suspend the constitution in 1993. In one of the stranger grabs for power in Guatemalan history, Serrano tried to take full control of the country; a combination of protesters, government officials, and international investors stopped his dictatorial efforts. The full reason for his coup d'état remains unclear, but many speculate that the coup was Serrano's own way of avoiding corruption charges, which he continues to skirt today by residing in Panama (Steigenga 1999, 162).

Regardless of Montt's and Serrano's damaged presidencies, neo-Pentecostalism remains a politically viable religious movement, which is why the growth and influence of Guatemala City's neo-Pentecostal population are at the very center of this study. Neo-Pentecostals supported both Montt's and Serrano's presidencies, and they continue to foster Dr. Harold Caballeros's political aspirations. These men signal a wellspring of support, even a social movement; yet lingering solely on their political biographies would be a mistake. As I mentioned before, it is my intent to shift the analytical focus away from Christian formations of democratic leadership to Christian formations of citizenship. This is not to say that one can (or should) distinguish entirely what Dr. Caballeros says from what El Shaddai congregants do. Dr. Caballeros's sermons echo throughout this book, constituting a major line of evidence. The point is simply that far too much scholarly attention has been given to Protestant presidents in Guatemala and not enough to the everyday experiences of believers who form their citizenship through their Christian practices. This is why this book addresses these kinds of ethnographic questions: How do Christian citizens render unto Caesar the things that are Caesar's and unto God the things that are God's? What does this kind of moral deliberation look like in a democratizing context? And how does the believer perform, and in the process further constitute, his or her citizenship through Christian practices? Answering these questions begins with a particular understanding of citizenship.

CITIZENSHIP

Citizenship, for the purposes of this book, involves three dimensions that I distinguish here for the sake of analytical clarity but that are in fact interrelated at the everyday level of experience and practice. They are political status, cultural identity, and governing rationality. By political status I mean that citizenship centers on questions of belonging (Marshall 1950; Anderson 1991). Citizenship pivots on a cruel dynamic between inclusion and exclusion that asks: Who is (and who is not) a citizen? To be understood as a full citizen is to be a part of a nation-state and to have the right to participate as well as to fulfill one's responsibilities. Yet the right to vote, to organize, and to engage in political processes has traditionally been granted only to certain categories of persons, such as men as opposed to women and adults as opposed to children. The political construction of citizenship, historically speaking, has always been a contested category, involving great struggles for formal political recognition by marginalized groups.[17]

This question about political status bleeds into the idea of citizenship as a cultural identity. If citizenship as a legal status asks who is (and who is not) a citizen, citizenship as a cultural identity poses this question: What does citizenship look like? The idea here is that citizenship is not an ahistorical category that one can plug into any given context. Rather, the bounds and dynamics of citizenship are culturally constructed in specific social and historical moments (Rosaldo 1994; Young 1996). The practice and the performance of citizenship exist in constant relationship to formations of the nation-state as well as to race, class, gender, sexuality, and religion. From this analytical perspective, citizenship as a cultural identity becomes unstable, forever in flux, and, following anthropological thought, something made. The most important conclusion that emerges from this viewpoint is that the construction of citizenship in one particular locale can exist as almost unrecognizable from the perspective of another—as containing few, if any, familiar citizenship practices or performances of national belonging. The strangeness of citizenship continually emerges throughout this book. Though they seem almost nonsensical at first, Christian practices such as fasts, prayers, and examinations of conscience exist in Guatemala City as very real acts of citizenship. They are acts of Christian citizenship.

To fully appreciate the idea that Christian practices can constitute citizenship, it is important to understand citizenship from a third, and final, perspective. This involves reading citizenship as a kind of subjectivity that has certain responsibilities and dispositions—to be active and disciplined (Rose 1996b; Gordon 1991; O'Malley 1996), and to pursue what Michel Foucault understands as the care of the self (1986). Citizenship is not just a political status or a cultural identity but also a political rationality that constantly asks: What should the good citizen do? A critically important part of this question is its ability to nest in the hearts and the minds of Christians. This means that rather than the nation-state simply governing its citizens, citizens often take on the responsibility to govern themselves—to regulate their own conduct or to police their neighbors' behavior. The logic and the promise of citizenship prompt people to do things—to themselves, for their nation, and in the name of democracy.

Foucault's notion of governmentality lends some perspective on how citizenship can be understood as a kind of political rationality. His lasting contribution has been to see the problem of government as not only tied to state politics but also linked to the formation of the modern subject, especially the citizen, in a variety of ways and through certain modes of thought (Foucault 1991). Neo-Pentecostalism, this book argues at length, is one such "mode of thought" that provides a range of cultural practices through which citizens are both constituted and governed: "Governing people is not a way to force people to do what the governor wants" (Foucault 1999, 162). Rather, governing involves getting citizens to "evaluate and act upon [themselves] so that the police, the guards and the doctors do not have to" (Cruikshank 1996, 234). This observation rings especially true in societies with decentralized or weak modes of authority, such as postwar Guatemala. There the formation of citizenship as a political rationality involves the production of "autonomous and calculable members of society [who are] able to be left for the most part to regulate their own behavior" (Hindess 1996, 72; Dean 1996, 10). Neo-Pentecostalism is one such rationality that promotes self-governing subjects—citizens whom governments do not have to rule because these men and women manage themselves.

The significance of this analytical perspective is twofold, at least. The first is that citizenship, Christian or otherwise, is a moral beast, and that within the neo-Pentecostal context, Christianity provides a logic through which believers govern their thoughts, feelings, and words for the betterment of Guatemala.[18] The second is that understanding citizenship as a kind of subjectivity means that the moral weight of citizenship is ever-present. One does not (nor cannot) shed citizenship when exiting the public sphere to enter the private sphere, as many civil society theorists imply.[19] This division between the private and the public is an absolute fiction. Guatemalans of all stripes wear their citizenship (as well as their faith) like a thick skin rather than a light jacket.

Foucault's notion of governmentality is, of course, not without its limitations. Foucault's work is grounded in a vision of the independent nation-state that does not take transnationalism into account; yet the kinds of political rationalities employed and assumed by citizens of post-war Guatemala do not obey borders. True to Arjun Appadurai's estimation, citizens now exist within "new geographies of governmentality" (2001, 24). This observation cannot be ignored in postwar Guatemala City, where efforts at democratization and evangelization routinely come from afar. Guatemalan efforts at democratization, for one, involve a range of international actors, such as trained observers and technocrats from "more established" democracies who oversee its implementation.[20] These specialists, as one might expect, are not elected but instead hired as consultants to organize elections, write constitutions, and streamline bureaucracies. At the same time, neo-Pentecostalism exhibits a remarkable level of transnationalism: its church networks stretch throughout the Americas as well as parts of Asia and Western Europe. Knitted together across national borders by the sale and distribution of cassettes, Internet evangelization, and apostolic church structures, as well as migrant labor circuits, contemporary Christian communities maintain contact through a web of formal and informal relationships (Robbins 2004b).[21]

Addressing these dynamics through the language of political rationalities raises a number of theoretical and methodological possibilities. One particular direction that this book follows is the language of "transnational governmentalities" (Ferguson and Gupta 2002). This concept allows scholars of citizenship to understand how mega-churches "overlay and coexist with" efforts at democratization in postwar Guatemala—how each Christian's citizenship exists in constant tension with state and non-state efforts at political reform. Transnational neo-Pentecostal mega-churches exist as "horizontal contemporaries of the organs of the state—sometimes rivals; sometimes servants; sometimes watchdogs; sometimes parasites; but in every case operating on the same level, and in the same global space" (Ferguson and Gupta 2002, 994). This kind of analytical resolution allows scholars to understand Christian citizenship as something made through a range of local, semilocal, and transnational programs of government. This kind of complexity may challenge the bounds of any ethnographic study, but it also allows scholars of citizenship to take seriously the ways in which neo-Pentecostal Christianity provides an increasing number of believers with the means by which to participate in their emerging democracies as citizens, allowing for the conceptualization of what this book and what millions of believers understand as Christian citizenship.

These three dimensions of citizenship have become entangled in postwar Guatemala City, knotting to form a very palpable, public debate in a class-divided, multiethnic, and multilingual capital city of 3 million people. This uneven conversation begins with the fact that not everyone in Guatemala considers himself or herself to be a citizen. Guatemala is a country of 14 million people, and approximately half of the population is indigenous. Comprising twenty-three distinct linguistic communities, the indigenous are present in more than 90 percent of the country; there are reportedly a million indigenous people in Guatemala City alone.[22] For centuries Guatemala's indigenous communities have been excluded from the political sphere through racial discrimination. The roots of this unequal power relationship began almost five hundred years ago, with Spain's colonization of Guatemala in 1524; the Spanish conquest killed two-thirds of the indigenous population. Exclusion at the level of citizenship concretized in a legal sense during Guatemala's liberalization period, which began in 1871. In this era supposed universal ideas, such as equality and individual freedom, did not extend to Guatemala's indigenous communities or to women. Both were barred from the processes that led to the construction of Guatemala as a nation-state. The indigenous lacked, for example, the constitutional right to own land and hold political office in the same way that ladinos did. During the liberalization of Guatemala, the state also seized indigenous land and forced the indigenous to work on coffee plantations and construct much of the country's infrastructure. Women were not granted the right to vote until 1945.[23]

Guatemala's civil war, in the late twentieth century, exacerbated an already extreme level of political exclusion. The longest and bloodiest in Latin America, the war formally began after the failure of a nationalist uprising by military officers in 1960. It formally ended on December 29, 1996, with the signing of a peace agreement between the military and counterinsurgent forces in Guatemala City. Yet the war really began in 1954 with a U.S.–backed coup of the democratically elected government. Framed by the Cold War's fear of communism, President Jacobo Arbenz's practice of land redistribution threatened the United Fruit Company, a U.S.–based corporation and Guatemala's biggest landowner.[24] Following the coup, Guatemala's government became increasingly militarized, while other ladinos formed counterinsurgent guerrilla forces. The battle between the government and the guerrillas was at first articulated through the language of class conflict. In the 1960s, however, ladinos recruited Maya communities through a narrative that included ethnicity and also emphasized Guatemala's fight for freedom of organization, land rights, and democracy. The government's response to these demands was absolutely brutal, especially between 1978 and 1982. Large-scale massacres, scorched-earth tactics, and massive disappearances and displacements aimed at annihilating Guatemala's Maya population riddled the country.[25]

Global awareness of such systematic, large-scale human rights violations forced the Guatemalan government by the mid-1980s to adjust its tactics so that it could continue receiving international aid. Under the protective umbrella of general amnesty and impunity, civilian rule slowly began to shape the agenda alongside the military's, while human rights abuses increased and went unpunished. Guatemala's peace process began in 1986, amid political unrest, with a series of talks and accords that ultimately led to a United Nations–mediated peace process (1994–1996). The Oslo Accord, signed in 1994 as part of this peace process, initiated the Historical Clarification Commission (Comisión para el Esclarecimiento Histórico, CEH), a project created to investigate human rights violations and to make recommendations on how to promote peace in postwar Guatemala. According to the CEH, more than 200,000 people died or disappeared as a result of the armed conflict, of which more than 80 percent were Maya; the report also established that 93 percent of these human rights violations can be connected to the state (CEH 1999). The CEH established in light of the United Nations Genocide Convention that the Guatemalan state committed acts of genocide against Maya people.[26]

This brutal exclusion built on, and resulted in, material inequalities. Today 86.6 percent of the indigenous live in extreme poverty, 75 percent do not own land, and 34 percent of indigenous women are severely malnourished. Forty-two percent of the indigenous population is illiterate and, more striking, 65 percent of all indigenous women are illiterate. Forty percent of indigenous children have no access to school, and only 4 percent of the indigenous occupy public positions (CERD 2006). More generally, a USAID report has established that "education levels in Guatemala are dismal": only 1 percent of all children enrolled in primary school finish secondary school (2006, 76). Since the Peace Accords, the report states, "the Government's focus has been nearly entirely on primary education, with 90 percent of primary schools funded by the government. By contrast, 80 percent of secondary schools are private, and thus unaffordable to the poor" (2006, 16). In the face of these disparities and in the shadows of the country's genocidal civil war, Guatemala's postwar indigenous rights movement has sought full membership and participation in Guatemala's democratizing context, using the Peace Accords as a means to frame questions of political inclusion through the language of cultural identities.[27] Yet pan-Maya activism, it should be noted, even if only briefly, has not had the same kind of success as comparable movements in Bolivia and Ecuador (Postero 2004; Zamosc 2004). Though urban Maya activists have been relatively successful in leveraging international awareness to advance their goals, they have not been able to generate a grassroots movement, or at the very least a groundswell of support, that might draw people into the capital city to protest or even to vote (Fischer 2004, 92). A disconnect remains between the Maya movement's urban-based leadership and those indigenous who reside in or beyond the capital city.

This movement's key projects, regardless of the quality of its support, cut to the very core of citizenship in Guatemala. Signed on March 31, 1995, in Mexico City, one of the accords, the Agreement on the Identity and Rights of Indigenous Peoples, makes explicit that democratization means recognizing all identities (Peace Accords 2006). Yet many Maya activists believe that congressional legislation continues to perpetuate a kind of racial discrimination that precludes the full political participation of Maya communities. There are very real legal constraints that make citizenship in Guatemala look one way rather than another—that make citizenship look exclusively ladino/a rather than inclusively ladino/a and indigenous. One example among many is that Guatemala's official legal language is Spanish. In a multilingual country, this means that individuals cannot bear witness in court unless they can read, write, speak, or understand Spanish. One result is that some indigenous cannot legally fulfill their citizenship responsibilities because they are not entirely comfortable or able to speak Spanish. It is an example that animates an enduring distinction between formal and substantive citizenship (Bottomore 1992). Formal citizenship refers to a person's legal standing as a member of a nation-state. All Guatemalans, for example, have formal citizenship, which grants them full political rights. Everyone, in theory, can bear witness in court. Substantive rights, however, refer to a person's ability to access the rights guaranteed to a citizen; substantive citizenship is not the formal right to bear witness but the actual ability to do so. The fact is that the legal construction of Guatemalan citizenship results in a cultural category that is something other than indigenous; Guatemalan legal citizenship is literally Spanish-speaking.

This battle over Guatemalan citizenship is not only a Maya concern. As one might expect, the debate over indigenous rights and Guatemalan citizenship pushes on the sensibilities of ladinos as well. Questions about citizenship have generated a very conspicuous debate among a plethora of people in Guatemala. A ladino/a concern with Maya identity politics is the subject of Diane Nelson's *Finger in the Wound* (1999) as well as Charles R. Hale's *Más que un Indio* (2006). The title of Nelson's study speaks directly to the discomfort that ladinos feel when addressing the history and future of indigenous people in Guatemala. "A finger in the wound" is a metaphor that Guatemalans use to refer to Maya cultural rights activism; it is an issue, Nelson explains, that prods and pokes at an open and wounded body politic that is busy healing but far from being completely whole. Debates over citizenship, from a ladino/a perspective, are often said to irritate the healing process. Moreover, numerous developments have contributed to this irritation, placing the ethnic dimensions of citizenship in a distinctly urban frame. They include street violence, organized crime, and political corruption as well as increased postwar migration of indigenous peoples from the rural interior to Guatemala City. Once overwhelmingly ladino/a, the capital city is now becoming an urban representation of the country's diversity. Rapid urban expansion, failing infrastructure, mounting levels of urban violence, and increased participation in transnational capitalism all strain the substantive dimensions of Guatemalan citizenship. All these developments have created an urban context that contradicts democratization's rhetoric of increased freedoms. Amid the rhetoric of democracy, the brute fact is that residents of Guatemala City have gained formal citizenship, but their ability to access and practice these rights has lessened because of increased poverty, systemic racism, and political corruption. The result is a kind of "disjunctive citizenship," wherein the rhetoric of citizenship does not match the experience of citizenship (Caldeira and Holston 1999).

One major dimension of this disjuncture is urban violence. Guatemala City is one of Latin America's most dangerous cities. In 1999 Guatemala City's homicide rate was third only to Medellín's and Bogotá's, but by 2007 both Colombian cities had witnessed an impressive decrease in violence, whereas Guatemala City's homicide rates were soaring. As the Canadian Red Cross (2006) has reported, Guatemala City's number of homicides rose from 3,230 in 2001 to 5,338 in 2005, making the city's murder rate 109 per 100,000 inhabitants.[28] These numbers are almost certainly conservative. Informal conversations with police officers and firefighters reveal that officials tend to count only certain murders, such as those of laborers as opposed to gang members. Regardless of the altogether imperfect science of tracking violence, this incredible spike in insecurity leads to some startling calculations. For one, the city's murder rate is almost eleven times what the World Health Organization (2002) understands as a "crisis"; the number of violent deaths between 2001 and 2005 equals the death toll of the great earthquake of 1976; and Guatemala City's current murder rate is higher than the average number of Guatemalans killed each year during the country's genocidal civil war (Painter 2007). The numbers raise the simple but maddening question: How "post" is postwar Guatemala?

The violence's gendered dimensions have also become apparent: from 2001 to 2006 more than 2,300 women were violently murdered in Guatemala City. This number wildly outpaces the infamous situation in Juárez, Mexico, where activists have long argued for an international awareness of what has been called "femicide." As Victoria Sanford reports: "Between 2001 and 2006, while the female population [in Guatemala] increased by eight percent, the female homicide rate increased by more than 117 percent" (2008, 21). In Guatemala City the problem has proven more pronounced; hundreds of women have become the victims of gender-based violence, such as brutal sexual assaults, torture, and rape—all with near absolute impunity. According to Amnesty International (2006), only fifteen murders of women resulted in convictions between 2002 and 2004, and of the some six hundred women murdered in 2005, only two cases resulted in convictions. Overall, no arrests were made in 97 percent of cases of violence against girls and women, and more than 70 percent of the cases have not even been investigated. Women's lack of protection by the Guatemalan government forces one to question the bounds, legitimacy, and efficacy of formal citizenship in Guatemala. Are women full citizens of Guatemala? If so, then why are they not being protected as such?

In this way, Guatemala's postwar government has been unable to provide all its citizens with justice in the form of security and due process. Guatemala's conviction rate is less than 10 percent for all cases in which a complaint is filed (USAID 2006, 78). This judicial weakness explains the growing trend of private security forces, neighborhood watches, and extra-juridical executions, such as lynchings (García 2004). Thirty-one percent of Guatemalans, for example, believe that taking justice into one's own hands is an acceptable response to crime (Seligson and Azpuru 2004). And, according to a survey conducted in 2000, over 7 percent of households pay for their own private security; that year "the total budget for private spending on security [approximately $3.5 million] was at least 20 percent greater than the public security budget" (USAID 2006, 71). In

Guatemala there are approximately 80,000 private security guards, compared to 18,500 police officers. Of the 180 private security companies in the country, a USAID report announced, only 28 are legal (2006, 71). A report by the United Nations also notes that there were more than 400 cases of lynching between 1996 and 2002, and 75 percent of those acts resulted in death (MINUGUA 2002). Because of a rise in transnational street gangs and drug trafficking in Guatemala City, citizens have taken it upon themselves to do what the Guatemalan state does not do: defend and protect themselves. In these efforts at self-protection, the practice of Guatemalan citizenship, especially in the capital city, involves dramatic acts of self-governance. By doing the work of the government, citizens secure city streets and bring alleged criminals to "justice." They also govern themselves and their neighbors at the same time. Community policing and neighborhood watches are striking examples—community members come together to agree to watch, or to police, each other for the betterment of the community. Though lynching and extrajuridical executions are heinous activities, they involve a level of vigilance that speaks to the kind of active and responsible citizen that Guatemala's postwar context prompts.

NEO-PENTECOSTALISM IN GUATEMALA

Adding a final layer to Guatemala City's current debate on citizenship is a dramatic shift in religious affiliation.[29] It is a transformation that began with an act of God: at 3:03 a.m. on February 4, 1976, an earthquake measuring 7.5 on the Richter scale rocked Guatemala. The quake's epicenter lay to the west of Guatemala City, near Chimaltenango, but the entire nation felt the effects: 23,000 dead, 77,000 wounded, and 370,000 houses leveled. The seismic activity left more than 1.2 million people homeless and destroyed 40 percent of the nation's hospital infrastructure. Guatemala City, with a population of 1.3 million people in 1976, reflected much of the nation's damage, proportionally speaking. The earthquake wounded 16,549 residents and killed 3,370; it destroyed 99,712 homes, rendering nearly a half million residents homeless. Water was completely unavailable. The effect of all this was more than structural. In the capital people slept in the open air, considering it safer to be in the streets than in their homes (Olcese et al. 1977; Thomas 2006).

As residents braced themselves for aftershocks, Guatemala's now storied Protestant growth took root. The reason was not, as one might first guess, because an act of God scared a population into a millennial worldview.

This may have happened for some, at first, but fear is hardly a sustainable cause for conversion.[30] Instead, the earthquake set in motion a number of processes that all contributed to a sustained expansion of Guatemala's Protestant population. The first, and possibly most important, was that Protestant aid agencies from the United States came to Guatemala soon after the earthquake. They provided much-appreciated relief in the short term, while in the long term they "saturated [Guatemala] with Scripture" (Garrard-Burnett 1998, 121). As immediate relief gave way to efforts at sustainable development, many of these Protestant relief agencies established regional offices in Guatemala City, continuing their work to rebuild both the nation and its soul. The strategy worked. Protestant church membership jumped by 14 percent within the first few months after the earthquake, and the annual growth of Protestant conversion in Guatemala rose to 26 percent by 1982. This number was nearly four times what it had been a decade earlier (Garrard-Burnett 1998, 121–122).

The earthquake also initiated a wave of migration from the rural interior to Guatemala City, as survivors moved to the capital looking for work (Gellert and Pinto Soria 1990). Finding little, these newcomers were provided by Pentecostal churches with basic resources, such as food and shelter, as well as spaces where they could cultivate a sense of belonging in uncertain times and unfamiliar places.[31] The Roman Catholic Church did not respond to these Protestant efforts. One reason is that the Catholic Church proved itself too oafish, in a bureaucratic sense, to compete with the dexterity of grassroots churches. For Pentecostals, schedules were open, plans could be changed, and word of mouth carried news from church to church. The same kind of deftness could not be managed by the Catholic Church, in which tradition holds precedence over improvisation and change comes in slow increments.

The Catholic Church was also nowhere to be seen in Guatemala in 1976. In the rural areas, the institutional presence of the Catholic Church disappeared between 1880 and 1950. In the 1940s in Huehuetenango, there were only two priests for a population of 176,000 (Sierra et al. 1990, 9). In 1966 only 530 priests served a nation of 4 million Catholics, and 434 of those clergymen were foreign-born. Catholic priests chose to minister in the countryside instead of Guatemala City, for reasons that most likely ranged from the practical to the romantic; the ratio of priests to congregants in Guatemala City's poorer *zonas* was even lower—1 to 30,000 by 1978 (Garrard-Burnett 1998, 123). The Catholic Church, at this level, was simply outmanned and outhustled by Pentecostal churches willing and ready to provide material and social support to poor residents. A less calculable but no less real reason for Protestant growth was that Pentecostal Christianity delivered an unmediated, personal relationship with God that resonated with post-earthquake Guatemalans. The Catholic Church could not replicate the level of spiritual intimacy that Pentecostal communities provided the faithful. In times of crisis, the cavernous feel of Guatemala's Catholic churches, rife with a kind of distancing formality, lost out to the intensity and warmth of clamoring for God in a neighbor's living room or kitchen.

Virginia Garrard-Burnett also notes that the earthquake brought to clearer relief many of Guatemala's social problems: "unemployment and gross inequities in income distribution; the vast chasm that separated the nation's poor, largely indigenous majority from the wealthy and cosmopolitan elite; and the societal stresses of increased urban migration by the poor" (1998, 127). One result of all these changes was the rapid escalation of the country's low-level civil conflict, which would soon turn into genocidal war. Protestant growth ultimately took place alongside (and partly because of) political violence and brutal military governments (Sierra et al. 1990, 11). Although both Catholics and Protestants felt the brunt of this violence, many make the argument that Pentecostal Christianity kept the faithful out of harm's way by delivering a far less political message than that offered by the Catholic Church's popular brand of liberation theology (Garrard-Burnett 1998, 104; Steigenga 1999, 160).

At that time in Guatemala's history, amid an incredible level of instability, Pentecostal discourse began to capture the nation's imagination, providing hopeful interpretations of complicated societal problems. And so in 1981, when 20 percent of the population called itself Protestant, and as Guatemala steamed toward the highest per capita representation of Protestants in Latin America (Sherman 1997, ix), General Montt was confirmed president. Capturing the narrative that accompanied Montt's rise to power, a prominent Pentecostal leader and Guatemalan businessman preached in Quetzaltenango to a large crowd of Protestant Christians. The year was 1984:

In the years before the arrival of General Montt to the presidency of the Republic, we remember how it was in Guatemala. The nation was financially divided by the guerillas, and bombs were destroying the capital every day. People were being kidnapped, ambushed, assaulted all the time and thousands were being affected by the actions of the army and the guerillas. . . . The [Protestant] Church began to understand that Satan was robbing, killing, and destroying Guatemala and began to resist in the name of Jesus. God showed us that what we could see with our eyes was a visible part of a spiritual warfare and He wanted his church to dominate in this environment. During the next 18 months [after Montt's confirmation], the guerillas retreated from much of Guatemala. The economy began to get better; corruption began to come under control. God began a great harvest of souls. . . . Satan, in the name of Jesus, we grab you and we order you to leave Guatemala, from border to border and from ocean to sea, in the name of Jesus: LEAVE! (Sierra et al. 1990, 13).

At face value, much of this history is correct. Following Montt's confirmation, the civil conflict shifted from urban to rural, which placed indigenous communities at greater peril but took the fight out of the capital. The result, if only anecdotally, was that business improved for urbanites. Moreover, Guatemala's "harvest of souls" surged as more people began to affiliate themselves with Pentecostal churches throughout the country. What is important about this speech, however, is not that it demonstrates a historical development; a more direct citation would have been satisfactory. Rather, this speech animates how neo-Pentecostalism began to make hope in incredible (and incredibly painful) times. As the country's political, economic, and social unsteadiness continued to grow, the religion delivered an optimistic rereading of things: life was getting better. When the fog of war and genocide's gray zone began to make the civil conflict difficult to assess, the narrative offered two clear-cut sides: God and Satan. And when many felt all but powerless, this discourse placed the means for change in urban believers' hands or, more accurately, between their interwoven fingers: prayer. Neo-Pentecostalism did not provide an opiate for the people, masking the truth of the matter; rather, the religion did what hope does best: reorient already existing knowledge about the present in behalf of the future (Miyazaki 2006, 149). Through the practice of hope, this Pentecostal reorientation of knowledge sparked the imaginations of many Guatemalans in a way that enabled very small Pentecostal churches to grow into very big neo-Pentecostal mega-churches.

Emerging in the early 1980s with names like la Familia de Dios and la Fraternidad Cristiana, many of Guatemala City's neo-Pentecostal mega-churches blossomed through strong ecclesiastical connections to mega-churches in the United States and South Korea. Though the strong North American influence comes as no surprise (several founding pastors received ministerial degrees from North American seminaries, and Guatemala's Protestant growth has been strongly aided by U.S. missionaries), the Korean influence is slightly more oblique but no less important. South Korea is home to one of the largest and most influential mega-churches in the world: David Yonggi Cho's Yoido Full Gospel Church. El Shaddai models much of its ministerial vision after Yoido, especially the church's so-called cellular structure—the strategy of church growth through small groups. Each cell strives to have twelve members, and among these twelve members there is a single leader. When a cell grows to be more than sixteen people, the cell splits in half, and these two new cell groups work to double in size so that they can divide again.

Yoido's relationship with El Shaddai began because of trade relationships between industries in Guatemala and South Korea, and it eventually resulted in the El Shaddai community's hosting several Yoido delegations, and sometimes even Pastor Cho himself. During Jorge Serrano's short term as president (1991–1993), Korean Free Trade Zones in Guatemala attracted more than 10,000 Koreans to Guatemala City. Immigrants themselves, they managed Korean-owned *maquiladoras,* or foreign-owned factories that employ lower-wage workers (Petersen 1992). A tariff-free relationship between the two countries, as well as Serrano's own neo-Pentecostal identity, generated a ministerial cross-fertilization that eventually influenced, even if only slightly, the style of Guatemala's most prominent of mega-churches. The mutual influence can be seen in the songs played during church services, the books sold in church lobbies, and the kinds of prayer campaigns advanced by church leadership. There has also developed a degree of competitiveness between the two countries. Dr. Caballeros during a Sunday sermon in 2002 announced: "In Korea today 38 percent of the people are born-again [Christians]. I saw the other day that between the born-again population and the charismatic Catholic population, Guatemala is 40 percent [born-again Christian]. Who would have ever said that we would be 2 percent higher than [the Koreans]?"[32] El Shaddai's enthusiastic race against the Koreans for church growth contributes to the production of a new language for national belonging that is itself rooted in a Christian anthropology, one that sees the citizen as both in Guatemala and of heaven. This vision of dual citizenship is relatively new to Central America but one that Christian thinkers have considered for millennia.

CHRISTIAN THINKERS, CHRISTIAN CITIZENSHIP

Christian citizenship is a fresh ethnographic object of study, but the conversation has biblical roots.[33] For early Christians, formal government was not important because Jesus Christ would soon come a second time.

Government and citizenship existed outside the scope of their cosmological map as societal and pan-generational concerns gave way to mounting expectations of millennial salvation (Brown 1989). The second coming seemingly on hold, the idea of government quickly became understood as an interim structure that would order humanity between "the fall" and Jesus' eventual return (Romans 13:1–7; 1 Peter 2:13–17). This confessional perspective, expectedly, raised moral questions about the relationship between Christians and their government. What authority does a government have in relation to God's kingdom? 1 Peter 2:13–17 reads: "For the Lord's sake accept the authority of every human institution, whether of the emperor as supreme, or of governors, as sent by him to punish those who do wrong and to praise those who do right" (see also Romans 13:3–4). What are the moral responsibilities of the Christian citizen? To this, the Bible suggests that Christians are to be "good" citizens who subordinate their needs to those of their countrymen: "Be subject to one another out of reverence for Christ" (Ephesians 5:21; see also Romans 12:10; Philippians 2:3–4). 1 Peter 2:15 continues: "For it is God's will that by doing right you should silence the ignorance of the foolish." Here Christian citizenship includes participating in government (Jeremiah 29:7), praying for governments (1 Timothy 2:1–2), respecting persons in authority (Exodus 22:28; Acts 23:5), distinguishing between the things of Caesar and those of God (Mark 12:17; 1 Peter 2:17), and caring for one's neighbor (Philippians 2:4). The Christian citizen, biblically speaking, properly attends to God's work on earth.

These questions helped foster an altogether different conception of the human.[34] Paul Barry Clarke writes: "The Christian notion of the person, by contrast with either the Greek or Roman concepts, shifted personhood into the domain of religion and metaphysics. By modeling the idea of the human personhood on the personhood of God the idea of the human person began to acquire a status that no legal notion of citizenship or personhood could, itself, complete" (1994a, 10). Hannah Arendt makes a similar point but in stronger terms. She argues that the advent of Christianity in the Roman world fundamentally reversed the relationship between individual life and political life. Whereas under the Roman system any hope for immortality was located in the sphere of political activity, this possibility shifted with Christianity to the sphere of individual life: "Just as the body politic possesses only a potential immortality which can be forfeited by political transgressions, individual life had once forfeited its guaranteed immortality in Adam's fall and now, through Christ, had regained a new, potentially everlasting life which, however, could again be lost in a second death through individual sin" (1958, 314–315). This new understanding of the person resulted in the theological formation of two worlds—two cities, in the words of Augustine (1993)—that the Christian citizen negotiates constantly. An anonymous author of an epistle to Diognetus, for example, writes in 200 that Christian citizens are ostensibly indistinguishable from non-Christian citizens: "For the distinction between Christians and other men, is neither in country nor in language nor custom. For they do not dwell in cities in some place of their own, nor do they use any strange variety of dialect, nor practice an extraordinary kind of life" (Lake 1912, 359). Christian citizens, rather, are ontologically set apart from non-Christian citizens by their inherent displacement in the world. Theologies of Christian citizenship constantly try to reconcile this displacement, arguing that Christian citizens are forever searching for their homeland. The epistle continues: "They dwell in their own fatherlands, but as if sojourners in them; they share all things as citizens, and suffer all things as strangers. Every foreign country is their fatherland and every fatherland is a foreign country" (1912, 359). The trope of travel, of sojourning, contributes to the theological construction of Christian citizenship, both as active and as on a constant pilgrimage from this world to the next. Christians are the citizens of two cities and in constant migration from one to the other.

Augustine, in the fourth century, constructs the earthly and the heavenly cities as distinct locales. The earthly city "does not live by faith," whereas "the heavenly city, or rather the part of it that sojourns on earth and lives by faith, makes use of [earthly] peace only because it must, until this mortal condition which necessitates it shall pass away" (1993, 695). Fleeting, temporal, and fallen, Christian citizens of this world journey to a more heavenly place to which they are called: "This heavenly city, then, while it sojourns on earth, calls citizens out of all nations, and gathers together a society of pilgrims of all languages, not scrupling about diversities in the manners, laws, and institutions whereby earthly peace is secured and maintained, but recognizing that, however various these are, they all tend to one and the same end of earthly peace" (1993, 695). Earthly obstacles—the fallen tendency to quarrel over difference—are lifted to reveal a frictionless society comprising citizens equal in both nature and stature.

This is not to say, Thomas Aquinas would later explain in the thirteenth century, that the laws of these two cities are equal. Rather, one's obedience to the heavenly city must always trump one's allegiance to earthly cities. The Christian citizen can very well be a lawbreaker and even a revolutionary:

"Every law is nothing else than a dictate of reason in the ruler by which his subjects are governed" (Aquinas 1974, 24). Laws, he argues, can facilitate goodness and virtue, but this does not necessarily need to be the case: "For if the intention of the lawgiver is fixed on that which is not simply good, but useful or pleasurable to himself, or in opposition to divine justice, then the law does not make men good simply, but in respect to that particular government" (1974, 25). Tyrannical law is thus "a perversion of law" (1974, 26) that the Christian citizen should not obey. Desiderius Erasmus, two centuries later, argues for the Christian citizen's coproduction of the common good: "In his performance of kingly duties let him bear always in mind that as a man he is dealing with fellow men, that as a free citizen he is dealing with free citizens, and above all as a Christian he is dealing with fellow Christians. The citizenry on their part must act in such a manner that their respect for the king be motivated by the interests of the common good" (1964, 194). Thematically speaking, then, the theological construction of Christian citizenship has long involved pilgrimage from an earthly city to the heavenly city and the responsibility to seek goodness.

Theologians from Erasmus onward have wrestled with the moral bounds of Christian citizenship; yet this book suggests that it is time for anthropologists to grapple with this as well, making this theological anthropology into an ethnographic problematic. It is my belief that neither biblical scholars nor theologians have a monopoly over questions of Christian citizenship. If the anthropologist stops to listen, Christians ask and re-ask each other (and themselves) in dialogical fashion who the Christian citizen is and what the good Christian citizen should do. Julio is but one example. Without ever having read Augustine or Erasmus, he spoke to me often about his own vision of Christian citizenship—the way that his Christian citizenship makes him feel of two cities but of one body; of one nation but affixed to two worlds (i.e., the material and the spiritual). In many ways, Julio's theology is more difficult to understand than Augustine's, given that Julio theologizes in a desperately violent capital city where political and economic stability is suspect at best. Waiting for Sunday service to begin, Julio leaned into my audio recorder just as a Guatemalan breeze swept over El Shaddai's campus, explaining:

[The Bible] says that we have our citizenship in heaven, with the Lord. That's the kind of citizenship we have. With this kind of citizenship, we have an obligation to the land, and we also have a citizenship up there in heaven with Jesus Christ. It's different [from everyone else's citizenship]. What do I have to do [as a Christian citizen]? What do I have to do if I am a believer and have my citizenship in heaven with Jesus Christ? Well, God demands of me to steward the land well, to make it better. God demands me to help Him whenever I can and to take on this responsibility. It is my obligation here on earth. But why? Because God demands it from me. In heaven it is different; in heaven there is nothing to do. . . . There is nothing to worry about; everything is eternal; everything is different. But as the Word of God says, God opened the heavens, so that the earth would be filled. And, who has filled the earth? It's Julio. It's Kevin. It's humanity. And, then what does God say? He says: "I am going to bless Kevin and Julio so that they can make heaven on earth."

The remaining chapters, in a sense, recount the ways in which Christian citizens like Julio work to "make heaven on earth" or, more specifically, in postwar Guatemala City—a place that for many has proven itself to be far from divine. Yet, amid crime, a feeble economy, and slow efforts at political reform, neo-Pentecostals like Julio take up the weight of Christian citizenship. They pray and fast a new Guatemala into existence. What follows assesses this effort with a balanced amount of admiration and disbelief, with a clear sense that Guatemala's neo-Pentecostals are by all means active (as active as any citizens could be) but also with concerns as to what this kind of activity means not just for their church but also for Guatemala. Both respect and frustration abound throughout these pages, but it is just this kind of ambivalence that extended fieldwork tends to yield.

ONE

Shouldering the Weight
The Promise of Citizenship

> Social participation at the community level . . . enables [citizens]
> to shoulder their responsibilities and commitments in the quest
> for social justice and democracy.
>
> 1996 GUATEMALAN PEACE ACCORDS

THE PROMISE OF CITIZENSHIP LINES the streets of postwar Guatemala City. As commanding as the volcanoes that frame the city and as ubiquitous as the squat, broken architecture that defines the capital's cityscape, citizenship campaigns print, paste, and post the promise of postwar citizenship on every conceivable surface that the city has to offer: billboards, buttons, placards, T-shirts. They announce that *you* are the city, that *you* must love Guatemala, and that God has chosen *you*. Flyers marked with this promise—with a catchphrase as well as a cue to participate—can often be found balled up and pushed into an alleyway, shuffled there by the bustle of *capitalinos* walking to and from work. Authored by an array of organizations and institutions, some of them ostensibly secular, others unbendingly faith-based, each campaign presses its own vision of postwar citizenship—its own idea of how Guatemalans should imagine their relationship to the nation and, moreover, how they can contribute to the governance of that nation. Clusters upon clusters of campaigns propagate this grand attempt, to be sure. They work excitedly to spark change at democracy's most basic of levels: citizenship.

The loudest of all efforts, in some sense the most inventive of citizenship campaigns, emerges from urban elites. They are ladinos with a message as well as the means to broadcast every conceivable iteration of that message to willing (as well as unwilling) Guatemalans. Alongside a less flashy and decidedly less vocal pan-Maya movement for increased indigenous rights, ladinos of a particular means promote a distinct formation of participation; they pour money and sweat into campaigns that, when read from a certain anthropological perspective, come off as incredibly tacky. They are tacky in the popular sense, certainly. These campaigns are garish and brassy; they use huge banners and bold colors to grab attention. They dress windowsills, and even people, in neon greens and yellows, draping government workers as well as volunteers in uncomfortable smocks replete with a citizenship slogan.[1] Yet these campaigns are also, and more interestingly, tacky in a way that communicates viscidity, something that sticks to one's person, that takes a great deal of effort to shake off and wash out. Citizenship campaigns in postwar Guatemala, with their jingles and slogans, with their television ads and radio spots, work hard to make the promise of citizenship something that takes hold of each Guatemalan— that sticks to his or her person.

This attempt at adhesiveness makes sense on at least two levels. The first is that during the country's civil war, fear became a way of life, as Linda Green notes (1999). Guatemalans, especially those in the western highlands, questioned their very thoughts and actions, wondering if either would be read as subversive by the military and thus "justify" their disappearance. For many, "self-censorship became second nature—Bentham's panopticon internalized" (Green 1994, 231).[2] Postwar citizenship, in contrast, promotes an attractive level of activity independent of the state and apart from the threat of paramilitary action. In its most ideal form, postwar citizenship promises a sense of political empowerment as well as personal liberation, even motivation, to forge a new nation.[3] The second level arises from the fact that Guatemala has experienced a great deal of change over the last thirty years. Guatemala has shifted from a state-centric economy to the global free market, from a thirty-six-year genocidal civil war to supposed peace and reconciliation, and from authoritarian rule to a formal democracy. These transitions have built on while also fortifying already dragging social indicators that ultimately raise a powerful postwar question: With so much work to do, who will make democracy, prosperity, and peace for Guatemala? The increasingly popular answer from the government, urban elites, and even mega-church pastors is that the individual citizen will shoulder the weight; the citizen will do the mundane and often thankless work of making an uncertain nation stable and secure.

Three of postwar Guatemala's tackiest campaigns embody the audacious gamble that Guatemalans as citizens will eagerly bear the weight of transitional times. The first is from Guatemala City's municipal government; the campaign announces, "Tú Eres la Ciudad," "You are the city." The second is an urban civil society organization whose brand is its slogan. An obvious play on the country's name, GuateAmala roughly translates as "Guate, love it!" The third comes from the neo-Pentecostal mega-church El Shaddai. Two slogans approximate the church's larger effort at fomenting a particular kind of postwar citizenship. The first is "Escogé tú," or "He [meaning God] chose you." The second is "Soy la Revolución," "I am the revolution." These three campaigns provide contrasting but ultimately interrelated visions of postwar citizenship, which this chapter examines at the level of discourse—citizenship as a message, citizenship as what Louis Althusser would understand as a hailing ideology (1998, 301). Althusser's famous reflection on the experience of being hailed (of the police officer yelling, "Hey, you there!") is helpful because each campaign's use of indexical pronouns suggests a political project that carries a number of assumptions and expectations.[4] Several citizenship campaigns are aflutter in postwar Guatemala City, but they tend to address *you* (instead of *us*) to participate as a good citizen. This chapter, in fact, lingers on this seemingly innocuous narrative decision, asking: Why are *you* the city (but *we* are not)? Why should *I* love Guatemala (while *we* could love Guatemala just as well, maybe even better)? Why has God chosen *me* instead of *us*? And why am *I* the revolution when *we* could probably form a more radical movement? These questions bring to relief the narrative fact that citizenship's indexical project locates social change within each individual Guatemalan. They make clear that postwar citizenship promotes an entrepreneurial kind of personhood that is intimately complicit with postwar Guatemala, so much so that the possibility of social critique and mobilization becomes difficult. How could *I* ever critique or mobilize against what *I* own, what *I* am, or what *I* have made? One of this chapter's central observations is that this manufactured complicity makes postwar citizenship so very difficult to shake, so incredibly tacky.

Accentuating this tackiness means reading each campaign with an eye to continuity rather than particularity. The approach is slightly askew from anthropology's long-held (and deeply principled) interest in difference.[5] A more traditional approach, for example, might detail how each campaign provides unique formations of postwar citizenship. The truth of the matter is, of course, that each campaign does offer something different, especially when one looks closely enough, but pursuing the approach glosses over the fact that Guatemala City is a small and economically polarized capital.

There are not many people in the city with the money to produce a vision of citizenship in any meaningful way, and those who do have it, predictably, run in the same circles. They frequent the same lectures, read more or less the same literature, and rely on the same North American think tanks.[6] Reading these campaigns as interrelated yields an understanding of postwar citizenship—its production, its logic, and its commitments as well as its redundancy and remarkable minimalism. Each advocates boldly, almost nakedly, that Guatemala will change when *you* change. This seemingly unanimous formation of personhood leaves individuals (far too often, I argue) standing alone with the weight of postwar Guatemala on their shoulders—with fingers wagging at *you* instead of *us*.[7]

WEIGHT

There is a sustained buzz about the promise of citizenship throughout postwar Guatemala—in the offices of civil society leaders, government officials, and Maya activists, not to mention in Guatemala's numerous aspirational documents, such as the country's constitutional amendments, tax reform legislation, and two truth commission reports.[8] The 1996 Peace Accords announce that "citizen participation in economic and social development is essential" to "promote productivity and economic growth" as well as to "achieve a more equitable distribution of wealth and train human resources" (2006, 46). The charge is one that many governmental and nongovernmental organizations (NGOs) have accepted in surprisingly consistent ways. Before exploring the promise of postwar citizenship in more detail, through the analysis of three campaigns, it is important to understand in some concrete terms the weight that these campaigns ask citizens to shoulder.[9]

The weight, simply put, refers to Guatemala's transitional promises that are *not yet*. In Guatemala there is a strong sense—a collective, felt agreement—that prosperity is *not yet;* democracy is *not yet;* and peace is *not yet*. The promise of citizenship in postwar Guatemala, in fact, rides on a palpable sense of incompleteness, and these unfulfilled promises help constitute the weight that presses down on present-day citizens who find themselves called to participate—who find themselves chosen to make a change for the future of Guatemala. The call to "complete" Guatemala is, to be sure, a deeply colonial vocation. The idea that Guatemala is incomplete or even *not yet* invokes the myth of Europe, which is often taken not only as the paragon of development but also as the moral and cultural point of comparison with non-Western countries such as Guatemala. There exists a popular narrative in Guatemala that constantly reiterates the fact that certain indices of development have *not yet* been achieved, and this narrative finds density through the themes of failure, lack, and inadequacy in much the same way that Dipesh Chakrabarty (2000) understands these terms.[10]

The producers of this progress narrative include the United Nations Development Programme, the World Bank, and the International Monetary Fund—but also the residents of Guatemala themselves, who often assume and become subsumed by a discourse of incompleteness— who find a level of freedom and agency in their own efforts at shouldering this weight.[11] Though this study is critical of developmental narratives (and their colonial subplots) that point toward Guatemala as *not yet*, it is also important not to avoid (or soften) the ethnographic fact that the feeling of "not yet" (todavía no) is quite real in postwar Guatemala. It is this very weight that ordinary residents of Guatemala City accept to become extraordinary Christians citizens.[12]

The felt sense that prosperity is not yet, for example, builds on the fact that Guatemala continues to be a country of extremes. The World Bank categorizes Guatemala as a "low to middle income country" on the basis of its gross domestic product (GDP). Yet scholars make clear that among similarly ranked countries, Guatemala has the highest incidence of poverty and is the third most unequal country in terms of the distance between the rich and the poor (Chase-Dunn et al. 2001, 4). According to the U.S. State Department, Guatemala's wealthiest 10 percent receives almost one-half of all income, and its wealthiest 20 percent receives two-thirds of all income. Close to 80 percent of the population lives in poverty, and two-thirds of that number lives in extreme poverty. Almost 65 percent of Guatemalans subsist on less than two dollars a day.[13]

The informal sector is a major part of this polarized economy—a major part of the weight that citizens are asked to bear. More than two-thirds of those employed in Guatemala work in the informal economy, selling goods, shining shoes, and doing odd jobs; and of those living in poverty, three-fourths work in the informal economy (CIEN 2006; Offit 2008). One result of the informal sector's predominance is an exceedingly low tax ratio (i.e., tax revenue as percentage of GDP). Guatemala has consistently had the hemisphere's second-lowest tax ratio, next to Haiti, and currently has the lowest public investment in social services and the lowest tax collection base in Central America (USAID 2006, 73). In the year 2000, for example, only six hundred taxpayers represented 60 to 70 percent of all of Guatemala's income tax revenue, and the wealthiest class of so-called special taxpayers, as of 1999, represented 38 to 40 percent of the total revenue collected from all taxes.[14] At the same time, government spending in Guatemala in 2003 was lower in terms of GDP than any other country in all of the Americas (Sridhar 2007). The Guatemalan government, simply put, neither collects taxes nor invests in either infrastructure or social services. With an economy driven by nontaxable, informal activities, the most robust stream of income originates from an estimated one million Guatemalans living and working in the United States. In 2006 some $3.6 billion crossed into Guatemala from the United States in the form of nontaxable cash remittances (Dardón 2007). This development, combined with the above factors, has left Guatemala ranked quite low in the category of "potential for economic growth." One report states that Guatemala is seventieth of eighty countries (Chase-Dunn et al. 2001, 4).[15]

The historical context for Guatemala's present-day economic troubles includes the weight of its thirty-six-year civil war. The Comisión para el Esclarecimiento Histórico (CEH) notes that the authority and the efficacy of the state weakened alongside a serious "loss of infrastructure" that was due to armed conflict, which destroyed bridges and roads as Guatemala continued to lose irreplaceable human capital (CEH 1999). Today Guatemala's postwar rapprochement with crime is no less expensive. The economic costs of crime in Guatemala in 1999, for example, were estimated to be $565.4 million (USAID 2006, 37). At the same time, international development organizations experimented throughout Latin America with what is commonly understood as economic restructuring, or neoliberal reform. In the 1980s and 1990s, during Guatemala's early efforts at democratization and a peaceful resolution to its civil war, international organizations such as the Inter-American Development Bank encouraged the privatization of public industries, such as water and utilities. These efforts attempted to streamline the state, open the markets to trade, reduce government corruption, and make Guatemala more competitive on the world market.[16] Yet a common analysis found in critical Guatemalan circles holds that this increased reliance on the private sector simply layered bureaucracy on top of bureaucracy while making the state even weaker and the responsibility of the individual citizen more central to the Guatemalan context. Following the 1996 Peace Accords, a wave of NGOs arrived in Guatemala to begin doing the work of the state—to run schools and hospitals, for example. With neither coordination nor transparency, the state began to pay these NGOs through the national budget as consultants to do the very work that the state had otherwise been expected to do.

One poignant political cartoon animates the effects of neoliberal privatization and offers a glimpse of the public's perception of democratically elected officials in postwar Guatemala. In a seven-panel cartoon, the first six captions frame a high-ranking government official's chubby fingers. The first panel announces: "It was hard. Boy, it was hard! But little by little I achieved a great deal for my country." The next five panels list the governor's accomplishments, each counted with a fat digit: "I got Amnesty International to worry about my incarcerated opponents; I got UNICEF to help this country's tens of thousands of abandoned, malnourished, and illiterate children; I got the Red Cross to be in charge of helping the multitude of sick senior citizens." With three fingers fully extended, the official continues: "I got Greenpeace and their volunteers to stop this country's frightening ecological deterioration; I got DEA agents sent from Washington to direct a war against drugs and drug trafficking." The final panel shows the official lying back in his chair, arms raised in success, a bottle of liquor on his desk. He exclaims: "Finally, I can now govern in peace without worrying about anything or anyone."[17] This representation of the carefree, high-ranking government official and the weight that has been taken from his shoulders stops just short of naming where the weight has been placed: not just on the plates of NGO workers but also on the shoulders of Guatemalan citizens.

Increased decentralization and the withering of the Guatemalan state have not exactly invigorated Guatemalans with the promise of democracy. The public's overall perception of electoral democracy is quite dismal—lukewarm at best. At the very same time that some of the tackiest citizenship campaigns exhort Guatemalans to complete their nation, democracy itself remains a distrusted means to an end. If the cartoon exists as an approximation of the public's confidence in democratically elected leaders, then the following statistics provide a more calculated assessment of Guatemalans' opinion of democracy. The first telling indicator is electoral participation. Of those Guatemalans eligible to vote, 36.2 percent fulfilled their civic duty between 1990 and 2002 (UNDP 2004b, 85). In the 1990s, on average, only 29.6 percent of Guatemalans voted in each election, which ranks Guatemala dead last among twenty Latin American countries (IDEA 1998, 6). This strikingly low level of voter turnout makes sense when one glimpses the public's perception of democracy. The Latinobarómetro reports that a dismal 51 percent of Guatemalans in 1996 agreed with the statement "Democracy is preferable to any other kind of government." Only 16 percent of respondents answered "very satisfied" or "fairly satisfied" to the question "In general, would you say that you are satisfied with the way democracy works in [your nation]?" And only 56 percent of respondents answered "yes" to the question "Would you be willing to defend democracy if it was under threat?" When these three numbers are combined to form an "Index of Democratic Perceptions," Guatemala ranks last in a field of eighteen Spanish-speaking countries (IDEA 1998). Guatemala's apparent inability to wrap its optimism around democracy makes the following statistic less surprising: only 6 percent of respondents answered "fully established" to the question "Do you think that democracy is fully established in [your nation], or do you think that . . . there are still things to be done?" The overwhelming consensus that "there are still things to be done" presses down on postwar Guatemalans, highlighting a sense of incompleteness.

Ten years later, though hard-fought political victories have been won, the Latinobarómetro confirms that not much has changed in terms of democracy's overall popularity. Only 10 percent believe that in the future there will be greater equality in Guatemala, whereas 18 percent of those polled think that the future holds a more democratic Guatemala; some 50 percent even expect that Guatemala will be more corrupt than it is already perceived to be (Latinobarómetro 2007, 53). In 2006, 31 percent of those polled answered that they were "satisfied" with democracy (rather than "very satisfied" or "fairly satisfied"). In 2007 only 30 percent of those polled responded in like fashion (2007, 80). This lack of growth places the country last in a field of eighteen Latin American countries. Guatemala is also the country in which the fewest people feel that "democracy is the best form of government" and second to last in believing that "the government looks out for the well-being of its people" (2007, 81). These numbers suggest that the idea of democracy has not yet stuck—has not yet proven itself to be tacky enough.

Postwar violence in Guatemala is one reason the promise of democracy has not taken hold in the region. There are, for example, an estimated two million unregistered firearms left over from the civil conflict in the hands of 36 percent of the civilian population (USAID 2006, 79). This partly explains why 56 percent of Guatemalans, responding to questions about postwar insecurity, reported feeling troubled (inquieta); 60 percent reported feeling angry (enojada); over 50 percent reported having troubles sleeping; and only 54 percent reported that they "enjoy life."[18] And though the actual causes of such extreme postwar violence are unknown, a combination of factors is at least partly responsible. Among these include the migration of street gangs from Southern California to Guatemala City.[19] Stricter immigration policies in a post-9/11 United States have led to the continued deportation of undocumented Guatemalans from Los Angeles. The United States, for example, deported 9,487 Guatemalans between 2004 and 2005, of whom 2,210 had criminal records (USAID 2006, 77). Working closely with organized crime, many of those deported move billions of dollars of illegal narcotics through Guatemala to the United States, while also taking over large swaths of land in the capital city through violence. Minuscule life chances in a postwar context now mix with transnational street gangs, butting up against a continually shrinking and increasingly ineffective Guatemalan police force.[20]

At least in the capital city, where I collected testimonies from several people who had been assaulted, kidnapped, or mugged, my question whether they had contacted the police after being assaulted was always met with curiosity. Jaime, a key informant from the El Shaddai church, once told me about being carjacked at gunpoint. It was 9:00 a.m. on a Saturday morning in one of Guatemala City's safer *zonas* when three men pulled him from the front seat of his car, put a gun to his head, and then threw him into the backseat. They drove him around the capital city for a little over thirty minutes, waiting to see if a timed alarm would sound (a common security feature in Guatemala City automobiles, which allows the driver to secretly activate an alarm system that only he himself can deactivate). After threatening to kill Jaime and discard his body in one of the capital city's many *barrancas*, or ravines, they let him go. With no car and no money, Jaime ran to his father's house, which was quite a distance away. I asked Jaime what the police did when he reported the incident. I was (naively) surprised when he told me that he had not yet informed the police: "They don't do anything," he shrugged—his sentiment reflecting the statistical fact that 73 percent of those who live in or around Guatemala City believe that the police are directly involved in crime. This staggering number means that a mere 27 percent believe that the police are either indifferent or that they actually protect them (USAID 2006, 78).

The impunity found in Guatemala is almost as striking as the violence. Impunity, it should be noted, was an important theme during the 1996 Peace Accords, as many military officials and soldiers were charged with crimes against humanity but were protected from prosecution.[21] The overarching theme in Guatemala at the time of the Peace Accords was reconciliation rather than retribution. Peace was brokered only through the promise of impunity for those involved in the war—even though the Guatemalan state was found to be responsible for 93 percent of all human rights violations registered by the Comisión para el Esclarecimiento Histórico (CEH 1999). Today Guatemala's violence goes unpunished. As the introduction points out, violence against women continues to go unchecked, growing at a shocking pace: 317 homicides in 2002, 383 homicides in 2003, 497 homicides in 2004, 518 homicides in 2005, and 603 homicides in 2006 (Alvarado and Blas 2008). As Victoria Sanford reports, "The mortality rate of women in peacetime Guatemala today is reaching the very high levels of female mortality in the early 1980s at the height of the genocidal war that took 200,000 lives" (2008, 22). With no arrests in 97 percent of the cases of violence against girls or women and more than 70 percent of all cases involving girls or women having not even been investigated, reality forces many to think that if the government will not act, then each citizen must.

YOU ARE THE CITY

At the time of the inauguration of Álvaro Arzú as Guatemala City's mayor in 2008, the capital took on a new image as well as a new social experiment by way of a glossy citizenship campaign. The campaign, in all its simplicity, is arresting in the truest sense of the word. The campaign makes one stop; it calls to the pedestrian, charging *you* with a level of ownership and complicity. Tú Eres la Ciudad, the movement announces; you are the city. The campaign hails the pedestrian by way of bumper stickers, T-shirts, pins, banners, street signs, posters, television commercials, radio spots, and public service announcements. Walking down some of Guatemala City's major thoroughfares means confronting, or rather being confronted by, the announcement dozens of times. They all proclaim that *you* are the city; other street signs add, through sassy amendments, that so are "you, you, you, and you and all of you as well."[22] There is no obvious way to escape. *You* are the city.

Produced by Guatemala City's municipal government, and authored by its Department of Communications, the campaign is an exercise in branding the city. The effort is annual. In 2006, for example, the city's slogan celebrated Guatemala City's 230th anniversary as the nation's capital, which the municipal government complemented with efforts at restoring

Centro Histórico—the capital city's historic district, which has over the years fallen into some disrepair.[23] In 2007 the municipal government celebrated ten years of the Peace Accords and organized a series of community events, including a five-kilometer run and an outdoor performance, to celebrate their contribution to Guatemalan history. Implied in all this exertion is a kind of rhythm. With the municipal government's annual theme comes some level of action; anniversaries yield efforts at restoration and celebration.

True to tradition, the municipal government's 2008 effort at branding involved activity; yet the action implied is the very thing that makes this campaign also function as a social program. The municipal government, as far as its Tú Eres la Ciudad campaign goes, in no way pretends to do anything beyond pushing its message onto the masses. There is no development project (at least in the traditional sense) tethered to the campaign; there are no panels or parties to commemorate past events, or any new schools, clinics, or welfare programs. Rather, the very message—Tú Eres la Ciudad—has been framed in such a way as to prompt each individual to act as a particular kind of citizen. The municipal government can do only so much, the message implies; *you,* the citizen, must do the rest. Tú Eres la Ciudad is not just a catchy phrase but also a call to participate as a good citizen—as the very city itself.

Tú Eres la Ciudad, at the same time but through a possibly more critical register, is also a proposal for the creation of persons with a certain kind of relationship to *themselves.* As the city, *you* take on a range of responsibilities and relationships. *You* become the city's coproducer, maybe even primary author, alongside the municipal government. Understanding this rhetorical move as well as the participation it promotes helps to clarify the kind of citizenship advocated throughout postwar Guatemala. The municipal government's proposed citizenship advances an entrepreneurial relationship to the city and to the self; the narrative provides a new grammar for living, one that states in the clearest of terms that the citizen (as the city) must steward himself or herself—not just for the sake of himself or herself but also for the capital as well. Mayor Arzú introduced the slogan to much fanfare on January 12, 2008. He announced: "We hope that each Guatemalan feels every day that the municipal government is close at hand, from when they are walking down the streets in the morning until they return home at night after a long day of work."[24] The mayor's interest in the municipal government as ever-present through oneself and one's neighbors is a response to a long-held opinion that the government does very little for the city. The government, as the critique of many goes, is corrupt and without teeth; the municipal government easily forgets those in the capital and so, in turn, the government deserves little respect. The prosecution rates for the killing of women cited before are but one line of evidence. Another is the staggering fact that hundreds of people are killed in Guatemala City every month. But, in reality, noisy traffic and trash-strewn avenues also stoke the flames of frustration for those Guatemalans who work, commute, and live in challenging urban conditions.

The mayor, attentive to this popular assessment as well as to the city's shocking crime statistics, continued: "We are plainly aware of our daily struggle to regenerate urban life and to attend to problems promptly and professionally, but none of these concerns distract us from our ultimate objective: to make Guatemala City an international city that is prosperous and innovative, that is a model for the region." For a city with some of the most troubling social indicators in all the Americas, these are lofty goals, yet the mayor quickly complemented his optimism with a plan. At its most basic, the plan requires that each citizen take on the responsibility of doing the work that the municipal government simply cannot complete: "Today, while setting some goals and generating a little consensus, I want to tell you that, for us, as a team, it is fundamental that you are the city— not the streets, not the buildings, not the parks." *You* are the city, and so are *you, you,* and *you.*

At its most ideal, Mayor Arzú's logic is that without citizens, the streets are just empty spaces. Without citizens, buildings are vacant shells and the parks abandoned areas. Without *you,* the city would not exist. The mayor continued: "You are the city because you make it; because you transform it; because you suffer in it; because there, in the streets, is your childhood; because you raise your children in those streets; because there is your house, your work; because there is your life, your aspirations, your memories." You, the citizen, in all of your complexity, constitute the city—one biography at a time. Though the streets are its arteries and the buildings its organs, citizens—*you*—are the city's lifeblood: "For all those reasons and for many more that escape me now, you, as am I, as is the neighbor, as is the friend, the coworker, the person that you don't even know when you cross the street, even the child in the street . . . all of you are the city!" Concluding his speech, the mayor emphasized, pleaded in some sense, "It is vital that each one of you feels that you are the city." To reach the goal of becoming "a model for the region," you must become invested; you must recognize yourself as the city.

Arzú's director of communications, during an extended interview, clarified why recognizing oneself as the city is so very important: "The municipal government provides services, but it is not the city. The citizen is what makes the city. We can have a super-modern city, for example, but we can still be a cold city. We, or the government rather, deliver services, but the citizen makes sure that those services run well and will ultimately define the direction in which the city will go." The government, the director explained, can do only so much, and these limitations force the government to shift much of its responsibility onto the citizen. She continued: "Because really [Tú Eres la Ciudad] is a very powerful movement, with great reach. Our objective is rather clear. We want the citizen to identify with the city. We want the citizen to feel a part of the city." This rather general objective carries strikingly concrete metrics: "The goal is for people to say to themselves: 'I'm not going to throw trash in the street because I am the city. I am going to clean my sidewalk because I am the city. I'm not going to speed because I am the city; I'm going to use my seat belt. I'm not going to talk on the phone when I am driving."[25] The municipal government's intention is for Guatemalans to establish a new relationship with themselves through the language of citizenship—one that is thoughtful, observant, and, most important, self-governing. Tracking the pronouns reveals as much. Clear, for example, is the narrative fact that *you* are the city and that this decision means that *we* are not the city—in a collective sense; the city, moreover, is not immediately identified with *us*. Interesting, also, is the idea that *it*, meaning the municipal government, is not the city. Within Guatemala City, there exists an array of agents and networks of responsibilities; but the indexical emphasis here is on the individual and the work that the individual must do. Yet what is also clear is that this citizenship campaign wants you to establish a relationship with yourself— with *I*—so that *you* can tell *I* to do certain things. The director of communications, again, wants each citizen to speak to himself or herself, to adopt what Mikhail Bakhtin would call an internally persuasive discourse— "the monologue that lasts a whole life" (1981, 345). When you become the city and when you begin to address yourself, then you take on the responsibility to clean sidewalks and police speeding cars (even if it is just your own vehicle). This kind of citizenship promotes a personhood that literally does the work of the municipal government—that becomes complicit with the city itself because, ultimately, *you* are the city.

The director provided an instance of how this citizenship campaign might hit the ground: "If there is junk in the streets, for example, as a citizen one can arrange to have that trash collected [by the municipal government], but citizens can also participate. They can sweep and wash their sidewalks; they can collect the trash that has blown into their gardens. It is a way of participating . . . and with every piece of trash collected, we can improve the city." As Julia Paley reports, from the Chilean context, on the very topic of trash collecting, citizenship participation of this kind prompts individuals to do the work of the state (free of charge) while also deadening the possibility of social critique (2001, 146). Social critique becomes softened because Guatemalans, not just as members of the city but also *as* the city, must address themselves as well as the municipal government when voicing critique. Condemning dirty streets and speeding cars does not just point a finger at the municipal government. Such a critique also implicates oneself; critique incriminates *you*.

The municipal government, through its citizenship campaign, asks Guatemalans to establish a governing relationship between themselves and the city, one that ideally echoes the very internal dialogue promoted by the director of communications: "The goal is for people to say to themselves: 'I'm not going to throw trash in the street because I am the city; I am going to clean my sidewalk because I am the city; I'm not going to speed because I am the city.' " This internal dialogue between the self and the citizen is productive because this kind of discourse is always "half-ours and half-someone else's" (Bakhtin 1981, 345); in turn, it limits the ways in which citizens of postwar Guatemala can act as citizens. Though the semantic structure of such a dialogue, as Bakhtin argues, "is not finite" but "open," the rapport is nonetheless limited and limiting; the dialogue primes Guatemalans to take up certain modes of participation as opposed to others. The municipal government, for example, does not just want active citizens to pick up trash; the government also wants its citizens to engage in a range of proposed activities.

The first, according to its promotional literature, is to observe: "Walk around and observe closely your neighborhood. Look at the buildings, the houses, the people, the bridges, the open spaces, the businesses, the gardens, the parks, and the traffic. Observe how people use these spaces. Observe the rhythm of your neighborhood . . . take notes, if you like, about what you have observed." The second is to think (piense). The literature asks: "What do you think about the place in which you live? What do you like about your neighborhood? What are the places and buildings that you frequent the most? What are the aspects that you admire most, and what are those things that you would like to change?"[26] The active citizen (as the city) observes and thinks as well as speaks (hable), learns (aprenda), and evaluates (evalue).

These proposed activities, without a doubt, invoke a tortured history. Only a few decades earlier, Guatemalans lived under the threat of military informants, not knowing if a friend or a family member would identify them as guerrillas or rebel sympathizers. The idea of neighbors observing and taking notes, watching with the single intent of learning more about someone, cannot help summoning painful memories. Linda Green captures the tenor and texture of the Guatemalan civil war. She writes: "Denunciations, gossip, innuendos, and rumors of death lists create a climate of suspicion. No one can be sure who is who" (1994, 227). And the reality is, of course, that Guatemala's haunting civil war is impossible to shake; the war lingers in Guatemala City's streets—in the hearts of survivors, on the scarred bodies of victims; yet the municipal government advocates a different kind of governance from the one advocated during the civil war, even if this new form of governance is seemingly impossible to disentangle from the country's history. For the municipal government, the active citizen does not observe neighbors to learn who is (and who is not) a guerrilla. In many ways the knowledge produced through these activities is secondary to the political rationality formed through the very practice of observing and thinking as well as speaking, learning, and evaluating. If one reads the municipal government's literature closely, if one listens to its spokespersons, what becomes clear is that the intended outcome is not necessarily for the individual to learn anything per se about his or her city but rather to assume and become subsumed by a "thinking, acting, and choosing" self (Rose 1996a), replete with an internally persuasive discourse of Bakhtinian dimensions. The ultimate objective is for each citizen to solidify an intimate relationship between the self and the city while also recognizing an arena of action that counts as productive citizenship participation.

The municipal government works to form a particular kind of citizenship through a range of predictable techniques: self-esteem, empowerment, consultation, and negotiation (Dean 1999, 168). Reappearing often within postwar Guatemala is also the idea of the *attitude* as a constitutive element of citizenship; the attitude is one of ownership, responsibility, and activity. Or, as the director of communications explained: "We're going to see a change in people's attitudes [with Tú Eres la Ciudad]. . . . And [citizenship] is all about changing the attitude of people, because many times people walk by a place and they don't pay any attention to a monument, for example. But now [because of Tú Eres la Ciudad] they'll pay attention. Before, people saw a garden and it was half made. Now they are going to notice that there are really nice flowers . . . and they won't even think of destroying them."[27] The municipal government's citizenship campaign works to shape citizens with a certain mode of self-reflection, with a certain attitude, one that governs the self for the sake of Guatemala—one that manages the self as the city. This effort at making postwar citizenship resonates with several other postwar campaigns. The continuity of it all is often startling.

LOVE GUATEMALA

GuateAmala, another popular citizenship campaign, captures the moral dimensions of postwar citizenship in Guatemala. GuateAmala's emphasis on the interior dimensions of citizenship makes it an altogether representative example of how postwar formations of citizenship ultimately ask Guatemalans for a level of self-mastery—to rule one's own desires and to tame such interior realities as habits, attitudes, thoughts, and behaviors. GuateAmala's guiding message is that only when the individual has proper control over himself or herself will Guatemala achieve an acceptable level of prosperity, democracy, and peace. Guatemala will change for the better, GuateAmala announces, but only one person at a time—only when *you* change. In this sense, GuateAmala calls on individuals to participate not just in the remaking of themselves but also in the taming of themselves through distinct technologies of citizenship. These technologies yet again place the responsibility to govern Guatemala in the hands (and on the shoulders) of individuals.

Founded by urban elites in 2005, the GuateAmala campaign reportedly began during a conversation about Guatemala's supposed pessimism and how dreams of a new, more optimistic country could become a reality. With a clear sense of purpose, the twelve founding members grew to three hundred, clarifying their intention along the way: "We want to make Guatemala a country of citizens. We dream of a nation in which its residents practice responsibility and a full awareness of political, civil, and social rights. We understand that for this to happen, it is indispensable to understand the rights and the obligations that we all share."[28] GuateAmala places this commitment into the mold of a social movement; its central goal is to cultivate what the campaign understands as a "culture of life" with "the desire to transform the attitude of Guatemalans into a proactive and positive approach [to life], instilling in [Guatemalans] rules of citizenship behavior and inspiring them to live and act positively." GuateAmala's ultimate vision is not only to change the nation but also to make Guatemala a beacon of hope: "Our country will change and will be a model to the world. The dark times that we have lived through will be full of light, full of dreams, and full of opportunities."[29] GuateAmala, through the formation of citizenship, makes hope in abundant quantities, its promise almost within reach.

Enthusiastic, even inspired testimonies abound in GuateAmala's literature, and these testimonies reinforce the movement's central message. Otilia Lux, a member of GuateAmala and UNESCO, explains: "GuateAmala is a novel initiative, where optimistic people participate voluntarily. They persistently embody the values of agreement, harmony, and brotherhood." Juan Mauricio Wurmser, a member of GuateAmala and a businessman, adds: "I am convinced that the greatest obstacle to Guatemala's advancement is a negative and defeatist attitude. The GuateAmala movement has given us a very effective tool to achieve a change in our attitude, to develop our potential and wealth, to improve the living conditions for a great number of people in our country."[30]

Spokespersons, however, are only a small part of GuateAmala's vision for change. They do the technical work of organizing an increasingly complicated network of projects and message points, but the real work starts with the individual. Only through individual and interior change will Guatemala become a new and vibrant country. As one GuateAmala representative explained during a series of extended interviews: "If a person does not want to change, then that person will not change. It's that simple. . . . But the first step is the attitude. The first step is fundamental; it's saying, 'I want to change,' or, 'I want to leave this reality and I want to make my dreams a reality.'" Here again the decision to change begins with *you.* Throughout the literature, in fact, GuateAmala uses the indexical pronoun *you* to lasso its reader into the movement, conscripting Guatemalans to work for a culture of life, to work for the future of the nation by working on themselves. Just as *you* are the city, *you* must love Guatemala. The move is not surprising; scholars of Foucault understand contemporary social movements as principally concerned with formations of the self: "Those who undergo 'revolution from within' are citizens doing the right thing; they join programs, volunteer, but most importantly, work on and improve their self-image." (Cruikshank 1996, 234). GuateAmala is first and foremost a social movement that begins with the self—that actually begins inside people.

GuateAmala's narrative penetrates the model Guatemalan, speaking directly to his or her optimism, attitude, and values. This interior world, the campaign announces, is the plane on which social change will happen. GuateAmala can do only so much. The campaign can provide the tools to become a citizen, but the real work needs to take place inside every Guatemalan. The active citizen, ultimately, must become subject to himself or herself, which is a development that confuses a long-understood division. Subjects (as opposed to citizens) are said to "behave themselves because an external force exerts power over them," whereas citizens (as opposed to subjects) are said to act "as their own masters [because they] have the power to act for themselves" (Cruikshank 1999, 19–20). The difference is one of power. Yet campaigns such as GuateAmala make clear that citizenship involves citizens subjecting themselves to themselves. Citizenship in postwar Guatemala involves a range of self-governing practices. This is why working on oneself (and in turn participating in the formation of a new nation) begins with a personal decision. Linked by way of advertisements at bus stops and on widely distributed and brightly colored GuateAmala T-shirts, the campaign aims to be ever-present; in many ways, GuateAmala can feel ever-present. The movement forces residents of Guatemala to make a decision at every turn—to decide whether they are for or against GuateAmala's culture of life. At first blush, the decision is not very difficult; GuateAmala makes clear that citizenship begins with a passionate commitment: "We will realize our activities with passion. Passion is to be and to act. Genuine desire to change will allow us to have an influence. We will be authentic examples, credible and inspiring." With passion, desire, and authenticity, active citizenship will change the country, building a level of individual excitement that will grow beyond the city and into the countryside: "We will seek out multiple ways to release the spirit and passion in all of us: we will be in communication with the people, celebrating cases of success, we will record stories, we will present positive cases, we will identify heroes, we will define our identity, we will seek our new roots and will continue to make ourselves more capable of knowing and better executing the role that we have taken on to represent."[31] GuateAmala aspires to instill pride in Guatemalans and prompts them to care for their nation by caring for themselves. But how does one care for Guatemala by way of the self?

Citizenship participation, as scholars have made increasingly clear, involves a number of technologies. Barbara Cruikshank, for example, observes that "democracy is entirely dependent upon technologies of citizenship" and that "the constitution of the citizen-subject requires technologies of subjectivity, technologies aimed at producing happy, active, and participatory democratic citizens." Of interest for Cruikshank but also for this analysis is that "these technologies rarely emerge from the Congress; more often, they emerge from the social sciences, pressure groups, social work discourses, therapeutic social service programs and so on. Their common goal, nevertheless, is to get citizens to act as their own masters" (1996, 247). GuateAmala provides Guatemalans with technologies through which they may "act as their own masters."

One of GuateAmala's central technologies is a rubber band. Complete with instructions, the band allows Guatemalans to make (and remake) the decision to love Guatemala. The instructions announce: "Guatemala's change begins with you."[32] Depicting an extended arm with a rubber band worn around the wrist, the directions present a series of virtues, such as "respect," "punctuality," "love for Guatemala," and "tolerance." This constellation sets the tone; Guatemalans need to make a change on the inside before they can begin to make a change on the outside. The sheet explains: "When you are lacking [one of these virtues], give yourself a tug! To remember that a positive attitude is a daily promise, use this rubber band." The sheet also enumerates concrete steps toward becoming a better, more involved citizen: "(1) Place the rubber band around your wrist. (2) When you are feeling negative, when you are feeling down, without hope, give yourself a tug. (3) Discover your capacity to improve your attitude." Or, as one GuateAmala representative explained to me: "[The rubber band] makes one think: if I am doing something against the culture of life, like littering in the streets, then that's bad, and when I [litter] I need to snap the rubber band." The band prompts thoughtful action: "Again, the rubber band reminds you that you have to act like a good citizen; it says, 'Don't throw trash in the street, don't honk your horn for no reason, let people pass,' and it reminds you when you act to the contrary that you should really snap the rubber band." The representative, in mid-sentence, pulled an imaginary rubber band, stretching his pinched fingers back behind his ear, releasing air, and then announcing, "POW!"—as if the band had snapped his flesh. "It's a way to make you reflect," he added.

The band promotes a series of relationships: between the self and the nation; between righteousness and delinquency; between one's interior world and exterior world. The band exists as a striking reminder that the management of the interior world exists in constant relationship with the Guatemalan nation by way of one's attitude. The physical tug of the band—the brute pull of the band, even a possible "slap on the wrist" if the tug becomes a snap—brings the interior world into contact with the exterior world. From the perspective of GuateAmala, the tug on the wrist mediates these two thinly separated domains. Tugging at the band becomes a conscious decision to "discover your capacity to improve your attitude."

The band, of course, is intended to be a simple reminder. Be a good citizen; have a good attitude. Yet GuateAmala's citizenship technology also exists as an opportunity to discuss how the formation of citizenship in postwar Guatemala involves learning to govern the nation through the self—to master oneself. Such messages, of course, are not unique to postwar Guatemala. Nikolas Rose comments: "Liberal strategies of government thus become dependent upon devices (schooling, the domesticated family, the lunatic system, the reformatory prison) that promise to create individuals who do not need to be governed by others, but will govern themselves, master themselves, care for themselves" (1996b, 45). For GuateAmala, being a good citizen means managing one's level of respect, calibrating one's respect for others (e.g., punctuality and tolerance), and administering one's love for Guatemala. Its rationality links the interior, individual self to the collective: *My* attitude affects *our* Guatemala. GuateAmala's literature explains: "A proactive and optimistic attitude toward the future will be essential [to change Guatemala]. And as we seek the realization of each individual, our success will be based on collective force. Being together, united by one noble and challenging vision, we will make ourselves stronger, better equipped to fight, more human, better friends, better leaders, more creative, better Guatemalans."[33] Once again to chart the pronouns at play, it is fair to note that the work that *I* do on *my* self is for *us*—not just for *me* and not even for *you*. Moreover, the work that *I* need to do on *my* self is *my* responsibility, not *yours* or even *ours*. GuateAmala sets the parameters clearly: citizenship is an individual effort made in behalf of the collective.

In terms of a social movement, the logic of GuateAmala also paints a picture of millions of individual, interior social movements taking place alongside each other. This is not just because individuals make up Guatemala but also because there is a rich understanding that Guatemalans *are* Guatemala—that Guatemala comprises some 14 million individuals. And with 14 million individual attitude changes, Guatemala will be transformed. Samuel Pérez, a member of GuateAmala and a representative of Universidad Rafael Landívar, explains: "I believe in Guatemala, in Guatemalans, and that with the proper attitude we can transform everything together. We are doing something that will turn us completely around. Guatemala is going to change." As GuateAmala's literature explains, one must constantly survey one's own attitude, constantly assess the level of love one has for Guatemala, and measure one's respect as well as tolerance for others, making sure that at the same time one is punctual and proactive. Low levels of respect and miserly amounts of love threaten Guatemala. The rationality envisions the active citizen as a "calculative, prudent person" who understands himself or herself "in terms of calculable dangers and avertable risks" (Rose 1996b, 58). A bad attitude is risky for Guatemala.

This level of self-governance—this constant monitoring of one's inner world—brings to mind the image of a pilot who actively watches the dials, digits, and monitors in the cockpit of an airplane to keep the plane steady. To keep from going off course or inadvertently changing his or her altitude, the pilot makes adjustments—flips switches, types in numbers, turns a steering device from time to time. In the same vein, to make sure that the Guatemalan citizen does not go off course or inadvertently change his or her attitude, GuateAmala suggests the monitoring of emotions, tugging on the rubber band as a reminder to be punctual, respectful, and tolerant. While at risk of being overextended, the metaphor of the pilot also helps to locate GuateAmala's vision of the active citizen. Just as the pilot struggles with the dangers and responsibilities of flight while alone in a cockpit, the kind of rational subject that GuateAmala offers its country places the citizen in a similar cockpit of Cartesian dimensions. Alone to deal with the growing weight of postwar Guatemala, GuateAmala's ideal citizen fidgets with his or her attitude. While possibly connected to others, each citizen struggles alone with an unruly attitude, working to stay aloft and keep the nation afloat.

HE CHOSE YOU

Dr. Harold Caballeros and the El Shaddai congregation promote yet another vision of postwar citizenship that, along with its secular counterparts, maps social change onto the terrain of the self, asking each Guatemalan to develop the nation by way of self-improvement. The register through which El Shaddai promotes its vision of citizenship is, of course, explicitly Christian and ultimately hitched to a theological anthropology that gives priority to the individual by way of personal salvation and the saving grace of Jesus Christ. And at the very center of Christian citizenship sits the problem of free will, what Augustine narrates in his *Confessions* as an internal moral conflict that demands a fundamental reorientation of the self. Pitting rational moral discernment against sin as constitutive of the human condition, Augustine narrates the practice of Christian introspection to suggest, at the very least, that there exists an interior world in need of reform. The problem and practice of Christian citizenship in postwar Guatemala, in fact, begin with this interior world, identifying the will as the constant cause of postwar Guatemala's tremendous weight, while also recognizing citizenship as a technology through which the will can be harnessed. As many of this book's chapters attest, being an active Christian citizen means controlling oneself, or placing oneself under control through a range of practices that expose oneself to one's own thoughtful gaze.

Postwar citizenship, placed in a Christian key, prompts a kind of moral anxiety over the state of one's own will. From a neo-Pentecostal perspective, then, the site of democratic reform in postwar Guatemala is not really the public arena. Given the continued politicization of neo-Pentecostal Christianity in postwar Guatemala, mega-churches like El Shaddai spend a striking amount of time and energy detailing clearly how each person can best govern himself or herself for the greater glory of Guatemala. Saving Guatemala begins with saving the self, with controlling the self. And these acts of self-governance take place in a number of confessional settings: Sunday services, Christian concerts, reflection groups, praise and healing sessions, prayer and fasting campaigns, journal entries and moral manuals, and public as well as private testimonies that detail the shadowy corners of the broken and fallen self.

Dr. Caballeros frames this neo-Pentecostal formation of postwar citizenship with a charged observation: Guatemala is a fragmented nation, as broken as the Christian's will. At a private event Dr. Caballeros announced: "Guatemala needs the formation of an identity. We are Guatemalans, but what really is a Guatemalan? Do leaders hold the same concept of Guatemalans in [the village of] Santa Maria, the same concept of Guatemalans in a barrio? The same sentiment in the city? Some say that [the identity of] those in the upper classes is close to what it's like in Miami, while other [Guatemalan] towns are closer to Africa. . . . We Guatemalans are so distant from each other in terms of the formation of citizenship and the formation of an identity." Dr. Caballeros continued, proposing Christian citizenship as an identity that would unite Guatemala: "What better than the work of believers? What better than the link of the gospel to dissolve these sentiments and polarizations? We need to pursue a national consensus, and we have the tools to clean up [the polarization], tools like the gospel, love, and forgiveness—allowing us to construct this identity of Christian citizenship." Neo-Pentecostal formations of Christian citizenship work to bind the nation into one, assuming that if there is anthropological consensus (i.e., agreement on the human condition), then there will also be national unity.

A number of citizenship campaigns drive Dr. Caballeros's call for a single brotherhood in Christ, for an army of Christian soldiers capable of spreading not just the Gospel but also the means by which the faithful can govern themselves. The first to be addressed here is El Shaddai's "2020" campaign. It introduces the ways in which El Shaddai frames the idea of citizenship participation in postwar Guatemala. In the 2020 campaign the church refers to its explicit goal of making Guatemala completely born-again Christian by the year 2020; the goal also invokes the trope of vision. With perfect 20/20 vision, the church works toward making Guatemala a better (meaning more Christian) nation—a nation that sees its past, present, and future with focused attention. In terms of complete conversion, Guatemala's intoxicating church growth inspires the El Shaddai community; the numbers make the seemingly impossible goal of national conversion a relative possibility. The plan, in the end, is straightforward and repeated often. As one congregant explained: "Look, we are four people around this table. Right? One. Two. Three. Four. And, let's say that this table is Guatemala. So if you change and if you change [pointing to two people], then Guatemala is half-Christian. If we also convert, then Guatemala is 100 percent Christian. Person by person, we can change Guatemala." Developing the nation—changing Guatemala—takes place, as it does in the Tú Eres la Ciudad and GuateAmala campaigns, person by person; choice by choice; will by harnessed will.

Again, the individual is central to El Shaddai's vision of citizenship and celebrated by merchandise, such as bumper stickers and church pamphlets. One brochure clearly indicates Christian citizenship's very scales: "[The church of El Shaddai] wants to bless you with God's powerful message so that you will transform your life, your family, and your nation forever."[34] The message moves in units: from the individual to the family to the nation, implying that transformation forever begins with the person, that the nation comprises individuals, and that society will never experience complete change unless each person changes completely. In this sense, conversion literally makes Guatemala a better nation—safer, cleaner, more punctual. In fact, by becoming Christians, in and through their conversion Guatemalans become sinners (Robbins 2004a) and, in so doing, take on the responsibility for governing themselves.

Sharing space with El Shaddai's 2020 campaign is a more dramatic apocalyptic aim. As the church leadership states clearly, the El Shaddai community works to "place Guatemala on the list of nations that will survive the apocalypse." The stakes are high. The church's radical eschatology does not necessarily see the end of days as imminent. No dates are mentioned. But the church does not back away from the enduringly radical Christian vision of history that begins with Christ and ends with judgment. This worldview is rooted in Scripture: "The nations will walk by its light, and the kings of the earth will bring their glory into it" (Revelation 21:24). Dr. Caballeros, during a sermon, unpacked the citation's significance: "Revelation 21:24 says that nations will have to be saved. Nations will need to enter the light to be saved. We believe that Guatemala will be a saved nation. The vision of our heart is to be of this society, a Christian society, a saved nation, a new nation, and a nation transformed by the gospel of Jesus Christ."[35] Dr. Caballeros's vision of a new nation ultimately begins with the singular believer.

Another El Shaddai citizenship campaign is the church's "Jesus Is Lord of Guatemala" crusade. The campaign is El Shaddai's effort to raise Guatemalan citizens' patriotism through a movement that continually announces, "Jesus is Lord of Guatemala."[36] Almost a prototype for the GuateAmala movement, the campaign works to lift Guatemalans' spirits—to increase every Guatemalan's willingness to participate as a citizen. The language oscillates between faithfulness and citizenship, between people who believe and those whose faith commits them to change not only their lives but also their nation. This process, Dr. Caballeros makes clear, begins with a decision. Christian citizenship begins with a call from God to *you*. Dr. Caballeros, during a sermon entitled "Escogé Tú" ("He chose you"), announced: "I don't know why the world believes that we can't determine our future, that our future is determined by our past, our circumstances, our situations. The only person who can determine our future is *you*. Do you know who is *you*? Who is *you*? *Me!* In this phrase, *you* means every one of us. And the Bible says here, that amid life and death, I chose *you*. And between heaven and earth, between blessings and failings, between life and death, I chose *you*." He continued: "[God said] I chose *you*. *You* are responsible for your future. *You* are responsible for living in blessings or failings. *You* are responsible for life and death. *You* are responsible for living in accordance with the word of God because the decision between life and death is in your hands."[37] Again, postwar citizenship hails the individual, charging *you* with the power to change. Dr. Caballeros consistently links God's decision to choose *you* not just to the nation but also to each person's attitude: "Some people point to the situation of the nation, the situation of our currency [the quetzal], the situation of your employment, your place of work, your profession. They say that these circumstances mark your future. Your circumstances do not mark your future! Your faith marks your future! Your language marks your future! Your words mark your future!" By faith, language, and words, Dr. Caballeros meant largely attitude, which he quickly clarified: "God wants to change your attitude because when you change your attitude, you change your entire life. . . . My attitude determines my future. I will say it again. My attitude determines my future. Tell me. What can a person with a bad attitude say? Bad things. And what can he obtain? Bad things. And what kind of life can he live? A bad one. . . . Are you listening to me? Brothers and sisters, I am here to help you break the vicious cycle of a bad attitude."[38] Christian citizenship involves the formation of a Christian attitude alongside the forging of a Christian will. For Guatemala to change, *you* must change.

The logic boldly locates social change inside each Guatemalan, a mandate that Guatemala's neo-Pentecostal community has accepted with vigor. In the summer of 2006, for example, a neo-Pentecostal youth conference packed a Guatemala City hotel. For three days straight, young men and women dashed excitedly from conference room to conference room to chat with friends, both new and old, about the conference's stated goal: to save Guatemala. They listened intently and spoke passionately about a range of themes that concern their nation: gangs and youth violence (How we do we treat the problem?), discipline and punishment (How do we lift the fallen?), spreading the word (What are the changes we face?), pornography and masturbation (How do we help the youth?), and church attendance (Why don't the youth like to go to church?). The conference bubbled with a sense of possibility.

The conference's title, marketing the ideas of both social change and participation, reinforced this sense of possibility with a provocative phrase, Soy la Revolución, "I am the Revolution." The phrase was ever-present— on T-shirts, posters, banners, and booklets; yet a single illustration brought the phrase to life.[39] The logo depicts the silhouette of a man, standing with his legs wider than his shoulders; he balls his left hand into a fist, placing it firmly at his side, while his right hand stretches toward the sky holding a flag. The flag announces change, maybe even conquest, over a cityscape that serves as the revolutionary's backdrop. Buildings of varying heights can be seen in the distance. Their tops reach the revolutionary's knees, at best; the man towers over the city. At the same time, the sun is rising. It is early morning and the sun shoots lines of red and orange above the buildings. The obliquely communist colors frame the figure of resistance, and, if read from the perspective of scale and color alone, the image projects the message of a singular agent claiming victory over a city that bravado and courage have made small. The image announces a new day—a new beginning.

Donning a conference T-shirt, complete with this image of revolution, one thoughtful attendee explained: "I believe that being a Christian or believing in or loving God motivates me to be a better person, to be a better friend, to be a better son, to be confident, to be a better person every day. I motivate myself to be Christian by taking account of myself and knowing that everything I do carries a consequence. . . . [Revolution] affects me this way because I want to be a better person and citizen." This young man's interpretation not just of the image but also of the felt predicament of being a Christian citizen lingers at the level of the self, what Michel Foucault would call an ethics of the subject defined by the relation of self to self (2001, 242). The interpretation animates Dr. Caballeros's vision for social change—the idea that the Christian citizen participates in social change (even revolution) through continued work on the self. Many conference attendees echoed the power of interior revolution for the betterment of Guatemala, understanding themselves as both singular revolutions as well as Christian citizens. They understood that neo-Pentecostal Christianity is not just a religion but also a new style of living—a new way of life—and that this new lifestyle stands in contrast to the delinquency that neo-Pentecostals see as defining postwar Guatemala. Individuals must take control of themselves in order to take control of Guatemala.

HEY, YOU THERE!

Judith Butler, in *The Psychic Life of Power* (1997), raises a provocative question. She recounts how Louis Althusser, in his essay entitled "Ideology and Ideological State Apparatuses," maps the relationship between authoritative language and the formation of social subjects. Althusser's classic example, mentioned before, is of the police officer who hails the individual, who yells, "Hey, you there!" In the act of turning around, in the moment of recognizing that by *you* the police officer means *me*, Althusser argues that the individual becomes a subject. In response, Butler notes, "Althusser does not offer a clue as to why that individual turns around, accepting the voice as being addressed to him or her, and accepting the subordination and normalization effected by that voice" (1997, 5). Why, Butler ultimately asks, does the individual turn toward the voice?

Butler's question is the kind that generates several more. But first: *why?* Why would the Guatemalan turn toward the voice of, for example, the municipal government's charge that Tú Eres la Ciudad, or GuateAmala's call for a nationwide attitude adjustment? The ethnographic answer is that Guatemalans do not seem to "turn around" often or with much enthusiasm for either the municipal government's campaign or for GuateAmala. Almost everyone I interviewed understood how each person could be the city; yet I did not come across a single person who could narrate how identifying himself or herself with the city changed what he or she actually did as a citizen of postwar Guatemala. No one, to the best of my knowledge, kept a journal about his or her neighborhood—as the municipal government suggested. Likewise, those in the capital were quick to comment that GuateAmala is the brainchild of urban elites who do not understand the actual problems of real capitalinos. If they did understand, many added, they would propose real solutions. Though it was relatively common to see young men and women in GuateAmala T-shirts in some of the city's more rarefied *zonas,* I never spoke with anyone who put the campaign's principles into practice. I was never able to interview a single person, for example, who used the rubber band to train his or her attitude.

Christian citizenship is another story. This entire book rests on the ethnographic fact that the faithful do indeed "turn around"—do allow themselves to be hailed by their mega-churches as citizens of Guatemala. The reason the Guatemalan faithful willfully subject themselves to Christian citizenship, but not to the municipal government's campaign or to GuateAmala, exists beyond the scope of this study. Michel Foucault's observation that questions of causality can be embarrassing because "there are no definite methodological principles on which to base such an analysis" (1977, xiii) haunts every effort to explain why Christian citizenship effectively hails the Guatemalan—why Christian citizenship has become so incredibly tacky, something that sticks to one's person, that takes a great deal of effort to shake off and wash out. One effort at an answer, one that is deeply flawed (maybe even "embarrassing" by Foucault's standards), is that Tú Eres la Ciudad and GuateAmala both promise Guatemalans that the nation will change once each person has changed; real progress must wait. In contrast, Christian citizenship announces that the believer has already changed (through salvation) and that the country will continue to change through the work that each person does to himself or herself. This hypothesis, to be sure, is limited.

Yet Butler's *why* does generate more anthropologically sensitive questions, such as *How?* and *To what effect?* The following chapters, for example, detail how Christian citizens "turn around." They explore how neo-Pentecostals practice their citizenship through monastic pursuits that include prayers, fasts, and examinations of conscience as well as cell attendance (chapter 2), spiritual warfare (chapter 3), fatherhood (chapter 4), Christian charity (chapter 5), and world evangelism (chapter 6). *How?* is a question that the anthropologist can answer. So is *To what effect?* In regard to effect, all three citizenship campaigns addressed in this chapter achieve a great deal, even if their collective efforts at hailing individuals as citizens are remarkably uneven. Those citizens who do answer the call shoulder the weight of transitional times (and thus do the work of the state) while also becoming complicit in ways that limit social critique. The formation of postwar citizenship, again, promotes a level of ownership and complicity, an entrepreneurial brand of citizenship, that raises the question How could *I* ever critique or mobilize against what *I* own, what *I* am, or what *I* have made? But even for those who do not answer the call, these citizenship campaigns effectively displace entire fields of concern about postwar Guatemala. They effectively jam certain lines of analysis and interest, directing public opinion inward instead of outward. Public debate gravitates toward whether renovating the self does or does not contribute to national renovation, while an entire realm of concerns and mobilization strategies go untapped.

Nowhere in any of the campaigns' literature, rhetoric, or logic, for example, does there ever appear, or even get hinted at, what social scientists might call "material" or "historical" factors. Their construction of the active citizen is ahistorical and primarily concerned with the inner world—habits, attitudes, and thoughts. All three campaigns make general references to Guatemala's history but make no specific mention of colonialism or the politics of postcolonialism, of liberalization or neoliberalism, or of the country's thirty-six-year genocidal civil conflict and postwar context. These postwar citizenship campaigns tend to overlook the country's entrenched poverty, racism, and gang violence as well as the capital city's rapid urbanization and failing infrastructure. Flattened is the relationship between the United States and Guatemala vis-à-vis transitional capitalism and the signing of the Central America Free Trade Agreement. Police corruption, political scandals, and minimal levels of bureaucratic transparency are not among the campaign's talking points. The material and historical conditions that drive hundreds of thousands of Guatemalans to walk across the Mexican-American border—to travel through a desert in the height of summer—give way to a singular focus on one's ability to change one's attitude for the betterment of Guatemala. Each campaign's construction of postwar citizenship transforms the material and historical weight that presses down on a nation into a kind of emotional weight that the individual citizen must bear. It is in this sense that postwar citizenship campaigns can be understood as incredibly effective, as ever productive, because they keep a critical eye on *you* while allowing *us* to do whatever *we* want.

Policing the Soul

The Cellular Construction of Christian Citizenship

[Others] cannot lay their ears to my heart, and yet it is in my heart
that I am whatever I am. So they wish to listen as I confess what
I am in my heart, into which they cannot pry by eye or ear or
mind. They wish to hear and are ready to believe.

AUGUSTINE OF HIPPO

Confessions

It is only with the help of confession that I am able to throw myself into
the arms of humanity freed at last from the burden of moral exile.

CARL JUNG

Modern Man in Search of a Soul

AT FIRST I THOUGHT ESTELA was being silly—maybe even a little bit critical of the exercise. In a Guatemala City living room with a group of ten
neo-Pentecostals, each thumbing through what are called moral manuals,
Estela scribbled the number 8.33 into her workbook. The number—in all
its strange exactness—was Estela's evaluation of her own level of honesty on
a scale from 1 to 10. Others in the room gave themselves 3s, 5s, and 9s; Estela
felt deeply satisfied with 8.33. Later she would explain to me: "Well, I'm not
a 9 when it comes to honesty. But 8 seemed too low. I'm really honest.
Never lie, never cheat. I'm a good mother. But 8.5 [also] seemed too high.
8.33 felt right." The moral manual that prompted Estela to evaluate her
own level of honesty also provided her with questions for reflection and
self-evaluation charts. The questions asked: "Why did you give yourself this
score?" "What benefits are there for you in raising your score?" "What specific action can you put into practice this week to improve your score?"[1]

And below each of these questions there was printed a daily checklist so that Estela could keep track of her progress during the week. For this there were seven boxes, each labeled with a day of the week: Monday, Tuesday, Wednesday, Thursday, Friday, Saturday, and Sunday. At the very bottom of the chart there were two boxes that read, "Complete" and "Not Complete," allowing Estela to document whether she had accomplished all her assignments. To Estela's credit, pencil and pen marks—in the form of checks and x's, dashes and eraser smudges—stained her pages, suggesting a thoughtful plod from one exercise to another. They were markings that evidenced a considerable level not just of dedication but also of participation in postwar Guatemala.

Before I explain in greater detail how Estela's use of moral manuals could ever be read as a form of citizenship participation, it is important to note that her dedication to measuring and massaging her level of honesty is nothing new to the history of Christianity. Inspired by Plato and Aristotle but concretized in the work of Thomas Aquinas, virtue has long been understood by Christian thought as something practiced, as something made.[2] And at least since the twelfth century, moral theologians have attempted to translate supposedly universal principles to the individual case—principles that address the cultivation of Christian virtues, such as honesty but also humility, generosity, and moderation. As the first moral manual to appear in the English language states: "We ask the reader to bear in mind that the manuals of moral theology are technical works intended to help the confessor. . . . They are as technical as the textbooks of the lawyer and the doctor" (Harrington and Keenan 2002, 6–7). The monitoring and mapping of virtue have been Christian technologies of selfhood for centuries.[3]

Neo-Pentecostalism and the politics of postwar Guatemala, however, frame the use of these manuals in novel ways, providing a new model of community policing. Estela does not cultivate honesty out of some vague interest in living a better Christian life. Rather, what makes her efforts at self-policing, even self-improvement and self-help, so intriguing is that she pursues this kind of confessional work for the greater glory of Guatemala. It is a goal detailed in explicit terms nearly every Sunday morning. To quote Estela's pastor, Dr. Harold Caballeros: "God has called the church to disciple nations. . . . It is our principal intention to do all that we can to make nations into Christian nations. In all cases, brothers and sisters, we are working for the construction of a Christian society."[4] *Discipling* Guatemala, to be sure, means proselytizing. There is a very real sense among Guatemala's growing neo-Pentecostal community that national restoration will be complete when every Guatemalan is "born again." Yet *discipling* Guatemala also includes the work that born-again Christians do to themselves. For those who have already accepted Jesus Christ as their personal savior, participating in the construction of a new nation (a safer, more economically viable, and politically stable Guatemala—a more "Christian" Guatemala) means pursuing the kind of confessional work that Estela completed alongside her fellow believers. This Christian rationality parallels Martin Luther's sixteenth-century theological distinction between *salvation* and *sanctification*. Salvation, for Luther, is something bestowed by God on the sinner through faith, not works. Sanctification is a process of purification in which the Christian participates throughout life. Salvation happens in a moment through the conversion experience; sanctification takes a lifetime of work on the self (Luther 1961, 209–215).

Transforming Guatemala, from a neo-Pentecostal perspective, does not begin in town squares or even in the legislature. Though there is both a history of and an interest in cultivating neo-Pentecostal leadership for elected office in postwar Guatemala, Estela examines herself in order to corral and train what might best be understood as her interior world—her thoughts, habits, attitudes, and individual character. And much of this work takes place within church-organized cells, which meet weekly to learn and to police the neo-Pentecostal self. In fact, Estela's own self-reflection and efforts at ethical refashioning were made possible only because of her weekly meetings and the kind of intimacy generated in these settings. As a mix of classroom, self-help group, and emotional laboratory, cells allow believers to craft a sense of self, to link that self to the fate of their nation, and then to police that self for Guatemala. These Christian efforts at policing the self ultimately exist as manifestations of Christian citizenship; they allow Christian contemplation to constitute Christian action.

Alongside cellular formations of Christian citizenship, new forms of secular community policing and a reliance on private security have become increasingly popular in postwar Guatemala City (Frühling 2004).[5] Weighed down by soaring crime rates, minimal public trust in the police, and political instability, active citizens increasingly take it on themselves to police the very spaces that Guatemala's Ministry of Governance and the National Civilian Police do not and that the wealthy pay to have patrolled. Both state security forces, admittedly, are in their early stages of development, having come into existence through the signing of the 1996 Peace Accords, but neither has enjoyed much success. A USAID report announces: "Of the thousands of police investigators trained [since 1996], less than 15 are currently serving as investigators; of the 145 community-based police instructors who graduated from 'train the trainers' courses, none are currently serving in the Police Academy; and despite up to three years of management training, U.S. Embassy personnel assessed the managerial capabilities of the police as 'zero,' 'almost zero,' and 'the police couldn't care less'" (2005, 2). Community policing works to fill a void left by the state, and community policing, this chapter argues, is exactly what Christian citizens do in cells; as devout Christians, they are examples of concerned citizens who watch themselves as well as each other for the sake of the nation. These Christians, however, police not their neighborhoods but rather their souls; they count their levels of honesty, assess each other's confessions, and expose themselves to the group's gaze. Cells ultimately empower believers to participate in postwar Guatemala as "both the judge and the accused" (Foucault 1993, 206).[6] Cells prompt the faithful to act constantly on themselves for their nation.

COMMUNITY POLICING IN LATIN AMERICA

The implementation of economic policies, usually labeled structural adjustment, and efforts at democratization in Latin America have highlighted a distance that exists between the ideals of democracy and the practice of Latin American police forces.[7] As Latin Americans have gained formal citizenship rights, state police agencies have either compromised these rights by way of abuse (e.g., battery, death threats, torture, and extrajuridical killings) or failed to secure a public domain in which such rights can be actualized. One classic example is the distance between the right to walk freely through city streets, what the Universal Declaration of Human Rights would understand as "the right to freedom of movement," and the reality that street violence and police corruption (or inaction) preclude such liberties. This gap between ideal and practice, with its accompanying paradoxes (Caldeira 2002), has prompted both governments and international aid agencies to support police reform—in an effort to protect the citizenry but also in an attempt to continue decentralizing state control.[8] As a consequence of a dramatic rise in crime and violence, a number of Latin American countries, including Guatemala, have incorporated North American and European models of what is commonly known as "community policing" to ensure a level of oversight while also encouraging the citizenry to share the state's responsibility to secure and protect.

North American models of community policing emphasize decentralization and prevention. Rather than simply focusing on responding to crime, community policing works to prevent criminal activity from ever happening. This means that citizens work alongside trained police officers to patrol particular neighborhoods. In Bogotá, Colombia, for example, community initiatives have combined with local police departments to form networks of surveillance. Concerned citizens guard their neighborhoods informally, looking for suspicious behavior, with phone trees and neighborhood alarms installed in case of emergency (Llorente 2004). Working in conjunction with authorities, there are, for example, some 5,400 civilian patrolling networks in the city of Bogotá, which reportedly accounts for 13 percent of the city's residential area (Frühling 2007, 133).

In Guatemala City similar but far more informal patrolling networks have taken shape. Though some have dissolved into lynch mobs (García 2004; MINUGUA 2002), community policing has become a popular vehicle for securing otherwise insecure *zonas*.[9] Gated communities organize neighborhood watches, whereas more permeable neighborhoods, those without sturdy walls and with much less razor wire, patrol their streets on foot. In Villa Nueva, a particularly insecure suburb of Guatemala City, a pilot program, led by the Municipal Citizen Security Council, shifted law enforcement's focus from nominal efforts at crime fighting to concrete efforts at crime prevention (Chinchilla 2004). This was an effort to promote a level of transparency and accountability within Villa Nueva's already overworked police force while also extending the responsibility for patrolling neighborhoods and preventing crime to Villa Nueva's citizens. The activation and promotion of the Municipal Citizen Security Council involved meetings of community leaders to coordinate police efforts—to decide, for example, which areas demanded greater attention than others. These meetings also organized attempts at community outreach so that teachers and religious leaders could work with at-risk youths and even try to rehabilitate young men and women known to be involved in gangs. Though these efforts can be read as either positive or negative, as either an instance of holistic crime prevention or the state shaking free from some of its most basic responsibilities, the practice of community policing encourages a new relationship between the citizen and his or her community—one of vigilance, attentiveness, and discernment. Community policing constitutes what Gilles Deleuze would call "societies of control"—flexible and reflexive states of "perpetual training" that track the movement of people and the formation of places (1992).[10]

Within the El Shaddai community, there are no formal efforts to work in conjunction with either Guatemala's Ministry of Governance or the National Civilian Police—although the faithful would agree that cells do contribute to the prevention of crime and violence as well as to the policing and patrolling of certain domains. There are some five hundred organized cells throughout the capital city, each with as many as sixteen congregants; one can thus read the panoptic practices undertaken within the cellular context as an unexpected but nonetheless steadfastly pursued interpretation of community policing that links each person's self to the nation, polices that self for the sake of Guatemala, and constantly accounts for the self.[11] Cellular formations of Christian citizenship provide the faithful with terrains that they must patrol, with darkened worlds that threaten their families and nation, with what John Locke called camera obscura, or the dark room (1801, 135).[12] Cells generate a level of activity—they make the active citizen—through efforts at policing the self.

THE SELF AS NATION

I sat patiently in my chair for the next spiritual exercise to begin while dogs and chickens competed for our attention just outside the window. Sitting beside Estela and ten other middle-class ladina women, I found my patience beginning to wane as Carlota rescued a series of photocopied handouts from her bag. She passed the dog-eared sheets around the room, each of us taking one and then moving the pile along. "Look," Carlota said, "I want to go over this one more time." The sheets were familiar to the cell (as were their message points), but Carlota insisted that we all needed to be reminded of some basic assumptions now and again.

The handout provided an instructive image. Its simplicity conveyed a world of meaning, teaching the cell how each neo-Pentecostal self is tethered to the fate of his or her nation and how self-improvement fosters national development. The image presents a staircase with six steps ascending evenly from the bottom left corner to the top right corner of the page. Two men climb the stairs with some difficulty. The man who is farther ahead stretches backward, reaching for the other's hand. The less advanced man leans forward, grasping for help. The steps that they climb, from bottom left to top right, read: Thoughts, Actions, Habits, Character, Culture, and Destiny.

The handout, at its most basic, is a map. It plots the individual self in constant relationship to Guatemala, demonstrating how an individual's personal conduct ultimately affects the nation through an intricately established relationship between thoughts and destiny. As Carlota would rehash on that day as well as on many days to come, thoughts form actions, which congeal into habits and, ultimately, a character that defines not only a culture but also its destiny. The message had been cribbed almost verbatim from Dr. Caballeros's many sermons, in which he has announced with absolute certainty: "Be careful with your thoughts because they will become your words. Be careful with your words because they will become your actions. Be careful with your actions because they will become your habits. Be very careful with your habits because they will become your character. Be careful with your character because it will define your destiny."[13] Using Dr. Caballeros's logic, Carlota walked us through each step, reflecting on every buzzword for several minutes, highlighting her message points with carefully selected Bible passages, clips from Dr. Caballeros's many cassette recordings, and brief reflection questions that prompted conversations among cell members. This lesson plan allowed for the construction and maintenance of a neo-Pentecostal self that could ultimately be governed for the sake of Guatemala's destiny.

Cell members relearned in this particular meeting, for example, that *destiny* refers to El Shaddai's "20/20 vision"—the goal that the country will be 100 percent born-again Christian by the year 2020 and have its name on the list of nations that will survive the apocalypse. To highlight this destiny and the moral weight that it can place on each neo-Pentecostal, Carlota played a clip from one of Dr. Caballeros's more popular sermons. On the theme of destiny, the voice of Dr. Caballeros announced over Guatemala City's noisy streets, with their honking horns and growling dogs: "A Christian nation is one that has been constructed or established on principles or immutable laws from the word of God. [It is a nation] that is constituted by God's presence."[14] Guatemala's destiny is a safer and more prosperous country rooted in the loving grace of Jesus Christ.

As Carlota passed around a plate of stale cookies, she assured us that every great journey begins with a first step. Returning to the diagram, Carlota explained that Guatemala's destiny—that the goal of national salvation—begins with the everyday thoughts of each Guatemalan. Carlota asked us to sit in silence—to pray over the idea of literally thinking a new Guatemala into existence. Our collective stillness, rather than being empty or dead space, actually fostered a kind of activity—the art of listening, to use Foucault's terms (1997, 236).[15] In silence, cell members listened to themselves, linking their thoughts to Guatemala's destiny and, in so doing, availing themselves of a terrain of action that would allow them to exercise power on themselves (Cruikshank 1996, 234).[16] Far from being simple indoctrination or empty performance, sitting in silence allowed the group to do something (to reflect, to pray, to listen) for Guatemala. Or, as Estela would later explain to me: "[Sitting in silence] is what we have to do to break what is inside the human being. Because really there are things that form inside us, and when something forms inside our minds, then it begins to develop and to develop and to develop, and if that [thing] is good, well, it's good for our future. But [if it is bad] and continues for several years in that way, then that's not good." Sitting in silence allows the believer to distinguish between the good and the bad, between what can be salvaged and what needs to be broken.

Interrupting the stillness, Carlota read from her Bible, from Romans 8:6–7: "To set the mind on the flesh is death, but to set the mind on the Spirit is life and peace. For this reason the mind that is set on the flesh is hostile to God; it does not submit to God's law—indeed it cannot." The cell members began to reflect aloud on this quote. The discussion was brief but touched on the idea that thoughts are decisions that a person makes every day. Thoughts include the decision to feel happy as opposed to sad, the decision to be punctual as opposed to late, and the decision to be sober as opposed to drunk. Through this logic, thoughts become the first step toward constructing a Christian citizenry. One cell member, reflecting aloud to me well after the cell meeting, explained: "I do all this for two reasons. One is so that I can strengthen my spiritual life with God. The second is so I can clean the thoughts that come into my mind, my soul, my sprit. As human beings, we sin. We all do. But when we [attend cells] we learn more and we are able to see more. . . . [We are able] to expand our understanding. We have a greater understanding of how not to think negatively and how to do things more positively." She then summarized a quote from the very cassette recording that Carlota had played that night: "God needs a group of people—a critical mass—discipled people not only of the spirit but also of the mind, who do what God has mandated and who can serve the people of this nation to achieve a nation founded on justice, peace, and liberty."[17] The importance of the passage, the cell member intoned, is that a critical mass begins with thoughts—with the good Christian citizen's ability to train his or her own "inner dialogue" for good and not evil.

The idea that one can think a new Guatemala into existence is made salient by an agreed-upon relationship between thoughts and actions.

Thoughts lead to actions—on the one hand to individuals being depressed, late, and drunk; or, on the other hand, to individuals who are happy, punctual, and sober. At this point, one woman broke the meeting's flow to raise a question. Her husband drinks one beer every night. Just one beer, she insists. Is he an alcoholic? Carlota, bending the question into her lesson plan, framed the problem with the handout, narrating the following: The husband's thoughts about beer have led him to drink a beer every night, and the next step is for these actions to form a habit. The woman then asked if her husband's actions have formed a habit. This sent the group into a fit of nodding and a wave of opinions. Many disagreed, saying that two drinks (not one) is a sign of alcoholism; some quoted tidbits gathered from public health literature about alcoholism being a genetic problem, while others stuck to the idea that one beer a day is a habit because this man drinks every day.

From a certain analytical perspective, this excitement over thoughts and actions indicates just how successful cells are at getting believers "to write and tell their personal narratives with an eye to the social good," and how "narratives bring people to see the details of their personal lives and their chances for improving their lives [as] inextricably linked to what is good for all of society" (Cruikshank 1996, 233–234). With so much cellular interest trained on Guatemala's destiny, the husband's alcohol habit was not simply a problem for him or for his family but also for Guatemala. The husband's thoughts yield actions and these actions result in risky habits. The group even explained to the woman that the difference between a thought and a habit is the difference between being drunk and being an alcoholic. This is not to downplay drunkenness, Carlota added, since deciding to drink, or allowing oneself to drink, is the first step toward cultivating the habit of drinking—cultivating alcoholism. Yet the drinking that this woman's husband pursued *habitually* was dangerous—not just for himself but also for his family, church, and ultimately the nation.

Habits are critically important to achieving Guatemala's destiny because habits yield individual character. To say the least, the language of "character" is popular in Guatemalan cell meetings. There is a strong sense among neo-Pentecostals that Guatemalans suffer from bad character, which is evidenced by littering and tardiness, to name only two indicators that irritate neo-Pentecostal sensibilities. Murder and sexual assault are more egregious. Bad character has made Guatemala the country it is today, the logic insists. The consensus in each of the cell meetings that I attended, in fact, was that to change Guatemala, each Guatemalan must change his or her own character. Dr. Caballeros, on the topic of character, announced: "In reality, I need to train my spirit. I need to forge my character. I need to see my actions as being a direct result of my inner life . . . and a new life [with Christ] generates new works, produces new actions. A new person makes new fruits that are completely different. In this sense, we need to forge our character—and I use the word *forge* like one uses the word to describe the melding of metal with fire. I am using the word *forge* to say that we need to forge our character just as one breaks in a wild horse, to make the horse go in a certain direction. We need to make our conduct and our life subject to our control."[18] To buttress this bold idea, Carlota cracked open her Bible yet again. She read aloud from the Gospel of Matthew: "Jesus replied, 'And why do you break the command of God for the sake of your tradition?' " (15:3). She repeated the passage three more times for effect while the group actively listened in complete silence. Carlota then thoughtfully pointed at each cell member to reflect on how tradition can lead each of them to break God's law, adding: "They say it's like a fish that you want to eat. You have to clean it, clean it, clean it. You have to clean it. And when it is clean and you've put it through a process, you can eat it. It's just like the human. You have to clean the human; you have to put [the human] through the process, and this means having a good state of mind in which one has broken all the inner limits of human being." Cells prompt believers to clean themselves—to make themselves worthy and their nation stronger.

Naming bad character as the cause of Guatemala's postwar problems, to be sure, flattens a range of historical and material factors, such as a genocidal civil war, economic restructuring, and urban violence; yet, according to El Shaddai leadership and congregants alike, Guatemalans need to change the way that they think to make Guatemala a different place. The logic insists that Guatemalans must change their character in the same way that the early Christians changed their lives. Drawing on this message of cultural change through individual renewal, Carlota let her cassette recording play into the afternoon air. As the group sat around the living room, dusting their cookie crumbs from the tabletop onto their napkins, they listened to Dr. Caballeros's message: "I am speaking about the story of John, Peter, and Jacob. I am speaking about the story of the disciples. These were vulgar men and far from conversion; these were uneducated men." The cassette continued: "These were fishermen—simple men who in one evening changed, transformed, and as the Acts of the Apostles tells us, they became like Christ, and so much so that they began to be known as Christians." Dr. Caballeros stressed that these men changed their character and, in turn, their thoughts, actions, and habits: "They changed their lifestyles. They changed the form of their lives. . . . What did they change? They were not changing just their hearts. Of course they changed their hearts. But what else did they change? They changed everything!"[19]

Rising with Dr. Caballeros's cadence and tone was the cell group's own level of hope. The promise of change, as one might expect, is a particularly seductive message in a postwar context where urban violence and rural vigilantism make everyday life not just stressful but calculating, forcing each individual to assess constantly the riskiness of taking a particular city bus (as opposed to another) or traveling down one city street (as opposed to another). In this sense, neo-Pentecostals tend to welcome the idea that change begins with the self—literally within themselves. To consent to this logic shifts the ability to act from the streets of Guatemala City to the terrain of the self. This shift in some ways places the promise of change within reach of the Christian citizen. Commenting after the cell meeting, Estela underlined this sense of empowerment: "Yes, one needs to change one's mind first because if we change the way we think, we're going to be able to change our attitudes. Because here [in cells] is where we change our minds. And to change the mind means changing the way we think. And if we can change the way we think, then anything is possible."

Driving home the promise of change, Dr. Caballeros's recorded sermon continued: "This is what we mean by a 'believer'; this is what we mean when we say 'a Christian.' But how can a person change his habits? How can a person change his conduct? How can a person change all that he does? This change is an internal change, at the level of thought. It is a change in one's mentality. It is a change in one's thinking. When one changes on the inside, the change manifests on the outside."[20] With so much "on the outside" in need of change, cell members race "inside" to begin to do the work that they believe will make Guatemala safer, stronger, and stable. Or as Carlota, reflecting on her ministerial work during an interview, explained: "The real vision of [El Shaddai] is to change the Guatemalan lifestyle. There are so many cultures that have come to Guatemala over the years with negative principles, and this is not what God wants. What God wants is to clean the nation to make room for good principles. God wants a totally different kind of generation." Clean and totally different—cell members do the work of God every time they turn inward to rehabilitate themselves for something greater.

The logic gained even more strength once the voice on the cassette turned to a hypothetical example. Carlota smiled, pausing the cassette player and announcing that Dr. Caballeros was about to talk about alcoholism—the very theme of their earlier conversation: "[Take for example] 'Miguel,' who is an alcoholic. And as an alcoholic, Miguel has problems that alcoholics usually have: problems with his family, economic problems, et cetera, et cetera, et cetera." Cell members leaned toward the tape player: "If Miguel is a good Christian, hands his life over to Jesus, has converted, then what is the first thing we can hope for Miguel? We can hope for a change. It is not possible to say that Miguel gives his life to Christ, in this hypothetical example, on the first of January, and then in February, March, April, and June, we see that Miguel is fantastic since Miguel is now a Christian alcoholic." Here it becomes clear that simply believing is not enough: "Of course this is a contradiction, for one hopes that Miguel as a Christian has experienced a change in his life and that he is no longer what he was before. To use the words of Paul, the robber no longer robs but works with his hands. There is a change, there is a transformation, there is a notable difference in the conduct of a person."[21]

A change in conduct—this transformation—affects Guatemala's fate because conduct defines Guatemala's culture. But a true change involves serious work—the kind of police work that believers shoulder in cell meetings. This kind of work asks believers to craft painstakingly their characters, conduct, actions, and thoughts through elaborate efforts at self-governance. This chapter's opening vignette, the one that depicted Estela measuring her honesty in a strangely precise way, is but one example. As Dr. Caballeros announced: "We need to examine ourselves, engage in self-examinations. Then I can say whether, for example, I am good or bad with forgiveness. Or with truthfulness. Or with my fidelity. Or with legality. Et cetera. Et cetera. I need to examine myself for my own life and the life of my children and their offspring. And this is all to provoke a true change. And this doesn't mean we are accountants [of ourselves] but stewards [of ourselves]."[22] Accountants simply maintain; they count and parse. Stewards take responsibility. They act.

POLICING THE SOUL

Michel Foucault, commenting on Augustine's characterization of the sexual act, begins to approximate the difficulties of policing the self. Foucault notes that before the biblical Fall, "Adam's body, every part of it, was perfectly obedient to the soul and the will. If Adam wanted to procreate in Paradise, he could do it in the same way and with the same control as he could, for instance, sow seeds in the earth." But after the Fall, Foucault continues, "Adam lost control of himself. . . . His body, and parts of his body, stopped obeying his commands, revolted against him, and the sexual parts of his body were the first to rise up in this disobedience . . . his sexual organs were moving by themselves without his consent" (1994, 181). Like Adam in his struggle with his unruly erection, cell members work to tame their thoughts and attitudes, to make them positive instead of negative. Yet, as one might expect, this kind of police work can be both isolating and frustrating. Estela explained: "The change has to be singular, has to come from inside a single person, and if it doesn't, then it means the person really isn't trying or isn't really able to do the work they need to do." Cells, in response, allow individuals to distribute the weight of this unbending responsibility through the formation of panoptic social settings. Cells allow the faithful to police and to be policed—to embody what Foucault has called a "political economy of detail" (1977, 139).[23] The structure of cellular culture exposes the self; cells bring the self into focus for the world to see.

Efforts at teasing out the self abound in the cellular context. Confessing the self, exposing the self, is as critical to the neo-Pentecostal project of policing the self as are streetlights to the modern project of policing the city. Both involve the "mobilization of visual technologies designed to secure scrutiny of the entire surface of the body politic" (Joyce 2003, 109).[24] Although much of what threatens the faithful in postwar Guatemala City are such dynamic issues as urban violence and high rates of unemployment, neo-Pentecostal formations of the self successfully link these national concerns with moral questions, such as the regulation of conduct and the judgment of behavior. The reckless will that haunts Adam, stumps Augustine, and intrigues Foucault is the very one that neo-Pentecostals police by way of cellular activities. This means that policing the soul is not simply a negative activity "concerned with the maintenance of order and the prevention of danger," but also a positive program "based upon knowledge that could act as the foundation and the happiness of the State" (Rose 1999, 24).[25] One of cells' greatest functions, in fact, is their ability to open interior worlds to the external world and to commit each believer not just to a grid of standards but also to a sea of normative gazes.

One telling example of exposure, of disrobing the self for all to see, came at the end of a particular cell meeting. After completing some spiritual exercises, Javier asked if we could divide the group so that the women would remain in the living room while the men would stand in the hallway. We happily complied, and the group divided. Soon enough, I found myself with six men whom I had come to know over the course of several months. As the leader of this impromptu men's group, Javier turned off the lights and asked us to form a circle. Closing the group by holding hands, Javier instructed us to pray for the man to our left—not at once (he insisted) but one at a time. Made in complete darkness, the prayers were of the most personal order: marital engagements, father-son arguments, and missed business opportunities. A mixture of lament and hope filled the hallway as each man delivered his prayer for the other in a cracking voice. Javier then asked each of us to place his left hand on the other's right shoulder, keeping the circle intact but relieving us of sweaty palms. At the same time, from the other dark and equally weepy room, a Christian ballad could be heard. The women were lost (but at the same time found) in their own efforts at intimacy making as they sang along to a cassette recording of a popular Christian song. They were wailing into the night.

The music, the darkness, and the human touch combined to produce an excess of emotions. As my turn came, I struggled to pray for Emilio, the man to my left. I found it difficult to conjure the same emotion that the man to my right had generated in my behalf. As the man to my right had wept for my research and the safe travel of my wife to Guatemala, I felt the mounting pressure to perform. In prayer, I brought to attention Emilio's relationship with his girlfriend and his questions about whether he should propose to her. I asked for Emilio to stay focused on his relationship with his girlfriend, just as he is attentive to his relationship with God. Yet there was something missing. My prayer did not "connect" like the other prayers; my prayer for Emilio failed to generate the kind of closeness and camaraderie that the group demanded. With my prayer, the group lost momentum that Emilio fought to regain. It was a prayerful "misfire" (as John Austin [1975] might have called it) that highlights just how much effort it takes not only to police oneself but also to present the self of another so that it can be watched.[26] Not only does the actual performance of prayer need to be on point, but so too does the music, the darkness, the human touch, the hushed tones, and, when visible, the pinched faces. These are all strategies that allow believers to share themselves, to expose themselves, so that their selves can be policed not just for God but also for Guatemala. While I failed to expose Emilio's self with much clarity and, in turn, kept my own self at bay, I learned that cellular efforts at community policing work only if *you* let *me* watch *you,* and if *you* watch *me* while *I* watch *my* self.

This Christian panoptic was, of course, a calculated effort. Yet many times, maybe more times than not, policing the self does not take place in darkened hallways but rather begins with unscripted questions, such as the one that Maria asked aloud with some trepidation: "Am I a Christian?" Earlier in the night, the cell group had been lumbering through a popular moral manual, and some important distinctions were becoming a little fuzzy. The manual was a Spanish translation of *How Do You Know God's Your Father?* Written by Kay Arthur, a North American pastor, the workbook brings the insights of John the Apostle to bear on the reader's everyday life, helping the individual to cultivate what the book calls the "lifestyle of genuine Christianity." The manual fits well into the already established cellular protocol of weekly meetings; the workbook (itself divided into forty-minute lessons) acts as a foil for larger conversations about attitude and character. Setting the general tone, the manual explains: "There are two kingdoms in this world: God's and the devil's. There are two fathers and we belong either to one or to the other. So many say 'I'm a Christian,' but how can they really know God's their Father—and that heaven's home?"[27] To discern the quality of one's own Christianity, the manual asks cell members to answer questions about certain biblical passages, and to engage the text itself by flagging particular words—to circle the word "love" any time it appears, to cross out the word "hate," and to draw triangles around "greed." This kind of textual work then gives way to conversation, prompted frequently by discussion questions.

Late into the evening, its members dragging after a long day of work, one group took up the following question: "Do you know anyone who claims to be a Christian but walks in darkness as a habit of his or her life? What does 1 John 1:10 tell you about this person?"[28] In these kinds of conversations, cell members wrestle over what it means to be Christian—over what it means to know the neo-Pentecostal self and to manage the self, reform the self, and police the self. These kinds of conversations also allow cell members to assess each other's Christianity. Maria herself was stumped. Yet before anyone said a word, Javier, the cell leader, prompted the group to read 1 John 1:10 in silence—to literally read to themselves. The text contends, "If we claim we have not sinned, we are calling God a liar and showing that his word has no place in our hearts."[29] Maria read the passage, later confiding to me that she would never want to call God a liar; she would never want to place God outside her own heart. Her fear of offending God prompted her to ask her question: Am I a Christian?

After reading the passage, Javier asked each person to write his or her immediate responses in the margins of the manual. Discussion did not begin instantly, nor did biblical insights erupt from the group; rather, after quiet reflection and note taking, cell members such as Maria shared their insights and questions. There was a distinct rhythm and tempo, which the cellular practice of writing fostered. Slowly, by way of thoughts and scribbles, insights and marginalia, a self that could be governed came into focus. For many cell members, such as Maria, the act of writing their thoughts and reactions, engaging in a kind of bibliotherapy (Cruikshank 1996, 233), was a new and unpracticed technology that yielded snippets of themselves.[30] In the margins of one book, a cell member scribbled two bullet points: "The person is a liar. The person betrays God." The notes in another workbook read, "Lies. Lies. Lies." They are simple notes, to be sure, but they nonetheless demonstrate a level of introspection and activity—the practice of turning inward to survey one's inner terrain.

Notes having been written, Javier then narrated his own experience of a coworker who claimed to be a Christian but who never went to church on Sunday. From the cell leader's perspective, his coworker could be at best a believer but not a true Christian. It was a flippant comment that inspired Carolyn, a fellow cell member, to mention the supposed Christianity of her classmate. The classmate talked a great deal about being a Christian, but her works suggested otherwise: infrequent church attendance and no effort to participate in church activities. As both Javier and Carolyn made an increasingly stronger case for why some people's faith was suspect, they playfully made quotation marks in the air with their fingers to describe their acquaintances as "Christian." There were, in fact, many evaluations made during the conversation that night. Yes, these people may be "believers" but, no, they were not "disciples." Can one be Christian if one does not do the things of a Christian? Christians do more than just believe, right? The questions began to pile up. Cell members also drew from their own lives, placing their own Christianity under scrutiny. This is actually when Maria began to question the quality and character of her own faith. "I think I'm a good Christian," she testified, "but I'm very busy and can only develop my own faith. I can't help other people [with their faith]. Is that bad?" The group responded critically but comfortingly. No, it was not bad, but, yes, she should work harder to be a better Christian. The group, in the words of Nikolas Rose, policed Maria through "the calculated administration of shame" (1999, 73), allowing her to become anxious about her own Christianity while also charging her to cultivate her faith with more vigilance.[31] The condemnation, for sure, was a passing moment during an otherwise busy meeting, but, for what it is worth, Maria did not miss a cell meeting for months to come.

These kinds of conversations also indicate a dense field of social relations replete with questions, answers, debate, and uncertainty as well as action (writing, thinking, observing, and talking). These conversations mark a social process that involves digesting with some struggle the nature of the human condition from the perspective of faith while also opening oneself to judgment, to being policed by fellow cell members. Struggling over the question of whether God is in fact "my father" is a way for cell members to learn how they can make God their father; how they can become true Christians (and not just believers); how they can learn that the neo-Pentecostal self is something ultimately worthy of redemption through Jesus Christ. This learning process routinely involves linking the individual self to the fate of the nation. Moral manuals, such as those authored by Kay Arthur and fervently employed by Guatemala City cells, provide opportunities for believers to relate their thoughts to Guatemala's own destiny and, in turn, to allow their thoughts to be trained for Guatemala's future.

One example came during an exercise that addressed the biblical David. The manual lingered on 2 Samuel 11–13, which tells the story of King David's seduction of a married woman named Bathsheba. The biblical tale ends with David sending Bathsheba's husband into battle (and to certain death) when she becomes pregnant from their affair. David sins gravely against not only God but also his nation, the story explains, and the manual also makes clear that just as David's decision to sin compromised his nation, cell members' decisions to sin threaten their nation. The manual states, "Without a doubt, confession and repenting cannot stop the severe consequences of David's sin; the sins not only affect him but also his family and his nation."[32] The manual then guides cell members through David's own decision-making process with specific, open-ended questions: "What happened to David when he stayed in his home and did not go off to battle as all kings should do?" In response, cell members paused to think and then wrote in their books. "What decisions could David have made to change the end results of those events?" Writing continued. Shorthand sat in the margins of their manuals, spilling over onto other pages. "When David decided to sleep with Bathsheba, on what did he base his decision?" Blank stares preceded the jotting down of an idea or two. "When people confront a moral decision, what direction do they usually choose and on what do they base their decisions?"[33]

These were questions that led many cell members to narrate and then scrutinize the decisions that they had made in life. Javier, for example, drew on the story of David's infidelity to narrate in a confessional tone a recent trip to Costa Rica. His friends, Javier explained, are not Christian, so they drink and dance, and while they were in Costa Rica his very close friend celebrated his birthday. Javier did not drink, and he danced only a little, he assured the group, but he did spend a great deal of time talking with women at the bar. As he told his story, Javier drew on David's biblical missteps, explaining that "Costa Rican women are beautiful . . . absolutely beautiful, like Bathsheba." Javier then began to recount how he decided not to flirt openly with the women. He had a girlfriend and did not want to jeopardize that relationship. He also confessed that he was attracted to the women but that he did not pursue any of them. Javier then linked his decision-making process to the same values promulgated by the moral manual: Christian discipline, biblical morality, and individual responsibility. His decision not to sin was difficult but the right one.

The story of Javier's trip to Costa Rica and his carnal temptations was quickly echoed by Sabrina, who, she explained, had always had friends who were boys—not boyfriends, but good friends of the opposite sex. She confessed how her eventual husband was not comfortable with her spending so much time with other men. She and her male friends would just go drink coffee together, she assured the cell. It was harmless, she repeated. Ultimately, Sabrina admitted that she made the difficult decision not to be friends with other men; these friendships placed too much strain on her budding relationship. She made the decision, she explained, by sitting quietly in prayer, by listening to what she understood as God's will for her, and by struggling between her flesh and her spirit. She simply needed to change her past life for the sake of her new life, choosing family over friends. Her testimony prompted Javier to read aloud a reflection question from the moral manual that asked: "We saw last week that personal sin can have large-scale consequences. Sin can impact our families, churches, communities, and nation. Because of sin, David became distracted and forgot about the well-being of his nation. How can our personal decisions— morally speaking—impact our nation?"[34] Javier, on the subject of his experiences in Costa Rica, explained that his decision not to sin against his girlfriend was also a decision not to sin against his family. The family, he quickly reminded the group, is the building block of the nation. In a dark bar, with loud music and gorgeous, willing women framing his experience, Javier made a decision for, not against, Guatemala. Sabrina agreed, editing her life experiences to fit the immediate conversation. She made her decision, she explained, not to be friends with other men not only for her relationship but also for Guatemala. Linking logics, she announced that her decision not to be friends with males led to actions (i.e., actually not being friends with them) and that her actions resulted in habits (i.e., she is now not friends with males), and these habits now form her character (i.e., a good wife). And good character makes the culture of Guatemala better and its destiny of national salvation possible.

The weight of this responsibility can be profound, as much of this book notes; yet cells teach that through an established relationship with oneself, one can begin to change and, by doing so, change the nation. Moreover, cells provide the faithful with technologies of citizenship that allow each believer to shoulder this weight for the sake of Guatemala. The goal is not small, of course, but the ability to know and police the self is one key component to living as a Christian citizen in postwar Guatemala City—to building the City of God.

CALCULATING CHARACTER

Numbers are not simply descriptive; they are productive. Estela's 8.33 on the honesty scale reveals as much. Rather than simply documenting her actual level of honesty, a project as slippery as weighing the amount of happiness in a given room, the art of calculation constitutes new terrains of the self that need to be managed. The art of calculation provides the faithful with a new vocabulary of computation as well as novel avenues through which to act on themselves. Numbers pushed through a Christian register provide Estela and her fellow cell members with a new way of making and engaging the world. To appreciate the extent to which neo-Pentecostalism has transformed the faithful's relationship to themselves, it is necessary only to keep in mind that Estela would tell me often that she once had no idea she could track her honesty; before attending her cell group, she never knew that she could chart her virtues. Estela, like so many other converts, came to neo-Pentecostalism from a nominally Roman Catholic family who did not attend Mass regularly, let alone weekly support groups or Bible study. This new level of activity ultimately provides a third answer to this chapter's enduring question: What do Christians *do* as citizens within the cellular context? As I have shown, they link themselves to the nation and they police themselves for the nation. Third, neo-Pentecostals count themselves for (and in doing so make themselves accountable to) postwar Guatemala; neo-Pentecostals estimate their levels of virtue in a way that recommits them to policing themselves. This kind of cultural work drags this chapter to the rumpled and sometimes yellowed pages of moral manuals, to their charts and graphs, and to the kind of textual practices that these manuals prompt— the kind of labor that allows for the production and management of postwar Guatemala through the calculation of character.

A cursory glance of El Shaddai's bookstore reveals a preponderance of titles on the theme of character: *The Pillars of Christian Character, The Character of a Virtuous Woman, The Character of the Christian, The Character of the Lord's Worker, Good and Angry: Exchanging Frustration for Character in You and Your Kids,* and *The Character of God.* Rather than forming a distinct section within the bookstore itself, even though there are more than enough titles to warrant such categorization, books on or related to the theme of character pepper every imaginable subgenre of Christian literature: marriage, parenting, sexuality, leadership, and the youth. Yet two titles consistently emerged throughout my time in the field, both in the cellular context and as points of reference in interviews and public sermons. Estela, for example, assigned herself an 8.33 because of the first of the following two books: *Character: The True Colors of Character* and *Vision: The True Colors of Character.*[35] Other than playing a significant role in the lives of my informants, and therefore a major part in my own fieldwork, these two manuals also provide the clearest examples of how neo-Pentecostals assign numerical values to themselves and why evaluating themselves often means calculating character.

The two manuals share a publisher as well as an introduction. Aside from pagination, the first dozen pages of both books are identical. Although published in Guatemala, they pitch their message to a generic Latin American readership, explaining that "Latin America is one of the most bio-diverse and culturally rich regions on the planet. Studies demonstrate that Latin Americans have a great spontaneity, passion, ability to adapt, resourcefulness, and a fighting spirit. Many of those attributes, if not all, have come to form what it means to be Latino." But the texts continue: "These aspects have not been sufficient to solidify a just, prosperous, and peaceful society."[36] The books then enumerate material factors, such as racial inequality, abject poverty, and political exclusion; they quote the International Development Bank to make the case that violence and insecurity have direct costs to Latin America's health services, criminal system, and social services as well as indirect costs that include high rates of depression, homicide, and suicide. These are problems that result, the texts continue, in a flurry of economic and social problems: "In a certain way, [violence, poverty, and corruption] have formed true barriers to well-being and productivity. Moreover, we have become accustomed to a kind of mentality, a mixture of conformity, insincerity, and lies. This condition has seriously compromised our social and economic development, with enormous effects on our future and on future generations."[37] The books then make clear that Latin America has both potential and a problem: "There is now a great urgency to advance [as a society] by breaking cleanly from our past. We need to affirm the values that will deliver character to our culture." The books remind their readers, "We are all part of the problem," and so everyone must be "part of the solution."[38]

What should not be overlooked, but certainly is by many neo-Pentecostals who incorporate these manuals into their daily lives, is that the framing of both questions and solutions is itself a kind of activity. If taken point by point, the texts themselves do not propose anything terribly egregious. Stereotypes of Latin Americans often include such flat-footed characterizations as "spontaneous" and "passionate." Latin America also has witnessed increasing levels of violence and insecurity, and these developments have compromised Latin America's social and economic development. The text's effectiveness is its ability not to document Latin America's supposed reality but rather to arrange general statements in such a way as to invite the reader to see himself or herself in not just the problem but also the solution—to see Latin America as riddled with bad character, to identify bad character as a cause rather than as an effect, and, moreover, to see character as something that *you* have and that *you* make: "Our profound mission is to transform our immediate world with a forthright character and with the highest of ethics. The mission is to begin the construction of a healthy, productive, and prosperous culture in all aspects, from the material to the ethical."[39] In no uncertain terms, the narrative asserts that character—the character of each person—constitutes a nation's infrastructure. Not just bad character but *your* bad character, as well as *his* and *her* character, either hurts or helps Guatemala.

The fact of the matter is that one can find bad character whenever and wherever one wants, but if one is trained to look for it, examples abound in the most mundane ways, in the simplest and sometimes silliest of events. When ordering food with Julio in a small Guatemala City eatery, for example, I asked for a side of avocado, but the waitress would not give it to me because such an option did not exist on the menu. After the waitress left, Julio stared into my audio recorder, as if funneling his words directly into the machine so that none of them would be lost: "My children will live in a totally different generation from the one we are living in. They'll have good principles. If I am taught negative principles, then I will have negative principles when I grow up. You have to understand that this change has to happen to reestablish our nation. Like right now, in this restaurant, you wanted something specific to eat and they couldn't do it. That's a problem. There are cultures that have formed in the minds of people. . . . There are problems that need to change for this culture to change." It is important here to recognize that Julio was frustrated; Julio, like so many of my neo-Pentecostal informants, is not so much a curmudgeon as a concerned and empathetic believer. He barked into my recorder because he was (yet again) fasting and in the middle of a long workweek. His was an unexpected but nonetheless understandable rant. Important also were Julio's willingness (1) to read this ever-so-minor incident from the perspective of culture, (2) to generalize the situation to the national level, and (3) to locate the means for national change within every person. Unable to argue definitively whether books such as *Character* and *Vision* initiate or respond to this worldview, I can state with the utmost clarity that moral manuals such as *Character* and *Vision* provide neo-Pentecostals like Julio with an array of metrics and nomenclatures to chart progress, map virtues, and assess frustration—to "produce a degree of autonomization . . . from the state" that results in an "autonomization of society" (Barry et al. 1996, 11–12).[40] Although I never asked Julio, I would not be surprised in the least if he were able to ascribe a numerical value to the waitress's work ethic. This is plausible only because I have sat with Julio during cell meetings and have watched him rate his own work ethic on a scale from 1 to 10, as well as his levels of generosity and moderation. He is not kind to himself.

Understanding the mechanics of such Christian calculations means turning to the manuals themselves. *Character,* for example, provides the tools to evaluate one's own reliability, work ethic, honesty, humility, generosity, moderation, motivation, patience, productivity, and temperament; whereas *Vision* supplies the means to track thoughts, attitude, emotions, moral parameters, goals, ability to plan, common sense, ability to dream, and potential for prosperity. To sample the kind of statistical and textual work that these manuals ask of their readers, it is helpful, if only for the sake of continuity, to linger at the level of honesty by returning to Estela's cell group.

Embellished by a cartoon image of a man walking proudly and freely, the chapter's opening page begins its meditation on honesty with a quote from Proverbs: "The evil are snared by the transgression of their lips, but the righteous escape from trouble" (12:13). Carlota continued to read the following pages: "Overall, people who are honest do not lie, do not trick, do not rob, and do not manipulate. . . . While all of that is true, the definition [of honesty] is still much higher. Honesty also includes the intention that accompanies the truth of our actions. This means being transparent. If a person is honest, then there will not be even the slightest sign of anything other than respect for others."[41] Estela nodded along with the discussion's vagueness. The definition's generality (and inherent flexibility) struck a chord, reminding the cell members that, at the very least, honesty is more than what they originally thought it was. A bold woman who routinely remarked aloud "the common sense of it all" blurted out: "Makes sense. What else?" Carlota went on: "Honesty is the highest virtue of all human values because it allows us to enjoy excellent personal benefits; it is the best gift to both the community and the nation. It is a solid building block for each of us and society."[42] Honesty makes a good nation, but only when each person is honest.

The next several pages list the traits of an honest person—nine things that an honest person does, six ways in which an honest person acts, and so on. The group took the lessons at face value. The observations were at times either too extreme or too shapeless for many in the group to respond to: "An honest person does not traffic or use illegal drugs. An honest person does not waste time, talent, or money."[43] This group did not dispute these statements. Conversation began in earnest, however, when it came time to evaluate each person's own level of honesty—ascribe a number and, in turn, a level of density to one's honesty. *Character* reminds the cell members about the meta-importance of honesty before the actual self-evaluation: "The honest application of the principles makes habits; in time these correct habits become values."[44] Values constitute character, the manual argues, and character makes a nation good or bad. The stakes are high.

The manual then asks its readers to consider the following two questions as they evaluate their honesty: "What aspects of an honest society affect you the most? What can we do personally to help a community improve its honesty?"[45] As cell members reflected on the preceding forty-five minutes of reading, listening, and praying on the quality of honesty, they marked numbers on their score sheets privately. Some did not hide their scores well; some clearly wanted others to see the numbers they had given themselves: 4, 5 and 7, for example. Estela gave herself an 8.33—because it "felt right." The significance of this is that cell members, through their participation in self-evaluation and -assessment, through the calculation of character, gain not only a language for how to govern the self but also a sense of what "feels right" when governing. While rating the amount of honesty that one person feels he or she possesses may seem rather strange, cells successfully inculcate members with a logic that makes this kind of self-evaluation and self-governance not only possible but intuitive. Many cell members do not flinch at the numbers they give themselves. Some are brutal, ascribing to themselves 2s and 3s, while others flatter themselves with 8s and 9s. Important is not the score, but the ability for members to manage themselves for the sake of the nation—to be able to quantify the current state of their honesty.

The numbers signal a melding of logics, teaching each neo-Pentecostal how to manage himself or herself as well as to see the most intangible qualities as quantifiable. These manuals provide neo-Pentecostals such as Estela with a taste of expertise—with the ability to give an account of the self in the most literal of ways: a record, a report, a bill, a score. The manual asks the faithful to reflect on such truisms as "Corruption is a grave social ill that can be cured only with honesty" and in so doing form a new realism—a depiction of reality "as it appears."[46] This reality is based on making honesty visible and linking one's own honesty to such dynamic social developments as political corruption. For it is through such efforts at reflection and calculation that a novel accountability becomes instilled within the hearts and minds of each neo-Pentecostal, reframing how neo-Pentecostals see as well as relate to society. The active Christian citizen shoulders an accountability for himself or herself but also larger responsibilities for the production of the nation, which is an attempt not only to maximize accountability but also (deliberately or otherwise) to quell dissatisfaction. Christian citizenship means not only seeing *your* self in society but also understanding that *your* brokenness, your less-than-perfect level of honesty, is one important source of society's failures. Almost reversing a hackneyed consumer warning ("you break it, you buy it"), cellular formations of Christian citizenship recognize that "it" (meaning Guatemala) is already broken, which means that you (the Christian) must have already bought it. The calculation of character, ultimately, provides an organizing rationale that links the opportunities and demands of a future Guatemala with a revised perception of how today's individual relates to today's nation.

The effects of this new relationship, this Christian citizenship, can be haunting, especially as postwar Guatemala continues to experience a rise in political and economic insecurity alongside increasing levels of distrust of state security forces and an increased reliance on the private security industry. Given that active citizens in Guatemala have taken it on themselves to police the very areas that Guatemala's Ministry of Governance and the National Civilian Police avoid, it is important to note that El Shaddai–organized cell groups make a conscious decision to police their own neighborhoods through a Christian register, recognizing that the violence outside begins inside each person. Christian citizens take the time and energy to patrol themselves for the sake of postwar Guatemala while also marking themselves as culpable—at least partly responsible for the poverty, for the violence, for the corruption. The degree of activity and ownership is striking. It is an astounding level of citizenship participation, which brings to mind the epigraph that Hannah Arendt chose for her seminal work *The Life of the Mind* (1978). She quoted Cato: "Never is a man more active than when he does nothing, never is he less alone than when he is by himself" (Arendt 1978, 8). The Christian citizen neither takes foot nor walks a beat but rather sits quietly in reflection; the Christian citizen neither joins a mob nor accomplishes his true police work en masse, even though cells themselves are distinct forms of sociality that contribute to the end product of introspection. The Christian citizen, as Cato might have observed, is "never more active than when he is [ostensibly] doing nothing." "Never" is the Christian citizen "less alone than when he is by himself." The cellular context demonstrates just how much activity is involved when the Christian citizen polices and calculates the self; the cellular context makes clear just how crowded the Christian citizen can feel when linking the self to the nation.

ACTION AND AMBIVALENCE

In May 2006 I sat with Estela, Carlota, and eight other devoted women as they prayed against Guatemala City's unremitting postwar violence. A cell member's friend had been murdered earlier in the week. The victim was a single mother of two young children who, while at home on a workday, had been surprised by an intruder rifling through her bedroom drawers for money. A brief struggle ensued, which ended when the intruder slit her throat. She bled to death on the kitchen floor and, the cell members speculated, in front of her children. The event was cause for grief, pain, and the perpetuation of what many understand as a "discourse of fear"—one that divides people from their city and estranges certain classes from the promise of democracy.[47] Yet here, in this cell meeting, and at the lip of such raw emotions, the group met this senseless murder with renewed purpose. With my recorder long turned off, with never having felt comfortable taping in the cellular context to begin with, one daring statement found its way into my notes—not as shorthand or by way of paraphrasing, but verbatim: "Praying to God is the only way to stop this." And so the women prayed. With their Christian music turned up a little louder than usual, they paced the room with their hands pressed to the ceiling and with their eyes shut, tears streaming down their cheeks. They spoke in tongues, the hum of which slowly became unnerving as I sat watching them. Their thoughtful efforts made my own inaction—my observation rather than participation— appear increasingly useless, even lazy and callous. I sat. They acted.

Across town, throughout the capital, hundreds of like cells, facing similar threats, acted as well—praying, pacing, and protecting their loved ones, against insurmountable odds. They continued to augment as well as reimagine more mainstream efforts at community policing, efforts that the Guatemalan media report constantly in a lame effort at pairing chaos with control—balancing the unpredictability of postwar violence with groups replete with schedules, beats, and phone trees. Those who police their communities—underneath bridges, down darkened alleyways, in abandoned lots—struggle with the same dangerous postwar conditions. A resident of Zone 6, an area hit hard by drug trafficking and organized crime, mentions: "We are never relaxed. At any moment the gangs can come and begin killing without a care in the world about who is in the streets."[48] Those who take it on themselves to do something are active citizens who understand how risk and danger dominate not only their neighborhoods but also their lives, forcing them always to be vigilant and on guard. They are active in the very way that Michael Walzer uses the term—to denote citizens who assume individual participation in and attention to governance (1989).

Just as active, possibly more vigilant, however, are Carlota, Estela, and their fellow cell members. From their perspective, they police something far more fundamental than the streets. Zone 6, for these women, is the effect rather than the cause; moldy bridges, darkened alleyways, and abandoned lots emerge from perverted thoughts, broken attitudes, and reckless character. Their participation in making a new, more Christian Guatemala means attending cell meetings, praying together, and forging a sense of self that each governs constantly. These Christian efforts, of course, yield something far different from Guatemala's growing number of civilian patrols. Though many are quick to point out how community policing develops "exclusivist spatial practices" (Cattelino 2004, 115), the kind of cultural work prompted within the cellular context promotes a unique construction of an interiority that is constantly exteriorized, that is, in fact, the presumed engine of Guatemalan history.[49] This is not another Christian vision of the sovereign agent, but a kind of concerned citizen who willingly shoulders the weight of postwar Guatemala, knowing that whatever is "out there" could never be as broken as what lurks inside each thought, each habit, each imperfect virtue. As I mentioned in the introduction, Christian citizenship's effectiveness centers on its ability to generate a deep sense of meaning, whereas its productiveness lies in its tendency to limit the avenues through which neo-Pentecostals act. The familiar critique of community policing is that citizens do the literal work of the state free of charge; yet neo-Pentecostal efforts at policing the self raise a different concern. After learning of the tragedy, of a mother killed in front of her children, the cell group immediately acted, which is what democracy (in its most ideal state) asks of each citizen. But the cell did so in response to the following charge: "Praying to God is the only way to stop this." They acted through prayer and, in the months that followed, by calculating their levels of honesty, humility, and generosity. Again, this is not inactivity, but rather a swirling world of movement—of bustle and commotion undertaken with considerable gusto. These cell members are engaged citizens; they are invested in their nation, working daily to make postwar Guatemala livable—literally, a place where one can live without being murdered in one's own home. They participate through weekly meetings, moral manuals, and testimonies rather than through protests, marches, and community organizing. Prayerfully engaged, cellular formations of Christian citizenship embody the promise of postwar citizenship in all its unevenness—in a way that evokes contradictory emotions such as love and hate; encouragement and disbelief; respect and disappointment. Christian citizens act within cells but in ways that raise questions not just about the quality of their participation but also about the relevance of citizenship in postwar Guatemala City.

THREE

Onward, Christian Soldier

Solitary Responsibility and Spiritual Warfare

Finally be strong in the Lord and in the strength of his power.
Put on the full armor of God, so that you will be able to stand
firm against the schemes of the devil. For our struggle is not
against enemies of blood and flesh, but against the rulers, against
the authorities, against the cosmic powers of this present
darkness, against the spiritual forces of evil in the heavenly places.

EPHESIANS 6:11

We were all at once terribly alone; and alone we must see it through.

ERICH MARIA REMARQUE,
All Quiet on the Western Front

A YOUNG NEO-PENTECOSTAL PASTOR surprised his mega-church congregation early one Sunday morning. Deep in the heart of Guatemala City, he dimmed the lights during a church service, making his four thousand parishioners sit expectantly in the dark. Unafraid to mix theater with theology, the pastor, dressed in army fatigues, rappelled from the towering ceiling to the church floor. Once safely landed and behind his pulpit, the pastor proclaimed: "We are going to be Kaibiles for Christ!"[1] The congregation erupted with applause, meeting this bold announcement with unbridled bravado. The Kaibiles are the Guatemalan military's most elite commando unit. Modeled after the U.S. Green Berets, the Kaibiles played a terrifying role in Guatemala's thirty-six-year genocidal civil war, which formally ended in 1996. They were charged with a litany of human rights abuses; their well-known training techniques included "killing animals and then eating them raw and drinking their blood" (CEH 1999, 42). The

Kaibiles are also responsible for the genocide's most gruesome massacres, in one of which they killed some three hundred civilians in a matter of twenty-four hours, decimating a pueblo and stuffing as many of the bodies as they could into the town's well (CEH 1999, 42). According to the commando unit's own motto, the Kaibiles are "killing machines."

With this infamous history as background, the young pastor announced—indeed, explicitly enlisted—his congregants to be Kaibiles for Christ. He assigned them a singular mission: to soldier for Guatemala. And the congregants greeted the mission with enthusiasm. The audience wept; they screamed in praise and spoke in tongues, recommitting themselves to being Christian soldiers not only for Christ but also for the greater glory of Guatemala. In the context of neo-Pentecostalism, warring on behalf of Guatemala as a citizen-soldier means praying for Guatemala, fasting for Guatemala, and examining one's own conscience for Guatemala. Soldiering for Guatemala means practicing what is understood as spiritual warfare.

A subset of demonology, spiritual warfare is an age-old, biblical metaphor for the Christian life. At its most basic, the metaphor provides Christians with a combat-centered vocabulary through which they can articulate their own prayerful efforts at goodness.[2] In his letters to the Ephesians, Paul details this battle between good and evil and, through analogy, equips the believer with the means to fight: truth is the believer's armor; righteousness is the believer's breastplate, and the Holy Spirit is the believer's sword (Ephesians 6:10–17). The metaphor of spiritual warfare, however, has lost its moorings in postwar Guatemala City. For a growing neo-Pentecostal community, spiritual warfare has become the felt reality that Christians fight against Satan every day in their prayer lives for the soul of Guatemala City. Bearing titles such as *Victorious Warfare, Prepare for War,* and *Taking Our Cities for God,* dozens of internationally distributed spiritual warfare manuals instruct believers on how to fight Satan for their city and nation. Their weapons of faith include prayers, fasting, and spiritual cartography—the practice of mapping a city along moral lines. Bars, liquor stores, and Catholic churches are the devil's strongholds. Neo-Pentecostal churches and Christian-owned businesses are signs of victory.

At first glance, the practice of spiritual warfare seems to be having little effect. Guatemala City continues to be a dangerous place: there were some 20,000 gang-related homicides between 2002 and 2007 (Fuentes 2008). With violent crime and its impunity on the rise, it would be tempting to dismiss spiritual warfare as an opiate—as a moral logic that can shift responsibility from the individual to the underworld. This is in fact the guiding thesis of Michael Cuneo's sociological study of exorcism in the United States (2001). What could be more American, he asks, than blaming the devil for your moral failings and then paying to have those demons exorcised? In Cuneo's study, exorcism in the United States provides a fresh start at a reasonable price. This is not the case in Guatemala, nor is it an adequate rendering of religious experience in the Americas, as it flattens a complicated cultural manifestation to the logic of market exchange.[3]

It would also be easy to dismiss, or at least fixate on, the practice of spiritual warfare as boldly inappropriate. Given that Guatemala's Peace Accords were signed in 1996, thus ending Central America's longest and bloodiest civil war, the slippages that routinely occur are astounding. Parents and small children, strolling hand in hand through church lobbies, are often dressed head to toe in camouflage, the phrase "God's Army" stitched across their chests. On church grounds, children play with stage-prop swords that are eerily the size and shape of machetes—weapons used to mutilate enemy combatants during the civil war. Biblical quotes decorate the blades. One quotes the Book of Revelation: "But they have conquered [Satan] by the blood of the lamb and by the word of their testimony, for they did not cling to life even in the face of death" (12:11). And when asked to describe the similarities between Guatemala's civil conflict and the spiritual war, informants have begun their responses, "Look, war is war."

This chapter addresses neither spiritual warfare's audaciousness nor its potential to shirk responsibility. Instead, its focus is on spiritual warfare's tendency to make the individual believer shoulder the weight of transitional times by praying, fasting, and performing rituals as a soldier—all to slay the demons that haunt Guatemala City. This surprisingly heroic kind of participation produces an observable battle fatigue and sense of solitary numbness, the kind of "1,000-yard stare" that Erich Maria Remarque describes in his antiwar novel, *All Quiet on the Western Front* (1929). This solitary and sometimes friendless struggle builds from the Greek notion of the citizen-soldier—the idea that "if citizens want the rights and liberties that come with living in a free society, they must also share the duties of defending that society from its antidemocratic enemies, whether foreign or domestic" (Snyder 2003, 186).[4] The citizen-soldier tradition now coincides with neo-Pentecostalism in a way that asks each Christian citizen to fulfill his or her responsibility by fighting Satan for the soul of the nation.

These prayerful efforts ultimately speak to the quality of neo-Pentecostal engagement in postwar Guatemala, as opposed to other secular efforts across the country, to cultivate an active civil society. The contrast is often quite sharp. The 1996 Peace Accords, for example, advocate what Iris Marion Young might understand as the eroticism of democracy: "an attraction to the other, the pleasure and excitement of being drawn out of one's secure routine to encounter the novel, strange and surprising" (Young 1990, 238–241). Efforts at postwar participation have long been about unity through difference—about seeking out and organizing with "the other" in a multiethnic and multilingual nation. Yet ethnographic research in postwar Guatemala's spiritual trenches repeatedly evidences a model of participation that is not just Christian but also exceedingly forlorn—one that seems hesitant to reach out to another. While exploring how the practice of spiritual warfare exists as a mode of participation in postwar Guatemala, this chapter also lingers ethnographically on a manufactured kind of aloneness. The observation builds from Robert Putnam's familiar sociological observation, one that argues, in broad strokes, that more U.S. citizens are bowling alone (rather than in leagues), and that this suggests a growing disconnect between individuals and democratic structures (as well as friends, family, and neighbors) (Putnam 2000). Something analogous, I argue, can be observed in postwar Guatemala City. An increasing number of neo-Pentecostals, for example, enlist in God's army, surrounding themselves with fellow soldiers, but the missions that they are sent on—the battles that they are expected to win—are so remarkably singular, so deeply heroic, as to make one question the place of community even in postwar Guatemala City's largest of congregations. This chapter, ultimately, taps ethnographically spiritual warfare's solitary dimensions to suggest something about the formation of Christian citizenship in postwar Guatemala City: an increasing number of neo-Pentecostals are warring for their nation, but they tend to do so alone.

GUATEMALA'S MILITARY

A quick glace at the Guatemalan military makes curious the ministerial decision of neo-Pentecostal churches to lean on the metaphor of war—not just to articulate the Christian life, but also to capture a demonological worldview that pits good versus evil. There is, in fact, a surprising level of ambivalence directed toward postwar Guatemala's military. Though the Guatemalan military directed a war ostensibly against guerrilla insurgents throughout the 1970s and 1980s, international human rights reports have long demonstrated that the military was nonetheless responsible for the vast majority of the war's violence (Carmack 1988, Falla 1992, Manz 1988, C. Smith 1990). The Roman Catholic Church's truth commission report (REMHI 1998) as well as the UN–sponsored Commission for Historical Clarification (CEH 1999) assert that state forces and paramilitary groups were responsible for some 93 percent of civilian deaths, disappearances, and tortures—the strongest waves of repression being best characterized as acts of genocide against the Maya (CEH 1999). The testimonies that underpin these reports are painfully graphic: fetuses pulled from wombs, men castrated, women gang-raped. One of thousands of testimonies reports: "Before murdering her, they nailed her to a cross they had made. They stuck huge nails in her hands and chest, then they put her inside the house to burn her up. They found her burned, still nailed to the cross; her son was beside her, also burned—badly burned" (REMHI 1998, 2:215). Jean Franco, writing about rape as a weapon of war, comments on the Guatemalan military's use of violence: "Accounts of massacres in Guatemala describe orgiastic scenes as, for example, the events in 'Dos Erres' Petén in 1982, after the kaibiles were ordered to 'vaccinate' the population, first children and women and then men, all of whom were then hit on the head with a hammer and thrown into a pit; pregnant women were beaten on the stomach; and women, including children, were raped. After finishing off the survivors, the kaibiles 'were laughing as if nothing had happened'" (Franco 2007, 28). In the aftermath of these atrocities and alongside institutional efforts at memory making, military officials have proven to be without much remorse, darkening their already notorious personae. Jennifer Schirmer, in The Guatemalan Military Project: A Violence Called Democracy (1998), quotes several high-ranking military officials, who are self-identified architects of the counterinsurgency. They deny that the endeavor was "excessive" but do describe them as intentional efforts at annihilation (1998, 59).

The UN–brokered Peace Accords reduced significantly the reach of the Guatemalan military. In one agreement, entitled "The Strengthening of Civil Society and the Role of the Military in a Democratic Society" (September 19, 1996), the Peace Accords insist that the Guatemalan military shift its focus to external threats and international support and that the newly formed National Civilian Police accept responsibility for domestic security. Since 1996, some eighty Guatemalan troops, for example, have contributed to the United Nations' stabilization missions in Haiti, and Guatemala's infamous Kaibiles have had a sustained presence in the Congo.[5] The Peace Accords also suggested disbanding the Kaibiles altogether, to reduce the military's size and budget by some 33 percent, and to increase military oversight with the appointment of a civilian minister of defense. Some of these goals now having been accomplished, the place and significance of Guatemala's military within the nation's postwar context have shrunk; yet a strange ambivalence lingers, one that demands that the military remain accountable for the violence it wrought during the civil war but also one that seeks the military's continued presence.

In 2007, for example, the president-elect, Alvaro Colom, announced that the Guatemalan military would support the National Civilian Police's efforts to stem the tide of domestic violence. The National Civilian Police had proven ineffective in the face of growing postwar violence. Colom argued that he would expand the scope of the military in spite of the 1996 Peace Accords. Colom emphasized that he would need the military to regain large parts of rural Guatemala that were under the control of drug cartels: "It's a fact. It's not just that it could happen; it will happen. There are cartels that have their own armies. You can't go in there with the police alone; you have to go in with the army like a war operation if you really want to get the territory back." Colom continued: "The demobilization [of the military] left corridors from the Caribbean to the border with Mexico completely uncontrolled. I believe [these vulnerable points of entry] were planned."[6] Colom's comments reflect the public's interest in a strong hand, or *mano dura,* when dealing with questions of security. Colom, in fact, narrowly defeated for the office of president Otto Pérez Molina—a former military general whose very campaign slogan was *mano dura.*[7] Yet in 2008, just as he expanded the military's role in domestic life, Colom applied pressure to the Guatemalan military, making several army files public for the first time. Colom's intent was to expose many of the civil war's details, such as those related to massacres and torture. He wanted a level of transparency that reflected the public's own concern for justice, the public's own interest in dragging those guilty of war crimes into the light of day. Colom explained: "We are going to make all of the army's archives public so we can know the truth, to start building on a foundation of truth and justice."[8]

Striking is an observable ambivalence. On the one hand, there exists a sustained call for demilitarization and civilian oversight—the result of an overwhelmingly violent history. On the other hand, postwar violence raises a seemingly practical but nonetheless ideological interest in the military—a fighting unit that can presumably protect citizens more effectively than a civilian police force. In many ways, amid this ambivalence, maybe even because of it, spiritual warfare captures the imagination of a growing number of Guatemalans. Spiritual warfare allows many to displace the Guatemalan military with God's army but nonetheless find solace in a brand of Christianity that fights as fervently as the Kaibiles.

Spiritual warfare is one of neo-Pentecostalism's clarion calls to act, to do something heroic. The head pastor of El Shaddai, Dr. Harold Caballeros, has trumpeted a battle cry for decades, professing that every Christian is at war with the devil for the very fate of the nation. The charge is neither infrequent nor casually constructed. Spiritual warfare, rather, is systematically detailed, meticulously studied, and deeply felt by leaders and congregants alike. One dutiful soldier, for example, at the end of an interview, enumerated all that she had done for Guatemala as a "Christian warrior," ending her list with a brief moment of self-consciousness followed by steadfast resolve: "And we've been to all the departments here in Guatemala and have prayed for each mayor, especially when new administrations take office. There are a lot of prophetic things that go along with whatever the Lord tells us to do. It's basically . . . it basically sounds crazy to the natural mind and to outsiders, but if the Lord is leading us to do this, then we have to do this." The logic of spiritual warfare insists that there is no other choice but to fight, no matter how taxing or strange the missions may seem. Dr. Caballeros, in a fiery sermon, declared: "I have been telling you for the last hour that we are at war! And that we are the conquerors! Moreover, we are conquerors in the name of Jesus, who loves us [*applause*]! Aaaah, you must understand this, you must understand. . . . From the day that Jesus saved you, your enemy, the devil, lost you. [The devil] was once your father, had tied you up, was never going to free you, wanted you to be eternally lost." The tables have turned, Dr. Caballeros insists, which provides the Christian citizen with an incredible sense of agency as well as avenues by which to participate in postwar Guatemala: "Before [salvation], you were his slave, but now you are the devil's executioner. And your activities, your life, your words, and your daily routine are all meant to take souls away from the devil [*applause*]."[9] The battle is fought every day and at the most commonplace levels: activities, words, and routines.

The reason for such rhetorical flare, if not force, is the resolute belief that individual souls are at stake. The devil, it is understood, conspires against every person to lie, to cheat, and to steal. Yet through the practice of spiritual warfare, each individual can resist the devil and at the same time constitute his or her soul as a distinct battlefield in a larger war. The struggle is one that keeps the faithful pacing their bedrooms late at night while speaking in tongues and pressing their palms to the heavens; the struggle is over the soul as well as Guatemala's future. The two are inseparable.

To spiritual warfare's credit, the faithful routinely shoulder this weight; they take it on themselves to invest their time and their energy in fighting an enemy that they cannot see directly. They wake up early and go to bed late, all for war. One soldier reflected aloud to me about the weight of it all: "There's a very real weight *(peso)*. There's a responsibility for each Guatemalan because really it is our nation, right? And if we want something pure and good for our nation, then we have to fight for it. It's a weight; it's a weighty burden *(carga)*. But really it's a responsibility that each of us has to take upon ourselves personally as an individual." Like so many other manifestations of Christian citizenship in postwar Guatemala, the responsibility presses down on the individual. I—not we—fight the battle for us—not just for me and not just for you. Dr. Caballeros declared in a sermon entitled "A Battle between Two Kingdoms": "Today, more than ever, our country is in need of intercessors. And the country depends on the body of Christ. The nation certainly depends on those who pray. In all of biblical history, nations have depended on intercessors; without intercessors, we are out of luck." He continued: "Sometimes, one suffers so much [as a warrior] that, in the end, the burden is dropped. As your pastor says here, take up that weight!"[10]

The vision of a new Guatemala emerging through the power of prayer, through the practice of spiritual warfare, is palpable within the El Shaddai community. A renewed, even saved, Guatemala lies just beyond congregants' fingertips. This is a future worth fighting for, Dr. Caballeros insisted in a sermon: "We are very excited. Now we can visualize a great change for this nation. We are going to have the first saved nation in the entire world [*applause*]. We are going to see a new and different Guatemala, and we are going to fulfill our promise not to let our children inherit this country as it is now. We are going to have them inherit a different, new, and distinct country, renewed by the grace of God and the Holy Spirit."[11] The promise of postwar Guatemala abounds throughout neo-Pentecostal communities and is made possible through the practice of spiritual warfare.

Making this future a reality begins with understanding that neo-Pentecostalism sees the human condition as comprising the spiritual world and the material world. Dr. Caballeros notes in one of his many writings:

"There are two kingdoms at war. [They] oppose one another in open confrontation. One kingdom belongs to God and the other to the devil. . . . Spiritual warfare is the conflict between these two kingdoms, the kingdom of light and the kingdom of darkness, which contend for the eternal destiny of mankind."[12] Spiritual warfare rests on a series of Christian dualisms: material and spiritual; good and evil; lost and found. And along these long-established lines, the will of Satan and the will of God wrestle. Dr. Caballeros continues: "Because our lot has been to live in the times in which two wills coexist, the basic characteristic of the world in which we live is dichotomy, dualism, and duality."[13] Spiritual warfare portrays the faithful as tugged, pulled, and stretched by two great forces, and the righteous Christian—the self-aware believer—participates in this struggle by leaning toward God and away from Satan. Married to this dualism is the steadfast conviction that the spiritual world affects the material world and that the Christian soldier, by praying and fasting, can manipulate the material world. This very assumption, in fact, makes neo-Pentecostalism so remarkably utilitarian—almost magical in an anthropological sense.[14] One believer explained: "That is the point! God takes a position in our spiritual lives so that we can win the battle along with his son, Jesus Christ. Because there are real results! When one begins to pray, there is a result. When one begins to fast, there are results. All that comes to us is what we have won in battle."

The only hitch is that Satan continues to stump Christian efforts. A spiritual warfare manual written and published in Guatemala City explains: "If there is no immediate response [to your prayer], this does not mean that God does not hear you and does not answer you. God has sent an answer, but the answer has not been able to arrive. Satan guards the answer, blocks it. Satan keeps us captive in defeat."[15] The rhetoric of spiritual warfare insists that devils and fallen angels reside in Guatemala City. They make the city run less efficiently, causing corruption, fomenting urban violence, and wrecking families and marriages. Dr. Caballeros writes: "What determines the future of a country, a city, or a person? Spiritual forces determine those results—forces that do not obey barriers of space or time."[16] Guatemala's own depressed social indicators, Dr. Caballeros daringly asserts, "are due to spiritual circumstances—to the direct action of forces that were hidden to the human eye but that are absolutely real."[17] The neo-Pentecostal argument is that Christians have let demons run amok. Not enough Christian soldiers have answered the call to participate; they have been asleep on the watch.

Consistent with the logic of spiritual warfare is El Shaddai's grim projection that the current state of Guatemala is not good—that the devil and his army of fallen angels have overrun the country. The effects of this are clearly seen in the city's inordinate levels of violence, corruption, and lawlessness. Christians are losing the battle, the El Shaddai community insists, and the Christian commitment to war cannot wane. Believers have an unending responsibility to fight for Guatemala. Dr. Caballeros writes: "It is important to understand the type of participation God expects from His church in spiritual warfare. What a great responsibility we have! In God's creation, the human being is the only one who possesses the ability to speak and the mandate to do it, pronouncing the Scripture to principalities and powers."[18] One manual, hailing its subject as a citizen-soldier, announces: "You, who read this book, can change the destiny of your country, beginning today, at this very moment, by interceding for your government, and for those in authority, in accordance with the Word of God."[19] Reminiscent of James Montgomery Flagg's 1917 poster of Uncle Sam pointing a finger at the viewer as the United States entered World War I, the narrative in postwar Guatemala is clear: God wants *YOU*.

Dr. Caballeros insists that believers have the responsibility to change the current state of affairs in Guatemala: "It is we who are in charge of making the manifold wisdom of God known to principalities and powers. . . . In our example, God would be the legislator; the Church would be the judge, and the angels the police force."[20] God's foot soldiers, the logic assumes, are the congregants: "God has given us all of the responsibility [to fight Satan]. . . . How good is it to know that a homemaker, an office worker, a child or an elderly person can collaborate in fulfilling God's desire [to save Guatemala]?"[21] Spiritual warfare prompts believers to shoulder the weight of Guatemala's future: "The opposition can and must be conquered through prayer and fasting. . . . We have a very active role in obtaining our blessings."[22] And as this chapter argues, it is this activity—this "active role"—that constitutes Guatemalans of faith not just as Christian citizens but also as heroic, muscular, and surprisingly solitary warriors for God and for Guatemala.

CONQUER THE PAST

One of spiritual warfare's more troubling narratives is its framing of the Maya as enemies of Guatemala. There is a distinction to be made, of course. Church leadership has no problem with the indigenous; in fact, they constitute a growing percentage of El Shaddai's expanding congregation. Rather, the logic of spiritual warfare expresses grave concern for (and resentment against) Maya spirituality. Amid a postwar pan-Maya movement for the continued celebration of indigenous rights and cultures, Dr. Caballeros routinely refers to Maya spirituality only to frame the church as being at war with Maya spirituality. The El Shaddai community insists that one of the most catastrophically detrimental developments in the history of Guatemala has been the growth of pre-Columbian religion. This "false worship" opened Guatemala's borders to the devil. Dr. Caballeros writes in his book *Victorious Warfare:* "The Maya went through all that degenerative process which is provoked by idolatry. From the adoration of God, they placed their eyes upon man, and with this sin, they became corrupted. . . . They lowered themselves to worshipping birds (the quetzal), animals (the jaguar), and ended up worshiping reptiles (the rattlesnake)."[23] Guatemala, as a nation, derailed itself from God's grace, according to Dr. Caballeros, and centuries of idolatry have had a material effect: "Many of the Latin American countries have experienced revolutionary or guerrilla movements, and in each of these cases, the process is the same. They are fratricidal wars with Guatemalans killing Guatemalans, Nicaraguans against Nicaraguans, etc. [Like pre-Columbian human sacrifice,] brothers shed their brother's blood, thus defiling the land (Numbers 35:33)."[24] The belief is that Maya tradition primed Guatemala to be a negative rather than a positive culture, and that neo-Pentecostals must now counter (as well as conquer) this past through distinctly Christian practices. The charge is one that Dr. Caballeros leads by example.

Dr. Caballeros, in his *Victorious Warfare,* delivers a Christian story of once being lost and then being found, of having to wrestle with evil to lay claim to a righteous path. He tells how he sought out land in the 1980s so that he could construct the very mega-church that stands today in Guatemala City's Zone 14. But in the beginning times were hard: "Once again I prayed (and cried) saying, 'God, why don't you help us? We need the money for your church.' But there seemed to be no answer. I was a step away from desperation." He then had a vision: "What I lived in the following moments was absolutely real for me." While he was "submerged in prayer," the stool on which Dr. Caballeros sat "started to elevate and [then] quickly disappeared." In its stead sat "an enormous white snake. . . . It looked furious and its eyes looked straight at me. . . . Its eyes were charged with hate." Shocked, Dr. Caballeros recounts that he "was trembling with fear" and that his first instinct "was to leave the place immediately and to find help." Yet in the end he did not. He felt something swell inside his chest: "It was the voice of Jesus Christ that said, 'Isn't my name enough?'" Dr. Caballeros writes how he then began to rebuke the snake in the name of Jesus Christ: "The intensity of the battle increased and I noticed how the Word of God that came off my lips and in the name of Jesus Christ began to fill me with faith. . . . I was obtaining victory."[25] Dr. Caballeros actively fought down the devil.

Once the serpent disappeared, the story goes, the church purchased a large parcel of land and built the El Shaddai mega-church. Victorious, Dr. Caballeros stood proud; he had conquered the devil and had cleared the way for his church's progress. Dr. Caballeros, however, observes: "It is interesting to recognize that in our case, the greatest lessons and the greatest battles have been linked to the land we have purchased as a ministry." He refers to the fact that El Shaddai's new plot of land contains the Montículo de la Culebra, a colonial aqueduct as well as a pre-Columbian snake mound of archeological significance. These were findings made after purchasing the land—findings that soon frustrated construction with claims to historic preservation. Linking his own visions of a serpent with the snake mound that now slithered through church property, Dr. Caballeros framed the entire confluence of histories as a biblical battle over land: "We realized that our country had been handed over to, dedicated to, or given over to this evil [serpent] spirit." Heightening the rhetoric, Dr. Caballeros adds: "Now I understand what really happened to these cultures of pre-Hispanic America. God, in His mercy, had given every man an opportunity. He had given His testimony, but they rejected Him and in their self-deceit, they became corrupted, leaving an inheritance of curse, darkness, and pain to the next generations."[26] Guatemala had failed God, and now its history makes the country's future stumble.

Dr. Caballeros's narrative in *Victorious Warfare* moves quickly, weaving his own spiritual life with an archeological record that reportedly stains not only his church but also his nation. The tale leaves one very little room to catch one's breath; there are problems with his church, but then there is a serpent; they wrestle only to end with Dr. Caballeros as victor—until the snake reappears as an inconvenient archeological site. Open to any number of interpretations, the story could be read as folklore, as Christian allegory, or even as metaphor. But quibbling about genres would obfuscate the world of activity that accompanies Dr. Caballeros's Christian story of redemption. The El Shaddai community, for one, fought a legal battle with Guatemala's Ministry of Culture and Sports to ultimately build their mega-church over the archeological ruin. The legal battle, accompanied by its own flurry of activity, framed the eventual construction of the mega-church, as every brick laid for Christ and against the Maya constituted a material moment in what Mary Louise Pratt has called "the contact zone"—"contexts of highly asymmetrical relations of power" (1991). The El Shaddai mega-church, with its sleek architecture and floor-to-ceiling windows, stands as a monument to victory.

Litigation and the eventual construction of the church, however, are just two of the more striking instances of conquering the past. The fact of the matter is that spiritual warfare does not consist merely of court battles and storytelling. There is also a great deal of action that individual Christian citizens pursue as soldiers. Dr. Caballeros's story of wrestling with the devil, for example, serves as a brief introduction to his own manual for spiritual warfare—his own step-by-step guide on how to push Maya tradition out and thrust Guatemala forward. For example, Marta, a particularly committed congregant, found herself "on the ground" and "in the trenches" during the church's battle over its new parcel of land, employing many of the techniques that Dr. Caballeros advocates in his spiritual warfare manual. Listening to her own account of those days, to what she did as a Christian warrior, one begins to understand not just the level of activity that spiritual warfare demands from the faithful but also the kind and the quality of that activity. Marta, neither an architect nor a lawyer, responded to my question about what she did to "win the battle" against the snake mound, explaining: "There were many things we did, but one of the most effective things I found was to do spiritual mapping." Spiritual mapping, Dr. Caballeros explains in his manual, is "a technique that provides us the equivalent to military espionage and intelligence. Spiritual mapping is the way to discern, with precision, the powers in the spiritual kingdom, the structures in the cultural realm and its effects in the natural field. What an x-ray is to a physician, spiritual mapping is to an intercessor."[27] Marta continued: "You don't have to be so thorough, depending on what you want to do, even if you are sent to do it or if you are doing it by yourself (which I don't recommend). For example, we did spiritual mapping [here in Guatemala City], and it started with the serpent mound."

Marta then detailed her efforts at researching the possible spiritual forces at work in Guatemala City. A paper chase took her to libraries and archives as well as into conversation with archeologists and pastors: "One of the first things we found out was that the city was laid out like a serpent coiled up. The zones go 1, 2, 3, 4, 5 [she made a coiling pattern with her fingers] instead of being like a grid or something, like in a more orderly manner." The tempo of Marta's story picks up as she bends casual associations into grounds for causality: "And we saw a serpent pattern throughout the history of Guatemala, especially with Quetzalcoatl being the main god of the Maya. And when we found that out, we discovered that there were key places in each zone where Maya people went and offered sacrifices and made processions through certain streets." Marta then listed, with astounding clarity, the dates, times, and locations of these processions. She confessed to having researched this extensive information while balancing her part-time job and parenting her three children. She read books, took notes, and interviewed experts: "[Through spiritual mapping] we came to know the routes [of the processions] and [how the processions] retake and reclaim the neighborhood. And we found that there are many monuments and buildings that are dedicated to different purposes that you wouldn't even know."

As Marta made clear, spiritual warfare involves a cartographical imagination that asks the Christian soldier questions about place and about how the spiritual world marks communities, building, and nations: "Ours is not such an ancient city, although we have our share of things, right? Underground or above it. We have the obelisk in Zone 10. The archeological ruins. The tower [in Zone 4], which is like a phallic symbol. When you carry out spiritual mapping, you find those key places that could be touch points for the demonic." Marta then added in a hushed tone: "Or [you find] activities or carnivals that foster certain types of activities. It happens here during Holy Week for Easter. It's religious, but not really, and there is a lot of drinking and all those things. So you locate and you figure out what are the key points or key activities that happen through the demonic, and then you know what they cost the neighboring areas. You pray for God's will to be manifest and destroy whatever works of the devil might take place there." Critically important here is Marta's legwork—her archival and even ethnographic labor, which gathered reams of information about her city and about the demonic forces that threaten her nation; also important is Marta's addendum that "you pray for God's will to be manifest" and "destroy whatever works of the devil." Concerned neo-Pentecostals such as Marta layer an active prayer life atop their reconnaissance missions. The neo-Pentecostal identification of Maya spirituality as the cause of Guatemala's political and economic instability is deeply troubling. What should not be overlooked, however, is the reality that Guatemalans of faith understand clearly that their nation is in disrepair and that they have a responsibility to act. What also cannot be disregarded is that Guatemalans such as Marta decide to act—to devote time and energy to change the conditions of their nation—through the means they think most effective. There are few outside the neo-Pentecostal fold who would argue that such efforts are not misplaced, but of real anthropological significance here (at least for the purposes of this argument) is the reality that these neo-Pentecostals do act in the name of citizenship. They pray, they map, they learn, and they read—all for Guatemala.

El Shaddai's efforts at warring against demons to change Guatemala, no matter how off-putting those efforts are, reinforce one of democracy's central assumptions: democracy's ideal citizen is active, responsible, and willing to participate for the greater good. This ideal citizen owns societal problems and works to solve those problems. This vision of the citizen is the very one that Alexis de Tocqueville notes in his foundational work, *Democracy in America* ([1835–1840] 2004), and one that neo-Pentecostal mega-churches, such as El Shaddai, actively cultivate through the logic and practice of spiritual warfare. The active citizen for Tocqueville, as well as for neo-Pentecostals, is not governed per se, but is self-governing for the greater good. This means that the citizen organizes and accomplishes tasks to help society ([1835–1840] 2004, 123). Democracy, with its freedom of association, encourages the individual to cultivate a sense of concern for the public good. In some sense, this is what spiritual warfare advocates, demonstrating that even neo-Pentecostal visions of democracy rely on a productive rather than a repressive form of governance (Cruikshank 1996, 242). Democracy as a mode of governance needs people—like Marta—who are willing to subject themselves to society, to take on the responsibility of governing themselves for the sake of society—feeding the hungry, keeping neighborhoods safe with citizen-patrol units, and cleaning the streets. For neo-Pentecostals in postwar Guatemala City, this also means conquering the past and praying, which the faithful certainly pursue for the public good but do through rather private means. Prayer yields a model citizen who is active and well-intentioned, but nonetheless alone more often than not.

LET'S PRAY

The practice of spiritual warfare promotes a striking level of individuality that allows complicated societal problems with deep historical roots to be moralized—to be defined as a matter of character, individual failing, or sin and temptation—or some combination thereof. To enlist in God's army means engaging in a kind of participation that "extends [the believer] away from political institutions and economic relations" and "towards the terrain of the self" (Cruikshank 1996, 236). Through the moralization of drug trafficking, for example, Satan becomes the culprit instead of the dynamically complicated relationship among the United States' consumption of illegal narcotics, transnational street gangs that regulate the flow of drugs across borders, and hypermilitarized drug cartels that govern the industry. Once the material and historical dimensions of drug trafficking are flattened and its purported demonic dimensions are heightened, the neo-Pentecostal can war earnestly against the problems that trouble Guatemala by warring against demons. Through the logic and practice of spiritual warfare, congregants shoulder the moral weight of dynamic societal problems and in so doing become responsible citizen-soldiers.

Examples of this responsibility are not hard to come by in Guatemala City. One came while I was driving home from a mega-church service with Marco, a devoted El Shaddai congregant. It was late into the evening and we passed a crime scene. Police lights swirled as two corpses lay on the ground. Both had been shot to death. The reason was (and remains) unknown. Onlookers formed a crowd. "How ugly," I remarked. Eyes trained on the scene, Marco, not missing a beat, responded earnestly, "Yeah, but that's why I pray." It is a short statement worth taking seriously; he said, "Yeah, but that's why I pray." Of interest is Marco's use of pronouns, those both stated and implied, and what these indexical decisions reveal about the practice of spiritual warfare. Marco as well as an overwhelming majority of El Shaddai congregants insist that *I* [not *we*] am praying for *us*—not just *me* and not just *you*. The responsibility is singular but nonetheless taken in behalf of the collective. His prayerful comment recalls a popular quote from Fyodor Dostoyevsky's *The Brothers Karamazov:* "We are all guilty of all and for all men before all, and I more than the others" ([1880] 1957, 264). The practice of spiritual warfare makes "all guilty of all" and "I [the individual] more [guilty] than the others."[28] The Christian soldier prayerfully fights his or her battle against Satan all alone in Guatemala City, but in behalf of Guatemala—in behalf of the entire nation.

One prayer project that allows neo-Pentecostals like Marco to engage in the war as valiant but solitary warriors is *Oremos,* which is short for *Oremos por la nación que queremos,* organized by the El Shaddai community. The phrase translates two ways. The first is "Let's pray for the nation that we *want*." The second is "Let's pray for the nation that we *love*." El Shaddai intends for the model believer to see both translations at the same time. Promoted since the early 1990s, Oremos provides Guatemalan neo-Pentecostals with a body of literature that instructs believers on how to wage war against the devil. The project's pamphlets, manuals, and leaflets—pieces of paper that congregants carry in their back pockets or fold into their Bibles—go to great lengths to equip believers with the necessary tools to win back their nation from the devil, and to recover the capital as well as the nation from violence, drug trafficking, poverty, and broken families.

The logic of spiritual warfare insists that the successes or failures of each person in this battle will result in the success or failure of Guatemala. Participating in the battle for a short time is nonsense. Every waking minute demands that the believer pray, fast, and speak in tongues. The Oremos project emphasizes constant participation. Hesitating for a moment means certain defeat. Dr. Caballeros writes: "Spiritual warfare really constitutes the normal way of life for believers who have been redeemed by Christ from the slavery of the devil. . . . While we remain on the earth we will have an enemy that is in continual war against us." The time to act is now: "We were suddenly invaded by a sense of urgency. God was putting before us a revelation, giving us a great responsibility."[29] And, as the Oremos literature makes clear, El Shaddai congregants, as soldiers for Christ, face an unprecedented battle: "Now more than at any other moment in the history of mankind, God is looking for men and women who are able to place themselves between God and this world, to intercede for Him for a more just world, for a nation with government officials whose hearts are right with God, for a Church that is always on the offensive, for a strong and united leadership."[30] All that is needed are Christians willing to fight.

Oremos materials conceptualize this particular kind of participation through the language of intercession. Intercessors place themselves between God and those who need God's help. An intercessor is "one who is always at war, always at battle against Satan, and in that war, one cannot battle with carnal weapons. One needs to dress oneself in the armor of God." At the same time, the Oremos project reassures those who might wonder why God would need "the fallen" to help him defeat Satan and redeem the world: "God could do it all. He is everything. But in His great love, He made us, He filled us with His grace and chose to work with us for salvation. These [men and women He has chosen] are his intercessors.

What an immense privilege!"[31] The flip side of great privilege, of course, is great responsibility.

Interceding amid a spiritual war is not a collective activity; neither is it public or external. Intercession is individual, personal, and internal. The Oremos prayer sheets are not used in groups or during church services, but are kept at bedsides and work areas, in pouches or knapsacks. Fulfilling one's responsibility as a soldier for Christ takes place while praying alone. One poignant example came during a series of conversations with Julio, to whom I had complained about the noise in my neighborhood, noting that I felt helpless against the disturbance of discos playing music into the early morning. While flipping through his Bible, dragging his fingers across each page, Julio patiently explained to me that I needed to pray every day against the devil, being specific in the words that I chose and the images that I brought to mind, to rout out the bars in my neighborhood. To this I responded, "But then I should also go talk to the owners of the bars, right?" Julio's response gave a glimpse of the individuality and isolation that the practice of spiritual warfare produces. He looked at me quizzically, admonishing: "You shouldn't go to talk to the owner. He's not going to listen to you. You need to pray. In your apartment. Against the demons in the bars." Julio later continued: "So what I am talking about does not need to be done in front of a person. Pray against the demons that are manifesting themselves inside a person, but do this very discreetly. You need to be discreet to crush the demons that have come. When I am waging war discreetly, within myself, the demons leave. They leave. You see?" Spiritual warfare, Julio insisted, is set apart from other church activities. It is a daily responsibility that every congregant must pursue on his or her own time.

With almost never-ending patience, Julio then taught me how I might accomplish my own small victory over noise pollution. Prayer sheets in hand, Julio pointed out that spiritual advancement takes effort, painstaking effort, which begins with praying an hour a day. The hour-long spiritual exercise has six phases of active prayer. Phase 1 asks the Christian soldier to give thanks to God "for the privilege of entering into His presence." In this first phase, the sheets ask the warrior to recite God's many biblical names, invoking the power that accompanies each name. Phase 2 involves praying for the manifestation of God's kingdom in the present world. Here the believer presents his or her petitions to God; there is but one caveat: "Remember that we should not pray about a problem without having a solution in mind. The solution to the problem? Yes, examine the Word to encounter what solution God has for this situation. The solution should be placed in your mind and then confessed."[32] This is an active, not passive, practice that demands answers from *you*.

In the third phase, "We pray for a resolution for the needs of our family, church, and nation. This is the intercession." Phase 3 begins the specific prayers made in behalf of Guatemala, which turn a devout believer into a citizen-soldier; the sheets provide a prayer, but Julio explained that the goal is to have one's own prayer melt into glossolalia, or speaking in tongues—to fade from specific words and move toward direct communion with the Holy Spirit. Phase 4 asks the Christian soldier to put himself or herself at the service of God and neighbors, focusing on the importance of praying for the needs of others. Phase 5 returns to the explicit language of spiritual warfare: "Dress with the armor of God. Also, pray for God's protection (Solomon 5:12) in our lives, in our family, in our possessions, etc. (John 1:10)." The final phase asks the believer to pray on a specific theme. In my case, Julio said that this would be the elimination of loud music from my neighborhood. Julio assured me that if the Christian soldier is without a specific theme, Oremos literature provides an extensive archive of salient topics for the Guatemalan context. This archive, available both online and at the El Shaddai main office, provides congregants with a wealth of prayers on a wide range of themes, recommending specific topics each week, from marriage and the nation to particular Guatemalan departments—the northern jungles of Petén and the western highlands of Huehuetenango, for example.[33]

To my own observation that this all seemed so formal, so deeply ritualized as to simplify the fog of war, Julio agreed, saying that the daily struggles of a Christian warrior are far more unruly than the approach the Oremos project advocates. In some effort to substantiate his own bravado, Julio told me about a recent conflict that placed him on the front lines. He was in Guatemala City's Zone 21, "talking to a friend, teaching him how Jesus is really with us." But just as Julio was citing a biblical passage to his friend, "there came a guy our way with negative ideas. He had such negative ideas. The guy had tattoos, bad ideas; he came with different ideas, negative ideas." In an interesting moment of profiling, of seeing this man with tattoos as a gang member, Julio revealed his fear of being assaulted, explaining: "I prayed, and since I had positive ideas and since they are better [than negative ideas], the guy was rid of the demons that were inside him because inside him were demons that wanted to rob us. To rob us and hurt us." Julio added for good measure: "So when you confess the Word of God, it makes the demons leave; they die. In this moment, when I started to speak the Word of God, the guy with the tattoos left; he said, 'I don't want to be here with you guys, so I am going.' So I crushed, knocked down, and conquered the demons that were inside that guy." All of which, Julio pointed out, did not involve any face-to-face interaction. Citing the Book of Psalms to me, Julio insisted that when he confessed the Word of God against the demons, he did so to himself and in complete silence: "Confuse, O Lord, confound their speech; for I see violence and strife in the city. Day and night they go around it on its walls and iniquity and trouble are within it; ruin is in its midst; oppression and fraud do not depart from its marketplace" (55:9–11). Julio, leaning back in his chair, closed his Bible, announcing again how he had defended himself as well as his friend from demons, from the dangers that define much of postwar Guatemala.

Julio's efforts, of course, are a very different kind of participation from, say, protesting outside federal buildings for increased police security. The practice of spiritual warfare as something done not only in isolation but also inside oneself (and discreetly, to use Julio's word) can be seen as participation only when one understands, as I mentioned in the introduction and explored in chapter 2, that everything neo-Pentecostal begins with the believer's own heart and mind. Neo-Pentecostalism in Guatemala City has taken the form of a moral rationality based on a causal logic whereby one's thoughts and feelings form one's actions. These actions eventually congeal into habits, molding character and, ultimately, the nation's destiny. This rationale not only links individual states of mind with the nation-state, but also makes Christian practices such as fasts, prayers, and examinations of conscience very real acts of spiritual warfare. Julio's efforts at self-defense, no matter how imperceptible to anyone else but Julio, were actual efforts made in behalf of himself, his friend, and his neighborhood. And these acts of spiritual warfare make neo-Pentecostals like Julio increasingly responsible for the successes and failures played out in the streets of Guatemala City—for the successes and failures that result from praying (or not praying) an hour a day for Guatemala. As Oremos literature states: "As conscientious citizens who need an intervention from God for our nation, we are driven to a life of prayer for Guatemala." The conscientious citizen engages in the spiritual war: "The proposal, of course, is to win the spiritual war, to knock down the principalities and authorities that have dominated our country for far too long; we clamor for God that the heavens may be opened so that the power of God may descend and that we may have the greatest spiritual advancement of all time."[34] Participating in the war means being active—but active in a rather solitary way, in a way that involves praying discreetly against disturbances rather than addressing people and problems directly.

TAKING BACK THE STREETS

In the winter of 2006, a little less than a year before Guatemala would hold its 2007 general elections, El Shaddai announced its affiliation with a new political party: VIVA Guatemala: El partido político con visión y valores. VIVA is the "political party with vision and values." Soon thereafter, Dr. Caballeros announced his own candidacy for the presidency of Guatemala, running as VIVA's newly minted candidate. His candidacy did not come as a total surprise. Secular and Christian newspapers had been abuzz for months about Dr. Caballeros and how his vision for the country could be read along both political and spiritual lines.[35] In fact, the big question in the capital was not whether Dr. Caballeros was qualified to be president; the general assessment was that his education, training, and experience were excellent. The question was also not whether Dr. Caballeros could get enough votes to be elected. Many astute commentators, in fact, shuddered at the thought of Dr. Caballeros's ability to mobilize Guatemala's Pentecostal and charismatic populations as a unified voting bloc. The looming doubt was whether he could appeal to those who were not charismatic or Pentecostal Christians. Could Dr. Caballeros's vision and his values be relevant to Guatemalan Catholics as well as to the non-Christian indigenous?

This electoral anxiety motivated the El Shaddai community to do something for Dr. Caballeros's candidacy. After much deliberation, church leaders decided that Guatemala City needed a surge of optimism and success before Dr. Caballeros could launch his campaign. As Dr. Caballeros had explained during an interview with the Christian press several years before: "Six women in my church have been kidnapped recently for money . . . and the drug trafficking has increased dramatically. Recently police found Q14 million in one house where drugs were being sold. . . . When you look at the Guatemalan church you see big numbers. . . . But we have passed the point of focusing on the numbers. The point is that we Christians have not transformed society."[36] Something needed to be done, and done soon, to spotlight Dr. Caballeros's campaign—to prove to the nation that he could be an effective leader. So the El Shaddai community chose a select group of congregants to participate in what might best be described as a covert spiritual warfare campaign. The mission aimed at taking back the streets from crime, drugs, and corruption; it was intended to prepare the ground for Dr. Caballeros's political campaign. The project lasted one month and employed the neo-Pentecostal strategy of spiritual mapping. Most important for this study, the effort demonstrated how congregants worked to improve their nation and elect a president through explicitly Christian practices.

The effort, at least for me, began with a sound—one that was at first unrecognizable. The noise as I approached El Shaddai was like a large machine or generator working overtime, creating a strange buzz that floated across El Shaddai's expansive parking lot. It was not until I stood at the threshold of El Shaddai's prayer room that it became clear. The industrial noise came from a small group of dedicated congregants. Overwhelmingly women, they spent their mornings and early afternoons, from 7:00 a.m. to 2:00 p.m., praying in tongues over a basket of smooth, black rocks. Eight congregants at a time hovered over the small rocks, each keeping one palm facing the heavens and one palm facing the stones. What was most striking was that the women never stopped, even for a moment, to catch their breath or engage with each other. A steady, rolling wave of noise splashed over the rocks for seven hours a day.

During one particular visit I made to the prayer room, Telma (the group's leader) pulled me aside to describe what was happening. She explained that this was an effort at intercession for the country, for the city, and, ultimately, for Dr. Caballeros. She explained that congregants, each of whom had signed up for a shift of at least an hour, prayed seven hours a day for three weeks straight. Their mission was to pray over the rocks constantly, charging the small stones with the power of the Holy Spirit. And what would happen after they completed three weeks of prayer? Telma explained that congregants had been selected to place each stone at the doorstep, or in the general vicinity, of seventy-two carefully selected locations throughout Guatemala City. The sites included Guatemala City's airport and zoo, the Supreme Court building, the national palace, and the cathedral. Added to the list were hospitals and midlevel government offices, such as the office of immigration, the offices of the police and national defense, and the headquarters of the tax agency. The locations selected were for the most part political, with an assortment of Catholic churches and cultural centers added for good measure. Guatemala City's cardinal points were also included; stones would be placed in the city's north, east, south, and west regions.

After three weeks of prayer, the stones would be placed in their strategic locales and then lie in wait until they were activated, or "detonated," as Telma called it. The stones, in Telma's words, were capable of "exploding" the demonic strongholds that governed the city. They would be detonated on the first day of the New Year, setting a precedent for the year to come— creating opportunities for the church to change the country for the better. To activate or detonate the stones, leadership assigned individuals to each of the seventy-two stones and their respective locations. In one covert mission, for example, Julio—my earlier guide to prayerful intercession—was in charge of placing one stone at or near the doorway of the Department of Immigration office in Guatemala City's historic and bustling Zone 1. He did just that, he explained to me, quietly tucking the stone in a potted plant near the front of the building. No one saw him do it, Julio insisted, and the stone was in an inconspicuous enough place not to be touched or moved until it was time to detonate it. When asked what the stone could do for the city and the country, the Julio explained: "A lot! When detonated, the stone will break down the strongholds and principalities that govern the city . . . the stone will change everything. . . . No more corruption. No more violence, muggings, bad ideas."

On New Year's Day Julio returned to the Department of Immigration. With no one in sight on a quiet New Year's morning, Julio found his stone and then poured wine, water, and salt over it, praying in tongues as he completed the project. The water represented the Holy Spirit; the wine signified Christ's blood, which washes away the sins of humanity. The salt, Julio explained, acted as a coagulant that brought both the Holy Spirit and the blood of Jesus Christ together. Having bathed the stone and murmured the prayers, Julio left the stone in front of the government office, knowing that his work was done and that seventy-one other congregants had completed their missions at that very moment. Spiritual explosions of sorts were then peppering the capital, allowing the El Shaddai community to take back the city with acts of spiritual warfare.

The use of stones (as opposed to woodchips, or just wine and oil) deserves some attention. The biblical tale of David and Goliath forever framed this effort at taking back the streets: "When the Philistine [Goliath] drew nearer to meet David, David ran quickly toward the battle line to meet the Philistine. David put his hand in his bag, took out a stone, slung it, and struck the Philistine on his forehead; the stone sank into his forehead, and he fell face down on the ground" (1 Samuel 17:48–49). The story is popular with Christian soldiers because of the narrative's flexibility.

It highlights, for example, the Christian need for precision. One spiritual warfare manual states: "David had five stones when he met Goliath on the battlefield, but he used only one of his sharp stones to conquer the giant. We need the highest precision of aim to hit the enemy at his most vulnerable point. Wisdom in battle is to win the victory without wasting ammunition."[37] For the El Shaddai community, this meant selecting only seventy-two strategic sites instead of inundating the city with thousands of stones. With precision in mind, El Shaddai leadership also hand-selected seventy-two congregants from a field of volunteers to carry out the mission. Rather than inviting the entire congregation, the church formed a commando unit for Christ—a select fighting unit, much like the Kaibiles and the biblical David.

The dynamic that exists between Goliath and David adds yet another layer of meaning. As the story goes, Goliath is in control. He is large and threatening, able to defeat any opponent who crosses his path. At the same time, David is divinely chosen and inspired, though also noticeably vulnerable and young. The El Shaddai community reads itself through this biblical lens: Goliath stands for all that is wrong with Guatemala. Julio explained: "What does Goliath represent? The corruption, muggings, assaults, drugs, violence, death, bad ideas, hunger, alcoholism, and fraud." The biblical figure of David, therefore, inspires the El Shaddai community to read itself as a lanky shepherd chosen by God to do battle against a terrifying foe. Julio continued, "And what is important is that David cut off Goliath's head with [Goliath's] own sword." David felled Goliath with his stone, just as El Shaddai aimed to stun those who govern Guatemala. And just as David decapitated Goliath with Goliath's own weapon, El Shaddai worked to do the same—to dismember prayerfully that which disturbs the capital city and the nation: demons and devils. El Shaddai, through Dr. Caballeros's campaign for presidency, worked to become the head of government, to usher in a new era of peace and prosperity.

This particular effort at spiritual warfare comes in part from a cluster of spiritual warfare manuals. Primarily published in the United States, Guatemala, and South Korea, they are translated into dozens of languages and distributed throughout the world. These books provide what participants understand as the basics not just for spiritual warfare but also for the realization that their participation in spiritual warfare is a way to participate in postwar Guatemala. One central assumption in all these manuals is that spiritual warfare has actual effects in the material world. Dr. Caballeros, in one of his own publications on spiritual warfare, writes about the effects of prayer on political corruption, detailing how strategic prayer upended three reportedly crooked people in Guatemala City: "I can say that as a direct consequence of on-site prayer, the first [corrupt man] has lost all his power and is in jail waiting to be judged for his crimes. The second one is about to be impeached and thrown out of office, and the third one, at a critical time in his political career, suffered personal problems and has now lost most of his influence and power."[38] This belief in spiritual warfare's effects explains what happened next. On the day that the El Shaddai congregants detonated their stones in their seventy-two locales, the church celebrated an apparent reduction in crime, violence, and corruption. The air was even crisper, one informant told me. Another explained that there were five people murdered on Christmas Day in 2005; during the church's prayerful efforts at taking back the streets, only three people were murdered on Christmas Day in 2006. After New Year's Day the church continued to report a decrease in crime and murder in the city, even though the crime statistics said otherwise. Just one week into the New Year, ten women had already been violently murdered, continuing the pace that the country's "femicide" had set.

Regardless of the numbers, spiritual warfare's focus lingers on concrete effects. Dr. Caballeros writes: "Spiritual warfare brought forth fruit, not only spiritually, but also naturally, and the result has been a scriptural one. Having bound and defeated the strongman, we could then proceed to take from him all his armor in which he trusted, and divide his spoils."[39] The fruit included a reduction in crime and even air pollution. The message is consistent: things happen when congregants participate as good Christian soldiers, and so congregants must get involved. These opportunities include the Oremos project as well as more clandestine missions. And these efforts at participation through the practice of spiritual warfare produce effects that are not merely apparent to the faithful, but also capable of being documented by social scientists. One effect is a sense of citizenship—the felt reality of belonging to the nation, of being responsible for that nation, and of having the means to act in behalf of that nation. Julio would explain to me often that he never felt more involved and more useful than when detonating his stone for Guatemala. Another effect is the kind of membership that comes only through one's participation as a soldier: "When citizens serve their country [as soldiers], they gain the sense of community that comes from sharing a common cause" (Strauss 2003, 68). Telma routinely mentioned this to me. Yet another is a deep sense of responsibility for the nation, for all its successes and failures—for the crime, for the poverty, for the violence. This kind of responsibility weighs on the individual Christian soldier, making life as an active neo-Pentecostal in postwar Guatemala City sometimes overwhelming.

ALL QUIET ON THE WESTERN FRONT

Erich Maria Remarque wrote *All Quiet on the Western Front* to capture the absurdity of war while at the same time exploring a number of other subthemes. One is isolation; the suggestion is that the experience of war contributes to the distancing of the soldier from the life that he or she left behind—friends and family who could not possibly understand what the active soldier has experienced. War changes a person, making him or her unrecognizable to loved ones. Paul, the novel's narrator and a World War I German soldier, recounts this sense of isolation: "A terrible feeling of foreignness suddenly rises up in me. I cannot find my way back, I am shut out though I entreat earnestly and put forth all my strength" (1929, 176). Paul's struggle is with the emotional distance that war has created between him and those who knew him before the war. Paul's growing sentiment throughout the novel, in fact, is that the individual experience of war isolates the soldier—makes him forever alone. Interestingly, one of spiritual warfare's observable effects is this same sense of isolation and same experience of separation. The distance that emerges is between those who know spiritual warfare and those who do not. For those Christian soldiers who find themselves in the trenches day in and day out, warring against demons in the streets of Guatemala City, the disconnect can sometimes be too much. Informants explain, at times emphatically to quell their listener's disbelief, that the demons are everywhere, living alongside us in our daily lives. They are wreaking havoc. Why doesn't everyone see it?

One example among many comes in the story of Julio's broken marriage. Julio, who quickly became one of my most trusted informants, narrates his story like so many other neo-Pentecostals in Guatemala City. Drawing on a Christian narrative of having once been lost and now been found, Julio recounts a life of drugs and alcohol as well as marital unhappiness. For years he and his wife tried to have a baby but could not. One day, however, Julio found God—met Christ—and quickly plunged himself into church life. Soon after, the couple's marriage improved, they had two children (miraculously, he attests), and he gained steadier employment. At the same time, Julio's involvement in the church, especially his participation in spiritual warfare, intensified. He could see and feel the demons that governed the city. He participated day and night in saving the nation through the conversion of lost souls. He warred for the soul of Guatemala because he knew he had to. It was his deep responsibility as a Christian citizen of Guatemala. Soon, however, the war took over his life. Declaring that it was his generation that was going to save Guatemala—to change Guatemala forever—Julio put long hours into spiritual warfare campaigns, spending more time at the church and increasingly less time at home. Meanwhile, his wife stopped attending services—"retiring from the church," Julio would tell me. Uninspired by the spiritual war that raged in Guatemala City as well as throughout the world, his wife broke away from the church and, in turn, broke away from her husband. Still married, they live separate lives. One raises their two children. The other wages a spiritual war for Guatemala's salvation.

Marriages are social unions that are far too complicated to dissolve for only one reason. Spiritual warfare is not the sole reason for this marriage's problems, nor am I implying that spiritual warfare contributes to the failures of marriages. Rather, I am suggesting that there exists not simply an epistemological distance between "those who know war and those who do not" but an emotional distance as well. It is the emotional distance that *All Quiet on the Western Front* captures so beautifully. This kind of emotional distance emerged during a casual conversation I had with Julio. In a roundabout third-person hypothetical, Julio disclosed the emotional detachment that spiritual warfare can generate and the isolation that can emerge. Julio explained to me: "Let's say that 'Julioito' has a wife and two children and they don't believe and they don't go to church. What do we do? We pray for them . . . that they know Christ . . . that they go to church. We pray that they understand eventually." What is so touching about this remark is the admission that his wife and children do not understand. They do not understand that Christ saves, that Satan tempts the weak, and that Guatemala would be a better country if everyone, Julio's wife and children included, participated as Christian soldiers. They simply do not understand. What is also poignant is *how* Julio suggests that someone might change their hearts. Prayer made in isolation, possibly late at night when the three are asleep, is the way to enlist his wife and two children. The answer is not direct communication, counseling, or conversation, although all three (Julio insisted) have been tried—but rather prayer made in isolation in their behalf. This kind of strategy returns this chapter to the words of Remarque as he narrates the profound loneliness of battle; in the voice of an overextended soldier, the passage reads: "We were all at once terribly alone; and alone we must see it through" (1929, 12). Ironically, spiritual warfare delivers meaning and a sense of agency to the Christian soldier, at the same time limiting the avenues through which the soldier can connect with family, friends, and neighbors, let alone address the material and historical problems that continue to crush postwar Guatemala. Julio is more active for having found Christ, while he is more alone than ever.

The irony of Julio's Christian citizenship makes sense when one begins to link what this chapter has described as the individualizing and isolating effects of spiritual warfare with the commonsense observation that much of this book addresses the collective through the language of "the nation," the "congregation," and even "the Church as the body of Christ." At first glance, the vision of Julio alone in his home praying for Guatemala stands in stark contrast to the busy crowds that meet every Sunday morning at the mega-church to pray for Guatemala—to change Guatemala. But, in reality, the two images fit well together if one remembers that the practice of spiritual warfare, as it is understood in the neo-Pentecostal imagination, comprehends the collective as comprising individuals. It understands Guatemala (a country of 14 million people) as being made up of 14 million individuals, and understands neo-Pentecostal Christianity as not a single social movement, but as the collection of millions of individual (and interior) social movements made in behalf of Guatemala. To play with pronouns yet again, neo-Pentecostal efforts at social change through the practice of spiritual warfare do not say that *we* are the revolution, but rather, that *I* am the revolution. Julio has hitched himself to a new kind of sociality, a new kind of citizenship, one that charges him with incredible levels of responsibility to change Guatemala—to war constantly but discreetly, fervently but interiorly. What becomes clear, ultimately, is that an increasing number of neo-Pentecostals participate in the making of their postwar nation, but they tend to do so alone.

FOUR

The Founding Fathers

The Problem of Fatherhood and the Generational Imagination

To a father who asked how he might best bring up his son,
[the answer is given] "By making him the citizen of a state
with good laws."

G.W. FRIEDRICH HEGEL

The family becomes an instrument rather than a model: the
privileged instrument for the government of the population
and not the chimerical model of good government.

MICHEL FOUCAULT,

"Governmentality"

THE PASTOR SAT ON A STOOL at the very center of the mega-church. One spotlight shone on him as thousands of young men and women sat in the dark. They had all assembled for an event whose theme proved attractive: "The Fatherhood of God." Their interest had been piqued earlier in the week by small booklets. Serving as the event's invitation, the booklets presented six black-and-white photos of young fathers and stated: "As a child . . . I wanted to learn from dad . . . feel close to dad . . . play with dad . . . walk like dad . . . and even though I have grown up, I know that I continue needing Him." The last of the six photos depicted a young man reading the Bible, suggesting that one must always complement biological fatherhood with God the Father. The pastor confessed that he had done just that. In a quiet voice, from his perch he described his own father as loving but schizophrenic—well-intentioned but deeply troubled. He explained between long sighs that his father's mental disorder deeply affected his childhood and made his young life traumatic: the mood swings, the rage, the sadness. Emotional scars lingered, he admitted. He sat quietly for moments at a time, staring into the crowd as if lost in thought. Breaking his own silence, the pastor then revealed—weaving his own conversion narrative into and through the theme of fatherhood—that he often turned to God the Father to supplement his own unhealthy and unsteady father. When his father would become very ill, the pastor would feel God speak to him in his heart; the Lord would say, "I love you like a father loves his child." The pastor, in these moments, would recommit his life to God.

The spotlight then dimmed. In its place, the church's audiovisual team projected a home movie onto the mega-church's two-story screen. What emerged was a multigenerational family portrait, one in which an old man cuddled his grandson while a proud father sat watching. It quickly became clear that the home movie presented the pastor, his newborn son, and his elderly father. A theme of forgiveness emerged. Even with such a difficult history, with so much pain and opportunity for resentment, the three could come together as a family to celebrate their lives. A hug between the baby, the pastor, and the grandfather concluded the movie—played in slow motion for emotional effect.

The pastor then brought his seven-month-old baby onstage. Father and son sat quietly while a trio sang a slow melody that celebrated fatherhood. The three singers wore bright red T-shirts that read, "The Father in My Heart." The entire congregation's attention was rapt by the performance, and the pastor began to cry; he reflected aloud, between sobs but squarely into his microphone, "I can't believe I have my own baby now—a healthy baby boy." As the trio continued to sing, the pastor moved from the stool to the pulpit, playing with and kissing his son. After pacing for some time with babe in arm, he handed his son to his wife and walked toward an overweight young man who was crying furiously, heaving to catch his breath between sobs. The pastor brought this weeping young man to the front of the church as the spotlight followed their every move. Turning to face the crowd, looking over his shoulder with some strain, the pastor commented: "This might look weird, but I don't care." He then sat and placed the chubby young man on his lap. Wailing like a baby, the young man wrapped himself around the pastor, trapping the microphone between their bodies. The effect was a muffled groan that made each person in the church feel like the man was crying on his or her own shoulder. The pastor hugged him for a long while, saying, "I love you. Your Father loves you," and stroking his head like a father might caress his son, rocking him back and forth. The young man's lament filled the mega-church as thousands watched.

This chapter addresses the problematization, the practice, and, ultimately, the paradox of neo-Pentecostal fatherhood in postwar Guatemala City—how neo-Pentecostalism makes fatherhood a problem that requires attention, and how men with children attend to this problem not only for their families but also for the nation. Guatemalan neo-Pentecostals make it clear that the family is the nation's nucleus and that the father, not the mother, is responsible for stabilizing the family—for instilling in his children the right values, which will produce a generation of active citizens. Neo-Pentecostalism stresses that gang leaders and homosexuals, for example, were all once children capable of goodness. They lacked only a strong father who would love them tenderly and provide them with the ability to discern right from wrong. This particularly active vision of fatherhood constantly brings to attention the absent (or implied) mother; women, I found, have much to say about their place in this schema. This neo-Pentecostal formation of fatherhood does not just re-place (not replace but literally re-place) motherhood in postwar Guatemala but also generates a great deal of anxiety that deserves analytical attention. Competing and sometimes contradictory notions of masculinity press on even the most mundane corners of men's lives. The stakes, remember, are high. Strong but sensitive fathers will save Guatemala by producing a generation of active citizens. Absent fathers, neo-Pentecostals insist, will only breed more gang leaders and homosexuals.

Understanding fatherhood as a problem and, in turn, as intricately related to citizenship, begins with Michel Foucault's essay "Governmentality" (1991), in which he notes a historical shift in the relationship between the family and Western government. The shift is from model to technology. As a model of government, the family was at one time a replica, even a metaphor, for how a prince should govern his principality with "transcendent singularity" (Foucault 1991, 94). For centuries, the prince was to his principality as the father was to the family. Foucault writes: "The art of government . . . is essentially concerned with . . . the correct manner of managing individuals, goods and wealth within the family (which a good father is expected to do in relation to his wife, children and servants) and of making the family fortunes prosper—how to introduce this meticulous attention of the father towards his family into the management of the state" (92). This logic changed in the eighteenth century, when "the family becomes an instrument rather than a model: the privileged instrument for the government of the population and not the chimerical model of good government" (100). Rather than being a vision of what good government might look like, the family actually began to contribute to the governance of populations.

Foucault's emphasis on the population is important here. During the eighteenth century, as the relationship between the family and governance shifted, "population" became an object of knowledge—something counted, analyzed, and appraised: "The population now represents more the end [i.e., the goal] of government than the power of the sovereign" (100). Government began to strive toward the well-being of a given population and to use technologies, such as the family, to achieve particular ends: increased birthrates and higher literacy rates, for example.[1] The significance and practice of fatherhood followed this shift from model to instrument. Fatherhood no longer replicated the prince but rather existed as a means of control—an "ensemble formed by the institutions, procedures, analyses and reflections, the calculations and tactics that allow the exercise of this very specific albeit complex form of power" (102). Just as the family became a means to good government, fatherhood became a necessary component for the well-being of a population.

The perceived centrality of fatherhood to the governance of democracies has been well documented.[2] Inattentive fathers not only are bad citizens but also rear generations of failed citizens. The problem of bad fatherhood is viral, many suggest, a self-propagating practice that starts small but ends horrifically. Since bad fathers routinely fail to instill in their children democratic values and character, broken citizens threaten a range of populations, including the nation-state. In this sense, discourses of the derelict father are common. They are absent, alcoholic, abusive, adulterous, and asexual (or even homosexual). Good fathers are the exact opposite: present, sober, principled, committed, and heterosexual. Connected to this, but in an entirely different social and historical context, is an explosion of neo-Pentecostal experts who link the successes and failures of fatherhood not only to the well-being of children but also to the fate of postwar Guatemala.[3] Neo-Pentecostalism, as this chapter details, contributes to the formation of fatherhood as a particular kind of problem (and mode of governance) amid efforts at postwar democratization. Parenting experts from Guatemala, as well as from North America, frame fatherhood as Guatemala's problem (instead of a range of other potential problems—such as the economy, history, multinational corporations, or even the United States, for example). These very same experts also provide any number of practical solutions that men with children can adopt—even when the realities of postwar Guatemala make the practice of neo-Pentecostal fatherhood nearly impossible.

FATHERHOOD AS A PROBLEM

"Why do you think we have so many people who do not know whether they are men or women? Do you ever wonder?" Dr. Caballeros posed the question to his congregation in a sermon entitled "The Father: A Special Being." The faithful often replay the sermon, delivered on a breezy Sunday morning that has long since passed, in cell meetings and listen to it over El Shaddai airwaves. Dr. Caballeros answers his own question with a striking sense of anxiety about supposed sexual delinquents as well as other kinds of moral *delincuencia* that neo-Pentecostals understand as plaguing Guatemala: "It frightens me to see these poor children having surgeries [sex-change operations]. They are half-man and half-woman. It frightens me. This really frightens me." After asking God to help him regain his composure, Dr. Caballeros continues: "But they do not have themselves to blame. They have their fathers to blame. Their fathers never outlined the role of the woman and the man in the home. They did not see [those roles]. They did not live [those roles]. And they don't know how to act." Dr. Caballeros points to Guatemala's supposed problem with "sexual disorders" as a sign of bad parenting and explains how improper parenting has led to confusion about gender roles.[4] He argues that a generation of Guatemalans, having been preceded by fallen generations, does not know its role (or its place) in society. Without fathers, Guatemalans (as well as Guatemala) remain confused and half made.

In his sermon Dr. Caballeros performs a kind of moral apprehension that many have come to expect from neo-Pentecostal Christians in and beyond Guatemala. Like so many conservative Christians, he places a broken masculinity at the center of perceived social chaos: girls thinking they are boys, and boys becoming half-girls through surgery. The narrative follows North American Christian movements, such as James Dobson's Focus on the Family and the Promise Keepers.[5] These groups argue, in broad strokes, that a return to biblical gender roles will reinvigorate society with moral righteousness. An ordered family yields an ordered society. Dr. Caballeros echoes this logic directly but does so within a radically different context, advancing the idea that bad fathers not only produce sexual delinquents but also are partly responsible for Guatemala's postwar problems: violence, political corruption, and drug trafficking, for example. When men start acting like fathers, the logic presumes, then Guatemalans will start acting like citizens.

Neo-Pentecostalism in postwar Guatemala problematizes fatherhood, framing fatherhood as "a problem requiring attention" (Rose and Valverde 1998, 545).[6] *Bad* fatherhood, neo-Pentecostals insist, is responsible for some of the nation's most pressing concerns, and *good* fatherhood serves as the answer to such problems. The interpretation can be surprising, completely astounding from a certain perspective: neo-Pentecostalism makes fatherhood the source of postwar Guatemala's larger problems not simply in spite of more structural causes, such as free trade agreements and systemic racism, but also in spite of (but with no mention of) Guatemala's lost generation of men. Of the 200,000 people killed in Guatemala's civil war, upwards of 80 percent were men (CEH 1999); hence, many young fathers of today are not likely to have known their fathers themselves, because of violence, forced disappearance, or abandonment. Fatherhood, then, could be read as a certain kind of postwar problem from the perspective of public health or even public policy, for example, but neo-Pentecostalism sidesteps this history by focusing on responsibilities accepted (or declined) by individual men with children.[7]

Rodrigo, for example, is a middle-class El Shaddai congregant and father of two. Old enough to remember the civil war and fully cognizant of the war's toll on Guatemalan society, he announced: "There is a lot of work to be done by people in terms of the cultures that have formed inside them. Right now, if we form a new culture inside our children, our children's generation will be totally different. But there are so many people who are thirty or fifty years old who still live the way that they have always lived. But this generation could be totally different. It is all about the power to transform this nation the way God wants." Rodrigo continued: "And the role of the father is to be the head of the family, and the father really is the person who guides his family in a good or bad direction. And if we think in this way, then the father is the head of the family. He is the spiritual leader of his wife and his children. He has to instruct them. He has to teach and guide his family. The father has 100 percent of the responsibility." The father, rather than the war or the economy, rather than gangs or corruption, is 100 percent responsible—for his children and for Guatemala.

A generational imagination is an important subplot in the problematization of fatherhood. There is a rich sense in neo-Pentecostal communities that one generation affects the next. Dr. Caballeros announces: "The chaos that one creates in the home and in the family is bound to repeat itself in future generations. Listen to what I have to say: if you plant order and organization in your child, your child will plant those virtues in his children and so on."[8] Congregants own this narrative, noting in very concrete terms how the actions of a father mold the next generation. Andrés, building on Rodrigo's comments while waiting for Sunday service to begin, added: "It's so profound to think about. You need a father with principles to form children into people who can make decisions. The right decisions. You see! Guatemala needs a generation of fathers to make the next generation and then the next generation and the next generation." Fatherhood becomes a vehicle through which neo-Pentecostals grapple with the weight of transitional times, through which they come to own and answer their responsibilities. Andrés continued:

> Well. Here the church is not making anyone do anything. It is something that we have to learn to do for ourselves. The desire to search for God has to well up inside each and every person because the Word says that if we search for God with prayer, we can break this generation. You see, there are old generations and new generations. An old generation is a culture of twenty years or more where one feels like one can't change. But a new generation has Jesus Christ as its rock and is moving forward with help from Him. There's a difference. This means that their participation is personal. It's not obligatory.

The neo-Pentecostal imagination asserts that for generations, witchcraft, Maya spirituality, and Roman Catholicism have kept Guatemala broken—as "half made" as the transsexuals who concern Dr. Caballeros so much. Generations of Guatemalans have wandered through a spiritual desert of sorts, but they have now come home to God as a chosen people. Congregants announce that the growing number of charismatic and Pentecostal Christians in Guatemala evidences this transition. And, through difficult but deliberate work, neo-Pentecostals firmly believe that the sacrifices made today—that the changes made in *this* lifetime—will make Guatemala's future generations better. Moreover, this generational imagination places the father at the center of societal change—fatherhood as clearly the problem but also as the most obvious solution. Fathers affect future generations through the transmission of moral values, Christian principles, sound personalities, self-esteem, and self-worth. Congregants explain often and with much resolve that fathers have the unending responsibility to save (as well as to form and to govern) the nation, one child at a time.

The problem and promise of fatherhood have biblical precedence. The Gospel of Matthew, for example, presents Jesus' own genealogy, stressing the centrality of fatherhood. When pressed on why the father (rather than the mother, or any other social actor or force for that matter) must be Guatemala's guiding agent of change, the faithful invoke the following text as proof: "Abraham was the father of Isaac, Isaac the father of Jacob, Jacob the father of Judah and his brothers, Judah the father of Perez and Zerah, . . . Hezron the father of Ram, Ram the father of Amminadab, . . . and Jacob the father of Joseph, the husband of Mary, of whom was born Jesus, who is called Christ" (Matthew 1:1–16). Abraham is linked to Jesus through fatherhood, generation by generation, which is what neo-Pentecostals want. They pray that their country's transitional generation will one day link today's half-made nation with a Christian future.

As we might expect, the problematization of fatherhood corresponds directly with the naturalization of motherhood. For Guatemalan neo-Pentecostals, mothers are natural caregivers; they have always been an integral part of the family, providing the very conditions for life and production. Motherhood is not in question, since the mother's role has become understood as a logical extension of a natural order (Yanagisako and Delaney 1995). In contrast to fatherhood, motherhood literally is not a problem. As one congregant observed to me: "You don't need to tell a mother what to do. . . . Mothers love their babies. It is what they do." Fathers, however, have a problematic role in the cultivation of future generations. Whereas mothers care for their children and support their husbands with reported ease and panache, fathers must impress character, self-esteem, and personality on their children; the task is not an intuitive one, which makes fatherhood "strange"—something that one has to learn. And fatherhood's problematic strangeness allows for explicit conversations about the practice of attentive fatherhood as opposed to a kind of absent fatherhood. The communication of good fatherhood as a social process relies heavily on Christian parenting manuals that detail an unsurprisingly gendered but unexpectedly technical conversation. These manuals announce that individuals constitute the nation, and that the character of each individual determines the quality of a nation. The father, as the conduit of character, transmits to his children either good or bad character. Rife with "bad character," the logic continues, Guatemala has been the victim of bad fatherhood for far too long. Generations of bad fathers have begotten delinquent children who have, in turn, become bad fathers and have themselves begotten more delinquent children.

From the neo-Pentecostal perspective, making a new generation begins with fathers who are active, which largely means affectionate. Dr. Caballeros insists: "The father needs to hug, touch, and caress his children, because the touch of the father is the first entryway to the personality of a person."[9] It is commonplace, for example, to see El Shaddai fathers—rather than mothers—holding babies during church services, laying hands on their children, and hugging their teenage sons and daughters. Fathers, rather than the mothers, attend to their children in church settings. At stake in a father's constant affection is the child's personality. Dr. Caballeros continues: "This affection is absolutely necessary to develop a human personality. We have all been confronted with problems in our lives, at different times in our lives, and in different circumstances. But I say that you have to work hard to make a baby who is loved, adored, touched, appreciated, and cared for by its father."[10] A child's personality will be strong when the father hugs, kisses, and caresses his child. At the same time, a child's personality will be broken (or fragile at best) when the father is distant and cold.

Fatherhood works, many argue. Dr. Caballeros, mixing confessional with scientific registers, makes the point that affection generates better (more stable) children and, ultimately, citizens: "Scientifically speaking, the child forms his or her personality in the first seven years but obtains self-esteem and a basic self-confidence in the first nine months. . . . [These first nine months are when] the child should not feel like an intruder, when the baby should not feel overlooked, but on the contrary, should come to be loved, desired, and cared for as part of the family."[11] Again, broken personalities make for broken citizens, which result in a broken nation.[12] One congregant could not avoid using the word "responsibility" to describe the relationship between fatherhood and the future of the Guatemalan nation-state: "Oh, what a responsibility! Thirty years ago there were bad ideas and bad character. This is where we are, thirty years later, with more bad character. Now, we fathers can make a difference. We can make the choice [to change Guatemala]. What a responsibility!"

Fulfilling one's fatherly responsibilities means assuming and becoming subsumed by neo-Pentecostal technologies of fatherhood. Fatherhood as a technology—as something taught and learned, as something mapped and outlined—means doing certain things at certain times and in certain ways (as opposed to doing other things at other times and in different ways). Like Heideggerian notions of technology, neo-Pentecostal fatherhood is "a resource that aims at efficiency—toward driving on to the maximum yield at the minimum expense" (Heidegger [1949] 1977, 15). Yet neo-Pentecostal fatherhood also resonates with Foucault's notion of *technē*; neo-Pentecostal fatherhood as a technology produces a different kind of subject who does not just approach the world through technology but who himself becomes formed by way of the technology (Dreyfus 1984).[13] This means that there emerges from church doctrine as well as Christian publications a technical language for how to be an active father, and this language produces certain kinds of subjects. These fathers not only act in certain ways but also own the problem of fatherhood, seeing themselves as both the cause and the solution. Dr. Caballeros preaches: "And when I had my [four] children, from Harold to David, we made a point in the mornings, beginning with Harold, every day in bed, to have a 'love session' with the baby. We would invest fifteen to twenty minutes in them, first with Harold, then with Andrea, and then with Cristina, and finally with David. We would invest in them some minutes of love, affection, and time."[14] Neo-Pentecostal technologies of fatherhood encourage men with children not simply to be affectionate but also to approach affection in a particular way. Affection becomes ordered, calculated, administered, and managed—all for particular ends. Dr. Caballeros's use of the phrase "invest in them" (*invirtiéndoles*) suggests a kind of financial or economic mentality: the affection advanced toward children accumulates as a kind of asset and, ultimately, generates a future return. Like responsible investments, affection is not spontaneously administered or haphazardly distributed. Fathers make and apply, manage and assess, affection daily; the time becomes regimented, even measured—"fifteen to twenty minutes." Neo-Pentecostal technologies of fatherhood are similar to what Pat O'Malley has termed "the new prudentialism" (1992); they encourage men to invest in their children for the sake of the future, creating a new industry of both risk and return that asks the individual father to take individual responsibility not only for his children but also for society.[15] Fathers cultivate the child's self-esteem, personality, and ultimately his or her ability to participate in society at the most mundane of levels.

EXPECTANT DISCOURSES

Expectant couples often worry about their ability to be good parents. This is hardly exclusive to Guatemala or neo-Pentecostalism. So it comes as no surprise that in Guatemala, excited neo-Pentecostals, upon discovering that they will soon have a baby, often scramble for advice. They storm their youth pastor's office for private meetings on how to prepare themselves. They attend church activities focused on the theme of parenting, at the same time looking to wise elders for counsel. These couples, informed by a sense of the cross-generational implications, understand the stakes of it all and so seek out as much information as they can handle from parenting books, church sermons, and quirky anecdotes. Amid this cacophony of uneven voices, a wave of proscriptions and prescriptions, there emerges what this chapter understands as a fatherhood technology. The following analysis, in fact, focuses on such technical conversations and practices that relate child rearing to the fate of the nation through the language of "expertise," making good fatherhood not only Christian citizenship's crucible but also a form of Christian citizenship itself. One of this chapter's central observations, in fact, is that the growing prominence of neo-Pentecostal parenting experts in postwar Guatemala provides men of faith with a new vocabulary for responsible citizenship, allowing their own selves to serve as sites of restoration, while their children are understood as fields of concern and action. The practice of good fatherhood allows the faithful, in the words of Nikolas Rose, "to govern without governing society—to govern through the 'responsibilized' and 'educated' anxieties and aspirations of individuals and their families" (1999, 88). The analysis begins with an ethnographic vignette.

A young female cell leader, with husband in tow, announced sheepishly to her Monday evening group that she was pregnant with their first child. The eight people seated in a Guatemala City eatery shrieked with excitement: "We are going to have another cell member!" The group then peppered the expectant pair with obvious questions: When is the baby due? Are you feeling sick in the morning? Were your parents very excited to hear the news? When will you tell the pastor? Before praying for quite some time over the pregnant woman, for the health of her pregnancy and for the future of her family, the husband, Javier, admitted to his own concerns about becoming a father. Much of the cell over the preceding months had been devoted to the generational imagination—to the strong influence that one generation has over another. Keenly aware that Guatemala is in the middle of a transitional generation, the young man often noted aloud and with a great deal of earnestness that Guatemala is a country where individuals, fathers included, bear a weight that is heavier than usual. A few months earlier, before the big announcement and during an interview, Javier, a young, middle-class ladino man, explained to me confidently:

> A new nation has principles and morals, and the father brings the principles. The principles begin with the father. If the child wants to be a businessman, if the child wants to be president, mayor, whatever profession the child wants to be, the womb and the family are where the child will form. And this means that the nation forms in the womb. Part of the new generation is forming in the womb. This is why we are going to teach our children not to throw trash in the street, to speak well, to be disciplined. . . . But it is necessary to have Jesus Christ in your heart because that is the base. He is at the center of it all: Jesus Christ.

The young father-to-be, seemingly overwhelmed by what he himself had long branded "the great responsibility of fatherhood," appeared to be heavily burdened by his own future. Fiddling with his soda cup and looking to his wife, Javier asked the cell group a question that began his own quest for answers: "What do I need to know about being a father?" The question, asked in a moment of emotional vulnerability, is telling; it suggests that the church promotes a vision of active fatherhood that congregants easily parrot, but one that ultimately needs to be learned. Javier could rehearse with ease and clarity fatherhood's centrality to Guatemala's past and future, but he demonstrated a striking degree of flat-footedness when it came to the actual practice of fatherhood in his life—what he actually needed to do as a father. An avid reader of neo-Pentecostal guides, manuals, and self-help treatises, Javier found refuge in El Shaddai's bookstore. A brief look at the manuals Javier purchased gives us a glimpse of the kinds of expertise and technologies being advanced.

Javier's first book was Davíd Hormachea's *Father or Progenitor?* [16] Hormachea, a Chilean-born North American pastor who now resides in Southern California, has several Spanish-language publications available for purchase at the El Shaddai bookstore. The book's back cover announces: "Many men believe that being a father is only a question of providing for their family's physical needs. These social and cultural paradigms have created a crisis in the formation of our children and in the stability of our families." The continuation of Hormachea's logic, as well as that of his fellow parenting experts, is that the destabilization of the family leads to massive fault lines in society and that the father exists at the precise center of this crisis: "Sadly, the family's very structure is crumbling because of a lack of healthy values and Christian morality. The family is being destroyed by a general lack of knowledge, by inadequate interpersonal relationships between relatives, and by irresponsible fathers. This bad model of family produces severe effects between parents and children and among siblings."[17] Poised to save not only the family but also society, Hormachea explains to his reader: "I want to tell you [the father] that it is possible, and that it is your responsibility to act knowingly in your family's life, to actively form healthy principles in your children's minds so that they can make good decisions and live with integrity."[18] The pressure placed on fathers like Javier is to deliver good values to their children, so that they can make good decisions not only for themselves but also for their families.

Being a bad father, the manual explains, is rather common, even easy: "Sadly, there also exist absent fathers. This kind of father is always overwhelmingly busy with his work, and because of this not only fails to spend time with his children but also exudes an incredible amount of tension. . . . [He] is constantly angry and irritable."[19] Beleaguered with the pressures of providing for the family, this type of father is unable to love—to hug, to kiss, to laugh, and to tickle—yet, these are the very practices that define neo-Pentecostal fatherhood. Hormachea continues: "This [kind of] father does not dedicate any time to his family, does not pass time with or play with his children regularly. He only wants to give things to them. He wants to give them the fruits of his labor but does not want to be with them [or share with them], emotionally speaking."[20] In Hormachea's estimation, this kind of man is merely a "progenitor" rather than a father, and, in his expert opinion, this kind of man fails at his responsibility to show affection to his children. The absent father forms neither good children nor good citizens: "When citizens defy the police without any respect for the laws of the land, society experiences anarchy. The same happens in homes where there are no laws and limits."[21] Hormachea associates chaos in the family with chaos in the streets.

To form good children, Hormachea instructs young fathers to do certain things. Basing his suggestions loosely on biblical examples of fatherhood, both good and bad, Hormachea prescribes fatherly regimens: "My parents, for example, would dedicate 15 minutes of our day [as a family] to prayer and to the reading of the gospel."[22] Recalling Dr. Caballeros's morning routine of expressing affection to his four children, Hormachea encourages young fathers to construct similar routines: fifteen minutes a day of hugging, twenty minutes a day of speaking in tongues, twenty-five minutes of father-son or father-daughter sharing sessions. The cultivation of fatherly discipline quickly becomes dependent on timetables, schedules, and programmed routines concerned with controlling not just bodies and space but also personalities. These routines attempt to manage the ways in which men conduct themselves and their relationships with their children, which is how fatherhood becomes so deeply entwined with what Foucault understands as governmentality. In postwar Guatemala, fatherhood becomes a technology through which neo-Pentecostals govern themselves and participate in the formation of a postwar nation. As a representative example of an expansive field of Christian parenting experts, Hormachea works to inculcate an uncontestable code of conduct, placing the locus of authority squarely on the father's shoulders, all for the sake of good governance. Hormachea incites the will to govern the family through the practice of fatherhood.

The men of El Shaddai eagerly take up fatherhood as a mode of citizenship as well as a means to generate future citizens. They explain the seriousness with which they take their "daily conversations" as a family. From anywhere between ten and twenty-five minutes, fathers direct their children to sit around the kitchen table while mothers sit alongside, quietly but supportively. Fathers ask their children about their day—about their studies, prayers, and friends. Fathers also report that they read Bible passages and pray while family members link hands. Of importance here is that families pray together and that the father leads these prayers. They begin inwardly with the self but work outward toward the family, the church, and the nation. A common prayer made during these moments would be: "Celestial father, bless each and every one of us. Bless our thoughts and emotions. Bless our self-esteem and personality. . . . Bless the work of El Shaddai and the work of Pastor Caballeros. And, Lord, bless Guatemala. Bless this nation, our land. Make Guatemala your chosen nation."

Active fathers employ the power of prayer early and often. Rodrigo, for example, explained to me: "The father has the ability to speak positive words when the baby is inside the wife. It starts a change in the nation, in the human being, in the family, et cetera, et cetera, and et cetera. It's because of this [potential] that it is necessary to minister to the baby inside the woman for all nine months. It is possible to begin this development at a very early age. It's possible to make a change in the culture, to make a new generation." The father's work begins immediately, soon after conception, as he molds the fetus's development throughout its gestation. Rodrigo continued, explaining the power of laying his prayerful hands on his wife's belly: "When my second baby was inside my wife, it was different from my first. With the first, I ministered only a little bit to the child and this is why he was 'only 50 percent' [what North Americans might understand as a colicky baby]. Eventually the child grew stronger and is now doing really well. But now with the second child, he was totally 100 percent. Totally different in his actions, attitudes, in everything, emotionally, as a child, you know?" With this, he reinforced not just the centrality of fatherhood but also the problem of fatherhood. He strengthened the idea that the actions of a father weigh heavily on the life of his child: "Look, let's say I'm a father who drinks and smokes—what kind of children will I form? And so, this child I formed as a father is going to live in a generation that also drinks and smokes. So probably, children living in a negative context are going to form negative children. It's a chain that we have to understand. We also have to understand that it all begins with the family and inside the home." The father's work is not simply constant and somewhat contagious, but also moral—assessed as either positive or negative and in continuous relationship to what neo-Pentecostals understand as delinquent habits, such as smoking and drinking.

To make Guatemala a chosen nation, fathers must also cultivate their own attitudes, their own self-esteem, so that they may exude confidence, leadership, and affection. To cultivate their attitudes—to make sure that they are active and not passive—neo-Pentecostal experts such as Hormachea enumerate (often in bullet points) what good fathers do. Good fathers, for example, "Provide, Administer, Discipline, Restore, Educate."[23] As a mnemonic device borrowed from typical North American self-help discourses, the first letters of these five characteristics spell padre (father): *Proveedor, Administrador, Disciplinador, Restaurador, Educador.*[24] Each of these characteristics also goes beyond the assumed bounds of fatherhood: good fathers not only provide financial resources; they also provide for the emotional needs of their children. The active father restores not simply his own family but also society and the nation. The Christian father educates his children on topics that schools cannot: character, values, and morals, for example.

Expectant men also learn from neo-Pentecostal publications that good fathers constantly pray for their children—when they are with their families, while riding Guatemala City's public buses, and late at night when the rest of the family has fallen asleep. These prayers are sometimes impromptu but more often are part of neo-Pentecostal regimens. One very popular manual includes a telling testimonial: "For the longest time, I have had regular prayer groups meet in my home with the sole purpose of praying for our children. Each participant has seen an endless amount of prayers answered. This is because prayer works! And there does not exist a more powerful prayer than one from a father for his child."[25] This logic came to the fore when a congregant at El Shaddai attended a cell meeting one night; he testified that his son had had emergency surgery that very day to remove his appendix. The father asked the cell group to pray for his son, focusing the power of the Holy Spirit toward his son's well-being and health. Later, when I asked the father why he had not just skipped the week's meeting so that he could be with his son as he convalesced, the man explained: "My role as a father is to pray for my children. And the cell is the most powerful place for that." The active father balances affection and proximity with the power of prayer, assessing which is more appropriate at any given time.

The prayers that men deliver for the sake of fatherhood ask God for wisdom: "Transform me into the kind of father that I want to be and teach me how to pray and intercede for my child's life. You said in the Gospel: Have faith that you will receive whatever you ask for in prayer."[26] In another instance, experts ask fathers to pray: "I want to become closer to you and take part in your gifts of well-being, discernment, revelation, and direction. I also need your strength and patience, together with a generous portion of your love."[27] Fathers-to-be also take it on themselves to pray often and furiously for their own formation, knowing that their child's development depends heavily on their own. Through prayer, these young men imagine the kinds of children they want to form: children who feel "loved and accepted," "secure with eternal salvation," who "honor their parents and resist rebellion," and "develop a hunger for God." Praying early and often, these men lean on the advice of parenting experts, following technical counsel about which words to choose. They are fathers who fervently believe that their prayers will cultivate children who will one day steward postwar Guatemala.

FATHERS WITHOUT BORDERS

Neo-Pentecostal fatherhood is ultimately (and rather unexpectedly) about intimacy—touching, kissing, hugging, holding. It is a supremely active social relationship that demands both time and proximity—two things challenged by migrant labor circuits. Guatemala, like so many other Central American countries, continues to bleed men and women to the United States. Looking for better opportunities for themselves and for their families, an estimated one million Guatemalans live in the United States, in growing communities in California, Florida, Illinois, New York, and Texas. They send upwards of $3.6 billion back to

Guatemala each year in remittances, making undocumented emigration the country's most lucrative "trade relationship" (Dardón 2007). Yet the very nature of undocumented emigration strains neo-Pentecostal formations of the family. Coyotes, or paid guides, lead young Guatemalans across the U.S.–Mexican border, but they do not work on schedules. Sudden word that a popular coyote is in Guatemala City, even in a particular *zona,* sends men and women counting their money and conversing hastily about the possibilities that wait for them in the United States. Questions swirl over kitchen tables: Why return to the fields to cut cane, or to the streets to sell goods, when there is more money to be made in the United States? There aren't any jobs here in the capital, are there? Wouldn't the family be better off if we made this sacrifice?

One day whole, a family can be divided the very next night as a family member decides to try his or her luck against the increased militarization of the U.S.–Mexican border.[28] With the real possibility of never seeing their loved ones again, those who remain in Guatemala promise to pray constantly for the traveler's journey and new life. When fathers leave, the family experiences an understandable sense of disconnection. Yet even with distance between them, the practice of neo-Pentecostal fatherhood often continues. Though Guatemalan neo-Pentecostals generally disapprove of undocumented emigration because these men and women break U.S. law, church communities know full well that a vast majority of their congregants have immediate and often familial connections with undocumented emigrants in the United States. A close look at migrant labor circuits suggests that, contrary to folk theories about religious participation, religion is not a feminine domain that Latin American men find difficult to accept. Rather, fathers are often absent at church on Sunday morning because they are in Chicago, Houston, or Los Angeles working in restaurants, fields, or factories. Many of these men, however, still stretch their prayerful arms southward, toward their children, every chance they get.

In 2002, for example, an indigenous neo-Pentecostal family living in one of Guatemala City's poorer *zonas* made the difficult decision to separate. The family decided that the father and the oldest son would travel to California, leaving behind the family's mother, two daughters, and three remaining sons. Frustrated by limited opportunities in Guatemala City and made optimistic by stories of steady work in Fresno, these two men left their homeland, promising to send a constant stream of money to their family. The separation proved difficult. Devout neo-Pentecostals, the family—from father to youngest child—realized the separation's significance. How would the father fulfill his important role as the patriarch? How could he leave his five children, between the ages of thirteen and twenty-two, to develop as adults without his immediate guidance? Because of the ways in which the category of fatherhood has become situated in neo-Pentecostal communities not only as problematic but also as technological, these anxieties generated an open conversation about how to father from afar. The family, with help from an El Shaddai associate pastor, decided on three general strategies.

The first involved monthly phone conversations. Though not ideal, they were opportunities for the father to continue to influence his children—to tell stories of hard work in the United States, of personal sacrifice, and of dedication. These brief phone calls were opportunities not only to "stay in touch," but also to cultivate daughters and sons who would one day be responsible Christian citizens. The second strategy was to shift much of the day-to-day fatherly responsibilities onto the shoulders of the second-oldest son, Francisco. At the age of twenty, Francisco not only used his paycheck to support the family but also took a prominent role in the El Shaddai community, playing in the band and volunteering with the youth ministry. In addition to these church-related activities, Francisco also started his own cell group. Graduating from El Shaddai's leadership course, this young man began a weekly group composed of his own family members. Mother, aunt, sisters, and brothers met every Friday evening to discuss the relationship between their own faith and Guatemala's future. These cell meetings provided Francisco with an opportunity to actively "father" his brothers and sisters under the supportive gaze of his mother and aunt. Christian morals, values, and vision became the cell meetings' guiding themes.

During cell meetings, Francisco would pose questions to his brothers and sisters about his or her hopes and dreams. They were questions that forced each brother and sister to imagine the future aloud and then to describe how he or she might achieve these dreams. The older daughter wanted to be a schoolteacher, and the youngest son wanted to play soccer professionally. These exercises, pulled from the pages of El Shaddai leadership manuals, allowed Francisco's brothers and sisters to expand their horizons and plot their futures. They prompted each cell member to try his or her hand at managing his or her life, setting goals, and cultivating a vision of what he or she wanted to achieve. Francisco, as their surrogate father, led these sessions while also providing the kind of intimacy that neo-Pentecostal fatherhood demands. Francisco administered hugs, kisses, and pats on the back to his younger brothers and sisters in a very deliberate, even calculated way: one hug here meant another hug there, and a pat on this brother's back demanded a playful scratch on a sister's head. Constantly calculating the amount of affection administered, Francisco assumed a tremendous amount of responsibility while his older brother and father continued to labor in the fields of Fresno.

The third strategy acted as a steam valve, of sorts, for Francisco, who was in many ways left behind in Guatemala City to address the problem of fatherhood. This strategy recognized God the Father as the ultimate father. As long as his brothers and sisters had a personal relationship with God, then Francisco's efforts would complement God's work. This third strategy followed Dr. Caballeros's advice, including a lesson that he often delivered during sermons on the theme of fatherhood: "I'm going to talk to you about something that is very important. It's likely that there are people here who did not have fathers who lived past the age of forty, like mine. It's also likely that some of you didn't have fathers because your parents divorced or because they had problems. But, brothers, to change our future and our lives we need to realize that God is our father."[29] When he realized that God the Father was each person's true father, the pressure of being ever-present decreased slightly for Francisco. As he explained: "It's a big responsibility [to care for my siblings like a father] but I'm not the only one doing it. God helps me. God is their father, too." Nevertheless, Francisco's stress level—as both provider and surrogate father, as well as student, musician, volunteer, and employee—resulted in debilitating migraines, and he was forced to disband the Friday night cell meetings after eight months. "The doctors tell me it is stress," Francisco mentioned as he explained why there would be an indefinite break from the cell. Palpable, the moral weight that presses down on devout fathers can at times be crippling.

Families like Francisco's pursue active fatherhood even when separated by immigration policies and miles of Mexican-American border. But neo-Pentecostal formations of fatherhood do not totally satisfy the problems that the formations themselves raise. The pain of being apart, for example, came to a head when I was scheduled to return to Northern California for a short stateside visit. Having offered to deliver a package to Francisco's father and brother in Fresno, I met him and his younger brother at a nearby shopping center. They brought letters and CDs of Christian music as well as a plastic container that held a whole chicken, baked just as their father liked it. "They don't get enough good food in the fields, and this is their favorite," the brothers told me. As I explained that customs would probably not allow meat or poultry through security, it became clear (as one would expect) that the distance that separates families tests even the most concerted efforts at surrogate fathering through neo-Pentecostal technologies. It became obvious in our frustrating conversation that there was a very real need for the human connection that neo-Pentecostal fatherhood demanded but could not completely provide—a connection that even God the Father could not deliver through a personal, intimate relationship with Him.

The flow of Guatemalans across borders goes both ways. As thousands of Guatemalans leave for the United States, thousands more continue to be deported from the United States, separating Guatemalans from their established lives and families in that country. In 2004, for example, the Department of Homeland Security's Office of Immigration and Customs Enforcement sent 72,173 criminal and 64,520 administrative deportees to Central America (USAID 2006, 20). Juan Carlos's story is not uncommon. Affected deeply and personally by Guatemala's thirty-six-year civil war, Juan Carlos fled Guatemala for the United States, seeking amnesty. His brother had been violently murdered and Juan Carlos himself felt that his life was in danger. Arriving in the San Francisco Bay Area in the mid-1980s, Juan Carlos quickly became involved with raising international awareness for the crimes against humanity that defined wartime Guatemala. Along the way, Juan Carlos learned English, became trained as a paralegal, and earned a steady salary. He married a Salvadoran woman with U.S. citizenship and had two daughters. Life was good.

In the late 1990s, Juan Carlos made a mistake, he admits. He "sinned against his family," involving himself with a female coworker who eventually charged him with sexual harassment and assault. Although he would not find God until 2003, Juan Carlos now explains from his born-again perspective that those distant days were influenced by the devil and his own weakness as a sinner. Both his temptation and sinfulness would change his life forever, he would later remark. Charged with a felony, Juan Carlos was arrested and held in a U.S. federal prison for several months, separated from his life in San Francisco by the seriousness of the charges. He was unable to pay for proper legal counsel, and federal courts deported him back to Guatemala to live with his sister, working at a small diner in a middle-class section of the capital, while his wife and children remained in the United States. His life in shambles, Juan Carlos stumbled across both the Bible and El Shaddai at a time when he thought divorce would be the best solution to his problems. Divorce would offer a clean break from his past life—a new beginning, of sorts—so that he could begin to make a new life for himself in Guatemala. Juan Carlos's new mentors at El Shaddai said differently, reinforcing the importance of fatherhood, marriage, and family—stressing the responsibility that he has to his daughters, his wife, and Guatemala.

Juan Carlos took up the mantle of fatherhood as best as he could, given the distance that separated him from both his wife and his children. What became the most stunning dimension of Juan Carlos's renewed commitment to family was his own assessment of how good fatherhood can affect the nation. Juan Carlos explained: "My daughters don't know Guatemala, but they are Guatemalan. They speak English more than Spanish. I think they do it because I do not speak English very well." Smiling knowingly, he continued: "They are teenagers, you know? But I have the responsibility to be their father and to make sure that they know they are Guatemalan." For Juan Carlos, his two daughters remain critically important to Guatemala's future. While thousands of miles from Guatemala and fluent in English, not Spanish, Juan Carlos's daughters are two more foot soldiers in a war against Satan for a new nation.

With distance a problem, Juan Carlos extended his fatherly reach to California by way of e-mails and written letters. Often asking me to translate his letters from Spanish to English, he sprinkled the correspondences to his daughters with biblical quotes. Concerned that his daughters were befriending the "wrong crowd," Juan Carlos made sure that he angled his letters toward the Christian values that El Shaddai advocates—the values that will save not only the family but also the nation. The letters asked his daughters to pray to Jesus daily, to read the Bible, and to attend church services. Mimicking the logic learned in El Shaddai leadership classes, Juan Carlos challenged his daughters to cultivate their self-esteem and personalities, noting that individual character makes a nation like Guatemala stronger. As I sat with Juan Carlos one day, in between efforts at translation, he reflected: "It's possible to change the nation through the family. Of course. The family is the most important. You can't wait for a school or for a university to teach your children. The father has the responsibility, before God and before the family, to be the one who teaches his kids. Because if we don't have principles and values, then where are we going to get them? It starts with the father." The problem and the promise of fatherhood constantly vie for attention.

The distance between Juan Carlos and his daughters, however, proved frustrating. Teenagers will be teenagers, Juan Carlos confessed to me after learning from his wife that his younger daughter had defaced her Bible. "This isn't how it should be," Juan Carlos explained; "I know she didn't mean [to deface the Bible], but I am not there to tell her what to do. . . . My wife also thinks that my daughter is joining a gang." Compounding Juan Carlos's sense of frustration was the repeated message from El Shaddai that the father is the sole transmitter of values and principles from one generation to the other. The more Juan Carlos internalized this message, the more frustrating his reality became—the distance between California and Guatemala City seemed to grow with every church lesson on fatherhood. He was handcuffed by immigration laws, unable to apply for a tourist visa because of his criminal record, and his family existed permanently out of his reach, which is a reality that confounds the very logic of neo-Pentecostal fatherhood. Dr. Caballeros preaches: "Fathers need to hug their children, you need to love them . . . you need to hug and kiss your children and go look for your children and embrace them."[30] It is a level of intimacy that Juan Carlos cannot, and most likely never will, achieve.

Critical here are, first, that deportation frustrated Juan Carlos's ability to care for his children and, second, his awareness that he was failing not just his family but also his nation. Juan Carlos admitted, at times as an afterthought but in other moments as his central focus, that he was unable to contribute to the next generation of Guatemalans like some of his fellow congregants, whose children lived under their own roofs. This paradox exists at fatherhood's very core: neo-Pentecostalism problematizes fatherhood—making fatherhood Guatemala's problem—while also making fatherhood the answer and, thus, charging men to pursue what constantly seems to be the impossible task of raising not simply a child but also a nation. After I pointed out this tension—the impossibility of fatherhood—to Juan Carlos, he replied: "Look, for me it is a responsibility— the responsibility that we have as citizens and as Christian citizens. For us, we have a burden (*carga*) and a weight (*peso*), but whatever we cannot carry, we give to Jesus Christ. He will never give us more than we can ever carry. And we should depend totally on Him to take up the weight that we cannot. So, when the weight of fatherhood becomes too much for me, Jesus helps me pick it up." Juan Carlos, well aware of the weight that neo-Pentecostal fatherhood bears, asks Jesus, from time to time, for help.

It would be absurd to overlook the role of motherhood in the construction of fatherhood—even if motherhood (as opposed to fatherhood) is not a problem, is not something that Guatemalan neo-Pentecostals have made into an observable technology. Fatherhood, like any gendered category, is about social relationships, not only with children but also with wives and mothers. During women's groups' gatherings, before Bible study sessions and in passing sighs about the difficulty of raising children in Guatemala City, neo-Pentecostal mothers continually demonstrate their commitment to the formation of their children as Christian citizens. For example, women (and not men) are usually a family's first contact with the mega-church. The composition of any given service evidences this. Women outnumber men, both in the pews and in the church's volunteer and paid staffs, which makes women both gateways to and gatekeepers of the mega-church.

As gateways to the church, mothers, not fathers, tend to bear the responsibility for introducing the family to the Christian faith as well as bringing the family to church service every week. The enduring narrative heard repeatedly in the Guatemalan context is that a rapprochement between faith and family begins with the mother. Having attended a friend's cell group or having been invited to attend a Sunday service, the mother, taken by the cell's intimacy or the service's energy, then "drags" the begrudging husband to service. In the narratives collected from churchgoing families, there is an initial sense of masculine resistance that gives way to personal conversion and a reported relationship with the Holy Spirit on the part of the husband. This resistance is sometimes performed in a coy way to highlight the before-and-after of a man's conversion. As some husbands explained to me: "My wife asked me if I know [*conoce*] Jesus. 'Sure,' I said, 'Who doesn't know about [*sabe*] Jesus?'" The difference here is definitional. The Spanish verb *conocer* means to know but denotes deep familiarity, whereas the verb *saber* also means to know, but in a way that one knows a fact. The difference is between *knowing* Jesus as one might know a true friend and *knowing* that many people believe Jesus to be a historical figure. Other times, the resistance is naturalized as simply being part of manhood. As one woman explained: "Women are much more organized than men, so they go to church . . . but men need to be disciplined into going to church. It's not easy for them." It is a narrative often followed by a great deal of drama and pain. This preconversion resistance to church often is proportional to a husband's level of sexism or abuse toward his wife.[31] A husband's alcoholism, infrequent work, and adultery are commonly reported reasons for women to seek out the mega-church. Attracted by stories of men converting and then quickly becoming sober and less abusive, women work hard to get their husbands to church and, ultimately, to God.

Women also serve as gatekeepers, filling the volunteer and paid staffs of the mega-church as administrative assistants, office directors, and associate pastors. Although it is the category of fatherhood that dominates neo-Pentecostal constructions of Christian citizenship, it is striking that the very navigation of a mega-church's bureaucracy brings one into contact with women much more often than with men. Women, not men, grant access to interviews, archives, and activities. Women, not men, facilitate informal conversations and helpful contacts. Women, not men, keep the church clean and the stores humming with activity. The mega-church's organizational structure, in fact, exists as a metaphor for the structure of the family: The church, just like the family, aims to construct a generation of Christian citizens. Men in both the church and the family enjoy positions of authority.[32] Yet women provide the organizational and managerial support necessary to keep both the church and the family upright. Describing to me the role of the mother when it comes to fatherhood, one woman explained: "The first responsibility of the wife is to be obedient to the husband, but this doesn't mean being a slave. Because there are men who will have affairs and run this way and that, but the wife is supposed to complement the husband." It is a predictable kind of domestic politics that finds itself present and operative within the mega-church community.

The woman's auxiliary role has biblical roots. Ephesians 5:22–24 reads, "Wives, be subject to your husbands as you are to the Lord. For the husband is the head of the wife just as Christ is the head of the church, the body of which is the Savior. Just as the Church is subject to Christ, so also wives ought to be, in everything, to their husbands." Neo-Pentecostal women, such as those who volunteer at the church or those who meet weekly in women-only cell groups, emphasize that "submission" does not mean passivity. Women are quite active and powerful in their "submissive" role, they assert. They support, even buttress, the man's efforts at being a father—at raising children with good values.[33] Implied in this supporting role is the notion that women are natural nurturers and inherently more organized than men. Men, by the same token, are believed to be unruly by nature: "This is why men and women make such a good union," another woman explained. "Men are all over the place [*waving her hands above her head and making a funny face*], but women are serious and responsible." Women's natural qualities complement the sociological processes by which families come to know neo-Pentecostal Christianity. As I explained above, the dominant narrative of familial conversion is of the woman saving the family, especially the drunk, lascivious, and out-of-work husband, through conversion. In these narratives of familial renewal, prototypical constructions of motherhood and fatherhood emerge: wives submit to husbands, ceding to the head of the family his "God-given" authority; but at the same time, wives take on the responsibility of governing their husbands—when they attend services, how often they pray, if they volunteer with the church, and what cell groups they join.

This biblically infused relationship between husbands and wives (between fathers and mothers) is intimately linked to children—to Guatemala's next generation of Christian citizens. One recurring anxiety emerges in cell groups; when parents assume slightly different roles from those traditionally expected, the fear is that children will become confused. One among many examples begins with money. Rodrigo explained: "Let's say that the man earns Q.3,000 [monthly] and the woman earns Q.5,000 [monthly]. What happens? The woman begins to believe that she is the head of the household and then the children become confused about the family." This is not to say that neo-Pentecostal women never earn more than their husbands or that there is always shame attached to such a situation. The ethnographic interest here is in neo-Pentecostal formations of fatherhood and motherhood and the tendency for both constructions to generate observable levels of anxiety. During one women-only cell group meeting, the leader often would trumpet the fact that she earned a great deal more than her husband. The cell group as a whole rarely questioned this relationship as negative, only with curiosity: "What does he think about you earning more?" Her response always asserted a level of pride that also hinted at the very anxiety against which she was obviously working: "He knows I earn more than he does, but we have a good marriage nevertheless." In these moments of resistance ["I earn more than he does"] there are also moments of submission ["We have a good marriage nevertheless"]. Submission is part of the ideal "Christian" relationship between a man and a woman. It is necessary to create order—for the marriage, for the children, for the nation. And, even within this effort at order—at smoothing out the wrinkles that haunt each relationship—neo-Pentecostal women understand their faith as a vehicle for equality. To the question of whether neo-Pentecostalism is improving the lives of women in Guatemala, one woman explained: "The church helps change the minds of men here in Guatemala. The church is where women have roles of authority, and men see this and children see this. And when men and children see this, then they change their minds. It's like a chain reaction." She continued: "The same is true for spousal abuse. Machismo is a big part of our culture, and in generation after generation, men are *machistas,* but the church breaks this by giving the woman a voice in the community."[34] Even amid this qualified degree of self-reported advancement, the ultimate responsibility for societal change remains with the men. The woman concluded: "The life a child lives is the result of the father and so it is his responsibility to keep the child out of gangs and social conflict. It is all very complicated, but it is ultimately the father's responsibility." Present but supportive, peripheral but irreplaceable—neo-Pentecostal formations of motherhood happen in constant relationship to fatherhood and in such a way as to demand from women of faith a proper balance.

THE PARADOX OF RESPONSIBILITY

Neo-Pentecostalism problematizes fatherhood. The religion makes fatherhood one of postwar Guatemala's most pressing problems while also electing fatherhood as Guatemala's answer, charging men with children to pursue what constantly appears to be the impossible task of raising not simply a child but also a nation. Challenged by the dynamics of migrant labor circuits, Francisco parented his brothers and sisters until stress paralyzed his efforts. His own disappointment in himself is difficult to communicate; having shouldered such a heroic project, he finds that the idea of failure often leaves him speechless with both embarrassment and frustration. Whenever asked to talk, he would always defer the conversation to a later date, wanting instead to chat about soccer or contemporary Christian music. Juan Carlos, deported back to Guatemala on felony charges, parents from afar—too distant to administer the very kind of affection that neo-Pentecostalism demands of him, but too committed to his children and nation to soften his Christian responsibilities. While I was translating his letters, Juan Carlos's emphasis on the promise of fatherhood—on the need for fathers, for all fathers, to be more active— often amazed me. Fatherhood as a mode of governance subsumes men like Juan Carlos into a world understood as long since broken by bad fathers but one that active fathers will make whole again. Andrés, Juan Carlos, Rodrigo, and Francisco accept a deep commitment daily in the name of their families and nation. This kind of Christian responsibility paradoxically provides these men with a call to act, while at the same time restricting the ways in which they can contribute to postwar Guatemala's future. Andrés speculated:

> Fatherhood is a lot of work; it is a tremendous responsibility. But look. . . . The responsibility is enormous, of course, but we have to do it. We have to do a lot of things to place Jesus at the center of our families. So one can say that it is a lot of work, but how many of us have complained about this work? Now, Jesus helps us to understand better why we need to do this work for our children. To make them normal and excellent. Right? So this work that we have to do is not too overwhelming because Jesus gives us the health and the intelligence to form ourselves into better human beings.

The paradox—the one that makes fatherhood both the problem and the answer; both a weight and an honor; both an avenue and a dead-end—highlights just how successful neo-Pentecostalism can be at inculcating men (but also women) with a kind of responsibility that makes them deeply accountable for so very much. Andrés chose his words carefully, for example, saying that: "Jesus gives us the health and the intelligence to form ourselves into better human beings." This responsibility is fundamentally individual. This responsibility declares that the father must form himself; he must form his children. Moreover, the father—and not anyone else—must use the resources that Jesus provides to him to make Guatemala anew. Postwar Guatemala's gritty conditions can often be lost amid this narrative of fatherly concern and neo-Pentecostal regimes of care—both of the self and the child. Juan Carlos, Rodrigo, Francisco, and Andrés—a mixture of ladino and indigenous men, middle-class and poor—do not accept the mantle of fatherhood in, say, the middle-class suburbs of Southern California, even though this is where many neo-Pentecostal parenting experts (such as Davíd Hormachea) write their advice. Rather, these men live in a uniquely violent postwar culture. Guided by their pastors, but also by their own moral compasses, they accept the idea that they are the problem, that their own fathers were also the problem, and that they must vow to be better husbands, fathers, and friends. They accept all this in the hope that they can reverse unprecedented levels of street violence, jumpstart a national economy, and correct a legislature that continually proves itself incapable of governing.

This paradoxical abstraction of postwar Guatemala ultimately leads to the biblical account of Elijah and the Elisha—a tale frequently invoked by El Shaddai congregants and leadership alike. Elijah and the Elisha, the story goes, are two prophets whose relationship embodies the moral weight that fatherhood places on devout congregants. The Book of Kings announces that Elijah was a great prophet. He raised the dead, performed countless miracles, and foretold the future. The importance of Elijah, a major figure in the Bible's pantheon of prophets, is attested in biblical records as well as the Qur'an through his close proximity to Jesus and Moses during the transfiguration of Christ (Matthew 17:1–6; Mark 9:1–8; Luke 9:28–36). Elisha was Elijah's disciple (1 Kings 19:16–19) and God's unlikely choice to be Elijah's successor. 1 Kings 19:19 reads: "So [Elijah] set out from there, and found Elisha son of Shaphat, who was plowing. There were twelve yoke of oxen ahead of him, and he was with the twelfth. Elijah passed by him [Elisha] and threw his mantle over him." This mantle, is a ceremonial cloak draped across the back of the neck, allowing the weight of the cloth to rest on the shoulders. Elisha, the narrative continues, took up Elijah's mantle to prepare more prophets for future generations.

The story strikes a chord with Guatemalan neo-Pentecostals. Central is the transfer of authority from one generation to the next, as well as the responsibility accepted by the younger generation from the older one. The gendered dimensions of the narrative are also not lost; men transfer authority and responsibility to other men. There is, of course, also ethnographic significance to the notion that generations transfer the *weight* of this responsibility in a tangible way, from one set of shoulders to another—from Elijah's mantled shoulders to Elisha's bare neck. The weight of the mantle mirrors the kind of moral weight that neo-Pentecostals shoulder for their families and for the nation. During a conversation on fatherhood, Rodrigo explained: "We have a vision! It's not 4040 or 3030. It's 2020. We want to place Guatemala on the list of nations that will survive the apocalypse by 2020! This means forming the next generation. It is our responsibility as fathers." The moral ownership of this responsibility produces an observable weight for those who are best understood as "Elijahs," for those adults struggling to rear children not only as believers, but also as active Christian citizens of postwar Guatemala.

FIVE

Hands of Love

Christian Charity and the Place of the Indigenous

On the country has gathered the idea of a natural way of life:
of peace, innocence, and simple virtue. On the city has gathered
the idea of an achieved centre of learning, communication, light.
Powerful hostile associations have also developed: on the city as a
place of noise, worldliness, and ambition; on the country as a
place of backwardness, ignorance, limitation. A contrast between
country and city, as fundamental ways of life, reaches back into
classical times.

RAYMOND WILLIAMS,
The Country and the City

Wonderful charitable proclivities. Charity is unbelievable. I
appreciate it. I admire it. But charity is not justice. Two different
things. Two very different things.

CORNEL WEST,
Democracy Matters

I THANKED MARIA FOR THE glass of water as I took a seat in her office.
The photographs on the walls displayed some of the mission trips that her
organization had completed in Guatemala's rural highlands to help poor,
indigenous communities with basic social services, such as medical and
dental care, building projects, and educational programs. As the assistant
director of El Shaddai's philanthropic wing—Manos de Amor, or Hands
of Love—Maria exuded an earned sense of pride in her work. At a time
when the Guatemalan nation-state continues to relax its commitment
even to the most basic of social services and relies increasingly on the

global free market to provide for its people, her organization motivates the El Shaddai community to take on the Christian responsibility to help its neighbors with acts of charity. For some urban congregants, this means actually volunteering their time with the indigenous in the highlands of Guatemala; for most, it means responding to weekly requests for donations (big and small) through the church's bulletin. As I sipped my drink, Maria reviewed the social services that Manos de Amor provides, showing me more pictures of the indigenous communities that the organization assists. As Maria flipped through stacks of photographs, featuring smiling indigenous women who were decidedly poor but who seemed unmistakably grateful, the centrality of such images to Manos de Amor came into focus. The pictures themselves centered on a conspicuous fascination with alterity—with communities *over there* that needed help from those *here* in the capital.

In response to these images, I initiated a conversation that I would have many more times during the course of my fieldwork, each discussion winding through similar talking points. I asked whether Manos de Amor works with communities in the capital city. No, Maria answered; she explained that Manos de Amor helps those in grave need and that in Guatemala this kind of need exists in the rural countryside. But what about Zone 18 or Zone 3, I asked, mentioning some of Guatemala City's poorest and most ethnically diverse areas. Maria nodded, explaining that there was some talk of working in Guatemala City, in Zone 18, in fact, but that there was not enough interest or financial support. The capital was simply outside the scope of their project. Moving away from my questions, Maria shifted my focus back to more program reports and another series of images from the countryside, where young, indigenous boys and girls received dental work—their smiles as wide as the presumed divide between Guatemala City and country.

This chapter explores the charitable dimensions of Christian citizenship, with a particular eye to ethnicity and place. Amid the continued privatization of social services in postwar Guatemala, neo-Pentecostal charity both divides and connects as well as orders and ranks Guatemala City and country.[1] This two-part observation rests on the fact that mega-churches tend to direct their charitable interventions toward Guatemala's rural indigenous rather than Guatemala City's indigent, and that this decision to serve those in the country rather than the city evidences a shared moral geography with an agreed-upon sense of place.[2] In its use of the word *place*, neo-Pentecostalism evokes two interrelated meanings: "Place understood as both a location in space and a rank in a system of social categories (as in the expression 'knowing your place')" (Ferguson 2006, 6). First, neo-Pentecostal charity places the biblically deserving in the country as opposed to the city. From a neo-Pentecostal perspective, the city is a site of delinquency (laziness, thievery, and corruption), whereas the countryside is a locus of pure biblical need, the kind of need most clearly represented by images of poor indigenous children smiling and laughing. Second, neo-Pentecostal charity ranks the rural indigenous as less well developed (culturally speaking) and, in turn, more deserving of Christian charity than the urban poor. Neo-Pentecostalism, that is, tends to make the rural indigenous a charitable priority over and above the urban poor, while also contributing to the framing of both populations as less well developed than (as ranked below) El Shaddai's mega-church congregation.

These divisions and rankings emerge in a range of mega-church settings, during formal and informal interviews as well as public sermons. They crest most clearly, however, in a series of images that Manos de Amor produces and distributes in El Shaddai's Sunday bulletin. In these widely circulated pamphlets, photos of the indigenous are surrounded by community announcements, advertisements, and suggested prayer regimens. They provide some of the most potent, even iconic, representations of the biblically deserving—the orphan, the widow, and the stranger—that currently shape neo-Pentecostal understandings of, and responses to, Guatemala City and country. These images (as well as the short texts that frame them) speak directly to issues of ethnicity, place, and deservedness in postwar Guatemala, prompting Christian citizens to empathize in one direction as opposed to another. In a sentence, they teach congregants (both ladinos and the urban indigenous alike) what the rural indigenous need, and what the Christian citizen's responsibility (and relationship) is to the countryside.[3] Neo-Pentecostal charity ultimately foments a curious relationship between Guatemala City and country. On the one hand, neo-Pentecostalism divides city from country, placing the deserving *over there* while also ranking them below middle-class capitalinos in terms of progress or development. On the other hand, despite this division, neo-Pentecostalism cultivates an understanding of the city as in constant relationship to the country vis-à-vis Christian charity. Interestingly, even astoundingly (and sometimes ironically), neo-Pentecostalism is not only the social imaginary that divides city from country and capitalinos from the rural indigenous, but also the glue that holds the two together.

This observation about interconnectedness through divisions makes sense when connected to Georg Simmel's essay "Bridge and Door" ([1909]1997). Simmel suggests that bridges and doors are not just material constructions but also images of boundaries that both separate and connect. Bridges and doors speak to the human desire to connect while also marking the reality of separation: "Without bridges connecting separated places in our practical thoughts, needs and fantasies, the concept of separation would have no meaning" (Houtum and Struver 2002, 143). Bridges that connect one locale to another also mark the two as separate. Nothing could be truer about Manos de Amor. The organization reinforces the idea that the Guatemalan countryside is an entirely different kind of place from the capital, and at the same time it announces to the urban faithful that they are responsible for (and, in turn, in constant relationship to) this rural countryside. This chapter assesses this tricky relationship.

Before moving forward, however, it is important to note, even if only briefly, that this reading of Manos de Amor is not intended to undermine the kind of work that the organization pursues. To be sure, holes can be poked in any charitable project if one tries hard enough. The fact of the matter is that Manos de Amor is a small shop with limited resources. The need in postwar Guatemala is so great that its decision to work in the country rather than the capital is as good as any. The analytical interest of this chapter is in the cultural logics and social imaginaries that lead Manos de Amor to help those in the country as opposed to those in the capital, and what this decision means not only for neo-Pentecostal Christianity's continued rapprochement with postwar Guatemala but also for neo-Pentecostals themselves as they try to navigate the moral contours of their nation as good (even charitable) Christian citizens. At the same time, one could never displace Cornel West's haunting words on and about charitable practices—Christian or otherwise. His comments sting with clarity: "Wonderful charitable proclivities. Charity is unbelievable. I appreciate it. I admire it. But charity is not justice. Two different things. Two very different things" (2004). Manos de Amor is charity, not justice. The organization does the work of God in postwar Guatemala only because it is God's work that the country so desperately needs. Charity is a response to a particular kind of weight; charity is not a solution that reduces the weight's density or relieves its load. Charity helps shoulder the weight, but only for a moment—only with sugary bursts of help. Charity is not justice. They are two very different things.

Popular imagination in Guatemala routinely understands Guatemala City and country as being two distinct worlds ("la capital es otro mundo," many informants suggest). Urban geographers, on the other hand, argue instead that the two are one region—that it would be ethnographically untenable to speak about either city or country as a bounded entity.[4] The following section, in response to this tension, sketches Guatemala City and country's imagined division (by way of ethnicity, class, and even aesthetics) as well as their material connections. This sketch contextualizes how Manos de Amor participates in the division and connection as well as the ordering and the ranking of Guatemala City and country through Christian charity.

Present-day Guatemala City is neither an ancient nor a beautiful metropolis.[5] Aesthetically, Guatemala City has been set apart from the rural interior because the capital (in contrast to a lush countryside) has long been a gray and ugly city—beaten down by earthquakes, unplanned development, and violence. Its narrow, congested streets, with their squat architecture, sprawling developments, and shortage of public space, bespeak an itinerant life that has produced many—but maintained few—monuments, memorials, and museums. The capital, as history notes, currently stands in its fourth location because of moves prompted by natural disasters. From 1543 to 1776 the third capital of Guatemala, La Antigua, was the cultural and economic center of what is today known as Central America; yet its location proved fatal. The site was vulnerable to natural disasters, such as floods and volcanic eruptions, and two massive earthquakes in 1773 destroyed the city, driving residents to present-day Guatemala City, or La Nueva Guatemala de la Asunción, in 1776.

The construction of the new capital, like all Latin American cities under Spanish rule, followed the ordinances established by Spain's Felipe II in 1573; a plaza mayor was built, surrounded by ordered city streets. But the two hundred years that separated Felipe II and Guatemala City's construction provided room for improvisation. The city's buildings, for example, drew very little inspiration from colonial, baroque, or neoclassical styles of architecture; instead, more modern, even functionalist, approaches were taken. The constant fear of earthquakes also kept the buildings modest, sturdy, and single-storied; the city's cathedral was completed slowly (finished in 1815) and without its planned towers; and developers never properly considered the capital's eventual growth. Urban congestion became a serious problem as the city continued to grow, from 11,000 in 1778 to 55,728 in 1871.

Following Guatemala's independence from Spain in 1821, and until the beginning of its liberal period in 1871, the capital experienced very few modifications, remaining a relatively undersized capital city. By the end of the nineteenth century, however, modern urbanization in Guatemala City began with the reorientation of the national economy toward the cultivation of coffee. The city's infrastructure developed rapidly, and new barrios were built to accommodate a rapid influx of immigrants from Guatemala's rural departments. Buildings for banks, municipal offices, and commercial agencies emerged by way of function and utility (rather than beauty and grandeur). Early efforts at liberalization prized factories over cathedrals. A rather different phase of development followed the election of President José María Reyna Barrios in 1892. With images of Paris in mind, Barrios constructed some of Guatemala City's major avenues, which still stand today (e.g., La Reforma); he also attempted to beautify an otherwise drab city with gardens, parks, a replica of the Eiffel Tower, and Guatemala City's own Temple Minerva. His goal was for Guatemala City to become a "tropical Athens" and to be known throughout the world as "Little Paris."

A series of earthquakes in 1917 and 1918 devastated Barrios's Parisian dreams. The city's reconstruction period began soon thereafter, but cholera and political instability frustrated every effort. President Manuel Estrada Cabrera was overthrown in 1920 amid a crumbled cityscape, and construction once again prized function over splendor as migrants from the countryside entered the city looking for food, work, and shelter. The city's population swelled to 112,086 in 1921, and the capital's deteriorating infrastructure both limited and defined its urban development. Political instability throughout the 1920s ultimately gave way to corruption under President Jorge Ubico (1931–1944), which subsided briefly when voters elected Juan José Arévalo president in 1944. When the 1954 coup sparked Guatemala's civil war, Guatemala City had more than quadrupled in size since Barrios's presidency, during a stretch of history that allowed little time for sustained urban development, let alone attractive public works projects. The city was still reeling architecturally from the 1917 and 1918 earthquakes when it underwent yet another moment of destruction and reconstruction at the time of the 1976 earthquake. Following that quake, thousands migrated from rural areas to the capital looking for refuge; they found little, and the organized reconstruction period began alongside informal attempts by Guatemala City residents to build shelter from whatever materials were available.

Thirty years later, Guatemala City has once again doubled in size, to some 3 million residents; the city is home to one-fifth of the nation's total population, and people are moving to the city daily. Many of these recent arrivals are squatters, which means that Guatemala City has mushroomed in disorganized ways—without infrastructure, without planning, without permits. Even today, approximately one-fourth of the capital's population lives in what Guatemalan authorities define as "precarious settlements" (Morán Mérida 1997, 8). "Built with fragile materials such as cardboard, tin, or, in the best of cases, cement blocks" (Murphy 2004, 64), these settlements exist beyond the reach of property rights and the most basic municipal services. Infrastructure remains a problem as public transportation and water systems struggle to keep up with the city's demands. All this strain amid a history of construction, destruction, and reconstruction has left Guatemala City without Spanish architecture, towering churches, and cobbled streets lined with "local color." Polluted with diesel fumes, the capital currently stands as a city once built (and continually rebuilt) with an eye toward industrial function over beauty.

Guatemala City's gray facades and smoggy atmosphere contribute to an imagined divide, drawn along the lines of color as well as culture—not to mention class and ethnicity. As I mention elsewhere in this book, roughly half of Guatemala's population is indigenous. For many, this demographic fact calls to mind the colorful *traje* (traditional indigenous clothing) that the postwar Maya movement celebrates and that the Guatemalan tourist industry continues to market. In contrast to rural areas that are as much as 80 percent indigenous, the capital has been overwhelmingly ladino/a: 99.1 percent in 1930, 98.2 percent in 1960, and 96.4 percent in 1990. Though there are now a reported one million indigenous people living in or around the capital city, this historical trend perpetuates an imagined division between the cultureless (and colorless) ladinos of the capital, with their "sophisticated" sensibilities and stylized Spanish, and the culture-full (and colorful) indigenous of the countryside, with the kind of linguistic and ethnic diversity that has long enthralled tourists, artists, and anthropologists alike.

This kind of imagined imbalance between grayness and color has led to a neat division between city and country—a division that has dissuaded both Guatemalans and ethnographers from seeing "culture" in Guatemala City. Diane Nelson makes this point in *A Finger in the Wound* (1999), noting that ladinos have for far too long been understood as without culture (in much the same way that whiteness becomes deracialized in the United States), whereas Guatemala's indigenous communities are understood as a wellspring of alterity. The dissection is one that authors have long reproduced. The travel writer Paul Theroux describes Guatemala City from his hotel balcony: "Guatemala City, an extremely horizontal place, is like a city on its back. Its ugliness, which is a threatened look (the low morose houses have earthquake cracks in their facades; the buildings wince at you with bright lines) is ugliest on those streets where, just past the last toppling house, a blue volcano's cone bulges. . . . [The volcano's] beauty was undeniable, but it was the beauty of witches" (cited in Lutz and Collins 1993, 114). Another travel writer adds: "Guatemala City is a rough place. . . . The buildings and infrastructure are more or less intact, but the city is tired and world-weary. It [lies] supine in the highlands valley, beaten down by earthquakes, volcanic eruptions, civil war, revolution, economic devastation, and dictatorship. The city is hung over. Its eyes squint at the sun. It groans with depression and exhaustion."[6] This kind of division between urban blight and the natural (even supernatural) beauty "of witches" in nature contributes to the idea that Guatemala City is set apart from the rural and apparently magical countryside that is its backdrop. Jean Franco notes, using Guatemala City as an example of an impenetrable fortress of high culture: "The [Latin American] city, once imagined as the polis, had long been an image of repression and confusion, . . . a panopticon surveyed by the all-seeing eye of a dictator as in the Guatemala City of Miguel Ángel Asturias's *El Presidente*" (2002, 11). Literally above the rest of the country like a guard who stands watch in his tower, Guatemala City has long been imagined as not just set apart but set above the rural highlands.

At the same time, travel literature on Guatemala's rural areas does not disappoint. Collectively, the story is of a paranormal, maternal world of mystery in a lush jungle setting. The dominant narrative begins at the very edge of Theroux's description, at the foot of blue volcanoes. Martín Prechtel writes:

> The Indian girl was like an archaic Mayan clay figurine coming alive
> before my eyes. She was dressed in traditional clothing, her eyes both
> gentle and untamed, her long black hair carefully coiffured. Her appear-
> ance bespoke a ten-thousand-year-old pool of ancestral Mayan women.
> Her luxurious red and purple *huipil,* made by her own hand on a back
> strap loom, belied other secrets embodied within. Her hips were wrapped
> and bound by an indigo *murga,* a tubelike ankle-length skirt held fast by a
> wide sash where she tucked her little things: her comb, her money, weav-
> ing pick, and so on. Three large holes in her earlobes were laced with
> hanging shanks of red and violet yarns from which were suspended old
> Spanish *piastres* and *reals,* seventeenth-century silver (1998, 78).

Besides objectifying his subject ("the Indian girl was like an archaic Mayan clay figurine") and sexualizing her with a peculiar interest in the young lady's hips and "untamed eyes," important here is the author's use of color: clay, black, red, purple, indigo, red, violet, and silver. This kaleidoscope of culture paints a radically different portrait from the one commonly drawn of Guatemala City. Though the countryside explodes with color—in travel literature, through indigenous-made and -marketed textiles, and in Guatemalan tourist brochures—Guatemala City continues to be portrayed in shades of gray, as hung over. As one popular travel guide explains, "The best part about Guatemala City is leaving" (Lonely Planet 2001, 114).

The last thirty years of Guatemalan history, however, perforate this imagined divide. The 1976 earthquake not only drew indigenous migrants from rural areas to the capital city but also contributed to the escalation of what was then a low-level civil war. At first, the armed conflict peppered Guatemala City's streets with bombs and forced disappearances; yet the earthquake quickly contributed to a new kind of struggle that placed rural indigenous communities between two armies (Stoll 1993). As the violence moved from the city to the country, refugees relocated from the country to the city, once again poking holes in the shared belief that the capital city is an exclusively ladino/a place.[7] There has also been a continued spike in the number of Guatemalans, indigenous and ladinos alike, who have left Guatemala for the United States as undocumented migrants. International labor circuits tend to use the capital city as a first step in the journey from the countryside to the States. These international circuits have developed alongside *intra*national labor circuits that bring the indigenous from rural areas to the city for days at a time—to work as private security guards or to hawk wares in the city's informal economy. After working in the capital for two or three days, these migrants return to their families in Huehuetenango or Chichicastenango, only to return to Guatemala City for another stretch of time (Dickins de Girón 2006). Public buses brimming with rural migrants, their bodies dangling from the doors, shuttle between the countryside and the capital city. Their very travel documents the fact that the city and the country are not distinct entities—although they have come to be imagined as such—but are, rather, interrelated social formations. So too are a range of other bridges and doors, in Simmel's words: cell phones, political campaigns, gangs, and private security industries.

Another development that breaks any easy divide between Guatemala City and country has been the establishment of neo-Pentecostal church networks.[8] These networks use the capital city as a kind of headquarters for satellite churches that dot rural departments. El Shaddai has dozens of active satellite churches in the Guatemalan countryside, from the mountainous regions of Totonicapán to the lakeside vistas of San Marcos, from the jungles of Petén to the semi-urban regions of Chimaltenango, from Retalhuleu of the Pacific coast to the commercial center of southwest Guatemala known as Quetzaltenango. Tethered together by an apostolic network, these smaller churches minister to indigenous communities in their respective languages. Connected by Internet, radio, and television broadcasting, El Shaddai's rural communities keep in constant contact with their urban mother ship by participating alongside fellow congregants with live audio broadcasts of important sermons and conferences. Pastors and church leaders from rural areas also travel to the capital city for training sessions, workshops, and meetings about church growth, and pastors and church leaders from the capital city return the favor at special events in the departments. And through Manos de Amor, El Shaddai's main church in Guatemala City also organizes mission trips to the countryside to aid those El Shaddai communities in need of basic social services. This constant flow of ideas and people, faith and action, money and skills, perforates the imagined divide between city and country—between drabness and color, between ladino/a and indigenous. Neo-Pentecostal Christianity contributes to the formation of Guatemala City and country as interrelated spatial formations that draw on (and pull at) each other. Philanthropic interventions, moreover, suggest a new kind of relationship forming between these worlds—one that announces, at one and the same time, that the capital city is different from but nonetheless in constant relationship to the countryside. This relationship is clearly observed through the images and texts that Manos de Amor produces and distributes to the El Shaddai congregation.

VIEWING THE COUNTRY FROM THE CITY

Every Sunday at 8:00 a.m. and 11:00 a.m., El Shaddai opens its megachurch doors to thousands of believers. The size of the church's expansive parking lot obscures the fact that the vast majority of churchgoers come by public buses that snake through the city and dock at the church's front gates. El Shaddai's unbelievable growth since the late 1980s has bent bus routes to its front doors, forcing drivers to remap their routes to meet public demand. The number 82 bus, for example, makes its way from

Zone 2, through Zone 1's historic center, through Zone 4's efforts at urban renewal, right on past Zone 10's shopping centers, to the open arms of El Shaddai in Zone 14, where hundreds of people walk patiently through the front doorway, past the lobby, and into their seats. Those who arrive a little late for service are greeted as soon as they take their first step from the bus to the pavement by rolling waves of high-energy music, the density of which grows with every step the latecomer takes toward the church. Along the way, somewhere between the lobby and the main auditorium, a volunteer hands each churchgoer a glossy Sunday bulletin. Six to eight pages in length, the bulletin announces the service's theme as well as items for sale at the bookstore and other upcoming events. Sandwiched somewhere between these announcements and advertisements, there is an entire page devoted to the work of Manos de Amor.

Each Manos de Amor page tells a story and teaches a lesson through images and text. Although there exist innumerable interpretations of any given set of Manos de Amor images, the stories reported are overwhelmingly about need—about how poor indigenous communities in rural Guatemala need roofing materials, need better trained teachers, need food, or need medical care. At the same time, these images also deliver a lesson that is directed toward El Shaddai's viewing public—toward those who linger on these colorful announcements during the less riveting moments of Sunday service, on their bus rides home, or while relaxing afterward. The images teach the model viewer how to read the country from the city and, in the process, how to understand the city as being in constant relationship to the country. They promote a limited universe of ideas about ethnicity and class and how ethnic difference should be placed within postwar Guatemala. To study these images is in fact to hear a powerful voice in an ongoing cultural discussion about charity, space, and ethnicity in Guatemala—about the place of the country's deserving. The most basic assumption here, moreover, is that these narratives and images are not clear-cut representations of poverty (or even indigenousness), but a much more complicated kind of cultural work.

Deservedness is the first of three lessons derived from these images. With whom is God concerned? The answer is biblical for Manos de Amor—the orphan, the widow, and the stranger (e.g., Exodus 22:21–24; Leviticus 19:34, 25:35; Psalm 10:14; Deuteronomy 10:18; Proverbs 15:25). Maria, during one interview, explained: "We are called to help our neighbor. We read in Isaiah 58 that you need to 'share your bread with the hungry, and bring the poor and homeless into your house; when you see

the naked, cover them.' Isaiah 58 is our base. It's our fundamental principle." This sense of responsibility to the biblically deserving repeatedly
comes to the fore in El Shaddai Sunday bulletins—in the text and in the
images produced by Manos de Amor and distributed every week to a viewing public. The story of Zacarias Cuc Tuc is but one example.[9]

Zacarias is a five-year-old indigenous boy from the highlands of Cobán
whose story embodies Manos de Amor's philanthropic mission: to transform Guatemala one child at a time.[10] Images begin to tell the story. The
largest of the pictures introduces Zacarias, with his big smile turning
upward and a long scar on his forehead frowning downward. A row of
smaller pictures anchors the narrative with scenes of recovery: Zacarias
with his father at the hospital, Zacarias bandaged but with friends,
Zacarias again with his father, and Zacarias with his classmates. Zacarias's
face tells a story not just of hope and childlike wonderment but also of sincerity and potential. His scar cuts across his shaved scalp, interrupting the
portrait's soft composition with a brute concern that ideally provokes
curiosity. Answering the very question that such a dramatic image raises,
the text explains that Zacarias suffered a terrible fall. A student in one of
El Shaddai's rural elementary schools, Zacarias was taken by his teacher to
a local emergency room, where it was determined that his skull had been
severely fractured and that he would need to be taken immediately to a
better-equipped hospital. There doctors operated on Zacarias as his classmates and family members prayed for his speedy recovery.

The Manos de Amor page also reports that one intercessor received a
direct message from God, who explained to him that Zacarias would one
day preach in not just one but two languages. This prophecy, the text continues, reassured the faithful that the boy's life was in God's hands. At the
same time, Zacarias's own father, a "true believer," was confident that the
surgery would be successful—not only that his son would survive, but also
that his intelligence would not be affected in any way. All these predictions
seem to come true, as the Manos de Amor story concludes by assuring the
reader that the surgery was a success—although Zacarias still needed to
take expensive medication to recover fully. Maria added in an interview:
"The boy is doing well. It's been a year and he's doing well. I was able to
visit him after his operation and things were okay, but by now he has had
a year of treatment, and he's taking a medication called Epamin. The
doctor actually said that the medicine carries the risk of seizures, but thank
God he didn't have any of those. He's fine." The message, advanced by the
Manos de Amor announcement and confirmed by Maria, was that

Zacarias received the care that he so desperately needed with the help of Manos de Amor.

The lesson is that Zacarias is emblematically deserving—of money, of medication, of a future. To this end, the unmistakably endearing photos of Zacarias and his healing wound are an effective pedagogical tool. As scholars have suggested, images of children are frequently used to convey hope; the face of a child often becomes the ambassador of hope in charitable solicitations (Malkki 1997). Especially for philanthropic agencies, which market an idea of deservedness alongside Christian charity's moral imperative to help, children become symbols of goodness and seeds of world peace. Children suffer unjustly, but they also see a truth that adults, jaded by their years, cannot. They are emissaries not just of tranquility but also of the future (Bornstein 2001, 601). As Liisa Malkki has proposed, children are depoliticizing agents; they erase the complexities of life to reveal the simplicity of need (1997, 17). The story of Zacarias, it is safe to say, functions in this exact way. Manos de Amor markets Zacarias as intuitively deserving of charity not just because he is poor, but also because he simply did what so many other children do every day. He fell. The story is one of simple needs that is far less complicated than those wrought by, for example, alcoholism, gang involvement, and Guatemala City's informal economy.

Having determined who is deserving, Manos de Amor advances a second lesson—their geographical place. Zacarias lives in the countryside rather than Guatemala City. The placement of the deserving in the Guatemalan countryside mirrors the kinds of division that James Ferguson observes in Zambia, where "ethnographies from the 1950s provide many examples of moral thinking that opposed moral 'village women' to immoral 'town women'; rural generosity to urban selfishness; rural cooperation and social ties to urban competition and monetary ties; and, most generally, rural morality to urban immorality" (1992, 81). This kind of contrast between city and country has become heightened in Guatemala's postwar context, where urban violence now threatens the welfare of the nation through both organized crime and drug trafficking. *Delincuencia,* or delinquency, is the word used by believers and nonbelievers alike to describe the capital city; the word hints at the moral dimensions of Guatemala City's separation from the rural highlands. In response to Manos de Amor's decision to work in the countryside rather than the city, Maria added: "Regrettably, *la delincuencia* in the capital has been increasing. It really has been getting stronger. So you can imagine the risks that a child faces by living in the streets of the capital. It's the kind of risk that children in the rural areas do not know. They have no idea. Thank God. They are guarded, more protected. Maybe there are other risks, like house fires, but the children in the rural areas definitely do not live amid as much *delincuencia* as people do here in the capital." Zacarias, Maria continued, has needs, but they are needs that are simple and pure; Zacarias is "guarded" and "more protected." His life is simple.[11]

Guatemala City is also the seat of government, which neo-Pentecostals agree is more corrupt than other parts of Guatemala. Dr. Caballeros, responding to a political scandal in which a congressman stole money from the government, announced in the local press: "Unfortunately, [the scandal] confirms everyone's suspicion that politicians act only out of self-interest and that none of them are working for Guatemala. It's a bloody struggle to pursue a strictly purposeful direction. Guatemala's problem is not poverty or issues of security, but rather the country's radical absence of ethics and morals. A lack of morals creates these political problems. It creates such enormous problems for the country."[12] The moral constitution of the capital city, in short, is weak when seen through neo-Pentecostal eyes. Rural areas, however, remain less complicated. Many congregants even describe the Guatemalan countryside and the rural indigenous as childlike, as full of potential but nonetheless underdeveloped. This analogy allows capitalinos to depoliticize and even infantilize the indigenous, making rural Guatemala a place that needs simple things to make life better: food, medication, small amounts of money, and building materials, for example. Much of this narrative rests on the second lesson, the idea that the deserving—these prototypical orphans, widows, and strangers—live outside the city and in a more primitive setting.

Manos de Amor communicates to urban congregants through weekly solicitations that the place of the deserving is the countryside. On one particular Sunday, for example, Manos de Amor announced that a rural elementary school in Río San José simply needed more money for a teacher.[13] The parents in this community had constructed a school with their own hands, building the structure out of nothing into something, from a simple plot of land to a modest schoolhouse. But the community still lacked the money to retain a qualified instructor. The three photos that animate the solicitation in the Sunday bulletin depict a scene far different from those at the El Shaddai mega-church in Guatemala City. Rather than tiled floors, drywall, and an urban backdrop punctuated by mega-church glamour, the pictures document dozens of indigenous children standing barefoot in colorful *traje* on a dirt floor under a tin roof. The pictures, taken at the school during the rainy season with its thick morning fog, also suggest that these children live somewhere far away from the capital. The contrast becomes even more apparent with El Shaddai's own advertisements for its capital city elementary school.[14] Also appearing in the weekly bulletin, often next to solicitations made by Manos de Amor for rural schoolchildren, these advertisements depict smiling ladino/a (not indigenous) children wearing crisp white T-shirts (not colorful *trajes*).

The contrast, while strange from a certain perspective, is quite natural when viewed from another. Akhil Gupta comments on anthropological conceptions of space in a way that speaks to the imagined distance between Guatemala City and country: "Concepts of space have always fundamentally rested on . . . images of break, rupture, and disjunction. The recognition of cultures, societies, nations, all in the plural, is unproblematic exactly because there appears an unquestionable division, an intrinsic discontinuity, between cultures, between societies, etc." (cited in Malkki 1992, 28). The division between Guatemala City and country rests on this kind of break. And this kind of cultural placement—the idea that the deserving exist in rural areas while less deserving ladinos occupy the capital city—leads (conceptually speaking) to a kind of ecological immobility that many capitalinos share. Arjun Appadurai explains: "Natives are not only persons who are from certain places, and belong to those places, but they are also those who are somehow incarcerated, or confined, in those places" (1988, 37). Urban neo-Pentecostals and middle-class capitalinos in general tend to echo this kind of ecological incarceration. The director of a small NGO that works to train community-based NGOs in Guatemala City, for example, sighed during an extended conversation about philanthropic intervention. She explained that capitalinos are a huge obstacle to sustainable development. They believe, she explained, that the poor live outside the city, not within it, and that the urban poor can thus be relocated from the city to rural areas, since they *belong* in the mountains.

This kind of worldview obviously flattens the politics of migration, whether international or intranational, as well as the emotional and infrastructural complexity of resettlement. The imagined simplicity and effectiveness of its philanthropic interventions allow Manos de Amor to market Christian charity successfully to its congregants. Though the felt complexity of urban politics paralyzes many neo-Pentecostals, sending them to their knees in prayer, modest donations can really have an effect on rural communities. Just one week after the publication of their solicitation for funds for the rural schoolteacher, Manos de Amor delivered another message to its congregation: thank you.[15] Reprinting the same pictures, the Manos de Amor page announced that God had provided a quick answer to their prayers. A Guatemala City cell group had taken the responsibility not only to pay a schoolteacher's salary, but also to provide funds to strengthen the sagging schoolhouse.

The third and final lesson that Manos de Amor communicates to El Shaddai's urban congregation is that neo-Pentecostals in the capital exist in constant relationship to the rural indigenous. This is by far the most surprising recalibration of city and country. Though many are eager to dub the city and the country as two entirely different universes, neo-Pentecostalism links these distinct social formations through the language of Christian membership and responsibility. Dr. Harold Caballeros spoke at a public event, forming the city and the country as one: "We are Guatemalans, but what really is a Guatemalan? Do leaders hold the same concept of Guatemalans in [the village of] Santa María, the same concept of Guatemalans in a barrio, the same sentiment in the city? Some say that [the identity of] those in the high classes is close to what it's like in Miami, while other [Guatemalan] towns are closer to Africa." The distinctions that separate Guatemalans from Guatemalans are class-driven, certainly, but also influenced by geography. The idea of Santa María sparks images of the rural indigenous, whereas the reference to the high classes directs the imagination to the capital city's business sector. Dr. Caballeros continues to communicate a need for unity: "We Guatemalans are so distant from each other in terms of the formation of citizenship and the formation of identity. What better than the work of believers, what better than the link of the gospel, to dissolve these sentiments and polarization. . . . We need to pursue a national consensus, and we have the tools to clean up [the polarization]—the gospel, love, and forgiveness, allowing us to construct this identity." Dr. Caballeros makes clear that collapsing this radical polarization begins with extending outward, linking city and country through, among many other things, Christian charity.

Manos de Amor encourages this kind of outreach through its images and texts, which allow congregants to participate in the bridging of two regularly disassociated regions with small donations. Project updates let the El Shaddai congregation know that their donations (big and small) make a difference. One Manos de Amor page exudes the message of success with a large photo of laughing indigenous boys and girls. The headline announces "the advances of our new school."[16] The text tells a story brought to life by three more pictures. They show children being children—learning, playing, and laughing with their friends and families. More important, the school has allowed the children "to be able to know God in a personal way." This rural elementary school not only became a house of learning but also a house of worship because of the charitable support and missionary work that Manos de Amor provides from the capital city.

Another, possibly less well-focused Manos de Amor announcement echoes this particular message of success.[17] Embellished with images of indigenous men having their teeth screened by Manos de Amor dentists, of mothers and daughters in *traje* holding donated clothes, and long lines of people waiting to visit Manos de Amor doctors, the bulletin announces that Manos de Amor makes a difference in the countryside. A long list of rural departments is the first of two sets of text that accompany these photographs. A passage from the Bible is the second. The list includes the regions of Tucurú, Chimaltenango, Huehuetenango, Quetzaltenango, and Totonicapán. The biblical passage is Psalm 41:1–3: "Happy are those who consider the poor, the Lord delivers them in the day of trouble. The Lord protects them and keeps them alive; they are called in the land. You do not give them up to the will of their enemies. The Lord sustains them on their sickbed; in their illness you heal all their infirmities." Those in the capital maintain a charitable relationship with those in the countryside and reap great rewards, such as the idea of empathetic Guatemalans who might one day be accountable to each other through charitable outreach.

RANKING THE DESERVING

Neo-Pentecostal philanthropic intervention places deservedness in the country rather than the capital, mapping biblical need onto the rural indigenous. Christian charity makes Guatemala's countryside the geographical place of the deserving. Yet place is not simply a matter of location, but also an issue of value and verticality—of being ranked within a cultural system. Louis Dumont's *Homo Hierarchicus* (1980) tells us this much: "Hierarchy [is] the principle by which the elements of a whole are ranked in relation to the whole, it being understood that in the majority of societies it is religion which provides the view of the whole, and that the ranking will thus be religious in nature" (10).[18] The practice of Christian charity ranks certain groups as higher, or lower, than others—as not just more or less deserving, but also more or less well developed; more or less modern; more or less proximate to God. The images and sets of ideas that Manos de Amor produces and distributes by way of Sunday bulletins hints at this cultural ranking, as do the kinds of philanthropic intervention that the organization pursues. Manos de Amor's promotion of hygiene among rural indigenous communities is one effort (among many others) at ranking the rural indigenous as less well developed, less modern, and less proximate to God than capitalinos. Hygiene is so very illustrative of this process because it invokes Mary Douglas's observation that "dirt is matter out of place" (1966), as well as the Christian cliché that "cleanliness is next to godliness" (an axiom popularized through the sermons of John Wesley, the eighteenth-century Anglican minister).[19] The spatial dimensions of both phrases are instructive when thinking through, and listening to, Manos de Amor's ranking of the indigenous in Guatemala's rural areas—as below capitalinos in terms of spiritual and economic development, but also above the urban poor in terms of righteousness.

Manos de Amor's Christian commitment to hygiene is not subtle; the narrative unabashedly exposes the organization's Christian compulsions as well as some of its most basic (and, at times, base) assumptions. Responding to a question about lice in indigenous communities, one Manos de Amor spokesperson explained: "Lice are dirty. Absolutely. As we know, there are values that slow down progress. There are values that limit the development of a culture and a population [such as dirtiness], and values that promote [development]. One of those values is the use of a schedule. Punctuality, responsibility, cleanliness—these are the values of efficiency, of progress, of one's level of development. And so, dirt for the indigenous represents a great obstacle." Manos de Amor leadership, however, fully understands that dirt does not make itself. As Mary Douglas usefully argues, conceptions of dirt are relative: "There is no such thing as absolute dirt: it exists in the eye of the beholder" (1966, 2). What is so egregious to the very Christian sensibilities that Manos de Amor attempts to impart is that many of the indigenous do not recognize themselves as dirty. The spokesperson continued: "They are accustomed to it. And since they are accustomed to dirt, they don't see the need to clean themselves. They see it as a total waste of time. Totally. And so the most interesting goal [for us] is to change the way that they think." Manos de Amor, besides initiating building projects and clothing drives, educates the rural indigenous, providing them not only with a sense of dirt, but also with new regimes of self-governance so that they can deal with their newfound filth.

Protestant efforts to indoctrinate the indigenous with Christian modes of purity and danger stretch back to colonial times, but they took on an eerily familiar, if not entirely modern, form during Guatemala's liberalization period. Edward Haymaker, Guatemala's second Protestant missionary, arrived in 1887 with a set goal: "When the people of Guatemala begin to develop [the country] along modern lines, when they learn sanitation, motherhood, education, thrift . . . Guatemala will be one of the greatest little countries in the world" (Garrard-Burnett 1997, 41). Identifying the rural poor as "the Great Unwashed," Haymaker published Christian pamphlets on health and hygiene, all for Guatemala's salvation and development.[20] The two goals were hardly distinct. In the 1880s President Justo Rufino Barrios injected Protestant Christianity into the Guatemalan context to bolster efforts at liberalization. As Virginia Garrard-Burnett notes, Protestant Christianity seemed "the ideal vehicle" to advance Barrios's liberal agenda (1997, 38). The religion would "civilize" Guatemala by undercutting Roman Catholicism and Maya spirituality while also contributing to the country's own efforts at industrialization, not only with a Protestant work ethic, but also with a more hospitable atmosphere for German and North American Protestants interested in business opportunities. With the nineteenth-century French sociologist Auguste Comte and Social Darwinism fresh in his mind, Justo Rufino Barrios saw Protestant Christianity as a means "to create a modern, unified nation from a mix of ethnicities, languages, classes, customs, and conflicting bonds of loyalty and association" (Garrard-Burnett 1997, 35). And central to this modernization fantasy was, and still is, a vision of the human as autonomous, rational, and free—the Enlightenment's very own philosophical anthropology, which pushes past magic and religion to stake its claim on science and democracy.

Christian hygiene existed (and still exists) as one small but ever-important part of this modernization project. Hygiene provides an incredibly mundane, deeply routinized marker of Christian civility; hygiene exposes not simply exterior enactments, but more important, the quality of one's interior will. Mary Douglas cites the Penitential of Archbishop Theodore of Canterbury: "If without knowing it one eats what is polluted by blood or any unclean thing, it is nothing; but if he knows, he shall do penance according to the degree of pollution" (1966, 75). The Christian predicament of knowing better—of understanding the difference between earth and dirt, as Jonathan Z. Smith would argue (1978)—places the moral responsibility for cleanliness as well as advancement squarely on the shoulders of the learned.[21] As the Manos de Amor spokesperson makes transparent, "since [the indigenous] are accustomed to dirt, they don't see the need to clean themselves." This Christian logic makes Manos de Amor's commitment to dental hygiene, among a range of other hygienic prescriptions, rather telling. As innocuous practices, brushing and flossing, using Manos de Amor's widely distributed "bags of personal hygiene" (filled with soap, toothpaste, and floss), attempt to shape the indigenous into modern citizens through regimes of self-governance. Complimentary brushes and paste, alongside Christian goodwill, recruit the indigenous into regimes of self-regulation that ultimately aim for a more advanced nation-state. Bolstered by instructions on how to brush gently in semicircular motions, Manos de Amor's promotion of dental hygiene contributes to the production of Christian citizens who have not only a greater awareness of their own inner terrain, but also the means by which to observe and clean that terrain—to actually scrub it with soft bristles. To quote Douglas: "Dirt offends against order. Eliminating it is not a negative movement, but a positive effort to organize the environment" (1966, 2). Christian charity not only marks the rural indigenous as "matter out of place," to quote Douglas once again, but also inculcates in them an array of self-governing rationalities to attend to the very filth they have been taught to see.

During a public presentation of Manos de Amor's charitable activities, a spokesperson walked a small group of El Shaddai capitalinos through some of the many ways in which the organization supports the rural indigenous. While explaining that the organization educates the indigenous to understand that taking baths, "even if they make you shiver," is proper and good, one photo among many confirmed the organization's spatial commitments. The photo is of a small, rural classroom with ten students and an instructor. The colors are muddied—dull blues and greens straddle the room's browns and grays. Yet red boxes of Colgate toothpaste, obvious donations from Manos de Amor, pop out of the scene. They break the photo's balance: the children stretch upward and toward the camera, stretching their smiling faces toward the viewer. Of particular importance is that the children lean forward and upward; their shiny boxes of toothpaste pull them from their seats and toward somewhere else. Their bright smiles suggest that Manos de Amor's commitment to dental hygiene is working—maintaining white teeth and producing self-regulating citizens.

It would not take a great deal of analytical effort to conclude that the photo's composition has everything to do with a tall cameraperson and decidedly short subjects, who are most likely elated to have received not only something free, but also a short break from schoolwork, but the photo nonetheless exists as a cultural artifact. The photo communicates a logic that is still present and operative in postwar Guatemala. The image evidences the rank of the deserving. Urban congregants are the photo's implied viewer; the rural indigenous, moreover, are the photo's obvious subjects. Additionally, the rural indigenous in this photo literally look up, reach outward, and lean forward—all in the direction of the implied capital. The directionality of it all—the photo's implied verticality and value—is meaningful even if unintentional.

President Justo Rufino Barrios studied the works of Auguste Comte, who was one of the first to argue that society matures much like an organism and that not all societies have developed along the same time line.[22] Different parts of the world, Comte reasoned, are at different stages of development. Comte concluded that individuals pass through three stages of development and that each of these stages has a distinct mindset. Children are devout, even magical, believers. Adolescents become metaphysicians; they are enamored with fate and first causes. Adults, however, are positivists. They rely on science and reason. Societies, Comte reasons, follow the very same stages of development, constantly moving upward and outward—away from childish magic and adolescent metaphysics and toward a mature realism. Understanding Guatemala's fragmented society as being at different stages of development, Barrios hoped that Protestant Christianity would propel his countrymen beyond Maya spirituality and Roman Catholicism and toward liberal secularism (Garrard-Burnett 1997). Protestant Christianity, for Barrios, was not an end but a means; he did not want his country to be Protestant per se, but to have Protestant Christianity provide his citizens with enough forward momentum not just to surpass magic but also propel all of Guatemala beyond religion altogether.

Manos de Amor's photo of stretching schoolchildren, kids apparently leaning from one place to another, underscores the directionality not just of Justo Rufino Barrios's use of Protestant Christianity, but also of Manos de Amor's efforts at Christian charity. As Mary Douglas notes, "When we honestly reflect on our busy scrubbings and cleanings in this light we know we are not mainly trying to avoid disease" (1966, 69). Dental hygiene does not simply keep teeth clean, but also works to *raise* the indigenous *up*—to rank them while also providing the tools for them to advance themselves. Responding to these interpretations of space, of seeing strained efforts at progress in the photo itself, a Manos de Amor spokesperson commented: "We want to untie them from their yoke of slavery; we see them as enslaved by their paradigms and their ways of thinking. Really. The same tradition, the same history, the same. . . . The history and their past; their traditions enslave them. So for me [the work of Manos de Amor] is a way to liberate them from slavery and break them free from the yoke of oppression."

Explaining that rural communities receive incredible amounts of support from international groups, but that the support nonetheless keeps the indigenous poor, the spokesperson continued: "It is more important that they meet their potential, their [inner] wealth, and that they see all of this in themselves. I want them to see the responsibilities that they have. If not, they are not going to progress beyond where they are now or how they now think. They just won't." The language of progress, of moving forward and upward, easily latches onto Christian concepts of salvation, of beginning with Christ's life here on earth and ending with judgment up there in heaven. Modernity, salvation, democratization, secularism—the accepted goals of supposedly developing nations—begin low and aim high; they advance societies upward and outward. Manos de Amor, by way of dental hygiene, aims to advance the rural indigenous in the same way.

Ranking, however, is a relational practice. Urban congregants who rank the rural indigenous also rank themselves along the way. Edward Said makes this argument in his seminal work, *Orientalism* (1978), explaining: "The relationship between Occident and Orient is a relationship of power, of domination, of varying degrees of complex hegemony" (6). The East forever exists in material and discursive relationship to the West—which makes the production of the East also very much about the production of the West. The same can be argued about Manos de Amor. Through its ranking of the deserving as lower—as less well developed, as less modern, as less clean—than urban congregants, those who attend El Shaddai's urban mega-church come to understand themselves as cut from a different cloth, so to speak.

Another spokesperson, responding to yet another question about why Manos de Amor does not do work in the capital city, explained: "We work *there* [in the countryside] because we are only a few people and we cannot be everywhere. We work *there* because we feel that we are called by God to work *there*. We said, we can do something as a church over *there* in the mountains where they don't understand our Spanish. So that's where we want to work." The spokesperson's repeated use of *there*, or *allí*, is telling. Beyond signifying the actual distance between the capital and more rural areas, or the literal difference between *here* and *there*, her use of the adverb *allí* also denotes a moral distance, suggesting that the urban congregation is *up here* while the rural indigenous is not just "over there in the mountains" but also *down there*, "where they don't understand our Spanish." The spokesperson continued: "That was our first challenge. It was: 'Let's go and do something.' Then, after figuring out that we could do something, we wanted to make a lasting change. We are a church that talks a lot about changing communities, so we wanted to put what we believe into practice. [The countryside] has been a laboratory for us": "Ha sido todo un laboratorio."

The spokesperson's notion that the countryside exists as the church's laboratory evokes regrettable images of colonialism, of experimenting on "lesser" societies in the hopes that they might "catch up." The image of Manos de Amor as a collection of well-intentioned mad scientists with Christ on their side, in fact, taints the promise of Christian charity with a naked self-assessment of Christian charity's own practice. It calls to mind the words of Joseph Conrad, who wrote on the theme of colonialism but nonetheless speaks to the practice of Christian charity: "[It] is not a pretty thing when you look into it too much. What redeems it is the idea only. An idea at the back of it; not a sentimental pretence but an idea; and an unselfish belief in the idea—something you can set up and bow down before, and offer a sacrifice" (1995, 52).[23] Manos de Amor believes in the idea of Christian charity, with all of charity's tendencies to rank the rural indigenous below urban congregants; yet this belief smoothes over an otherwise uncomfortable inclination to help at all costs. The spokesperson continued:

> We enter [a community] and we begin working. We don't have a specific goal. We only know that we have entered a place where there is an opportunity to help. It's all about serving and helping the community we enter. And then we stay there, returning often, because they want something, and so we do more and more. We ask them, "What do you want to change?" And they often say, "Nothing." And so we help them move forward. Why? Because God commands us. We feel a love for them, for Guatemala, and for God. God saves them.

From a neo-Pentecostal perspective, Christian charity saves the rural indigenous; yet from a perspective more critical, one best understood as anthropological, the practice of Christian charity also ranks those who participate with a hierarchy of strict divisions—either as volunteers or as deserving; either as below or as above; either as here or as there; either as arrived or as "not yet."

WEIGHTLESSNESS AND THE GIFT OUT OF PLACE

Marcel Mauss's *The Gift* (1990) dissects the nature of gift giving and exchange, noting that the obligation to give gifts and to receive gifts demonstrates alternating expressions of generosity and respect. Mauss's most important observation, at least for this chapter, is that gift giving is a moral practice that establishes enduring social relationships between communities. The gift is not a simple object, or commodity, but is representative, even constitutive, of society. Giving a gift maintains social relationships between communities while also binding them to one another. In postwar Guatemala, philanthropic intervention as a gift bridges the city and the country while also reinforcing the division between the two. A collage of ethnographic vignettes constitutes one final observation about the place of the biblically deserving in postwar Guatemala and the kinds of responsibilities that this moral geography lends to those Christians who live in the capital.

The first vignette begins with a walk through a depressed part of Guatemala City with three neo-Pentecostals. En route to a cell group, we walked along with a sense of purpose until two small children approached us with candy in their hands. Their faces were pointed upward toward me, their eyes as doelike as they could make them. They asked us to buy the candy, explaining that the money would support a local charity. Francisco, the group leader with whom I was walking, quickly turned the two around, spinning them on their heels and said, "Thanks but no thanks." I asked him what the problem was. He muttered to me that I could buy the candy, but only if I wanted candy. I simply should not expect the money to go to a charity.

The second moment came during an extended interview in one of Guatemala City's upscale malls. Seated in a food court, Pedro and I chatted about the power and efficacy of prayer when a middle-aged woman approached us with child in hand. She pressed a sheet of paper toward us, explaining that it was a prescription for medicine that she desperately needed. Pedro had extolled the work of Manos de Amor in earlier interviews, and I had filled my notebook with stories of his volunteer activities with Guatemala's indigent. But here he avoided eye contact with the woman and shook his head. He later explained to me that we could have given the woman food, but that her solicitation for money was probably bogus. "You never can tell," he shrugged.

The third scene came as I stepped out of a public bus and onto church grounds. It was Sunday morning and I was walking through El Shaddai's parking lot to attend service. A woman I had interviewed several months earlier approached me, hailing me as her brother in Christ, and asking me about my research. I explained that everything was progressing nicely, but then turned the conversation to her. She was a single mother with three children. She explained to me that times were hard and that she could not pay the rent. She repeated this fact several times, eventually asking me if I could help her and her children. As I gave her the equivalent of five U.S. dollars, what struck me was my own lack of confidence. Having been instructed by my urban informants for several months that those who ask for money in the streets are untrustworthy—are working a scam that my gringo sensibilities just cannot register—I questioned my own relationship with this woman. As she thanked me, we entered the church together, she with five dollars and I wondering whom to trust and whether I had been taken for a ride. At the very least, I knew that Pedro and Francisco would not have been happy with me. They would have scolded me, arguing that the money would have been put to better use if given to Manos de Amor. Perhaps it would have been.

What emerges from these three vignettes (selected from dozens of similar instances) reinforces some of the lessons that Manos de Amor communicates to its viewing public about the place of the deserving; they also say something about the needy (and gifts to the needy), who are literally out of place. In short, there is an obvious and observable disconnect in the giving practices of El Shaddai congregants. I found that urban neo-Pentecostals tend to dismiss Guatemala City's own widows, orphans, and strangers, but are compassionate to those whom Manos de Amor brings to life in El Shaddai bulletins. Dozens of reasons explain the divide. For one, Manos de Amor has earned a certain level of trust with the El Shaddai congregation. Guatemala has seen an explosion in the number of NGOs and not-for-profit projects, including many used for tax evasion.[24] In contrast, Manos de Amor offers a welcome degree of transparency. Congregants know that their donations will have an effect. Another reason is the context in which congregants often donate their money—during church services. Manos de Amor passes the hat between jubilant praise and worship sessions; congregants have mentioned that they are most willing to give when they feel themselves filled by the Holy Spirit. This explains, in part, why believers may be less inspired to give in the dusty streets of Guatemala City, late at night or during a long commute home. Yet another reason may simply be the complexities of walking through Guatemala City with a gringo who is forever a target for panhandlers.[25]

Among all these reasons for such a giving divide there is still something more interesting at work. As I have pointed out, Manos de Amor's moral geography tends to place Guatemala's biblically deserving in the countryside, not in the capital, and rank the rural indigenous as below capitalinos but above the urban indigent, bending congregants' hearts (and giving practices) toward poor indigenous communities and away from Guatemala City's own needy. And this kind of philanthropic intervention establishes a social relationship and hierarchy between city and country that not only reinscribes stereotypical characterizations of urbanites and country folk, but also links city to country in ways not previously seen. As this new relationship between urban congregants and the country's rural areas becomes more enmeshed through gifts, there is an obvious disconnect taking place as well. Christian charity encourages neo-Pentecostals to become emotionally and financially invested in the country's deserving, but there is also an observable disengagement that forms when it comes to helping their own neighbors, those who walk (or even sleep) in the streets of Guatemala City.

A striking example came while I was traveling by bus to a cell group one night. I rode with Julio, a trusted informant. We huddled together in a slow-moving, fume-congested bus that was lit only by a few Christmas lights that cast a red haze throughout the interior. Suddenly, a man called for everyone's attention. He waved one hand in the air while using his other to brace himself up against a seat. He was sick. His shirt was unbuttoned, and a colostomy bag dangled from his side, half-filled with waste. In a loud voice, he began to preach over the engine's noise about God's mercy and about his own struggles with illness, accidents, and near death. He was poor, he insisted, and his tired face did not suggest otherwise. As he spoke, Julio nudged me in the ribs, obviously taken by this dramatic scene—an incredibly performed plea for help that mixed Christian faith with a broken body. Taken by it all—the roar of the engine, the man swaying with every shift of gears, and the soft red lights—my own thoughts drifted to the philosophical work of Emmanuel Levinas, who reflects on "the face of the poor, the stranger, the widow, and the orphan" (1969, 251). Levinas sees this face as commanding us all to feed the hungry not just with "a gift of the heart, but of bread from one's mouth, of one's own mouthful of bread" (Levinas 1978, 74). His hyperbolic ethics is embarrassingly arrogant as well as productively impossible and one that I failed to meet, as I handed the man some coins.[26] Julio, however, did not move for his pockets. Instead, he stared straight ahead as the man walked up and down the bus, asking for small gifts. Yet later Julio would celebrate the man's faith to a surprising extent and note throughout the night (during the cell meeting, and afterward as well) how incredible this man's faith was and how dramatic his story. Julio was sincerely touched.

On our way home, after hearing just how much of an impression this poor man had made on Julio, I asked why he had not simply passed along one or two coins. The amount, I said, was not the issue so much as the gesture of giving. One centavo could have been enough. Julio's reaction to my question was one of moral ambivalence. This is not because I proved to be more ethical or compassionate than Julio (as Julio's own dedication to Manos de Amor is commendable) but because I saw the sick man with different eyes. I assessed the event through an admittedly romantic moral vocabulary, one that ethnographers assume far too often, but Julio kept true to the idea that Guatemala's widows, orphans, and strangers do not ride public city buses. Rather, the truly deserving live in Guatemala's rural countryside. Julio, turning to me, remarked that his money was better off in the hands of Manos de Amor. The sick man simply existed somewhere outside his moral grid.

SIX

Cities of God

International Theologies of Citizenship

We shall find that the God of Israel is among us . . . for we must
consider that we shall be as a City upon a Hill, the eyes of all
people are upon us.

JOHN WINTHROP,
A Model of Christian Charity

First ourselves, then the world!

PASTOR CECILIA CABALLEROS,
October 25, 2006

THE YOUNG MAN LAY PROSTRATE in El Shaddai's prayer room—his feet
facing the door, the top of his head pointing toward an oversized map of
the world. He was weeping, screeching at times, pushing his words out in
such a way that they bounced from the room's linoleum floor to its aqua
blue walls in what seemed like 101 different directions. Modest, window-
less, and cramped, the room houses an assortment of mismatched chairs as
well as three wall hangings. The first is the map of the world to which the
man supplicated—his laments so distorted by the room's acoustics that his
tears became mournful dirges and his prayers rattled around the room like
pebbles trapped inside a tin can. My own audio recording of this extended
moment, of this prayerful meeting between man and map, is haunting;
the tempo builds slowly, not unlike an approaching locomotive, until the
man roars with sadness, hope, and faith, his lament piercing the air like a
steam whistle. The second is a map of Guatemala; flagged pins mark each
rural town in which an El Shaddai satellite church ministers, so that the
wall hanging is more pincushion than map—a vivid testament to the

church's prickly presence in (and penetration of) the countryside. The third is a map of Israel, marking neo-Pentecostalism's steadfast commitment to the Holy Land—to the idea that the restoration of Israel is proof of Jesus Christ's second coming.[1]

The three maps dominate the space; their cartographical proclivities to name capitals, mark borders, and juggle scale and cardinal directions frame the kinds of prayers that the faithful practice and perform within and beyond the room itself. They help give direction, as well as meaning, to the men and women who find solace inside this room, who petition God by way of these maps, training their prayers on specific places and in behalf of certain people who live in particular spaces. The young man who lay in front of the world map, for example, prayed for a range of things, many of them completely indiscernible, but those that could be understood included family in the United States, his life in Guatemala, and, most interestingly for this chapter, Guatemala itself. He prayed for his nation, as opposed to any of the nearly two hundred other countries represented on any given map of the world. His was a prayerful concern for Guatemala— a nation situated among many, contiguous to some, monumentally distant from others.

Prayerful supplication to maps—of Guatemala, Israel, and the world— complicates the understandable impression this book has given thus far, that El Shaddai and other Guatemalan mega-churches are nationalistic projects, interested in reimagining Guatemala as a Christian nation and its residents as Christian citizens. The impression is, of course, correct; neo-Pentecostalism is supremely concerned with citizens who use their Christianity to generate a sense of national belonging and responsibility. Yet the prayer room, its congregants looking to the world, evidences the fact that El Shaddai's ministerial vision spills out beyond Guatemala— while at the same time respecting (as well as reinscribing) the very borders that the church often crosses. As this chapter argues, Guatemalan mega-churches such as El Shaddai constantly produce international theologies of Christian citizenship that are transnational in practice. These theologies insist that Guatemalans have a Christian responsibility to the world, and, as Christian citizens, congregants must engage the world one nation at a time—through prayer, praise, and evangelization.

What is significant, if not entirely surprising, is that these international theologies of Christian citizenship place Guatemalan neo-Pentecostals in relationship to the world through their Guatemalan identity rather than in spite of it. This observation stands in stark contrast to a great deal of scholarship on so-called global Christianity, which tends to argue that the religion's worldwide expansion flattens nationalism, replacing it with a global Christian identity.[2] Neo-Pentecostalism does the opposite in Guatemala, however; it contributes to the formation of a Guatemalan identity through the religion's very participation in Christianity's expansion. This is what makes neo-Pentecostalism so very international, as opposed to global—so very interested in actual nations rather than the globe, the global, or even globalization. Neo-Pentecostalism, for example, tends to narrate Guatemala as a city upon a hill—as an outstanding example of Christian growth that exists for all other nations to replicate. By continuing to renew Guatemala one soul at a time, neo-Pentecostals recognize their contribution (as well as their connection) to Christendom—to a world comprising distinct nations, each with thick borders.

Theorizing this Christian dynamic among the individual, the nation, and the world begins with the need for an analytical distinction between *internationalism* and *transnationalism.* The international dimensions of neo-Pentecostalism produce an "imagined community of nations," not unlike those constructed in Disneyland amusement rides, at the Olympics, or through beauty pageants (Malkki 1994, 43). Internationalism allows nations to be imagined not only as homogeneous units with precise borders but also corporeally—with personal characteristics, tendencies, and moods. Thus, Germany becomes punctual, even compulsive, whereas Mexico is caricatured as lax, comfortable with sighing "mañana." International imaginations allow Miss USA to compete against Miss India for the title of Miss Universe just as the United States competes for Olympic gold against China. Internationalism makes the world "small" after all—as one of Disneyland's most celebrated attractions puts it.[3] Neo-Pentecostal internationalism allows the faithful to speak about the character and quality of a nation's faith in much the same way that they might assess an individual's own Christianity, to say things like "Argentina's growing devotion was once strong, but it is nothing like South Korea's faith today." More important, neo-Pentecostal internationalism charges certain nations with uniquely Christian responsibilities. Guatemala as a good Christian nation, for example, often becomes responsible for saving other members of the international community. Through Guatemala's example, Mozambique will find its way.

Of equal importance is that discourses of Christian internationalism travel along transnational circuits that link one context to another; these circuits include media networks, apostolic churches, migrant labor circuits, and, as I will discuss shortly, world congresses. Neo-Pentecostalism's transnational dimensions consist of "a network of direct and indirect relationships, stretching out wherever they may, within or across national boundaries" (Hannerz 1996, 46). Much of the ethnographic material used at the end of this chapter, for example, comes from El Shaddai's satellite church in Chicago—a small community comprising mainly Guatemalan immigrants, though it also includes Mexicans and Bulgarians. One important effect of transnational international theologies of Christian citizenship is that they further compound the moral weight that congregants already shoulder. This is the process's ever-precarious achievement. Devout Guatemalans work hard to be good Christian citizens not only for themselves, their family, their church, and their nation, but also for the world. The Christian citizen's task becomes the construction of *cities* of God throughout the world by way of the construction of Guatemala as a *city* of God.

At least for El Shaddai, the concern for the production of cities rather than a city is plainly stated. El Shaddai's vision for social change involves incorporated satellite churches throughout Guatemala but also the world: the United States, Canada, Mexico, El Salvador, Aruba, Spain, Peru, and Portugal. These churches minister largely to Guatemala's immigrant populations, yet El Shaddai also takes pride in pushing its message outward, beyond Guatemala's imagined community, through Internet broadcasts, multinational radio stations, and television programming. CDs, DVDs, and print media, such as El Shaddai–published books and pamphlets, in both English and Spanish, also stretch the bounds of the church's project from Guatemala to the entire world. El Shaddai's imagined relationship to the world is even central to one of the church's most carefully branded images: Guatemala's silhouette superimposed on a larger, watermarked map of the world, which links the two and makes them indistinguishably interrelated. The image raises the question: How could one begin to separate Guatemala from the world? As this chapter demonstrates, leadership and congregants alike argue that it would be impossible. Guatemalans of faith are in constant relationship to the world by way of their Christian citizenship.

International neo-Pentecostal congresses reinforce the melding of Guatemala with the world. Congresses are events that mega-church leadership and scores of volunteers plan years in advance; they bring well-known neo-Pentecostal personalities to Guatemala for as long as a week to speak on a central theme: church growth, spiritual warfare, or salvation. These congresses generally attract thousands of participants from dozens of countries. El Shaddai, for example, holds a world congress every other year, wrapping its ministerial vision around much more than just Guatemala. Using an ethnographic account of El Shaddai's 2006 World Congress, as well as fieldwork I completed in Chicago, this chapter reflects on international theologies of Christian citizenship and how they place Guatemalans in relationship to the world through a deep sense of national identity.

NEO-PENTECOSTALISM'S INTERNATIONAL IMAGINATION

Both neo-Pentecostals and scholars of Christianity commonly talk about something called global Christianity. This enduring narrative suggests that neo-Pentecostalism is everywhere, spreading the world over, like butter on warm toast—evenly and with ease. Statistics claim that, for example, nine million people convert to neo-Pentecostal Christianity every year, and that much of this growth takes place in Asia, Africa, and Latin America (Barrett and Johnson 2004). The *World Christian Encyclopedia* reports that a quarter of the world's Christian population is best described as charismatic or Pentecostal (Barrett et al. 2001); David Martin estimates that there are some 250 million Pentecostals in the world today (Martin 2002). These statistics, regardless of their accuracy, sustain exaggerated headlines about the "coming of global Christianity" (Jenkins 2002) and "charismatic Christianity as a global culture" (Poewe 1994).[4] Of analytical interest, however, is that for all this talk about global Christianity, both neo-Pentecostals and scholars of Christianity tend to focus their rhetorical efforts on the nation far more often than the globe. Moreover, the actual movement of Christianity in the world is remarkably uneven, which makes the religion decidedly transnational rather than global.

El Shaddai, for example, remains trained on the nation even when making an effort to celebrate the global dimensions of its mega-church. In a souvenir pamphlet celebrating the construction of El Shaddai's mega-church, nations (rather than the globe) structure the discourse: "The steel beams are from Russia, Canada, and China; the roofing materials are from Venezuela; the chairs are from Mexico; the aluminum windows are from Korea and the glass from Colombia; the ceramics and the porcelain are from Brazil; the tiles are from Spain and Italy; the plumbing pipes and air conditioning units are from the United States; and the electrical system is from the United States and Canada."[5] This international narrative focuses on distinct nations rather than the globe: Russia, Canada, China, Venezuela, Mexico, Korea, Colombia, Brazil, Spain, Italy, and the United

States. The same is true of Dr. Caballeros, who often preaches in a deeply international frame, with an eye to nations: "There are other examples in the world where one can see Christian development. There is a wonderful example in Turkey; there is a wonderful example in Singapore; there are various examples, especially in Latin America. We have two fabulous projects in Chile and in Costa Rica, not to mention Barbados in the Caribbean. But this is not what interests me. I am interested in the case of Korea."[6] As excitement and optimism build along with Christianity's development, there emerges a level of anxiety about those nations that have not yet been introduced to the saving power of Jesus Christ. These countries must be saved, neo-Pentecostalism insists. This anxiety lingers at the level of the nation—not the globe. Though forever focused on individual Guatemalans, Dr. Caballeros and the congregants of El Shaddai, when looking beyond their own borders, are largely concerned with Mexico—not necessarily Mexicans—and Chile rather than Chileans. As I will explain shortly, neo-Pentecostalism's international imagination directs the faithful to see the nation as a unit of salvation.

Social scientific research on global Christianity tends to mirror neo-Pentecostalism's international predilections. These studies participate in what Ulrich Beck understands critically as "methodological nationalism" (Rantanen 2005). Donald Miller's *Global Pentecostalism* (2007), for example, is based on research in the following nations: Uganda, Kenya, Egypt, South Africa, Ethiopia, Thailand, the Philippines, India, China, Singapore, Hong Kong, Guatemala, Venezuela, Argentina, Brazil, Poland, Armenia, Turkey, Georgia, and Russia. The Pew Foundation's *Spirit and Power* project (2006) completed fieldwork in the United States, Brazil, Chile, Guatemala, Kenya, Nigeria, South Africa, India, the Philippines, and South Korea. And Paul Freston's ambitious work on evangelical Christianity and democracy covers Brazil, Peru, Mexico, Guatemala, Nicaragua, China, western and northeastern India, Indonesia, South Korea, the Philippines, Nigeria, Zimbabwe, South Africa, Kenya, Zambia, and Mozambique (Freston 2008; Ranger 2008; Lumsdaine 2008). Of interest (again) is that these studies remain focused on nations—not the globe. Much like neo-Pentecostals, these scholars reflect on Brazil—not necessarily Brazilians—and India rather than Indians.

An important contrast emerges. A global Christian imagination would take time to picture the globe—possibly as a sleek and slippery orb on which people and faith flow in a frictionless way, or as "flat," to quote Thomas Friedman (2005), or as at one's fingertips, as the Microsoft advertisement asks: "Where do you want to go today?"[7] There would be, in short, a developed imaginary attuned to the globe, the global, or globalization. But in practice the world for neo-Pentecostals tends to be neither slippery nor flat. The world instead is more like a quilt. Through an international Christian imagination, neo-Pentecostals have come to imagine the world as nations sewn together. As the world's basic building blocks, these nations are patched together, their borders serving as important but nevertheless awkward efforts at stitching. This is one reason maps tend to be such attractive images for neo-Pentecostals—distinct units pieced together like a quilt. Every nation has its place, and every person has his or her nation. Guatemala's piece, for example, is forever a different color from Mexico's and El Salvador's, a distinction that nonetheless fosters continuity—a sense of being separate but forever connected, of being autonomous but nonetheless tied together by way of an imagined community.[8]

This observable contrast between the global and international allows us to make at least two observations. The first is that both scholars and the faithful tend to assume that global Christianity is much like a tidal wave—a natural event that comes down from on high only to splash into the lives of every single person. Faith steadily saturates the world. Yet this assumption is analytically unhelpful when one is trying to understand with any kind of ethnographic clarity the kinds of worldwide relationships sustained by neo-Pentecostal Christianity. Again, most of neo-Pentecostal Christianity is not global in its relationships per se, but in fact transnational (Hannerz 1992) or translocal (M. Smith 2001; Diaz 2007), meaning that Christians and discourses of Christianity flow across borders and between nations rather than saturate the world evenly. The key terms used in this chapter bend toward this kind of analytical specificity; they refer to networks established between points on the globe rather than throughout the world. For example, even for all of El Shaddai's satellite churches, world congresses, and multinational media networks, the church's growth and influence largely follow (and build on) Guatemala's free trade agreements with the United States and South Korea, as well as the country's migrant labor pools, which have always circulated at the whim of militarized borders. The above-mentioned social scientific studies also have their rather unglobal approaches to studying the world. They took place in Brazil, Guatemala, and South Africa—long-celebrated neo-Pentecostal hotbeds—but none pursued research in Mexico, for example, a place long resistant to Protestantism. The idea of global expansion, in all of its intensity, obscures the ways in which a global narrative not only reinforces itself (by treading over already blazed national ground) but also limits the questions that the field asks. There exist copious studies on global Christian expansion, but there is practically nothing on disaffiliation or understanding how neo-Pentecostalism fails to gain traction in some contexts as opposed to others.

The second observation is that talk of global Christianity tends to reinforce the idea that Christians are becoming ever more connected as well as interconnected. The assumption is that national differences give way to Christian sameness: a single brotherhood in Christ. Though the latest iteration of global Christianity does strengthen individual relationships across borders through neo-Pentecostal multimedia networks, neo-Pentecostalism does not do so as evenly as the literature or the faithful would suggest. Christianity, for example, travels along well-paved media networks from Christian node to Christian node while often not touching the turf that exists between them. The point is the very one that James Ferguson makes about the global flow of capital:

> It is worth noting that the movement of capital that is entailed in such enterprises is "global" in the sense that it crosses the globe, but it does not encompass or cover contiguous geographic space. The movements of capital cross national borders, but they jump point to point, and huge areas are simply bypassed. Capital does not "flow" from London to Cabinda; it hops, neatly skipping over most of what lies in between. When capital is invested in spatially segregated mineral-extraction enclaves, the "flow" of capital does not cover the globe, it connects discrete points on it (2006, 379).

The same can be said of so-called global Christianity, which is as much about disconnections as about connections. Guatemala City megachurches, for example, are connected to a surprising extent to megachurches in South Korea and the United States, but they are largely disconnected from churches in Canada and Nicaragua. From the perspective of many Guatemalan neo-Pentecostals, Africa is somewhere "over there," despite a rapidly growing African church network.

Neo-Pentecostal world congresses play a considerable role in both the formation of an international imagination and the establishment of transnational points of contact (and missed points of contact) between Christians and churches. In Guatemala these conferences place the faithful in relationship to the world through international theologies of Christian citizenship. These theologies stress the making of one's own nation for the sake of the world: Guatemalan neo-Pentecostals will save the world by being better Christian citizens of Guatemala. Shuttling transnationally from one world congress to another in the form of a sermon, CD, or personal experience (which might be narrated at distant cell meetings), international theologies of citizenship contribute to the formation of neo-Pentecostal notions of belonging and responsibility— and the ultimate goal of saving Guatemala for the world.

THE WORLD CONGRESS

After years of planning and months of excitement, El Shaddai opened its doors to the church's 2006 World Congress, entitled Profecía. The event brought thousands of pastors and congregants to Guatemala City from throughout the world. As the faithful navigated El Shaddai's parking lot, teeming with cars, buses, and pedestrians, congress participants received a message from Dr. Caballeros in a glossy souvenir program nestled inside their complimentary portfolios: "We want to welcome you to the Prophecy 2006 World Congress. . . . We have been praying and fasting for the prophetic voice to be expressed at this time over each person and this beautiful country of Guatemala."[9] Taking this benediction to heart, Nina, an El Shaddai congregant overwhelmed by the opening night's energy and promise, ducked into a quiet corner of the church, took a deep breath, and sighed to me: "God has given us these few days for the World Congress so that we can put into practice His blessings, for our nation and for ourselves personally." Nina's gentle meditation on the self and the nation soon gave way to the congress's raucous opening ceremony and keynote sermon by Pastor Cindy Jacobs, one of eight neo-Pentecostal "prophets" who travel the globe from world congress to world congress, delivering spiritual visions about the fate of nations and what individual Christians must do to save their nations as well as the world.

During the opening ceremony the church leadership paraded into El Shaddai's main auditorium. All were present. Framed by bombastic orchestral music that lent a sense of gravitas to the event, Dr. Caballeros took center stage as individuals carrying twenty-two flags filed in behind him. Each flag represented one of Guatemala's twenty-two departments; their flapping presence at the ceremony was as gratuitously literal as listing each department here by name: Alta Verapaz, Baja Verapaz, Chimaltenango, Chiquimula, Escuintla, Guatemala, Huehuetenango, Izabal, Jalapa, Jutiapa, Petén, El Progreso, Quetzaltenango, Quiché, Retalhuleu, Sacatepéquez, San Marcos, Santa Rosa, Sololá, Suchitepéquez, Totonicapán, and Zacapa. Each flag staked its claim to a distinct part of Guatemala, making the nation as much a quilt as the world itself.[10]

Dr. Caballeros then welcomed the audience and, following a brief prayer, introduced Pastor Jacobs, who quickly set the tone for the entire congress. Pastor Jacobs, from Colorado Springs, Colorado, announced with energy as she was trailed by a Spanish translator who mimicked her every move and intonation: "Now let's talk about nations. We're in a season where God is changing not only individuals but also nations. We're in a great battle in the heavens over all the nations right now. Right now in all the lands, there is a restructuring of government." Those present could not keep their bodies in their seats. Cheers mixed with ecstatic tears as energy filled the church. The congress's overall force grew steadily. Noting that each nation has a God-given destiny in much the same way that each individual has a God-given destiny, Pastor Jacobs continued: "You know that God sometimes does something in one place that will affect the world. You in Guatemala are doing big things." From Pastor Jacobs's perspective, those "big things" included fighting poverty one prayer at a time, battling corruption through steady and mindful fasting, and promoting national renewal through evangelization and individual conversion. Individualism, nationalism, and the world fought for attention in Pastor Jacobs's narrative. She continued: "God is looking for a generation of leaders. He is calling you. God is choosing a people to be a great army of the Lord. You are a chosen generation! He is calling you to bring revelation! He is calling you in Guatemala to teach nations! It is a revolution of the Holy Spirit!!" Every word spoken by Pastor Jacobs tightened the congress's message points, developing its central theme: individual Christians sustain Guatemala's world standing as a chosen nation; and Guatemala, as a chosen nation, serves as an example to all other nations. World revival is possible by being better Christian citizens of Guatemala.

A stunning level of internationalism framed the congress's rhetorical as well as theological construction of Guatemala. Congress organizers counted and announced repeatedly the names of the twenty-four nations that the event hosted. A congregant or pastor from each of the following nations had registered and was participating in the proceedings: Argentina, Belize, Brazil, Canada, Chile, Colombia, Costa Rica, Cuba, Dominican Republic, Ecuador, El Salvador, Germany, Guatemala, Honduras, Mexico, New Zealand, Nicaragua, Panama, Peru, Puerto Rico, Spain, Switzerland, the United States, and Venezuela. A sense of something "global" emerged through reporting and rereporting this fact. As part of the congress's proceedings, the church's oversized screen often flipped through a video slideshow of each of these nations' flags, blowing in the wind against a blue sky. When one flag would replace another, a different section of the church would burst into in cheers. The Chileans in the upper left deck would shriek with excitement when their flag appeared onscreen, until the image gave way to Colombia's flag. Then those participants, some actually draped in Colombian flags, cheered at the front of the church, hugging one another and pointing at the screen. This happened daily, reminding those present that this was a world congress that knew no geographical bounds and that one's own national identity existed as the very door through which to engage others and the world. Dr. Caballeros, during one such effort at reinforcing this international imagination, walked the cheering crowd through the list of flags, leaving Guatemala's flag to the very end. The crowd, knowing that Guatemala's was yet to come, cheered in anticipation as Dr. Caballeros announced "and . . . GUATEMALA!" The church erupted, and each person (Guatemalan or not) applauded for the nation—for its continued rebirth and for its ability to ignite similar renewals across the world.

These stylized moments of national recognition fomented the proceedings' near obsession with internationalism. This mixture further concretized the notion that the faithful maintain their responsibility and sense of belonging to the world through their national identity. A brief list of those places mentioned during sermons and prayers over the course of the world congress begins to approximate the unrestrained geographical imagination that the event fostered: Africa, Asia, Australia, Bolivia, California, the Canary Islands, China, Egypt, Europe, French West Africa, Germany, Haiti, Hawaii, India, Indiana, Indonesia, Iran, Iraq, Israel, Italy, Japan, Jordan, Kansas, Kuwait, the Middle East, Mississippi, Mozambique, New York, North Korea, the Orient, Pakistan, Paraguay, the Philippines, Portugal, Russia, South Korea, Texas, Toronto, Uruguay, and Zambia. These references encouraged participants to think comparatively. In an imagined community of nations, Guatemala sits with its head high. One gentleman from New Zealand reflected between sessions: "In the West, we are very unspiritual, compared to the Orient or the East, and even here in Guatemala, where people are very hungry for God. In Almolonga [a small village in rural Guatemala that is more than 90 percent Protestant Christian], you could see the tears streaming down their faces—they are hungry for God." This man's reflection on the differences between the East and the West as well as between Guatemala and elsewhere rode the congress's rhetorical wave—a wave that placed Guatemala at the very center of Christian revival, even modern-day Christendom. Using the congress as proof, this gentleman noted that people craved God in Guatemala more than people in New Zealand did, that Guatemala's need for Christ outpaced other nations' desire for salvation. Implicit in this man's conclusion was a sense that Guatemala looms larger in the neo-Pentecostal imagination than other places, such as New Zealand, because Guatemalans are "hungrier" Christians than New Zealanders and, thus, better examples to the world.

Ecstatic nationalism emerged throughout the congress and during informal conversations with participants, as did a near obsession with internationalism. One morning during the conference, for example, I had coffee with the pastor of a small church in Venezuela. He described Guatemala as a "light among the nations" and extolled the work of El Shaddai. The pastor also proudly declared that he was Venezuelan, wearing a large Venezuelan flag like a cape. He said, "We are trying to create a network of churches in Venezuela, just like El Shaddai. I am here at the conference to pray for my nation and release the demonic hold of [President Hugo] Chávez." The pastor's love of and commitment to both Christ and country radiated throughout the conversation. It was also clear that he bore the weight of national salvation on his prayerful shoulders. From his perspective, Venezuela depends on his own efforts at being a good Christian citizen—evangelizing, praying, and fasting. His efforts, he explained, would break the rule of Hugo Chávez and transform Venezuela into another light in a constellation of saved nations in and beyond Latin America. Of particular interest is the fact that this Venezuelan came to Guatemala to save Venezuela. His journey evidences the new transnational social relationships and technologies of citizenship that neo-Pentecostalism presents to the Americas as well as the world. International theologies of Christian citizenship have placed this Venezuelan in relationship to the world not only through his own national identity but also through his participation in Guatemala's Christian revival.

Bold references to Christian citizenship emerged repeatedly throughout the congress. Pastor Emanuele Cannistraci from San Jose, California, for example, preached to thousands one afternoon about Jesus Christ, individual responsibility, and saving the world one nation at a time. He explained that each Christian must renew his or her nation to save the world. To this end, he instructed each participant to yell out loud: "Jesus Christ owns [name of nation]! Jesus Christ is the boss of [name of nation]!" He listed the United States as well as Mexico, Guatemala, Brazil, and so forth: "Jesus Christ owns Brazil! Jesus Christ is the boss of Mexico!" Pastor Cannistraci added, while wiping his brow and gesticulating wildly behind the pulpit, that individual Christians need to renew themselves to renew their nations. Specific acts of personal renewal will lead to national (and then worldly) renewal; according to the pastor, those acts include a range of sexual proscriptions, such as abstinence and a masturbation-free life.

Pastor Cannistraci then called all those participants not from Guatemala to the front of the church. As the audience quickly became a disordered mass of people, Pastor Cannistraci extended his sweaty hands. With a microphone in one hand, he reached out with the other, demanding: "Tell me the name of your nation! Everyone scream out the name of your nation!" Noise erupted as participants leaned toward the pastor, yelling: "Cuba!" "Belize!" "The Dominican Republic!" Over and above this noise, Pastor Cannistraci placed his free hand on participants and declared that their nations were now nations for Christ: "Mexico! Venezuela! Costa Rica! Chile!!! Chile needs a breakthrough! Breakthrough! Breakthrough! Breakthrough!" Brought to ecstasy, participants fell to the floor one by one. Pastor Cannistraci continued: "Who is the boss of your nation? Jesus Christ is the boss of the United States, of Guatemala, of Brazil, of Russia, of Germany . . ." Sweating over fallen bodies, leaning toward those still standing, the pastor then pulled back for a moment to address the crowd one more time. He explained the following lesson amid apparent chaos: "If the world's going to change, I have to change. . . . I'm a world-changer." By "I," Pastor Cannistraci meant every person in the room. "I'm a world-changer" meant that every individual has the capacity to change the world through his or her Christian participation in national renewal. The neo-Pentecostal logic, at its most basic, begins with *me:* I change; then my nation changes; then the world changes—all for Christ.

As I have noted throughout this book, the individual exists at the very center of neo-Pentecostal efforts at social change—whether national salvation or worldwide renewal. This is not a surprising observation, to be sure, given the Protestant roots on which neo-Pentecostalism stands. "The Protestant problematic," the *Blackwell Companion to Protestantism* reads, "is that it places priority on individual conscience in response to revelation—in the Bible and the experience of salvation—as its defining characteristic" (McGrath and Marks 2004, 14). This is why the question of Christian citizenship has historically been a Protestant (rather than a Roman Catholic) question: citizenship concerns itself with individuals and their sense of responsibility rather than with the common good, to which the Roman Catholic Church tends to give priority.[11] This is also one reason individualism sits at the core of Protestant theology and the individual exists as the vehicle for social change. As Pastor Jim Goll, yet another invited pastor from the United States, announced to the crowd: "I am taking Guatemala from personal salvation to Holy Spirit movements, and from Holy Spirit movements to societal transformation." The acknowledged scales of social change are important here. The point of departure is the individual—his or her personal experience of Christ, his or her change of heart, his or her awakening and rebirth. These individual and interior movements then become social movements, or "Holy Spirit movements," in the words of Pastor Goll. The world changes one individual at a time. As Pastor Cecilia Caballeros announced during the congress proceedings, "First ourselves, then the world!"

The responsibility to change begins with each person's decision to accept (or not accept) Jesus Christ. To recount an observation made earlier in this book regarding a neo-Pentecostal youth conference entitled Soy la Revolución, neo-Pentecostalism understands itself not as a single social movement per se, but as the collection of millions of interior social movements. From the neo-Pentecostal perspective, Guatemala comprises 14 million potential individual social movements made repeatedly for Christ but also for the greater glory of the nation and, ultimately, the world. The monastic activities employed by believers to change the world are the same ones used to change Guatemala: prayers, the laying-on of hands, speaking in tongues, and fasting, for example. Although shaped by transnational networks and placed in an international frame, acts of self-governance work toward the formation of a Christian world. Pastor Cecilia Caballeros echoes this logic—and the logic of self-governance—in her own published and distributed message to congress participants, which focuses on the individual's ability to change the world: "Each one of us is the author of our future; we are history makers. May I suggest a question: How can I make a difference? The answer is easy. If you pay attention to your surroundings and pay attention to your neighbor's needs and not your own problems . . . you will see the amount of opportunities at hand to be useful."[12] "Usefulness" here means the willingness to pray for a neighbor, fast for that neighbor, and speak in tongues in his or her behalf.

Ephesians 2:20 is a biblical citation that pastors quoted often at El Shaddai's 2006 World Congress; the reference provides some texture to the event's effort at constructing a sense of belonging and responsibility—all for the greater glory of the world, but through the formation of Guatemala as a city upon a hill. Ephesians 2:19–20 states: "So then you are no longer strangers and aliens, but you are citizens with the saints and also members of the household of God, built upon the foundation of the apostles and prophets, with Christ Jesus himself as the cornerstone." Many congress participants recognized that Guatemala exists as a world leader in church growth and that through their participation in Guatemala's remarkable Christian expansion, individuals would "no longer [be] strangers and aliens, but . . . citizens with the saints." And so hundreds of believers traveled thousands of miles to attend the congress, to witness church growth, and to imbibe both its energy and its promise. Through their participation in Guatemala's revival, conference attendees understood themselves as participating in world change.

This logic of world change, as one might expect, is not original. Since so much of what El Shaddai practices and promotes has deep roots in the history of Christianity, it is not surprising that the formal structure of El Shaddai's international theology of Christian citizenship can be traced back at least to a 1630 voyage across the Atlantic Ocean from Great Britain to New England. John Winthrop, governor of the Massachusetts Bay Company, authored an essay that would contribute to the formation of an "American" identity.[13] This sermon would also, many centuries later, bolster the ways in which Guatemalan neo-Pentecostals imagine themselves as being in constant relationship to the world through their own national identity. John Winthrop's basic theological disposition as a Puritan Christian dictated that each nation has a covenant with God. Winthrop and his fellow colonists, moreover, believed that England had betrayed its covenant with God through the Anglican Church's continued relationship with Roman Catholicism—however diffuse and confused the relationship may have become.[14] In the shadows of England's broken pact with God, the Puritans traveled to New England to forge a new covenant, understanding themselves as the Israelites of the Hebrew Scriptures who wandered through the desert until they came to their own promised land. Winthrop, seeing this new covenant as an exemplary relationship between God and His chosen people, famously wrote: "We shall find that the God of Israel is among us . . . for we must consider that we shall be as a City upon a Hill, the eyes of all people are upon us" (1838, 47). This "errand into the wilderness" aimed to renew, if not remake, the Puritans' own covenant with God while also putting forth a model for the world to witness and replicate (Miller 1956).

El Shaddai leadership and congregants do not shy away from making the very same argument that John Winthrop made during his passage to New England. For neo-Pentecostals, postwar Guatemala is as much a desert as was the Puritan's Atlantic Ocean. In one of dozens of sermons that refer to Guatemala's chosen status, Dr. Caballeros announces: "God called this nation. He made a calling, a choice, and called unto [Guatemala] with the goal of making it His own nation. You all remember, we have already been over Peter's letters. We have already been over Deuteronomy and seen how God tells you that *you* are My special treasure, a holy nation, a nation of kings and holy people. A nation chosen by God."[15] Congregants of El Shaddai celebrate Guatemala's chosen status, pointing to the country's remarkable church growth and worldwide standing as a Christian country. Pushing the notion that God's election of Guatemala will change the world, Dr. Caballeros continues: "[World change] requires a great effort on our part. But I hope that a group of people has the desire, energy, and force to generate a critical mass that can not only truly change the nation [of Guatemala] but also form the model of a Christian nation that will change all the nations of the world."[16] The idea of Guatemala as a city upon a hill constantly places the individual congregant in relationship to the world—a world that neo-Pentecostalism imagines as being in need of saving.

As I have demonstrated in previous chapters, neo-Pentecostals believe that the individual bears the responsibility to sustain Guatemala's chosen status, a belief that the El Shaddai 2006 World Congress ceaselessly reiterated, forcing participants to relate themselves to the world through their national identities. For Guatemalans, this meant recommitting themselves to making Guatemala anew by being active Christian citizens—by forging themselves into being better Christians one monastic practice at a time. For those visiting Guatemala or the congress, contributing to the world meant in part contributing to the formation of Guatemala as a Christian nation through prayer and fasting while also learning as much as they could about what makes Guatemala a chosen nation. Congress participants as active learners watched closely to gain nuggets of information on why and how neo-Pentecostalism continues to expand with such force in Guatemala. These lessons always included one of Guatemala's greatest success stories: Almolonga. This town's story constitutes a popular narrative that begins with vegetables but ultimately ends with a morality tale, one that insists that change begins small but ends big.

A table laden with colorful fruits and vegetables greeted World Congress participants as they entered the mega-church's main door. The counter brimmed with oversized carrots, tomatoes, and cobs of corn—so comically engorged that many did a double take, asking the indigenous men and women behind the display for an explanation. The answer, repeated often, was that the fruits and vegetables came from a small pueblo named Almolonga that lies a few hours from the capital city. The produce, they continued, was so large because the pueblo is itself a chosen pueblo. Almolonga is Guatemala's own model of Christian living—a model for national revival. As the story goes, drunks once lined Almolonga's streets, corruption threatened local government, and the jails teemed with violent offenders. Then a few decades ago, a wave of conversion took over the town, which pastors and congregants now report is over 90 percent Protestant Christian. Storefront churches replaced jails, and men returned to the fields to harvest what are now famously oversized fruits and vegetables. Dr. Caballeros explained to the Christian media, "The mentality, and the way of thinking, and the patterns of thinking of the people [in Almolonga] has changed so drastically! Changed from a culture of death, a culture of alcoholism, idolatry, and witchcraft, to a culture today where they think only about expanding the kingdom of God—prosperity, blessing, healing—and everything related to Revival!"[17] The vegetables are, as many proud men and women have explained, of export quality, and in many ways they represent Guatemala's faithful transition from a state-centric economy to the global free market.

An overwhelming success, Almolonga is known in neo-Pentecostal circles throughout the world as the small Guatemalan town that changed in an instant through the saving power of Jesus Christ. El Shaddai has a satellite church there, and it often uses Almolonga as a model within a model. During a stump speech, the very one that announced his own presidential campaign, in fact, Dr. Caballeros proclaimed: "Today I announce my victorious campaign for the president of Guatemala. [I'm announcing] here in Almolonga because Almolonga is a symbol of prosperity, of progress, of work, of productivity." He continued: "When we were walking earlier, we saw the fields and we saw how the men and women of this community work in the morning, afternoon, and evening to produce, and I dream that one day all of Guatemala will be as productive as Almolonga." Leadership and congregants look to Almolonga as proof of what can happen when nearly every resident is a born-again Christian—when everyone is a Christian citizen. The results are peace and prosperity. Noting that Guatemala is not yet 100 percent Christian, many dream about what Guatemala would be like as a Christian nation, using the cultural familiarity of Almolonga as an incentive. These dreams revolve around Guatemala as a developed country—one without violence, corruption, and poverty, but replete with produce fit for export.

Narratives of transition and development, supported by the story of Almolonga and the promise of Guatemala's church growth, defined the 2006 World Congress in its descriptions of Guatemala's potential and world standing. Pastor Jacobs, during the congress's opening ceremony, preached: "Latin America is in a transition right now. Transition is the most fragile time for a woman giving birth. It is a time when a mother does not want to have any more pain. The mother does not want to go on anymore." Resuming her analogy between postwar Guatemala and labor pains, Pastor Jacobs argued that though almost complete, Guatemala must push through the pain: "You are in transition. You in Guatemala are going to have a beautiful baby. And God has chosen you. I am speaking to you, Guatemala, as a mother. God has chosen you as a model. Guatemala is a model that will affect all of Latin America!" Eyes wet, congregants greeted this message with cheers and unbridled hope. Many congress participants continued to turn toward what they could do as good Christian citizens of Guatemala for both their nation and the world.

THEOLOGIES MADE TO TRAVEL

International theologies of Christian citizenship travel transnationally along media circuits and on the lips of modern-day itinerant preachers who spend their lives hopping from one world congress to another. Lingering on the actual movement of international theologies of Christian citizenship is important—if only to make possible the argument that Christian citizenship's moral weight exists in many more locales than postwar Guatemala, pressing down on the shoulders of many more people than Guatemalans. Because of certain neo-Pentecostal media circuits and rhetorical engines, international theologies of Christian citizenship also load believers in South Korea, Mozambique, and Brazil, for example, with the very kind of moral weight documented throughout this book. This transnational distribution of weight begins with a ministerial practice that dates back to colonial North America.

During an era of Christian revival, Methodist pastors took the ministerial responsibility of a *charge,* or particular geographical area, which would include more than two churches. The pastor's annual duty was to visit each of these churches at least once a year, while establishing new communities. These men had a dual focus—both to minister and to spark revival. Biographies and historical renderings of these itinerant preachers place them on the backs of horses, galloping across untamed American landscapes, sometimes at great personal risk. They were simple folk, the narratives insist, who renounced (almost by necessity) personal possessions and a home life to spread the word of God anywhere they could. Their historical imprint is romantic, daring, and heroic.[18] Today, transnational neo-Pentecostalism's own circuit riders travel not from colonial village to colonial village but from major metropolis to major metropolis, stopping to spread their message to the masses.

The pastors who participated in El Shaddai's 2006 World Congress are perfect examples of modern-day circuit riders and exemplify how this kind of travel disseminates international theologies. Eight neo-Pentecostal pastors from abroad, for example, participated in the 2006 World Congress: James Goll, Cindy Jacobs, Jane Hamon, Emanuele Cannistraci, Rony Chaves, Bill Hamon, Hank Kunneman, and Brenda Kunneman. Each of these pastors manages a successful multinational mega-church while also traveling the world to preach at services, congresses, and conferences, filling oversized churches and sports stadiums for an afternoon or a weekend. The travel itineraries of these eight pastors provide astonishing circuits. For many, the 2006 World Congress in Guatemala was not their first or last national or international trip of the year, or even of the week. In the same month that Pastor Rony Chaves of Costa Rica appeared at El Shaddai's 2006 World Congress, he also preached to churches in San José and Puntarenas, Costa Rica; Puerto Rico; the Dominican Republic; Florida; and Iguazú, São Paulo, and Manús, Brazil. In 2006 Pastors Hank and Brenda Kunneman preached to churches throughout Florida as well as in Irving, Texas; Oak Forest, Illinois; Norfolk, Nebraska; Washington, D.C.; Atlanta, Georgia; Lanham, Maryland; Redford, Michigan; Petersburg, Virginia; and Guatemala City. Pastor Jacobs's online itinerary notes the days she is away from her church to "preach the word of God." According to her calendar, she traveled (domestically and internationally) every day between September 1, 2006, and December 1, 2006, including trips to other parts of Latin America and to the Middle East. The year 2007 began in a no less demanding way; Pastor Jacobs trekked across the world during the entire month of January.

One vignette captures the frantic pace these pastors keep. It occurred after Pastor Cannistraci's final sermon at El Shaddai's 2006 World Congress. Waiting patiently backstage with several Guatemalans for an impromptu interview, I encountered Pastor Cannistraci coming out of his dressing room holding an oversized carrot—obviously a gift from the people of Almolonga. Escorted by two El Shaddai security guards, Pastor Cannistraci met my eyes with a look of panic. It was clear that I was waiting for him—for either an interview or a blessing. Tired and guarding his time, Pastor Cannistraci continued briskly past me, mumbling to me, "God bless you, brother, I love you," the next instant instructing his security detail: "Do not stop. Do not stop!" Shuttled from airport to hotel to church to hotel to airport, these pastors maintain schedules that do not allow for much cultural engagement with Guatemala or any other place they happen to land. They deliver the word of God in a virtual vacuum. Guatemala might as well have been Florida, so far as Pastor Cannistraci was concerned.

One result of this harried itinerary is the production and reproduction of neo-Pentecostal narratives that do not become acculturated—that are resistant to the kind of acculturation that so many scholars of global Christianity note.[19] In fact, the enduring scholarly paradox of global Christianity seems to be the religion's ability to maintain a level of narrative continuity in places as diverse as India and the United States, but also to become a part of a community's particular culture (Meyer and Geschiere 1999). Distinct communities throughout the world seem to make the religion their own and accept it on their own terms (Bastian 1993; Manning 1980). Much of this book argues that Guatemalan neo-Pentecostals practice Christian citizenship in Guatemala for Guatemala; however, El Shaddai's 2006 World Congress suggests some of the cultural mechanisms by which neo-Pentecostalism maintains a level of continuity across cultures and nations. For example, it is not obvious that Pastor Cannistraci or any of the other invited pastors at the 2006 World Congress adapted their sermons to the Guatemalan context, except to announce that Guatemala (rather than the United States or Argentina) is a city upon a hill. Some of the more obvious clues came during "ministerial misfires," when Pastor Cannistraci, for example, railed against Islamic terrorists, admonishing toward his conclusion that Christians must be as vigilant as Islamic extremists. The silence that met these pronouncements signaled, on one level, that post–9/11 politics is not as relevant to Guatemalan neo-Pentecostal communities as it is to those in the United States. On another level, it also signaled that the cultural dexterity of these pastors can be somewhat arthritic. The overriding sense from the 2006 World Congress, in fact, was that these pastors travel the world delivering the same sermon to different crowds, pressing square—albeit flexible—pegs into round holes. The prevailing impression is that these pastors may very well deliver similar "city upon a hill" speeches to a number of other nations similarly situated, such as the United States, South Korea, Brazil, and Mozambique. These nations—like Guatemala—all demonstrate substantial church growth and thus seem receptive to the very same kind of Christian citizenship promulgated in world congress settings. One of Pastor Jacobs's recorded sermons, one that she preached in and about the Philippines but that now circles the Internet, demonstrates how a sermon about the Philippines could very well be one about Guatemala, or even South Korea:

> The Lord would say to the Philippines, I am shaking everything that can be shaken, so no man would glory in what I will do. For I have waited for a generation that I could raise up a purity and a holiness in. And I am raising up firebrands—there is a forerunner anointing coming upon the youth of the Philippines that will prepare the way of the Lord even in the Middle East, says the Lord. Look and see what I will do in Mindanao. For I am going to visit in a way that you cannot imagine. I am coming to Mindanao, says the Lord, as the God and the Lord of hosts, and I am going to start appearing. The Lord says, as a sign, that I am going to truly change the nation. . . . And I am going to come with signs and wonders and miracles. And I am getting ready to pour out a miracle anointing upon the Philippines such as the earth has never seen.[20]

The frantic nature of travel by these harried pastors contributes to what Mikhail Bakhtin would call the *centripetal* aspects of these theologies (1981). His theory of the centripetal aspects of language describes how ideology consolidates a discourse and then flattens that discourse's diversity of voices and opinions.[21] His is a distinctly Marxist argument, and Marxist philosophies of language such as Bakhtin's do not provide this study with a very helpful lens through which to analyze international or transnational theologies of Christian citizenship. Yet Bakhtin's language of centripetal forces does provide a way to describe the flattening of what is largely considered neo-Pentecostal Christianity's multivocal community

(Burdick 1998, 123; Freston 1998, 81; Robbins 1998). World congresses, for example, provide powerful and intense venues for entrepreneurial pastors to recite their theologies of Christian citizenship without inviting many others to participate in a dialogue. These pastors, for example, constantly meet and network with each other at home and abroad. They participate in a sociality that is familiar to the professional academic who travels to annual meetings to exchange ideas and make contacts—all irrespective of the city in which the conferences take place.

From the passing comments made at the 2006 El Shaddai World Congress, it became clear that Pastor Jacobs and many of the other visiting pastors had been together in Hawaii that same year for a "prophets" conference. Pastor Cháves also mentioned having been at retreats with the other pastors in the recent past, including Dr. Caballeros. Pastor Kunneman announced proudly that he seemed to "follow Bill Hamon around to different conferences lately," and Pastor Cannistraci noted that he and Bishop Hamon had been together in Maui back in 2001. Pastor Cannistraci also remarked that he had been in Hawaii just a month earlier with Pastor Jacobs and Pastor Hamon. These connections ran rather deep. During conference proceedings, Pastor Cháves mentioned that he had been in Atlanta with Bill Hamon twenty years before and that Pastor Jacobs had written the prologue to one of Pastor Goll's books. Pastor Cecilia Caballeros observed during one of her own sermons that she had attended a conference in New York recently with Pastors Cannistraci and Hamon. She also mentioned that she had been "adopted" by Pastor Hamon's church and family in Florida. These personal and professional networks contribute to a level of narrative continuity that international theologies of citizenship sustain in spite of the places that the theologies travel. These proscriptive and prescriptive discourses travel from one world congress to another, from one distant city to another. These modern-day circuit riders, however, represent just one contributing element of neo-Pentecostalism's continuity—to a stability that delivers not only the word of God but also a degree of moral weight to believers throughout the world.

To return to this book's central metaphor, moral weight travels the world via these itinerant preachers and broader media networks. At El Shaddai's 2006 World Congress, for example, the church bookstore burst with attendees who bought books, manuals, CDs, and cassettes. The most popular authors included names familiar to a transnational neo-Pentecostal community: Cindy Jacobs, James Dobson, Rony Chaves, James Goll, Rick Warren, Ashley Smith, T. D. Jakes, Stephen Arterburn, Fred and Brenda

Stoeker, Joyce Meyer, Gene Edwards, Watchman Nee, Josh McDowell, Tim LaHaye, Kevin Johnson, Joel Comiskey, Andy Park, Oral Roberts, Antonio Cruz, David Solá, Osvaldo Carnival, Christopher Shaw, Félix Ortiz, Benny Hinn, Rebecca Brown, and John Maxwell. Translated into dozens of languages, these authors loom large in mega-church bookstores throughout the world. They contribute to the formation of a discursive well that congregants and pastors visit for instruction—on how to pursue personal and national salvation, build a church, minister to barren women, form after-school programs, exorcise demons, lose weight, and so on. The most successful of these authors are English-speaking North American pastors who distribute their literature through international presses. The most significant presses are in Colorado Springs, Miami, and Bogotá, cities that form neo-Pentecostalism's production capitals (García-Ruiz 2004). These centers also push their material from distribution centers to mega-church bookstores.

Theologies of Christian citizenship, simply put, travel beyond the borders of Guatemala along transnational networks. The observation ultimately allows for the expansion of this book's central argument: the formation of Christian citizenship prompts the Guatemalan faithful to shoulder the moral weight of transitional times not just for their nation but also for the world. Believers beyond the borders of postwar Guatemala also take on a similar kind of weight to save their own nations as well as the world. As much as this book is an ethnography of Guatemala, it also points toward the felt reality of Christian citizenship (with its moral weight) wherever neo-Pentecostal Christianity meets questions of citizenship. The following section documents ethnographically that Christian citizenship's moral weight does travel.

CHICAGO

As someone accustomed to seeing El Shaddai images in Guatemala, to speaking with El Shaddai's faithful in *la capital,* I found the storefront church "uncanny," in something of a Freudian sense—something denied and displaced that, much to my own surprise, surfaced in the most unlikely of places. Nestled between a music shop and a bakery, cattycorner to a hardware store, the El Shaddai church of south Chicago is nearly ten years old, with upwards of fifty congregants. The rented space, with its folding chairs and modest wall hangings, pales in comparison to Guatemala City's mega-church and its unflinching commitment to upward mobility and naked prosperity. Yet the satellite church's Guatemalan-born and El Shaddai–trained pastor, Raul, routinely delivers an unmistakably ministerial vision, one that clearly travels constantly from Guatemala City to Chicago not only by way of migrant labor circuits but also through new forms of media, such as electronic mail, MP3 downloads, and international phone calls now made affordable by Internet programs. These media allow not just words but also moral weight to shuttle between cities and ultimately onto the shoulders of congregants. Raul's ministry evidences as much.

Raul's personal story is circuitous. It is filled with intimate callings by both God and Dr. Caballeros that have pulled him and his wife from Guatemala City to the south side of Chicago. Along the way, he has founded not just one but two El Shaddai churches in the Chicago area and has stayed true to a familiar kind of moral weight that originates in El Shaddai's Guatemala City mega-church but that now travels from Guatemala to the United States on the backs (and in the hearts) of Guatemalan migrants. Important for this chapter is how this moral weight becomes imagined and distributed by Guatemalan immigrants in North America. The weight, as my interviews with Raul demonstrated, becomes multiplied and shared by Chicago's El Shaddai community—only to be pushed back into the world, even down south into Mexico, for a growing number of neo-Pentecostals to accept. As I will show, Raul wants to start his own satellite church in Mexico. But before documenting Raul's entrepreneurial efforts at spreading the Word in Mexico and his own concern not just for his new nation but for all nations, it is necessary first to listen to the kind of Christian citizenship that Raul himself helps manufacture for a small congregation comprising Guatemalans, Mexicans, and an assortment of Bulgarians who found themselves married to devout Guatemalans. The weight is as ever-present in Chicago as it is in postwar Guatemala. Raul explained to me:

> In different ways, we have seen the transformation of people [here in Chicago], especially in the last two years. So many people have changed their way of thinking and their vision. They are completely renovated people. We have taken on a tremendous weight [*carga*] to change all of the neighborhoods here in Chicago with the Word of God. And with the blood of Christ, we are going to be able to accomplish this change. We want to eliminate poverty where we live. We want our children to study more and graduate from high school. We want parents to inculcate their children with a different vision, with a will to succeed.

Raul's wife, Silvia, added, "Spiritually and materially, we want them to succeed in everything that they do." Silvia, performing the role of supportive wife to Raul in his dream of a burgeoning church, consistently and lovingly amended each of Raul's statements—even when Raul settled into his own vision for the United States. His was a tremendously unexpected Christian commitment to an adopted homeland, which further helps contextualize the bounds of Christian citizenship: "This is the way we want to live. This is the change in people's mentality [that we want]." Raul continued: "Our goal is to write the United States on the list of nations that will survive the apocalypse. We are from Guatemala but we live in the United States. So our weight is the United States. Our charge is to plant an El Shaddai church in each of the United States' fifty states." Silvia, closing some of the rhetorical openings that her husband left open, added: "That is the goal. Fifty states. Fifty churches. And we'll do this step by step." Raul continued: "We are just one example. In Chicago, there are two churches. One in the north and one in the south. And so the weight that we shoulder is to save the United States. This is the weight that we shoulder. All those in Guatemala are working for Guatemala. But we are working here in the United States with the Word of God to change the way people live and think." "Everything can be different," Silvia insisted. Raul, gaining steam, continued: "There can be a change in the people. We are working with children and with adolescents right now so that they can set goals for themselves. We want them to set professional goals that they can achieve. This is all so that they can move forward. We want to motivate children and the youth, especially the ones in high school. We want them to move forward." Raul, using the metaphor of weight throughout the interview, gave the image increasing density and relevance in the Chicago area, but the image nonetheless upset his wife. Frustrated by her husband's use of the term, concerned that it might sound pejorative or tedious, Silvia mentioned: "It's a blessing, not a weight. It's an opportunity that God gives us. It's not a weight. Because I'm sitting here and my husband keeps calling it a weight—a weight, a weight—but no. It is a blessing to serve the Lord like this. There's a great deal of need and we have the ability to help. It's not a weight." The point is not an unfamiliar one, especially in Guatemala, where the faithful consistently grapple over how to represent the felt reality of responsibility as not simply a burden but also as significant—that the weight is indeed heavy but nonetheless feels good; the weight is purposeful and full of meaning. Raul nodded in agreement only to continue the interview by leaning (at times even more insistently) on the language of weight. The conversation showed, at the very least, the difficulty of conceptualizing the responsibility of Christian citizenship any other way. And so Raul enumerated the ministerial goals that his church community set for the upcoming year, once again demonstrating that *weight* is a somewhat inescapable term for the kinds of responsibilities that Christian citizens shoulder:

> The vision of the Church [this year] is to establish cells within our congregants' houses. This lets us cover a great deal more territory. We are also preparing a group of evangelists so they can speak the Word of God to people in the neighborhood. And this year, we are planting the first groups; the first cells. For the last five years, we've been praying and receiving acts of God. And now we are teaching people how to be intercessors for the Lord and how they can take on the weight to do all that is needed. So as a church, we are praying for the state, for the nation. And there's another group building the cell structure of our church. They just started last year.

Raul continued, his own excitement expanding his vision by the sentence: "And we also want to buy our own church. We do not want to rent a space anymore; it's a vision that Pastor Caballeros has given us. We want to buy. We don't want to rent. And so this is our vision. And it is the same vision as the church in Guatemala—the same vision and the same weight." Midthought, Raul introduced a surprising development: "But now we also want to travel south and inculcate those in Mexico with El Shaddai's principles. That's the goal. And this is possible because our Chicago church in the south is almost one hundred percent Mexican." The Chicago church shares "the same vision and the same weight," in Raul's words, and the focus is on action—on the near-constant activity that this small church maintains for the United States. The church's participation appeared constant and fierce. Working multiple jobs, bound to a long commute from home, to church, to work, Raul and his wife manage a growing congregation alongside a frustrated (and frustrating) U.S. economy, mounting domestic responsibilities, including two children, and the challenges of raising children in a foreign city. Amid these concerns, Raul and Silvia placed their new nation—the United States—at the center of their own ministerial concern while also pushing even farther outward to other countries:

> And part of our vision this year is to enter Mexico. That's what we are doing right now. Right now, there are two El Shaddai churches in

Mexico. One is near Mexico City and the other is in Chiapas, close to the border. But we [the El Shaddai church of Chicago] want to start a church in Mexico. This is the first time that an El Shaddai church in the United States is starting an international church. It is the first time. And so now we are asking Mexico to take up the weight. This is part of our vision as a church. To start cells and to enter Mexico. It is a year of breakthroughs.

Raul added, explaining why Mexico is in dire need of El Shaddai's vision: "We're going to enter an abandoned country. A country with a great deal of witchcraft. And so all of this is the reason why we are also practicing spiritual warfare. We are working hard in this way. Basically, the church right now is praying, discipling people, practicing intercession and spiritual warfare. And we are also evangelizing." Moving into Mexico also means preparing those in Chicago—preparing the people *here* to intercede *there*. Raul explained:

In terms of spiritual warfare, we are warring over the neighborhoods [here in Chicago and in Mexico]. There is a struggle with the gangs. There are a lot of young people in the gangs and it's sad. But it's not only the gangs, but also the idolatry [in Chicago and in Mexico]. And God opposes all of this, so we work to save as many people as we can. We ultimately want to leave all of this behind. All we want to do is put people on the right path and just prepare people to leave [sin behind] on their own accord. There is a great deal of need, but Jesus Christ will help us. This is an active church, you see, and we are taking on an incredible amount of weight this year. But this is all part of our focus this year.

Revealing why an ecclesiastical move from Guatemala City to Chicago to northern Mexico is at all possible, Raul refers to the back-and-forth migration of Mexican immigrants and their families: "The heart of this one Mexican town [migrated to Chicago and now] attends our church in Chicago. So we want to move our vision to Mexico and prepare the people to practice spiritual warfare there. Here they do it, but we want them to do it in Mexico also. We want them to hear the word of God and learn how to pray to God. It's power. It is a way to change the people. It's a way to change the way they think." Raul explained why El Shaddai's main church in Guatemala City does not coordinate the founding of this new church in Mexico. Raul's connections to Mexican migrants in Chicago, men and women who travel as often as possible between the United States and Mexico, have provided an opportunity to export a Guatemalan-based vision of Christian citizenship to Mexico via Chicago without ever having to involve Guatemala City's mega-church community. Reinforcing his scale of salvation, Raul suggested: "Our vision is not just a town and is not just a nation, but is everything. All the nations in the world. So our vision is to plant churches all over the United States and Mexico. Geographically speaking, we are right now in the center of the United States." At this, Raul began to name all the places in the United States that have an El Shaddai church; his list of locales reminded me of El Shaddai's 2006 World Congress—each city rattled off feels like another pin pushed into a map. In a matter of minutes, Raul mentioned El Shaddai churches in New Jersey, Pennsylvania, California, Florida, Rhode Island, and Massachusetts, detailing to me the personalities of each of their pastors and adding: "There is such a weight that these churches are taking up. People enter the church never having been affected by the Word of God and then take up the weight. They ask, what do the people need to advance? What can I do to help them advance? It's because they feel that things need to be accomplished. This is the Holy Spirit that enters them. And so, after their hearts have been changed, they work to change their lives. This is about being obedient to the Word of God and about shouldering the weight." Raul went on optimistically: "And so I think in a short time, many children will think differently. They will have a different set of expectations. They'll understand their potential and have a different mentality altogether." Bringing me back to his main message point, Raul finished the interview with a degree of seriousness punctuated by extended eye contact: "It's a responsibility that we can't forget. It's a great weight. But God gives us the ability to work, to get up every day, and instill potential in the children. This weight is a blessing for the nation."

Disappointment

A Conclusion

The sense of something lacking or failing arises from the realization
that we inhabit a violently unjust world, a world defined by the
horror of war, a world where, as Dostoevsky says, blood is being spilt
in the merriest way, as if it were champagne. . . . This experience of
political disappointment provokes the question of justice.

SIMON CRITCHLEY,

Very Little . . . Almost Nothing

MORE THAN FIFTY POLITICIANS, ACTIVISTS, and party workers were
murdered and dozens more seriously injured during the heated months
leading up to Guatemala's 2007 general elections. One candidate from San
Marcos was shot, wrapped in left-leaning political paraphernalia, and then
stuffed in the trunk of his car. The Guatemalan press argued that the
bloodshed represented the continued influence of organized crime, a
seemingly unstoppable perpetrator of violence.[1] Terror fostered impunity
and resignation. As one international observer remarked: "It's sad to say,
[but] Guatemala is a good place . . . to commit murder."[2] A little more
than ten years after the 1996 Peace Accords, postwar democratization
seemed little more than a bloodied banner. In the face of an average of sixteen murders daily in Guatemala, who could say for sure whether any of
these particular fifty were the result of political antipathy or cruel chance?
And who would do anything about it?[3]

The dutiful congregants of El Shaddai would. Despite a corrupt judici-
ary, an ineffectual police force, and a broken penal system, El Shaddai's
congregants organized an eight-week prayer and fasting regimen that
emboldened each member to serve Guatemala through Christian practices. While the faithful fasted for peace and security, they also followed set

prayers that reminded them that Guatemala is a chosen nation and that they should all "wake up to [their] dream [of a new Guatemala] by throwing aside passivity and indifference." The effort asked good Christian citizens to analyze their "spiritual, emotional, and familial situations" and then link themselves to the events reported in the daily newspapers, making the personal explicitly political.[4] The overall aim was for each believer to remember that his or her fate was inextricably interrelated with the fate of the nation. Their spiritual restoration was for the restoration of Guatemala.

This book has addressed neo-Pentecostal formations of citizenship in postwar Guatemala City, and it has done so with both an observation and a pair of arguments. The observation is that neo-Pentecostalism provides an increasing number of postwar Guatemalans with their sense of citizenship—with a sense of belonging to Guatemala, of being responsible for Guatemala, and of having the means to act in behalf of Guatemala. Christian citizenship is what the faithful performed and maintained as they prayed and fasted against electoral violence in late 2007. This means that Christianity is neither incidental nor tangential but in fact central to citizenship in places like postwar Guatemala, a conclusion that goes against the grain of citizenship studies (K. O'Neill 2009).

The pair of arguments, based on this observation, is as follows. The first is that Christian practices, such as praying and fasting against electoral violence, not only constitute Christians as citizens but also shift the moral responsibility for postwar Guatemala from historical and structural factors onto the shoulders of believers. As cell members, as warriors, as philanthropists, as fathers (and as mothers who support fathers), Christian citizens shoulder the moral weight of postwar Guatemala, working feverishly to remake their nation through the remaking of themselves. Christian citizenship makes postwar Guatemala the believer's burden, not the burden of economics or history.

The second argument, at its most basic, is that the practice of Christian citizenship provides an increasing number of Guatemalans with a deep sense of meaning while also limiting the avenues through which they can act (Paley 2001, 146). The more Christian citizens link themselves to the fate of the nation—praying and fasting a new Guatemala into existence— the less time, energy, and interest they have for participating in more traditional modes of citizenship, what some commentators would call "real" politics, such as community organizing, public demonstrations, and voter registration campaigns. The promise of Christian citizenship produces an impressive level of bustle—a hive of activity—while also narrowing what Christians actually do as citizens of Guatemala. As I mentioned in the preface and substantiated throughout the subsequent chapters, Christian citizens in Guatemala are more likely to pray for Guatemala than pay their taxes; they tend to speak in tongues for the soul of the nation rather than vote in general elections; and they more often than not organize prayer campaigns to fight crime rather than organize their communities against the same threat.

The observation and the arguments are ethnographic. They are empirical in the rawest sense; although they are formed into a narrative through a series of interpretations, and they are surely capable of telling an altogether different story through an altogether different set of interpretations, this book is based on actual events, real people, and an extended engagement with postwar Guatemala City. The book, at its most basic, observes and argues that a growing number of Guatemalans practice and perform their citizenship through neo-Pentecostal Christianity and that this ethnographic fact has consequences—not just for scholarship but also for postwar Guatemala.

One unaddressed consequence—one emotional effect, even affect—that emerges from this research has been (and, I expect, will continue to be) a sense of disappointment. Both past and future audiences, both imagined and implied readers, both active Christian citizens and the most ardent of secularists will surely find themselves disappointed by neo-Pentecostal formations of Christian citizenship—by what Christians actually do as citizens in a democratizing context. It is disappointment with which I wrestled on more than one occasion. Questions already posed, only to be raised again, in professional and informal settings, by North Americans and Guatemalans alike, include: Why do Christians do so little as citizens of postwar Guatemala? Why do neo-Pentecostals fail to steward properly their democracy as citizens? And aren't those who take to their souls rather than to their streets just bad citizens? This registered (as well as expected) level of disappointment tends to be directed toward actual citizens, rather than the promise of citizenship itself. It is a distinction on which this conclusion lingers.

To contextualize this disappointment in citizens (rather than citizenship), it is important to remember, once again, that this book flies in the face of existing narratives describing postwar politics in Guatemala. Dusty reports enumerate Guatemalans' remarkably inactive citizenship, low voter turnout, sluggish civil society, shocking levels of tax evasion, high level of dependency on nongovernmental agencies and international aid, incredible levels of pessimism about democracy's promise, and faltering sense of nationalism. Yet fieldwork with neo-Pentecostals has made it eminently clear that members of this large subset of Guatemalans work constantly as citizens not just of heaven, but also of Guatemala, in the hopes of remaking their nation through the renovation of themselves. These Christian efforts, ethnographically speaking, are no less active than more expected modes of political participation such as voting and activism. Practice is practice, to the cultural anthropologist; performance is also performance. So from a certain anthropological perspective, the very one from which I write this book, it would be impossible (even irresponsible) to say that these neo-Pentecostals are inactive—that they are not doing anything at all. The fact of the matter is that they obviously do a great deal for themselves as well as for their families, church, nation, and world. They pray for reduced levels of crime; they fast for less political corruption; and they sermonize on the service of self to the nation.

Action by the subject, however, does not preclude disappointment on the observer's part. In many ways Christian citizens evoke disappointment because of *how* they act rather than *whether* they act at all. To note that Christian citizens are actually doing something is not the same thing as arguing that they are doing something productive or appropriate, or that they are making postwar Guatemala into something with which everyone can agree. This book's hard-fought ethnographic observation is simply that Christian citizens *have done* and *continue to do*—that they *are doing*. This is why I have left the theme of disappointment for the very end. Even though the kind of disappointment that Christian citizens evoke is as ethnographically palpable as its moral weight, it is not entirely productive to address disappointment ethnographically (as I have done with moral weight). Rather, I prefer to approach disappointment as an event, in something of a Badiouian sense—as a rupture in the established order of things, as an appearance of truth (2005).

Though disappointment could be approached as evidence and documented fastidiously to make a larger argument, disappointment-as-event provides an opportunity for reflection on why such an emotion seems so inseparable not simply from formations of citizenship, but also from the everyday lives of citizens, Christian or otherwise. Reading citizenship amid disappointment provides an opportunity for a meditation on citizenship's political usefulness and the kinds of metrics and empathy that Western scholars of liberal politics tend to employ when celebrating citizenship as an intuitive vehicle for social reform. Neo-Pentecostal formations of Christian citizenship, as a telling example of citizenship's cultural flexibility, political limitations, and maybe even downright failure, call into question the very category of citizenship itself. This conclusion, in short, recognizes as well as anticipates disappointment in postwar Guatemala City's Christian citizens, while also wanting to redirect that disappointment onto the very category of citizenship itself.

Disappointment, then, is a point of departure for a larger, more general reflection on citizenship, one that ultimately parrots Simon Critchley's philosophical conviction to "not begin in wonder, like Greek philosophy, but in disappointment. With a sense, to quote Wallace Stevens, that a fantastic effort has failed" (2007, 159). Starting a critical conversation about citizenship with disappointment rather than *promise, hope,* or even *wonder* allows both the scholar and the practitioner (citizens of both *here* and *there*) not to linger on how or why citizens have disappointed their democracies or even themselves, but rather to inquire why citizenship itself is so terribly (and repeatedly, even mechanically) disappointing. If we approach citizenship by way of disappointment rather than promise, in much the same way that Friedrich Nietzsche and Michel Foucault approach history by way of discontinuity instead of continuity, then the conversation becomes something entirely different. Citizenship becomes a clumsy artifact rather than a shiny promise—a constant reminder that there is always much more work to do.

DISAPPOINTMENT

Dr. Caballeros ran for office in 2007, campaigning as early as February 2006 to be the president of the Republic of Guatemala. He was ultimately not elected; a technicality disqualified his name from even appearing on the ballot. Sometime, somewhere, Dr. Caballeros failed to sign and submit one of the forms that would have made him an official presidential candidate.[5] In a country of suspect politics, when close to a dozen candidates were running for president, Dr. Caballeros's attempt at the presidency fell short because, as the story goes, he did not complete the requisite paperwork. His embittered supporters whispered that Dr. Caballeros was too principled to bribe the appropriate people at the appropriate time; others added that as the only Protestant candidate, he proved too great a threat. Since 60 percent of the country was either Pentecostal or charismatic

Christian, and since Dr. Caballeros was making connections with an increasing number of Roman Catholic politicians through mainstream civil society projects, he could easily be seen as a major contender. He had the numbers as well as rhetoric that could at least in theory mobilize the faithful to vote, and a deft sense of both community organizing and public relations. Rumors abound about how political corruption interrupted his 2007 campaign.

Dr. Caballeros's failed campaign became a wellspring of disappointment, an enduring feeling of dissatisfaction, when he and his supporters did not realize their presidential expectations. And the tone of Dr. Caballeros's disappointment was telling. Months after the elections, in a sermon entitled "Putting Our Values into Practice," he established two radically different poles of political participation: the secular and the Christian. The secular is without faith, whereas the Christian is without any kind of practical engagement with the material world. Advocating for a middle ground between the two, the sermon marked one of the first times that any member of the El Shaddai community seemed to question the spiritual world's authority over the material world's. Dr. Caballeros, through his sermon, suggested that the good Christian citizen must do more than pray, fast, and perform examinations of conscience: "I would like to speak about the equilibrium that should continually exist in the life of a believer. The life of a believer needs balance. The Christian life needs equilibrium. For example, there needs to be a balance between the spirit and the body. It doesn't work when someone is so spiritual, *so spiritual,* so very spiritual that they lose contact with the material world. In the same sense, of course, a believer can be so focused on the material that they lose sight of the spiritual." Dr. Caballeros assured his congregation that a church without faith is interested only in the rational and, moreover, that a rational church is a lost church. The answer is not to divorce the Christian citizen from the supernatural, Dr. Caballeros insisted, but to realize that there exists a well-grounded stance in the world: "Some place themselves totally within faith and exclusively with the supernatural; they cultivate a deep compassion for the Gospel through their faith but ultimately lose contact with reason. They lose any sense of rationality." Dr. Caballeros, in what can only be described as a raw turn of phrase, then commented, "Faith is more than just the music."[6] Uncomfortable laughter followed.

Dr. Caballeros's sermon exposed an observable level of disappointment in the very Christian citizens whom he had spent decades cultivating. His disappointment lay with his failed run for presidency, with the need to begin a campaign for the 2011 general elections, and with his congregants— who proved to be overwhelmingly active Christian citizens, but only by way of the supernatural and at the expense of the rational (in his words). Dr. Caballeros, however, was not the only person disappointed in Christian citizens. Christian citizens also proved to be rather disappointed in themselves. During an informal conversation with an El Shaddai congregant, a woman committed to Dr. Caballeros's campaign suggested disappointedly that the weight of it all had become too much. She was unable to do enough, and she questioned whether she would ever be able to do enough. The congregant then confided to me something rather telling not just about the 2007 campaign, but also about her life as a Christian citizen: "Siento el peso del mundo en mis hombros." "I feel the weight of the world on my shoulders," she said, linking the felt reality of moral weight with disappointment's lingering density.

The comment was difficult for me to hear. Over the course of my fieldwork, these men and women had become for me more than objects of ethnographic analysis or faceless civil subjects deploying religious discourse. During my ethnographic research, a certain form of intimacy had emerged from long conversations about life, theology, and national politics. Again and again, men and women confessed to me a surprising sense of responsibility for the state of postwar Guatemala—a surprising amount of moral weight that presses down on their shoulders—as well as an enduring kind of disappointment in themselves for never being able to shoulder it all. This woman's comment made me uneasy, as it seemed to me particularly self-flagellating for her to imagine the burden of postwar Guatemala as solely hers. Yet as I had witnessed repeatedly, Christian citizens pray, fast, and fidget with themselves (literally their selves) as if it were their obligation to manage chaos. It is the self, and not their state, that serves as the site of restoration.

In the face of incredible levels of urban violence, economic instability, and political corruption, why do Christian citizens take to themselves instead of the streets? I often asked this question of myself and my informants during the course of my fieldwork, registering my own disappointment in the Christian citizens who taught me so very much about life in postwar Guatemala City. While the faithful would re-explain to me the relationship that exists between the self and the nation as well as between the material and the spiritual, I often found myself returning unexpectedly (and uncomfortably) to Ayn Rand's *Atlas Shrugged* (1957). Although I do not advocate Rand's brand of rational self-interest, her prose provides a tempting rejoinder to neo-Pentecostal formations of Christian citizenship—to the very kind of weighted disappointment that taints El Shaddai's Christian citizens. Through the novel's protagonist, Rand asks: "If you saw Atlas, the giant who holds the world on his shoulders, if you saw that he stood, blood running down his chest, his knees buckling, his arms trembling but still trying to hold the world aloft with the last of his strength, and the greater the effort the heavier the world bore down upon his shoulders—what would you tell him to do?" Rand's other protagonist, stumped by the question, responds: "I . . . don't know. What . . . could he do? What would you tell him?" To this the first protagonist responds, "To shrug" (455).

Should Atlas shrug the weight of the world? Observing neo-Pentecostals in postwar Guatemala pressed me to question certain liberal assumptions that the social sciences and humanities seem unable to shake, assumptions also shared by development workers, aid agencies, political operatives, and church leaders who work feverishly to implement the promise of citizenship in places like postwar Guatemala, Mozambique, Brazil, and Iraq, among others. These are places where an array of actors place a seemingly unquestioned premium on citizenship—where the promise of citizenship is like a silver bullet or magic pill—but where there nonetheless emerges an enduring sense of disappointment in the men and women who fail to shoulder the responsibility of citizenship "properly" or in a timely manner. The disappointment tends to settle not on citizenship, but on the citizens.

There is a tendency, then, not just to lay blame but also to distribute a patronizing kind of disappointment at the feet of well-intentioned citizens—men and women who shoulder the moral weight of citizenship in uneven ways, or in a fashion nearly unrecognizable to citizenship's own liberal authors (as in the case of Christian citizenship). There is a part of me that deeply hopes that these neo-Pentecostals will shrug, that they will unfetter themselves from the impossible obligation of saving Guatemala and the world. But what does this disappointment, this hope for such a shrug, say about Christian citizens and, more important, about the promise of citizenship altogether? Said simply, disappointment in citizens for not being more active or for not shrugging obfuscates the more important conversation about why there should exist substantial disappointment in the very promise of citizenship itself. If extended fieldwork with postwar Guatemala's Christian citizens demonstrates anything, it is that citizens do not fail nearly as often or with as much gusto as the promise of citizenship itself. Before bringing this point into greater focus, however, it is important to concede (at least for a moment) that Guatemalan neo-Pentecostals are nothing new to the history of Christianity, and neither is the disappointment that follows them. Instead, they repeat a familiar history.

A FOOL'S ERRAND

In 1952 the historian and literary critic Perry Miller penned his essay "Errand into the Wilderness," which addressed a minor moment in American letters: the rhetorical disjuncture between the first colonial Puritans and their subsequent generations. The archives tell us that the second and third generations seem to have failed their forefathers. In these sermons of the second and third generations, "a deep disquietude" is conveyed; the sermons tell us that "something has gone wrong" (Miller 1956, 2). The task of "Errand into the Wilderness" is to explain the rhetorical difference between the bombast of the first generation and the seeming malaise of their progeny. To do this, Miller expands on a metaphor often invoked by Puritan writers, that of an errand, arguing that the difference between the generations is a definitional one. For the first generation, the errand is something one completes, only to return. In this sense, the Puritans who crossed the Atlantic could be understood as running an errand on behalf of God, an errand from which they must, to fulfill it, return: "[The Massachusetts Bay Company] was an essential maneuver in the drama of Christendom," Miller writes (1956, 11). The first Puritans wanted to complete the Reformation, perfecting it on the hills of Massachusetts for all of Europe to see.

Among the second and third generations of Puritans, however, *errand* referred to the journey itself, the errand at hand. "[The Massachusetts Bay Company] was, so to speak, on its own business," wrote Miller" (1956, 6). The purpose of the journey was the journey itself, not the return. Miller makes clear that the gap between the generations was one of disappointment. The errand boy had not returned; he had not even been seen. The second generation discovered what the first could not believe: No one in the Old World cared very much about the Reformation in the New. Miller writes: "If an actor, playing the lead role in the greatest dramatic spectacle of the century, were to attire himself and put on his make-up, rehearse his lines, take a deep breath, and stride onto the stage, only to find the theater dark and empty, no spotlight working, and himself entirely alone, he would feel as did New England around 1650 or 1660" (1956, 13). Too much European history unfolded to keep England's attention on New England. Civil wars, heresy, and the like made the Puritans' errand into the wilderness a fool's errand: "Their errand having failed in the first sense of the term, they were left with the second, and required to fill it with meaning by themselves and out of themselves. Having failed to rivet the eyes of the world upon their city on the hill, they were left alone with America" (1956, 15). It is at this moment that Miller closes his essay, suggesting that now the process of what he terms *Americanization* will begin (1956, 9). This "fool's errand" would become not a new Reformation, but a new empire.

The Guatemalan neo-Pentecostals of today are not entirely unlike Perry Miller's Puritans. They understand themselves as errand boys and girls for Christendom. They actively build on Guatemala's intoxicating levels of church growth to imagine postwar Guatemala as a city upon a hill. They imagine further a world witnessing, watching, and waiting for this city to achieve its most moral fruition. El Shaddai leadership and congregants alike do not shy away from the idea that they are completing the Reformation—that they are a part of Christendom's most daring of dramas. This is one reason Christian citizens of postwar Guatemala work so feverishly for Christendom, remaking themselves to remake the nation, only to remake the world.

Yet this book has made obvious that Christian citizens of postwar Guatemala are also the doers of their own errands. Christian citizens fast for safer streets, pray for less political corruption, and battle against demons for the soul of their nation. Simply put, postwar Guatemala provides Christian citizens with much to do. And though neo-Pentecostalism trades on the winds of a single brotherhood in Christ, Guatemala's Christian citizens do not flinch at giving their national identity priority over their global Christianity. Guatemala's faithful make it clear that they are Christian citizens of Guatemala before (but nonetheless for) the world.

A deeply ironic and seemingly unsustainable kind of rhetorical work perpetuates the fantasy that Guatemalan neo-Pentecostals are currently on both errands, as defined by Miller. The reality of the second errand makes curious the first. The first errand is the sense among Guatemalan neo-Pentecostals that they work hard as Christian citizens to create a replicable model for the world. This kind of imagining builds on neo-Pentecostal world congresses; it emerges from ecclesiastical structures that link Guatemalan mega-churches to storefront satellite churches throughout the Americas. The fantasy surfaces in a flamboyant sense of international-ism that bubbles up in sermons, radio broadcasts, and print media. The brief quote cited earlier from Dr. Caballeros is only the tip of a narrative iceberg: "[World change] requires a great effort on our part. But I hope a group of people has the desire, energy, and force to generate a critical mass that can not only truly change the nation but also form the model of a Christian nation that will change all the nations of the world."[7] These efforts are not just for Guatemala, but for Christendom.

My own research for this book has even participated in the idea that the entire world continues to lean toward Guatemala with curiosity and respect. My presence as an interested outsider constantly demonstrated to the faithful that Guatemala represents something important—something that each nation needs to understand. My informants, rather than wondering why I did not have something better to do with my time, would comment (often at length) about how there could not be anything more important than understanding Christian citizenship and how it can change the world. I existed as a kind of proof for their own self-impression. An early experience set the tone. Having diligently scoured the phone book and the Internet for addresses of Guatemala City Pentecostal churches, I eventually found myself chatting for hours with the pastor of a particularly small church. We talked about Christianity, democracy, and Guatemala's continued shift in religious affiliation. Yet nothing in our conversation prepared me for what would happen later that evening.

His small church brimming with congregants, the pastor stopped the service to introduce me as a university professor with a doctorate from the United States. Only a graduate student at the time, I flinched at the distinctions, but the pastor ignored my efforts to correct him. Pushing me in front of the congregation, he then announced that Guatemala is a shining example of evangelization and that *this* congregation meant something not only to Guatemala but also to the world. The pastor made his point by highlighting the presence not of his faithful, but of a scholarly interloper. Though I credited Google (not God) for my unlikely participation in their service that evening, the pastor nonetheless used my presence to advance the narrative that Guatemalans are on an errand for global Christianity. By simply pointing to me, the pastor demonstrated that they were a part of something great—that the eyes of the world were indeed upon them.

The world, however, is neither watching nor waiting. The world has long since turned its back on Guatemala. And this is how Guatemalan neo-Pentecostals have and will become the doers of their own errands. This is why they continue to fight against soaring levels of drug trafficking, gang violence, political corruption, and abject poverty. As a small country long tethered to more powerful economies, Guatemala has only recently been left alone by colonial powers. Guatemala surely held a certain amount of the world's attention in the 1980s and 1990s. The titles of published books mirror the intensity with which the Western gaze critically assessed the genocidal effects of U.S. intervention in Latin America during Guatemala's civil war: *Between Two Armies in the Ixil Towns of Guatemala* (Stoll 1993); *The Guatemalan Military Project: A Violence Called Democracy* (Schirmer 1998); *A Finger in the Wound: Body Politics in Quincentennial Guatemala* (Nelson 1999); *The Battle for Guatemala: Rebels, Death Squads, and U.S. Power* (Jonas 1991); *Fear as a Way of Life: Mayan Widows in Rural Guatemala* (Green 1999); *Harvest of Violence: The Maya Indians and the Guatemalan Crisis* (Carmack 1988). Later, however, the United Nations–brokered Peace Accords (CEH 1999) and the reconciliation that the Roman Catholic Church so poignantly scripted (REMHI 1998) signaled to the world that Guatemala is in a postwar context—that Guatemala has begun a transition from war to peace, from poverty to prosperity, and from autocracy to democracy. The dramatic events of September 11, 2001, and developments in global capitalism further shifted the world's attention from Latin America to the Middle East and also to East Asia, Africa, and India. President George W. Bush's own goodwill tour of Latin America in the spring of 2007 aimed to remind the region that the United States had not completely forgotten about it, despite the fact that Bush's flat-footed meetings and barricaded visits signaled to everyone that it had.[8] The violent reality of postwar Guatemala makes curious the idea that the world is watching or even at all interested. A country does not become "a good place to commit murder" without being more than a little overlooked. Guatemala is a good place to be forgotten, a good place for the world to forget.

TO BE LEFT ALONE

Like actors without an audience and strongmen without relief, Guatemala's Christian citizens have been left alone (alongside their secular counterparts) to do their own errands. Their aloneness is both a source and a byproduct of disappointment directed at them—at each Christian citizen for not doing enough, for not doing it correctly, or even for not shrugging. Yet to be left alone, to be lonely, is in some perverted sense citizenship's ultimate goal. As Alexis de Tocqueville announced more than a century and a half ago, using the United States as a case study, the difference between a subject and a citizen is that the subject must be governed, whereas the citizen governs himself or herself. While Barbara Cruikshank has rightfully collapsed this binary proposition by arguing that the active citizen must always be subject to himself or herself (1999, 20–24), efforts at democratization throughout Latin America and beyond consistently aim toward a citizenry that can be left alone to run on its own accord. The United Nations Development Programme, for example, in a report entitled *Democracy in Latin America: Towards a Citizen's Democracy* (2004b), announced that democracy is "in trouble" and even "in crisis"; it "calls for increased participation by citizens," and proposes a "citizen-centered State." Citizens are key ingredients to democratization; they are the cogs that keep the machine running.

The promise of citizenship in this sense advocates a vision of democracy not unlike that of the deists of the Enlightenment, who argued by way of Newtonian physics that the universe as a system behaves much like a clock: patterned and dependable. God, in his infinite wisdom, created a rational universe, one that is mechanistic and independent of divine interference. Set in motion, the universe runs like clockwork. Democracy has come to be imagined in much the same way. Detached authors set a democracy in motion, rational and mechanistic, with peace accords and free elections, and expect it to run well; it will, but only if all democracy's pistons fire in sequence, if all of democracy's cranks and gear shafts move smoothly, if every single component of this impressive machine functions properly. Democracy, the narrative implies, should be able to be left alone when citizens hum with energy and excitement—when they participate to their fullest abilities. The contrapositive of this story, of course, is that if a democracy such as Guatemala cannot be left alone, if Guatemala's efforts at democratization must be watched and tinkered with time after time, then its citizens have failed; they have not done enough and must do more.

Clocks, however, do not run on their own, and neither do democracies. The work of Bruno Latour tells us this much: "It is by mistake, or unfairness, that our headlines read 'man flies' or 'woman goes into space.' Flying is a property of the whole association of entities that includes airports and planes, launch pads and ticket counters. B-52s do not fly, the U.S. Air Force flies. Action is simply not a property of humans but of an association of actants" (1999, 182). This is to say that clocks can either be read heroically as technological achievements brought into being by a single agent, or they can be read in a much more sophisticated way, so as to bring out a clock's infrastructure—mainsprings, dials, bezels, springs, pendulums, weights, and quartz movements—as well as the repairmen who keep these objects in sync, the advertising agency that pushes the clock onto the masses, the salesperson who moves the clock from store's shelf to fireplace's mantel, and the unskilled laborer who cleans the repair store, the advertising agency, and the sales floor. In contrast to the deist's "mechanical universe," this is a world full of actors and activities, relations and relationships, people and professionals that all contribute to the workings of a single clock.

At the moment, citizenship tends to be read heroically, and democracy mechanistically. If citizens act, then democracies will run. But citizens need not carry so much weight—so much responsibility to act so heroically—when they can very well "read democracy as a clock" in such a way as to expose the machine's infrastructure. Though the promise of citizenship prompts individuals to stand alone, a robust network of agents and relationships deeply interrelated to the formation and the practice of citizenship can be easily enumerated: constitutions, elections, security, the courts, campaign reform, civil society, political parties, tax reform, and the congress, and also multinational corporations, immigration policies, the informal economy, free trade agreements, new forms of Christianity, unions, and public transportation. And this is only a cursory list. The actors and networks that contribute to the formation of citizenship would yield a text at least twice the length of this book. Again, the promise of citizenship prompts the individual—hails *you*—as both democracy's problem and its answer, both the cause and the solution. This, simply put, is disappointing.

Disappointment does not emerge because the vast majority of postwar Guatemala's Christian citizens do not shrug the weight of citizenship from their shoulders. I referred to Rand only in my most cynical of hours, when, for example, I was traveling by public bus to a cell meeting with informants who seemed unfazed by the fact that it was the rainy season, that the bus overflowed with people, and that not a single window was cracked for fear that rainwater might hit those fortunate enough to have a seat. As the bus's atmosphere became thicker, as the bus lurched forward tens of meters at a time, as the windows fogged and my back perspired, I would plead with my informants to shrug—to shrug off the weight of Christian citizenship so that we might hop off the bus and skip into a bar for a drink. But they never did, not once, assuring me that this was all for something greater. Why?

In the introduction I referred to the work of Milan Kundera to offer a glimpse of the kind of moral weight that Christian citizens shoulder in postwar Guatemala City. Building on Nietzsche's theory of the eternal recurrence, Kundera notes, "If every second of our lives recurs an infinite number of times, we are nailed to eternity as Jesus Christ was nailed to the cross." He calls it "a terrifying prospect" and notes that "the world of eternal return" is one in which "the weight of unbearable responsibility lies on every move we make." *Das schwerste Gewicht,* Nietzsche calls the idea: "the heaviest of burdens" (Kundera 2004, 5). In this brief but important reference to Kundera, I admittedly stalled. I held back, placing some additional information in an endnote rather than in the main text itself, in the hopes that the flip side of this "unbearable responsibility" would have more of an effect in this book's conclusion than in its introduction. The flip side to the "heaviest of burdens" is an image of life's most intense fulfillment. Kundera writes: "But in the love poetry of every age, the woman longs to be weighed down by the man's body. The heaviest of burdens is therefore simultaneously an image of life's most intense fulfillment. The heavier the burden, the closer our lives come to the earth, the more real and truthful they become" (2004, 5). Kundera and Nietzsche tend to advocate for weight; they philosophize on a need for significance. It is a need of which Christian citizens are keenly aware: "The absolute absence of a burden causes man to be lighter than air, to soar into the heights, take leave of the earth and his earthly being, and become only half real, his movements as free as they are insignificant" (Kundera 2004, 5). Love, for Kundera and Nietzsche, is a significant burden—as is, my informants argue, Christian citizenship. Christian citizens do not shrug because the weight is heavy. This moral weight makes their lives significant.

The promise of citizenship prompts the individual to accept a heroic level of responsibility, even when copious numbers of actors and networks constitute the worlds in which these citizens act. These actors and networks have not (maybe never will) shouldered even a fraction of the weight that individual citizens now bear. When the municipal government of Guatemala City, for example, announces that "*you* are the city" in a way that also suggests that *we* are not the city and that *it* (meaning the municipal government) is also not the city, there is cause for disappointment. When civil society organizations, such as GuateAmala, ask for a national attitude adjustment that begins with *you* rather than *us,* when this indexical move releases an impressively long list of people, places, and institutions from sharing in what could otherwise be read as a collective burden, then there is cause for more disappointment. When a popular megachurch asks *you* to change through the saving powers of Jesus Christ, charging *you* with the goal of improving your honesty, asking *you* to soldier for Guatemala, and prompting *you* to father a postwar nation, then there is cause for even more disappointment.

Disappointing is the fact that the promise of citizenship is predicated on *your* individual responsibility and not a kind of social obligation that the state may have for its people. Disappointing is the fact that the promise of citizenship excuses the kinds of responsibilities that could be ascribed to multinational corporations, the very ones that make money off Guatemala's tax-free zones. Disappointing is citizenship's relative flimsiness when it comes to making demands on the state and multinationals; citizenship was once understood as a vehicle for social change, an identity that had leverage. Disappointing is the fact that citizens rather than foreign investors or local industries, citizens rather than anyone else, in fact, have been saddled, or more important, prompted to saddle themselves, with a weight not of their making and not entirely of their choosing. This is why citizenship in postwar Guatemala can be read as a sham in the truest sense: an imitation that purports to be genuine. Citizenship, in theory, could be a vehicle through which Guatemalans could, for example, leverage the state, remind the state that it too has responsibilities, and charge those nonstate actors with a level of accountability as well. Citizenship could induce collectives to work with other collectives in an effort to share social burdens. Rather than prompting the state or multinationals, for example, to do things, the promise of citizenship makes people do things, to themselves and often by themselves. The promise of citizenship aims to make democracies run on their own, like clocks set by God, without much attention to the hordes of other actors and networks that should also contribute to this shared project.

NOTES

PREFACE

This book, like many other ethnographies, relies on both key informants and what David Pedersen would call brief events that "are saturated with qualities of immediacy, abruptness and the faltering of expectations" (2008, 58). It would be unsatisfying, analytically speaking, not to recognize the complexity of either, even if only in a short note. As for key informants, this ethnography is the result of an array of informants interviewed and observed over the course of several years. Though it is difficult to say why ethnography as an "improvisational method" (Cerwonka and Malkki 2007) tends to yield so-called key informants, my own study has benefited not only from those individuals who seemed to be in tune with my own temperament, making both interviews and friendship easier, but also from those who stood out because of their experience and reputation within particular communities. Because of these unique relationships, I often "name" my key informants in this book—not to identify them (as I always maintain their anonymity by way of pseudonyms) but to add a degree of narrative to them within the context of this text. Carlota in this book's preface is one example; Julio in the introduction is another. These key informants, moreover, are often part of brief events that either begin each chapter or serve as illustrative vignettes. Generally, I take these events as representative moments of a much larger research stay. They introduce, convey, or demonstrate (or some combination of these) the complexity of the ethnographic moment and, at times, even the anthropological questions that emerge from the field. Much of fieldwork, I have found and now argue, can be read as a pile of brief events eventually quilted together to form (and at times resist) a coherent narrative. In many ways, these moments and events can be an ethnography's most basic building block.

1. The bulk of this research took place over the course of sixteen months, from February 2006 to May 2007; it also consisted of shorter trips to Guatemala City in 2001, 2004, 2005, 2007, and 2008.

2. The distinction between an analytical and a folk category is the same one that drives anthropology's emic/etic dichotomy. An *emic,* or folk, perspective involves an effort to understand a given worldview. See Headland et al. 1990. Guatemalan neo-Pentecostals, for example, use the phrase "Christian citizenship" in their everyday lives. An *etic,* or analytical, perspective seeks a more comparative approach with generalizable categories. I propose throughout this book that anthropologists use the term "Christian citizenship" to describe what neo-Pentecostals in and beyond Guatemala do at the intersection of Christianity and democracy.

3. See, e.g., chapter 1 of this book, as well as IDEA 1998; Chase-Dunn et al. 2001; CERD 2006; Sridhar 2007; Latinobarómetro 2007.

4. As I discuss in the introduction, a constructionist understanding of citizenship leads to the use of the verb *to make* when describing the cultural processes that contribute to the formation of citizenship as both an identity and a form of subjectivity. See, e.g., Rosaldo 1994; Young 1996; Rose 1996b; Gordon 1991; O'Malley 1996.

5. Here, *mega-church* is defined as any congregation with a sustained weekly attendance of two thousand persons or more (Thumma and Travis 2007).

6. Paul Freston's ambitious and timely *Evangelical Christianity and Democracy in Latin America* (2008) is one such example. Comparative in scope, Freston's study notes that the spread of both democracy and evangelical Christianity throughout Latin America yields important intersections worth understanding; yet Freston and his fellow contributors tend to linger at the level of political parties and candidates. Little of this otherwise significant project reveals what Christians do at the everyday level in the name of democracy.

7. For research on the voting behaviors of Pentecostal and Charismatic Christians in Latin America, see Gill 2002; Martin 1990; Smilde 1998, Stoll 1990.

8. Dr. Harold Caballeros, "Hacia una visión de una nación Cristiana, el papel de la cultura" (June 13, 2004) (audiocassette); all translations are mine.

9. I do not understand *field* as a geographic locale but rather a distinguishable site where individuals and institutions wrestle over meaning and value. See Pierre Bourdieu (1984) as well as David Swartz's commentary on Bourdieu's conceptualization of the field (1997, 218–246).

10. Those churches include Casa de Dios de los Ministerios de Cashluna, Calvario, Iglesia Cristiana Verbo, and Iglesia de Dios Fraternidad Cristiana.

11. See, e.g., Garrard-Burnett 1998 (epilogue); Althoff 2005; García-Ruiz 2004. In the Guatemalan context *ladino/a* refers to an officially recognized ethnic group whose first language is Spanish.

12. See, e.g., "Christianity Reborn," *Economist*, December 19, 2006. See also Naomi Schaefer Riley, "Can the Spirit Move You to Join the Middle Class?" *Wall Street Journal*, October 13, 2006.

13. Methodologically, my use of contrast here is akin to the ethnographic work of Teresa Caldeira in *City of Walls: Crime, Segregation, and Citizenship in São Paulo* (2001). Caldeira accomplishes a cross-class analysis of fear and segregation by pursuing ethnographic research in three areas (13–15). Another analogue, in terms of method, can be seen in Saba Mahmood's *Politics of Piety: The Islamic Revival and the Feminist Subject* (2005). Over the course of several years, Mahmood completed cross-class ethnographic fieldwork in mosques located in distinct neighborhoods (40–78). Both efforts, as well as mine, aim not at ethnographies of these particular areas but rather at ethnographies of broader themes, such as fear, piety, and Christian citizenship. But as a final note it is worth recognizing that in Caldeira's case, areas (in the sense of the physical spaces of the city) matter a great deal: walls, buildings, gates, fences, security systems, and borders, for example.

14. See Sullivan-González 1998.

15. A note on sources: Ministerios El Shaddai records, produces, and distributes cassette recordings of each sermon. This provides a convenient way to cite public talks. In this study, when they are available, I cite El Shaddai recordings.

16. The celebrated journal *Citizenship Studies,* for example, observed its tenth anniversary in 2007, having never published a single article on or related to the theme of Christianity (K. O'Neill 2009).

17. The observation has been made but no research agenda has been systematically sought. Bryan Turner writes: "While [Michael] Mann (1987, 340) warns us that 'tradition matters,' he completely neglects the impact of organized Christianity and Christian culture on the structuring of public/private spaces, and how the typically negative evaluation of the political in mainstream Christian theology continues to place an individualistic brake on the expansion of active political citizenship. I have argued elsewhere (Turner 1986, 16) that both Christianity and Islam contributed to the development of citizenship by providing a universalistic discourse of political space (the city of god and the Household of Islam) which challenged ethnicity and kinship as the primordial ties of the societal community (Parsons 1971)" (Turner 1990, 197).

18. See, e.g., S. Coleman 2000; Robbins 2003, 2004a, 2004b; Bornstein 2005; Cannell 2005, 2006; Engelke and Tomlinson 2006; Smilde 2007; Keane 2007; Engelke 2007; Elisha 2008; Guadeloupe 2008; Tomlinson 2009.

19. See, e.g., Dwyer 1982; Clifford and Marcus 1986; Rosaldo 1989; Trouillot 1991; Tyler 1991; Abu-Lughod 1991; Scheper–Hughes 1995; see also Benson and O'Neill 2007.

20. For cultural Catholicism, see, e.g., Greeley 2000; Massa 1999; Orsi 2005; O'Donnell 2006.

INTRODUCTION

First epigraph: *The New Oxford Annotated Bible* (Metzger and Murphy 1991). Second epigraph: Lake 1912, 359.

Biblical passages used throughout this book come from Bruce M. Metzger and Roland E. Murphy, *The New Oxford Annotated Bible, with the Apocryphal/Deuterocanonical Books* (New York: Oxford University Press, 1991).

1. Local media covered Guatemala's 2007 general elections. See, e.g., Gema Palencia, "Diecisiete candidatos intensifican campaña," *Prensa Libre,* June 18, 2007; Luisa F. Rodríguez and Jéssica Osorio, "Candidatos discuten planes de trabajo en cuatro áreas," *Prensa Libre,* August 9, 2007; Luisa F. Rodríguez, "Candidatos con fuertes dispositivos de seguridad," *Prensa Libre,* August 16, 2007; Edgar López, "Menchú y Pérez atienden a indígenas," *Siglo XXI,* August 9, 2007 ; Otto N. Ángel, "Candidatos conocerán CICIG," *Siglo XXI,* February 2, 2007; Roberto Arias, "Candidatos y la mujer guatemalteca," *La Hora,* November 17, 2007.

2. In my use of *morality,* I follow Michel Foucault to mean practical ethics, or the art of living. In *The Use of Pleasure* Foucault distinguishes between ethics and moral codes. Though ethics is largely understood to mean rules of behavior, Foucault shows that in antiquity there were no rules. Ethics, rather, included guides for the forging of oneself. These guides established relationships between the self and the self. They were "intentional and voluntary actions by which men not only set themselves rules of conduct, but also seek to transform themselves, to change themselves in their singular being, and to make their life into an oeuvre that carries certain aesthetic values and meets certain stylistic criteria" (1985, 10–11). In terms of morality, Christian citizenship involves the art of living.

3. I follow Judith Butler (1999) in arguing that citizenship, much like gender, is a performance rather than an essential or universal identity.

4. The idea that neo-Pentecostal Christianity could depoliticize Guatemalans builds on the so-called withdrawal hypothesis. The general notion of this hypothesis is that Pentecostal and charismatic Christianity's rejection of the material world allows the faithful to withdraw from the public sphere into churches. Variations, or at the very least explorations, of the withdrawal hypothesis can be seen in the work of David Stoll (1990), David Martin (1990, 2002), Jean Comaroff (1985), and John Burdick (1993).

5. Caballeros, "Hacia una visión de una nación Cristiana."

6. Spiritual warfare, as I discuss in chapter 3, is a biblical metaphor for the Christian life that has lost its moorings. As Christian citizen-soldiers, neo-Pentecostals routinely understand themselves as fighting Satan every day in their prayer lives for the soul of Guatemala City.

7. In citing Kundera and Nietzsche, I am trying to capture Christian citizenship's felt pressure but also the notion that Christian citizenship as the "heaviest of burdens" is an image of life's most intense fulfillment. Kundera writes: "But in the love poetry of every age, the woman longs to be weighed down by the man's body. The heaviest of burdens is therefore simultaneously an image of life's most intense fulfillment. The heavier the burden, the closer our lives come to the earth, the more real and truthful they become" ([1984] 2004, 5). Kundera and Nietzsche both seem to advocate for weight, for the fundamental need for significance: "The absolute absence of a burden causes man to be lighter than air, to soar into the heights, take leave of the earth and his earthly being, and become only half real, his movements as free as they are insignificant" (Kundera [1984] 2004, 5). Love, for Kundera and Nietzsche, is a burden, as is, I argue, Christian citizenship.

8. Guatemala has long claimed all or part of the territory of neighboring Belize. See, e.g., Sutherland 1998.

9. See, e.g., Thompson 1985; Simpson 1978; Perry Miller 1956; Bellah 1992; Sullivan-González 1998.

10. See the second English printing of Marta Pilon de Pacheco's *Intercessory Prayer: Weapon of God: A Handbook on How to Intercede* (1998).

11. Many scholars make strong arguments against the accuracy of these numbers. In his review essay, Joel Robbins (2004b) identifies several (Corten 1997, 313; Levine 1995, 157; Stoll 1990, 6). These scholars note that the figures are hyperbolic and that religious conversion is a very difficult process to track globally, which allows statisticians to exaggerate the numbers. The statistical representation of Protestant growth in Guatemala is difficult to assess. The numbers range from the dramatic to the conservative. The Pew Forum on Religion and Public Life (Pew 2006) places the proportion of Guatemalans who report that they have "had a direct experience of the Holy Spirit" at 60 percent, whereas more conservative studies argue that the number of Protestant Christians in Guatemala is far fewer (see Grossmann 2002). Though nothing is definitive, I rely mainly on the findings and references used in the Pew Foundation's *Spirit and Power: A 10-Nation Survey of Pentecostals* (2006) as well as the work of Andrea Althoff (2005) and Jesús García-Ruiz (2004).

12. This commonly accepted four-part definition obscures the diversity of evangelical expression, effacing the fact that the term historically has been broad enough to include an assortment of distinct traditions: Dutch Reformed churches, Southern Baptists, some Episcopalians, and the majority of African American Protestant sects (Lofton 2008a, 224–228).

13. See "Weird Babel of Tongues," *Los Angeles Times,* April 18, 1906.

14. This history of Pentecostalism is based on Wacker 2001; Cox 1995; D. Miller 1997.

15. See Gustavo Gutiérrez, *A Theology of Liberation* ([1973] 1988).

16. The following history of Protestantism and, especially, Pentecostalism in Guatemala depends heavily on the Pew Forum's Historical Overview of Pentecostalism in Guatemala (Pew 2008).

17. The idea that citizenship rests on questions of belonging, especially national belonging, refers to a highly developed academic conversation not just on the formation of imagined communities (Anderson 1991), but also on the sociological construction of citizenship (Marshall 1950; Hindess 1993; Kofman 1995; Mann 1987; Turner 1993). See also Postero 2007.

18. Here it is appropriate to invoke Barbara Cruikshank's smart deconstruction of Alexis de Tocqueville's distinction between the subject and the citizen: "Whereas subjects behave themselves because an external force exerts power over them, citizens have the power to act for themselves; they are their own masters" (1999, 19–20). Though the two have long been understood as antitheses of each other, Cruikshank demonstrates that to be a citizen means being a subject to oneself—that there is no such thing as an inactive (or dependent) citizen since citizenship itself involves a range of self-governing practices.

19. This enduring division between the public sphere and the private sphere runs throughout the social scientific literature and is most acute when scholars speak about the division between Christianity and citizenship. See, for example, Parsons 1963; Berger 1986; Turner 1990. Will Kymlicka and Will Norman (1994) spot this assumption as central to the relationship between voluntary organizations and the formation of citizenship, while also pointing toward other advocates of this assumption, namely Michael Mann (1987), Mary Ann Glendon (1991), Michael Walzer (1992), and Susan Okin (1992). See also Nikolas Rose's genealogical deconstruction of the private-public divide in advanced Western democracies (1987).

20. See, for example, the work of Timothy Mitchell (2002) and Katherine Verdery (1998) for analyses applicable to the Guatemalan context.

21. Almost one million undocumented Guatemalans also currently live in the United States, and many of them sustain a connection to their homeland through neo-Pentecostal church networks (see chap. 6).

22. See Offit 2008.

23. Several very strong studies review the history of Guatemala in greater depth than I am able to do here. See, for example, the work of Carol A. Smith (1990), Rachel Sieder (1999), Arturo Taracena Arriola and Jean Piel (1995), David McCreery (1994), and Greg Grandin (2000, 2004). I have limited my historical discussion to those facts most relevant to the themes of neo-Pentecostal Christianity and citizenship.

24. See Schlesinger and Kinzer 1999.

25. This history is based on the work of Patrick Costello (1997).

26. The conclusion that periods of Guatemala's civil war are best understood as genocidal is not uncontested. Diane Nelson, for example, suggests that

questions of intent complicate the charge of genocide, given that genocide's legal construction pivots on the intent of the powerful to eradicate the powerless (2003).

27. See the work of Fischer and Brown 1996; Warren 1998; Handy 2002; Fischer 2002.

28. A brief note on violence and statistics in Guatemala: the numbers I employ throughout this book to approximate Guatemala's postwar violence are somewhat inconsistent. I am consistent with my sources, to be sure, but each organization uses its own methods to track crime and homicide rates. These methods included interpretive decisions about, for example, where Guatemala City begins and ends. For this reason, the statistics I cite may not present an entirely consistent statistical portrait of violence in postwar Guatemala, but they provide a trustworthy approximation.

29. This history is based on Virginia Garrard-Burnett's *Protestantism in Guatemala: Living in the New Jerusalem* (1998). Garrard-Burnett's work looms large in this section and this study.

30. See the work of David Smilde (2007) for a sociological exploration into why people convert.

31. The Pentecostal churches referred to here were not mega-churches but rather small family churches with relatively few congregants.

32. Dr. Harold Caballeros, "El desarrollo de una nación Cristiana" (December 12, 2002) (audiocassette).

33. This biblical review is based in part on a report of the Commission on Theology and Church Relations of the Lutheran Church (LCMS 1968). The conversation, it should be admitted, is both too much and too little. The intent is simply to introduce the fact that Christian and non-Christian thinkers have considered Christian citizenship to be an object of intellectual concern for millennia while also contrasting this relatively exclusive intellectual conversation with the everyday thoughts of Christians. The biblical and theological review of Christian citizenship is not meant to be exhaustive but rather suggestive of a field of intellectual concern.

34. This theological review of Christian citizenship is based in part on the work of Paul Barry Clarke (1994b, 61–68).

CHAPTER ONE

Epigraph: Agreement on the Strengthening of Civilian Power and on the Role of the Armed Forces in a Democratic Society (September 19, 1996). See Peace Accords 2006, 46.

1. The municipal government's citizenship campaign comes with neon yellow smocks that government workers wear. The smocks broadcast the campaign's slogan, Tú Eres la Ciudad.

2. Linda Green writes, further contextualizing the fearful and deeply complicated realities of wartime Guatemala: "I met several women whose sons had been in the military when their husbands had been killed by the army. In one disturbing situation, I interviewed a widow who described the particularly gruesome death of her husband at the hands of the army, while behind her on the wall prominently displayed was a photograph of her son in his Kaibil [a special operations commando unit] uniform. When I asked about him, she acknowledged his occasional presence in the household and said nothing more. I was at first at a loss to explain the situation and her silence; later I came to understand it as part of the rational inconsistencies that are built into the logic of her fractured life. On a purely objective level, it is dangerous to talk about such things with strangers. Perhaps she felt her son's photograph might provide protection in the future" (1994, 234).

3. See, e.g., Julia Paley (2001). She observes that civil society and citizenship have become key concepts both for countries managing transitions to democracy and for those studying such transitions (143–147).

4. In using "indexical," I follow the work of Charles Peirce to mean anything that points to something: "An index is a sign which refers to the Object that it denotes by virtue of being really affected by the Object" (1955, 102). This includes any sign that helps to create a social identity or social location; pronouns are classic examples. The difference between *I* and *you* is a difference of social location. See, for example, Emile Benveniste's "On the Nature of Pronouns" (1971, 217–232), in which he argues that *I* and *you* refer to the act of dialogue, which sociolinguistic's "pragmatic turn" would recognize as a distinct form of sociality (e.g., Silverstein and Urban 1996). In the act of dialogue, *I* signifies "the person who is uttering the present instance of the discourse containing I," while *you* means the "individual spoken to in the present instance of discourse containing the linguistic instance *you*" (Benveniste 1971, 218). For Benveniste, *I* and *you* function within the dialogic space of direct address, forming distinct conditions of personhood.

5. There are innumerable ways to footnote anthropology's commitment to difference, epistemologically and methodologically speaking, but Bronislaw Malinowski's famous depiction of the ethnographic predicament will suffice: "Imagine yourself suddenly set down surrounded by all your gear, alone on a tropical beach close to a native village while the launch or dinghy which has bought you sails away out of sight" (Malinowski 1922, 4). Anthropological research has long been predicated on an experience of disconnection and an interest in difference. Clifford Geertz adds: "The usual tack [of the anthropologist] is to begin with our own, more or less unexamined, everyday sense of what 'the family', 'the state', or, in the case at hand, 'religion' comes to, what counts for *us* as kinship, or government, or faith, and what, family-resemblance style, looks . . . well . . . resemblant, amongst those whose life-ways we are

trying to portray" (2005, 5). The anthropologist, historically speaking, has long begun with the familiar, has found the strange, and has used this disconnect as an epistemological point of departure for larger reflections about the nature of any given category.

6. Here it is useful to rely on what Mikhail Bakhtin would call the *centripetal* aspects of language (1981). His theory describes how ideology consolidates a discourse and then flattens that discourse's diversity of voices and opinions. Ethnographically speaking, this means that the authors of citizenship campaigns draw from a limited universe of resources, such as the ones already noted within the text: lectures, literature, and think tanks.

7. For a similar critique, see, e.g., Lemke 2001, 202; Burchell 1993, 275–276.

8. By *aspirational,* I mean forward-looking documents that aspire to something more, in terms of development, and that often use goals, replete with metrics, to assess where a country currently is and where that country wants to end. For analyses of Guatemala's aspirational documents, see Sridhar 2007 and K. O'Neill 2005.

9. I recognize that by framing the following information with the language of weight, the issues that I describe gain a certain kind of density, even an ontological status. This is intentional. The weight of postwar Guatemala, from an ethnographic perspective, does sit on people's shoulders—as an object, as something that people feel comfortable naming; informants, for example, often noted that they would "feel the weight of the world on their shoulders" ["Siento el peso del mundo en mis hombros"]. I comment on this sensation in this book's conclusion. In this chapter, however, I both construct and deconstruct—both confirm as real and expose as manufactured—what I understand as the weight of postwar Guatemala.

10. Dipesh Chakrabarty interrogates the myth of Europe, which is often taken as not only the paragon of development but also the moral and cultural point of comparison with non-Western countries. This imaginary is part and parcel of the social scientific imagination, Chakrabarty suggests. Guatemala is not simply "not yet" on its own; rather, it is "not yet" (or underdeveloped) because of its relationship to Europe. Seen from the perspective of Europe, postcolonial Guatemala will always be lacking.

11. It is helpful to use the terms *freedom* and *agency,* even if only briefly, during an exploration of postwar citizenship and the weight that citizenship provides postwar Guatemalans. It would be misguided, for example, to read this ethnography as simply an instance in which Guatemalans become saddled with responsibility. The image of "saddled" is important here: from on high, a weight is strapped onto someone. The enduring "paradox of participation," to quote Julia Paley (2001), is that the promise of citizenship delivers to postwar Guatemalans a deep sense of meaning that they themselves seek out, accept, and cultivate while at the same time limiting the ways in which they can participate

as citizens. If the work of Michel Foucault on the concept of governmentality teaches us anything, along with the work of Patrick Joyce (2003) and Nikolas Rose (1999), it is that one can never be simply a subject or a citizen—disempowered or empowered. Rather, freedom and agency are themselves techniques of control through which citizens willingly become subject to themselves.

12. This sense of incompleteness (todavía no) goes hand in hand with the idea that the postwar context promises Guatemala "something better" (algo más) (Fischer and Benson 2005).

13. A crisp consolidation of these statistics comes from the work of Archana Sridhar (2007). These statistics can be found through the U.S. State Department (2006) and the World Bank (2000).

14. The Comisión para el Esclarecimiento Histórico (CEH), one of the country's two truth commission reports, makes clear that the armed conflict "exacerbated the traditional weakness of the State regarding tax collection and intensified private sector opposition to necessary tax reform" (CEH 1999). The report demonstrates that during the height of armed conflict, from 1978 to 1984, when state violence reached genocidal proportion, taxes as a percentage of GDP "dropped constantly." In 1984 taxes as a percentage of GDP reached 7.1 percent, which is the lowest level in recent history.

15. Several very smart Guatemalan tax pamphlets and books provide the statistical backbone for this paragraph. Those citations include the work of Menaldo and Morales (2000), Martini (2000), Valdez (2000). Further statistical support was provided by an article through Reuters (2001) and a USAID (2001) document. See also Sridhar (2007).

16. See Fischer and Benson 2005; Gwynne and Kay 1999; Kay 1989; and Oglesby 2004.

17. Joaquín Salvador Lavado, "Quino," *Prensa Libre*, August 31, 2005.

18. Lorena Seijo, "Ciudadanos angustiados por violencia y falta de recursos," *Prensa Libre*, June 15, 2008. The numbers here are not particularly important. The study itself seems to have adhered to certain social scientific standards, but the real interest is the instinct to pursue such a study—that such a study would produce not just findings of social scientific interest but ones that would resonate with readers who are themselves made to feel anxious by their country's high levels of crime and violence.

19. Scholarship on gangs in Guatemala has varied in its quality and depth. One report on gangs in Central America, however, has been particularly well received (Arana 2005). Arana suggests: "In the past few years, as Washington has focused its attention on the Middle East, it has virtually ignored a dangerous phenomenon close to home. Ultraviolent youth gangs, spawned in the ghettos of Los Angeles and other U.S. cities, have slowly migrated south to Central America, where they have transformed themselves into powerful, cross-border crime networks. With the United States preoccupied elsewhere, the gangs have

grown in power and numbers; today, local officials estimate their size at 70,000–100,000 members. The *marabuntas,* or *maras,* as they are known (after a deadly species of local ants), now pose the most serious challenge to peace in the region since the end of Central America's civil wars" (2005, 98–99).

20. See, e.g., ERIC et al. 2001; 2004a; 2004b; Fyke and Meye 2008.

21. See Sanford 2003a, 2003b.

22. See the municipal government's pamphlet *Tú eres la ciudad.*

23. See Véliz 2006.

24. See Álvaro Arzú's public speech "Tú eres la ciudad" (January 15, 2008).

25. Director of communications for Mayor Arzú, interview by author, March 7, 2008, Guatemala City.

26. Ibid.

27. Ibid.

28. See GuateAmala's pamphlet *¿Quiénes somos?* (2006f).

29. See GuateAmala's pamphlet *Declaración de propósitos* (2006e).

30. For quotes by Otilia Lux and Juan Mauricio Wurmser, see *GuateAmala's* pamphlet *Cultura de la vida: Forum 2006* (2006c).

31. See GuateAmala's pamphlets *Cultura de los sueños* (2006d); and *Cultura de la ciudadanía* (2006a).

32. See GuateAmala's pamphlet *El cambio de GUATE empieza con vos* (2006d).

33. GuateAmala 2006e.

34. See the El Shaddai Sunday bulletin, *Fortaleciendo el vínculo del amor* (July 2, 2006).

35. Caballeros, "Hacia una visión de una nación Cristiana."

36. See Stoll 1994.

37. Dr. Harold Caballeros, "Escogé Tú" (December 18, 1991) (audiocassette).

38. Ibid.

39. See Guatemala City Municipal Government, *Soy la revolución* (August 4, 2006) (pamphlet).

CHAPTER TWO

First epigraph: Augustine 1961, 10.3.

Second epigraph: Jung [1933] 2005, 35.

1. Valderrama 2004a, 25.

2. Modern virtue ethics, in light of Aristotle and Plato, stresses the centrality of moral education. This should be understood as an emphasis not on rules but rather on training character (Carr and Steutel 1999). Thomas Aquinas's approach to virtue, moreover, stresses the will. Since humans are susceptible to evil and thus must wrestle with their will to make good rather than sinful judgments, it is important for Christians to cultivate virtues that will guide their

decisions in life. To be virtuous is a sign that the Christian has trained his or her will to be obedient to natural law (Pope 2002).

3. As Daniel Harrington and James Keenan point out, Pope Innocent III (1160–1216) understood the masses to be damned unless they confessed annually and openly to their sins. To meet this ministerial need, Innocent charged the Dominicans and the Franciscans to become trained as confessors. In turn, they developed confessional manuals based on the seven deadly sins. Martin Luther and John Calvin argued during the Reformation that the Ten Commandments were more important than the seven deadly sins. Neither disputed the centrality of the confessional act. At the same time, Erasmus's *Handbook for the Christian Soldier* appeared in 1503 to solidify the popularity and relative usefulness of manuals as a genre of literature (Harrington and Keenan 2002, 1–8).

4. Caballeros, "Hacia una visión de una nación Cristiana."

5. Avery Dickins de Girón (2006) argues that like most Latin American capitals, Guatemala City is considered a dangerous urban sprawl marked by crime and gang violence. Although the violence remains concentrated in the capital, it fuels a private security industry that connects rural populations to Guatemala City both economically and socially. This linkage is forged primarily by indigenous men from small towns who provide the labor for the police, military, and security agencies in the capital. Their role in combating urban violence stems from economic necessity, yet working as a security guard brings a young man status in his rural village; it allows him to support his family in a way that would otherwise be impossible. Her work contrasts postwar violence to the state-sponsored violence characteristic of Guatemala's civil war and places rural migrants working in the security industry within the longer history of rural migration in Guatemala.

6. Foucault uses this phrase to discuss Stoic examinations of conscience that at first seem similar to the Christian confession because the penitent is "both the judge and the accused," in that "the subject divides itself in two and organizes a judicial scene, where it plays both roles at once" (1993, 206). For the purposes of my own ethnographic examination, I maintain this meaning even though Foucault goes onto explain how this Stoic examination of conscience does not "judge" but rather "administers."

7. What follows in this section is offered not as an original contribution to the history of community policing in Latin America, but as a summary of research done by others—particularly those who have completed research in postwar Guatemala: Hugo Frühling (2004, 2007) and Laura Chinchilla (2004). This section is meant to make the overall analysis of cellular culture more relevant to community policing.

8. Teresa Caldeira (2002), for example, notes that in São Paulo there is popular support for "violent police" that coexists with the victimization of working-class people. Caldeira argues that this paradox emerges from a historical disrespect for civil rights as well as a cynicism regarding the justice system.

9. See, e.g., Olga López, "Crearán policía comunitaria," *Prensa Libre,* March 16, 2005; Lorena Seijo, "Policía será más accesible," *Prensa Libre,* October 9, 2007; Alberto Ramírez, "Tránsito, bajo el control edil," *Prensa Libre,* October 28, 2004; Acisclo Valladares Molina, "Policía Comunitaria, seguridad y municipio," *El Periodico,* July 7, 2005; Claudia Méndez Villaseñor, "Sitiados por la violencia," *Prensa Libre,* February 21, 2005; Grupo Seguridad y Justicia, "Atemorizados por inseguridad," *Prensa Libre,* July 14, 2004.

10. In a very short but altogether very influential article, Deleuze (1992) notes that Michel Foucault rightly captured the productiveness of disciplinary societies: prisons, schools, hospitals, and factories. Yet Deleuze argues that "societies of control" now replace disciplinary societies. The family, school, and army are no longer distinct spaces that converge toward an owner but are now something akin to a single corporation owned by stockholders. Deleuze's point is that physical barriers are not nearly as important as corporations that track movements. My analysis of the mega-church cell, then, suggests that the cell, or even the mega-church, functions not like a prison, school, hospital, or factory but like a flexible and fragmented corporation that seeks control over the individual through what Deleuze would call "perpetual training."

11. In using *panoptic practices,* I refer to Michel Foucault's analysis of the panopticon in *Discipline and Punish: The Birth of the Prison* (1977). The panopticon is a style of building authored by the utilitarian philosopher Jeremy Bentham in the late eighteenth century. The panopticon involves a central watchtower from which a guard has a view into each cell. The guard's dilemma is that he or she cannot observe every prisoner at every moment, but the panopticon's power lies in its ability to convince the prisoner that he or she can be watched at any given moment. This potential for continual surveillance proves, Bentham announces and Foucault concurs, an effective means of control. A prisoner does not need to be watched to be controlled. The prisoner must simply know that he or she can be watched at any given moment.

12. John Locke argues that our ideas result from sensation (i.e., the body) or reflection (i.e., the mind). In a famous lecture, Locke creates an analogy between the mind and a "dark room" that has only a narrow aperture. Locke then compares ideas to images projected onto the back of the room through the aperture. For the purpose of my own ethnographic analysis, what is important here is that the Western intellectual tradition, Christian or otherwise, has long imagined the interior world as a complicated and sometimes shadowy domain, as a place that can be explored. Augustine, for example, imagined the interior world, like so many other Christian saints, architecturally—as a large palace with rooms, stairways, and inner sanctums (see Cary 2003).

13. Dr. Harold Caballeros, "Pongamos en práctica nuestros valores" (March 9, 2008) (audiocassette).

14. Caballeros, "Hacia una visión de una nación Cristiana."

15. By using the phrase "art of listening," Foucault refers to a distinction between Plato's interest in cultivating dialogue and the Pythagorean cultivation of silence and listening (1997, 236). These are two very different activities that need to be cultivated, learned, and even practiced. Foucault's use of the word *art* is telling—listening is not inactivity but rather a certain kind of work that takes times to perfect.

16. My continued interest in the work of Cruikshank stems from her ability to identify the self as the field on which political action takes place. As I mention elsewhere in this book, my understanding of Christian citizenship rests on Cruikshank's collapsing the distinction between subject and citizen in such a way that one is able to understand the citizen as subject to himself or herself.

17. Caballeros, "Hacia una visión de una nación Cristiana."

18. Caballeros, "Pongamos en práctica nuestros valores."

19. Dr. Harold Caballeros, "El desarrollo de una nación Cristiana" (December 12, 2002) (audiocassette).

20. Ibid.

21. Ibid.

22. Caballeros, "Pongamos en práctica nuestros valores."

23. By viewing discipline as "a political economy of detail," Foucault is able to shift an understanding of power from a repressive and ideological model to one that is productive—that creates, or generates, certain kinds of persons: "[Discipline] produces reality; it produces domains of objects and rituals of truth. The individual and the knowledge that may be gained of him belong to this production" (1977, 194). The neo-Pentecostal cell does not deter the member from doing certain things as opposed to others but, more interestingly, makes the cell member into a certain kind of person, here a Christian citizen, as opposed to another kind of person.

24. Joyce's concern is with liberalism and the modern city and how governmental entities become scripted into a cityscape (as well as into the people who live in and through these cityscapes). Modernizing cities implemented lighted streets so that people could walk at night with a greater sense of security. Streetlights as a modern development pursued in the name of freedom, Joyce notes, fomented new forms of surveillance, such as the policeman's beat. Joyce notes that ultimately freedom contributes to the governance of people, which is an observation that I apply to the cellular context. Truth, the Christian adage notes, will set you free—but it is through this very freedom that people come to be governed.

25. Nikolas Rose builds on Foucault's notion of power's productive dimensions. See note 22.

26. John Austin demonstrates that language's performative dimensions actually accomplish things. Couples, for example, officially marry after saying, "I do." While exploring "how to do things with words," Austin also takes note of

those moments when words fail to do the things that they were intended to do, which he calls misfires (1975).

27. See Kay Arthur et al., *How Do You Know God's Your Father?* (2001), back cover.

28. Ibid., 9.

29. Ibid.

30. Bibliotherapy is not a new concept, although it has gained popularity in North American therapeutic discourse. At least since the 1930s, and especially after World War II, there was a sense that reading and writing were healing activities. See Hartman 1951.

31. The idea here is that shame contributes to the management of Maria's inner world, her sense of Christianness, and what she does in the name of belonging and responsibility. Nikolas Rose observes: "Shame here was to entail an anxiety over the exterior deportment of the self, likened to an injunction to care for oneself in the name of the public manifestation of moral character. These strategies govern all the more effectively because each individual is to play his or her part in the games of civility. Yet simultaneously they produce new spatial and topographical divisions between those within and those outside civility, and are linked to a whole set of new inventions for disciplining those whose transgressions are now seen as an affront to the order of proper comportment and propriety" (1999, 73–74).

32. Arthur et al. 2001, 9.

33. Ibid.

34. Ibid., 20.

35. See Valderrama 2004a and 2004b.

36. Valderrama 2004a, 8–9.

37. Ibid., 7.

38. Ibid., 6.

39. Ibid., 8.

40. By the "autonomization of society," it is generally meant that citizens do not need to be governed directly or constantly but can instead govern themselves.

41. Valderrama 2004a, 35.

42. Ibid.

43. Ibid., 37.

44. Ibid., 38.

45. Ibid.

46. Ibid.

47. See, e.g., Davis 1990; Caldeira 2001; Low 2001.

48. Villaseñor, "Sitiados por la violencia."

49. Neo-Pentecostals' concern for the interior world and the role of the self within history makes the self the presumed engine of Guatemalan history—the idea that *you,* rather than (or alongside) history or the economy, shape Guatemala.

CHAPTER THREE

First epigraph: *The New Oxford Annotated Bible* (Metzger and Murphy 1991). Second epigraph: Remarque 1929, 12.

1. In a flashy show of faith, Pastor Cash Luna of La Casa de Dios allowed spiritual warfare's narrative to mix with Guatemala's own recent history of guerrilla warfare, encouraging his congregants to make themselves elite commandos for Christ.

2. Images of battle and the language of warfare exist at the heart of the Christian imagination. Erasmus's *Handbook for the Christian Soldier* appeared in 1503 and solidified the popularity of spiritual warfare (Harrington and Keenan 2002, 1–8); Sabine Baring-Gould's nineteenth-century English hymn "Onward, Christian Soldiers" testifies to the importance of warring for Jesus Christ, of "suffering like a good soldier of Christ Jesus" (2 Timothy 2:3). As a metaphor rooted in biblical stories, spiritual warfare has proven a flexible image that communities have molded for their own purposes. Among early Christians, for example, monastic authors used the metaphor of combat to "make the monk"—to forge a sense of masculine devoutness and defiance in spite of Satan (Brakke 2006).

3. Finke (1990) and Iannaccone (1990) argue that the United States has a "free market" when it comes to religion: "Deregulating the market increases the level of religious mobilization" (Finke 1990, 622). The general idea is that the United States' religious plurality has led to a religious market best understood in economic terms, such as rational choice. My own concern is that a market approach to religion fails to account for unquantifiable dimensions, such as responsibility and belonging, in any meaningful way. The ultimate critique is that even if religion can be understood in market terms, then this approach is the least compelling, ethnographically speaking. For further critique, see Bruce 1993.

4. Every citizen in ancient Greece was either a soldier or a military officer trained and on call for active duty (Adcock 1957). Rachel Claire Snyder (1999), however, argues that modern notions of the citizen-soldier begin with Machiavelli, who provides modern republicanism with one of its first images of a citizen as an active member of a militia. Snyder notes that military service indoctrinated individuals with a particularly active sense of civic participation, which was (and arguably still is) masculine in both structure and function. The active citizen as well as the active solider, Snyder suggests, must have a certain degree of masculine bravado that has since defined what political scientists understand as the public sphere.

5. Alberto Mendoza, "Guatemala: Army Losing Fight against Crime," Inter Press Service, September 27, 2007; Dina Fernández, "Kaibiles en el Congo," *Prensa Libre*, January 30, 2006.

6. Frank Jack Daniel and Mica Rosenberg, "Guatemala's Colom to Attack Drug Gangs," Reuters, November 6, 2007.

7. See, e.g., Julieta Sandoval, "Ofreció 'mano dura' con sus propios fun-cionarios," *Prensa Libre,* May 27, 2007; Conié Reynoso and Gema Palencia, "Discurso y canción de mano dura," *Prensa Libre,* October 21, 2007; M. Rodríguez and O. Figueroa, "Mano dura contra mano aguada," *Prensa Libre,* June 4, 2007; Marielos Monzón, "Detrás de la mano dura," *Prensa Libre,* October, 23, 2007.

8. Herbert Hernandez and Brendan Kolbay, "Guatemala to Open Army Files to Probe War Crimes," Reuters, February 25, 2008.

9. Dr. Harold Caballeros, "La batalla entre dos reinos" (October 28, 2001) (audiocassette).

10. Ibid.

11. Ibid.

12. Caballeros 2001, 25.

13. Ibid., 60.

14. Bronislaw Malinowski, for example, writes in "The Role of Magic and Religion" that "magic is to be expected and generally to be found whenever man comes to an unbridgeable gap, a hiatus in his knowledge or in his powers of practical control, and yet has to continue in his pursuit" (1972, 108), whereas religion is "born not out of speculation or reflection . . . but rather out of the real tragedies of human life, out of the conflict between human plans and real-ities" (1972, 111). The magical dimensions of neo-Pentecostal spiritual warfare, from Malinowski's perspective, would be their faithful "pursuit" in spite of "an unbridgeable gap" and their lack of "practical control."

15. Pilon de Pacheco 1998, 6.

16. Caballeros 2001, 94.

17. Ibid., 22.

18. Ibid., 34.

19. Pilon de Pacheco 1998, 23.

20. Caballeros 2001, 8.

21. Ibid., 32. See also K. O'Neill 2007. In a textual analysis of one of the National Rifle Association's longest-running columns, I demonstrate how unlikely candidates, such as children and elderly persons, can indeed become not only heroes but also heroically masculine. Just as the biblical David's boyish features made him an unexpected model of biblical masculinity during his fight with Goliath, so too do the age, sex, and health of El Shaddai's Christian sol-diers make them unexpected (but nevertheless real) models of Christian mas-culinity. It is a soldier's ability to overcome his or her threat through manly action that allows him or her to achieve masculinity within a neo-Pentecostal worldview.

22. Caballeros 2001, 8.

23. Ibid., 20.

24. Ibid., 21.

25. Ibid., 5, 6.

26. Ibid., 11, 19.

27. Ibid., 139.

28. This quote from Dostoyevsky comes from an often-cited interview between Philippe Nemo and Emmanuel Levinas. Nemo asked Levinas whether "the other" is also responsible for the self. Levinas responded: "Perhaps but that is not his affair. . . . The intersubjective relation is a nonsymmetrical relation. It is precisely as the relationship between the Other and me is not reciprocal that I am subjected to no Other; and I am 'subject' essentially in this sense. It is I who support all. You know that sentence in Dostoyevsky: 'We are all guilty of all and for all men before all, and I more than the others.' This is . . . because I am responsible for a total responsibility, which answers for all the others and for all in the others, even for their responsibility" (Levinas 1985: 95). Of import here is not simply the language of responsibility that Levinas develops, but also the radical asymmetry that makes Levinas's philosophy so challenging. This asymmetry—this sense that I am more responsible for you than you are for me—has ethnographic salience in postwar Guatemala. The neo-Pentecostal imagines himself or herself to be responsible for it all.

29. Caballeros 2001, 24, 23.

30. See *Oremos Online,* www.oremos.net (accessed February 15, 2006).

31. Ibid.

32. Ibid.

33. Ibid.

34. Ibid.

35. See, e.g., Olga López, Coralia Orantes, and Jéssica Osorio, "Viva queda fuera de la contienda electoral," *Prensa Libre,* July 7, 2007; Jéssica Osorio, "Harold Caballeros: Estoy tranquilo, vamos bien," *Prensa Libre,* June 22, 2007; "Caballeros descarta participar" *Prensa Libre,* July 10, 2007; Jéssica Osorio and Wendy Ruano, "Viva, en riesgo de no participar en comicios," *Prensa Libre,* June 21, 2007.

36. Grady 2004.

37. Sjöberg 1993, 115.

38. Caballeros 1993, 136.

39. Ibid.

CHAPTER FOUR

First epigraph: Hegel 1954, 268.

Second epigraph: Foucault 1991, 100.

1. In *The History of Sexuality: An Introduction,* Michel Foucault notes that sexuality for reproduction became linked to the study of population growth. Morality's intent is not to eliminate sexuality but to harness sexuality for reasons

of health and procreation. He writes: "At the heart of this economic and political problem of population was sex; it was necessary to analyze the birthrate, the age of marriage, the legitimate and illegitimate births, the precocity and frequency of sexual relations, the ways of making them fertile or sterile, the effects of unmarried life or the prohibitions, the impact of contraceptive practices—of those notorious 'deadly secrets' which demographers on the eve of the revolution knew were already familiar to the inhabitants of the countryside" (1978, 25–26).

2. See, e.g., McClain 2002; Cott 2000; Dowd 2000; Hartog 2000; Nock 1998; Blakenhorn 1995; Dennis and Erdos 1993; Morgan 1995. See also Donzelot 1979. The work of Nancy Cott, for example, argues from a historical perspective that American political theory harbors an assumption that makes intuitive a link between the health of the nation and a particular kind of marriage: unions that are Christian, heterosexual, and monogamous (2000, 9–23). By no means endorsing this particular vision of marriage, Cott details how certain marital policies have contributed to the formation not just of social standards but also of the nation's citizenry.

3. W. Bradford Wilcox's *Soft Patriarchs, New Men: How Christianity Shapes Fathers and Husbands* (2004) is in many ways a response to this spike in evangelical conversations on fatherhood. The study contrasts fatherhood practices in mainstream Protestant households with those in evangelical households in the United States. His conclusion is that there does exist a dramatic difference between the sociological realities of these two religious spheres when it comes to fatherhood. There is a marked difference between how mainstream Protestants and their evangelical counterparts imagine fatherhood, even though there is very little difference between their actual practice.

4. Homosexuality is not a social issue that is "on the table" for discussion in Guatemala. Most probably, Dr. Caballeros draws from North American neo-Pentecostal conversations that place homosexuality at the center of social chaos. See Hardisty 1999.

5. For the Promise Keepers, see, e.g., Gutterman 2005; A. Smith 2008; Bartkowski 2004; Rhys Williams 2001. For Focus on the Family, see, e.g., Apostolidis 2000. Gutterman, for example, shows how the Promise Keepers, a conservative evangelical men's group in the United States, constructed its own American jeremiad during the so-called culture wars of the 1990s. The group saw the American family as in crisis and taught that Christian manhood was the answer. Inspired by conservative Christian ideals, the Promise Keepers educated the faithful about how to act like "real" Christian men for the sake not just of the family but also of the nation (2005, 108).

6. On the notion of problematization Foucault writes: "Problematization doesn't mean the representation of a pre-existent object, nor the creation through discourse of an object that doesn't exist. It's the set of discursive or nondiscursive practices that makes something enter into the play of the true

and false, and constitutes it as an object for thought (whether under the form of moral reflection, scientific knowledge, political analysis, etc.)" (1988, 257). See also Castel 1994; Collier 2001.

7. The mention of public health and public policy is to suggest not that there is a right or a wrong way to understand fatherhood as a problem, but that there is more than one way to make fatherhood a problem. Much of this chapter probes the strangeness of fatherhood as Guatemala's problem—when there could be so many other potential problems. At the same time it is important to note that even the very problem of fatherhood itself has a number of different kinds of potential formations and that neo-Pentecostalism provides one.

8. Dr. Harold Caballeros, "El padre: Un ser especial" (June 18, 2000) (audio-cassette).

9. Ibid.

10. Ibid.

11. Ibid.

12. Medical professionals duly note that young children need a great deal of affection from their parents for the sake of development. Without wanting to pursue the ways in which the medical profession generates a certain kind of discourse about child care that is itself a recognizable technology, I am advancing the point in this chapter that neo-Pentecostalism advocates a certain kind of affection that is forever linked with the fate of the nation.

13. The contrast between Heidegger's and Foucault's notions of technology is instructive. Heidegger, for one, is concerned mostly with our orientation to technology. If we accept this formulation of the problem, then it becomes clear that our response to the various problems brought about by technology cannot be solved simply by making the technology better. Heidegger reflects on the ways in which people relate to technology and how people think about technology (1977). Foucault, on the other hand, draws from the Greek work *technē,* meaning "art," to refer to practical rationalities. The emphasis here is on the intimate relationship among the subject, the *technē* (or art of living), and the process through which the subject becomes reconfigured as a subject by way of the *technē.* Foucault's emphasis on *technē* as a rationality rather than as an instrument that one can pick up and put down allows fatherhood to be understood as a productive technology that prompts men with children to live differently (Dreyfus 1984).

14. Caballeros, "El padre."

15. In using the term "the new prudentialism," Pat O'Malley (1992) leans heavily on a nuanced sense of risk as a form of social control. Neo-Pentecostal formations of fatherhood, for example, commonly employ the language of risk when discussing children. Active fatherhood lowers the relative risk that a child will be delinquent. Important here is that O'Malley develops the idea that risk is both a means of social control (e.g., risk makes men with children do certain

things as opposed to others) and a cultural artifact. Risk is not a preexisting fact. Rather, specific cultural and political contexts, such as the practice of father-hood, make risk.

16. Hormachea 2003.

17. Ibid., 21.

18. Ibid., 17.

19. Ibid., 24.

20. Ibid., 17.

21. Ibid., 88.

22. Ibid., 34.

23. Ibid., 92.

24. Foucault notes that mnemonic devices have long been technologies of the self: "Seneca's *De Ira* (book 3) contains some traces of the old tradition. He describes an examination of conscience. The same thing was recommended by the Epicureans, and the practice was rooted in the Pythagorean tradition. The goal was the purification of the conscience using a mnemonic device. Do good things, have a good examination of the self, and a good sleep follows together with good dreams, which is contact with the gods" (1997, 237)

25. See Omartian 2005a, 6.

26. Ibid., 10.

27. Ibid., 8.

28. Undocumented immigrants cross the U.S.–Mexican border each year in search of work that ranges from agricultural to industrial in American locales both rural and urban. These men and women, however, rarely return to Latin America. Aggressive immigration policies and the further militarization of the border have interrupted the two-way flow of migrant labor and currently force undocumented immigrants to settle in the United States rather than return to Mexico and Guatemala, for example. Douglas Massey et al. (2004), in fact, argue that that U.S. immigration policy toward Mexico attempts to stop a migrant flow that grows out of market forces but in fact simply restricts the movement of labor from returning to Latin America.

29. Caballeros, "El padre."

30. Ibid.

31. Here the work of Matthew C. Gutmann becomes instructive (1996; 2003). In *Changing Men and Masculinities in Latin America* (2003), a range of articles addresses "men-*as-men* in Latin America" (2003, 1). Of most importance for this study is how Gutmann's volume addresses the relationship between local and global changes on gender and masculinity. See also Elizabeth E. Brusco's *The Reformation of Machismo: Evangelical Conversion and Gender in Colombia* (1995).

32. An important amendment is that in 2007 Dr. Harold Caballeros gave control of El Shaddai ministries to his wife, Pastor Cecilia Caballeros. The Guatemalan government's separation of church and state does not allow active

clergymen or -women to run for elected office. Pastor Cecilia Caballeros's very public role in the El Shaddai community is one exceptionally strong example of women in high levels of authority in neo-Pentecostal contexts.

33. The work of Saba Mahmood (2005) addresses this tension between submission and resistance through a critique of liberal politics and challenges popular assumptions on freedom, agency, subordination, and resistance. Mahmood demonstrates that women's cultivation of pietistic attitudes and emotions cannot be reduced to either resistance or subordination. Something similar could be argued for those neo-Pentecostals who understand themselves as supportive wives but contributing members of Guatemalan society.

34. Matthew C. Gutmann (1996) offers a compelling corrective to stereotypical formations of *machismo* through a study of masculinities in Mexico City.

CHAPTER FIVE

First epigraph: Williams 1973, 1.

Second epigraph: West 2004.

1. In many parts of the world, including Guatemala, neoliberal reforms succeeded in curbing inflation, encouraging foreign investment, and generating new export industries (Portes and Roberts 2004). At the same time, neoliberalism has been implicated in nearly all the social, political, and economic ills that plague the developing world today. The policies opened up many Latin American, Asian, and African nations as essentially unregulated sources of cheap labor and natural resources for the United States and Europe, perpetuating colonial legacies of exploitation and inequality (Goldman 2005).

2. For more on the concept of moral geography, see P. Thomas 2002, as well as Ferguson 1992; Comaroff and Comaroff 1987; Raymond Williams 1973.

3. An influential study for this chapter has been Catherine A. Lutz and Jane L. Collins's *Reading National Geographic* (1993). Their theoretical approach to texts and the production of difference has strongly influenced the way I have situated Manos de Amor publications in this chapter.

4. See Frisby and Featherstone 1997; Soja 2000; S. Graham 2001. Also, it is important to note that many geographers would reject outright the ability of a city to be distinct from the country. The discursive construction of city and country can result in two imagined worlds, but the material reality is quite different, as the city and the country always function as interrelated social formations (Caldeira 2001; Soja 2000; Sassen 2001; Karsten 2003; England 1993).

5. The following history of Guatemala City is based on the work of Gellert (1995); Gellert and Pinto Soria (1990); Gellert and Palma (1999); Webre (1989); Orellana Gonzáles (1978); AVANCSO (2003); Bastos (2000); Camus (2002); Castillo (1995); Morán Mérida (1997); Murphy (2004); Nimatuj (2002); Pinillos (1977); and C. Smith (1984).

6. Michael J. Tottens, "In Guatemala City," *Middle East Journal* (November 25, 2003), www.michaeltotten.com/archives/2003/11/in-guatemala-city.php.

7. Santiago Bastos and Manuela Camus have produced a series of joint studies of Maya migrants to the capital (1995, 1997, 1998; see also Camus 2002) that document emerging urban Maya identities.

8. Here I rely on the scholarship of Ulf Hannerz and his understanding of how "boundary-crossings" and "long-distance cultural flows" contribute to the production of community. Of particular interest is his sociological understanding of networks: "In more sociological terms, the habitat of an agent could be said to consist of a network of direct and indirect relationships, stretching out wherever they may, within or across national boundaries" (1996, 46). See also Hannerz 1992.

9. "¡Feliz Día Papá!" (June 18, 2006) (El Shaddai Sunday bulletin).

10. Ibid.

11. This is not to say that Guatemala's rural countryside is in fact peaceful. One dramatic story provides a glimpse of the kinds of violence taking place beyond the capital city. Brent Metz, for example, reports on the abduction of a ladina girl in Camotán. I quote at length:

> The Thursday before, a 9-year old Ladina girl, Alba Mishel España Díaz, was abducted around lunchtime in neighboring Camotán, a hot Guatemalan town of about 1,000 people near the Honduran border. . . . Alba Mishel's mother, relatives and friends frantically searched for her door to door. . . . Then, the mother received a call, "I know where your child is." She recognized the voice as that of local Marisol Martínez, who had been suspected of child trafficking. A mob raced to her house and held her hostage until she confessed the girl's whereabouts. She claimed to have nothing to do with the abduction, but premonitions told her that the girl was at a crossroads village about 20 miles away. There the mob scoured every home, but no Alba Mishel. Enraged, the mob continued to pressure Martínez, but she pleaded ignorance. At 2:00 pm the next day, Alba Mishel's body was found outside of town. Her eyes, scalp and many internal organs, including heart and lungs, were missing, and according to a regional doctor, serving as coroner, the body showed signs of rape and death by a blow to the head. The mob responded by dousing Martínez in gasoline, forcing her to confess that two local sisters, Marciana y Jesús Interiano, had offered her 1,000 quetzals (about $130) to deliver the girl to them. The mob set on the sisters, lynching one and lighting the other afire before the police intervened to save her, but the police themselves were attacked and forced to flee. Both Martínez and the seriously burned Jesús Interiano were placed in custody (2008, 28).

12. Hugo Alvarado, "Harold Caballeros: 'Hay que expulsarlos,'" *Prensa Libre,* June 18, 2008.

13. "¡No te puedes perder!" (July 23, 2006) (El Shaddai Sunday bulletin).

14. "Jesús: La razón de la navidad" (December 23, 2006) (El Shaddai Sunday bulletin).

15. See "Concierto de exaltación" (July 30, 2006), also "¡Inscríbete ya!" (September 17, 2006) (both El Shaddai Sunday bulletins).

16. "¡Inscríbete ya!"

17. "Los pasos del hombre son ordenados por Dios" (February 4, 2007) (El Shaddai Sunday bulletin).

18. It should be noted, at least briefly, that Dumont in this quote addresses the Indian caste system and not Christianity and that Dumont's analysis has received two major strands of criticism. The first is that Dumont deals with traditional rather than contemporary Indian societies. The second is that Dumont's association of an individual with his or her caste does not hold up to ethnographic scrutiny. See Béteille 1986.

19. Kathryn Lofton notes that "even within Wesleyan lore, cleanliness was a minor thesis, as Wesley's own 1764 treatise, *Primitive Physick,* devoted no special part to bathing, despite its comprehensive discussion of home remedies" (2008b).

20. "The Great Unwashed" had a lively history as a term in the Western context, usually used to describe recent immigrants, non-Christians (i.e., the unbaptized), and those considered uncivilized. See, e.g., M. Williams 1991, who notes that "public baths were one of the many solutions proposed by nineteenth-century American reformers when they were faced with the numerous social problems presented by unprecedented urban growth and congested slums" (2). Lofton adds: "White women and men did their white washing (of clothes, of stainless steel, of selves). Ivory bars lay track to anyone, anywhere that desires that which the product assures: 'to cleanse without injuring.' The 'do no harm' Ivory bar became a symbolic sidekick to the history of Protestant missions, American expansions, and the widespread medicalization and sanitization of American culture" (2008b).

21. In *Map Is Not Territory* (1978), Jonathan Z. Smith discusses working on a small farm: "I would have to rise at about a quarter to four and fire up the wood burning stove, heat a pan of water and lay out the soap and towels so that my boss could wash when he awoke half an hour later. Each morning, to my growing puzzlement, when the boss would step outside after completing his ablutions, he would pick up a handful of soil and rub it over his hands. After several weeks of watching this activity, I finally, somewhat testily, asked for an explanation: 'Why do you start each morning by cleaning yourself and then step outside and immediately make yourself dirty?' 'Don't you city boys understand anything?', was the scornful reply. 'Inside the house it's dirt; outside, it's earth'" (291).

22. See, e.g., Elwell 2006.

23. Michael Taussig cites this very quote from Conrad in his *Shamanism, Colonialism, and the Wild Man* (1987, 16). My use of Conrad here builds on

Taussig's reading to suggest how colonialism as a horrifically violent experiment in domination actually persisted because it was understood in a certain era as good—as promoting progress. Although this is an uncharitable comparison to Manos de Amor, there are obvious parallels between colonialism and Christian efforts at charity.

24. See, e.g., Jennyffer Paredes, "Q67.33 millones cobra OIM en comisiones," *Prensa Libre,* September 11, 2006.

25. If anthropology's reflexive turn has proved anything, it is that the anthropologist cannot remove himself or herself from the equation (Rosaldo 1989; Clifford and Marcus 1986). When dealing with informants' giving practices on the streets of Guatemala City, I was approached far more often than my informants (and sometimes approached by my informants) for money. Though from one perspective this could be seen as an epistemological wrinkle in the study, the predicament (the "gringo-factor") opened up productive avenues to speak about giving and deservedness in Guatemala City.

26. In regard to "productively impossible," the work of Emmanuel Levinas allows for an ethically informed ethnography premised on an acknowledgment of risk and uncertainty over researcher control or reflexivity. See Benson and O'Neill 2007.

CHAPTER SIX

First epigraph: Winthrop 1838.
Second epigraph: Cecilia Caballeros, Guatemala City, October 25, 2006.

1. Christian eschatology is the theological study of the future—the study of what Christians hope for but have not yet received. Jürgen Moltmann, an eschatologist and liberation theologian, calls this hope "not yet": "Everything that comes into being must properly perish—not, however, because everything that is born is born for death, but because the true life, the full identity, was *not yet* born—*not yet* realized—has *not yet* appeared" (1996, 63–64). For much of Christianity, the end of history begins with Jesus Christ's return to earth (Luke 22:15; 1 Corinthians 11:26). For neo-Pentecostals, certain historical events suggest the second coming of Christ. This includes the formation of Israel as an independent nation. See, e.g., Wacker 1984.

2. See the following for an ongoing conversation on the relationship between nationalism and global Christianity: Martin 2002, 26; Englund 2003; Corten and Marshall-Fratani 2001, 3; Robbins 1998; Austin-Broos 1997, 111–112; Csordas 1992, 12; Gifford 1998, 341; Poewe 1994.

3. In her 1994 article "Citizens of Humanity: Internationalism and the Imagined Community of Nations," Liisa Malkki draws on fieldwork in Tanzania to explore the taxonomic dimensions of internationalism. Of critical importance to this study on neo-Pentecostalism, Malkki argues that internationalism can

homogenize the idea of nations. She contends that this homogenization solidifies nations as observable units. Malkki's analysis of internationalism as fomenting nationalism sheds light on how neo-Pentecostal nationalism depends heavily on a strong sense of internationalism.

4. Jenkins's enthusiasm is evident when he writes: "The era of Western Christianity has passed within our lifetimes, and the day of Southern Christianity is dawning. The fact of change is itself undeniable: it has happened, and will continue to happen" (2002, 3). He continues: "Since there were only a handful of Pentecostals in 1900, and several hundred million today, is it not reasonable to identify this as perhaps the most successful social movement of the past century? According to current projections, the number of Pentecostal believers should cross the one billion mark before 2050" (2002, 8).

5. *Reseña histórica* (El Shaddai pamphlet, 2006).

6. Caballeros, "El desarrollo de una nación Cristiana."

7. For the reference to Microsoft, much credit must be given to James Ferguson, who uses this advertisement in a syllabus to highlight globalization's exaggerated expanse. The advertisement makes sense, of course, when one imagines globalization along the lines of media and the World Wide Web. The very same advertisement becomes nonsensical, however, when mapped onto issues of political economy. It is absurd, for example, to ask a Guatemalan, "Where do you want to go today?" Militarized borders continue to prevent him or her from entering the United States.

8. Of interest here is Benedict Anderson's own use of maps when analyzing formations of the modern nation-state. Anderson writes: "Like censuses, European-style maps worked on the basis of a totalizing classification, and led their bureaucratic producers and consumers towards policies with revolutionary consequences" (1991, 173). He adds: "Map and census thus shaped the grammar which would in due course make possible 'Burma' and 'Burmese,' 'Indonesia' and 'Indonesians.' But the concretization of these possibilities—concretizations which have a powerful life today, long after the colonial state has disappeared—owed much to the colonial states' peculiar imagining of history and power" (1991, 178)

9. El Shaddai, *Profecía: La revista del Congreso Mundial 2006* (October 25, 2006), 6.

10. This procession recalls Olympic proceedings, especially the opening ceremonies, and the work of David Gilman Romano (2004) reminds us that the Olympics' pageantry has much to do with the religious origins of festivals and rituals.

11. It is important to note that the U.S. Conference of Catholic Bishops releases a document every four years entitled "Faithful Citizenship," which largely addresses "responsible citizenship" and the citizen's "responsible participation in public life" as "a moral obligation." It is argued by some, however, that Catholic social thought lacks a coherent account of citizenship (Coleman 2007).

12. El Shaddai, *Profecía*, 8.

13. For more on John Winthrop, see, e.g., Bremer 2003. For a more critical assessment of Winthrop's governance of the Massachusetts Bay Colony, see Howard Zinn, *A People's History of the United States* (1980, 108).

14. Puritans, by definition, were those traditional Anglicans who wanted to "purify" the Church of England. Puritans believed that the Church of England was corrupt because of the Roman Catholic Church's continued influence on Anglican rites and rituals. True Christians, Puritans argued, must reform the church. As Perry Miller writes: "[The Massachusetts Bay Company] was, so to speak, on its own business . . . to improve [their] lives to do more service to the Lord, to increase the body of Christ, and to preserve [their] posterity from the corruptions of this evil world, so that [the next generation] in turn shall work out their salvation under the purity and power of Biblical ordinances" (1956, 5–6).

15. Caballeros, "Hacia una visión de una nación Cristiana."

16. Ibid.

17. Sarah Pollak, "Guatemala: The Miracle of Almolonga," *Christian World News,* June 10, 2005, www.cbn.com/cbnnews/CWN/061005Guatemala.aspx (accessed June 23, 2008).

18. See, e.g., Hall 1994; Stout 1991; Lambert 1994.

19. The ways in which neo-Pentecostal Christianity adapts to specific cultural contexts has been the subject of many studies. See, e.g., Berger 1990, vii; S. Coleman 2000, 67; Meyer and Geschiere 1999, 159; Olson 2001, 24; Robbins 2001.

20. Cindy Jacobs Ministries, "Prophecy for the Philippines," www.youtube .com/watch?v=49ZoRiz3VEY (accessed June 23, 2008).

21. Bakhtin argues that any language has certain centripetal forces, which eventually congeal the language into a monoglossic, or unitary, language. Ideologies, for example, congeal any given language to embody a distinct view of the world. This process of consolidation depends on those who have the means to produce language, which properly captures how neo-Pentecostal discourses maintain a certain degree of continuity.

CONCLUSION

Epigraph: Critchley 2004, xviii.

1. Local media covered the violence of Guatemala's 2007 general elections. See, e.g., "Violencia contra los candidatos," *Prensa Libre,* August 9, 2007; "Violencia política preocupa a CIDH," *Prensa Libre,* September 1, 2007; Juan Callejas Vargas, "Elecciones y valores morales, Es un deber ciudadano construir ciudadanía," *Prensa Libre,* August 9, 2007; Óscar García and Mynor Cabrera, "Matan a dos candidatos," *Siglo XXI,* July 5, 2007; Rodrigo Pérez and Otto Ángel, "Temen violencia pero no llegaría a 'alto perfil,'" *Siglo XXI,* May 31, 2007; Rita María Aguilar and Otto Ángel, "Reportan 43 casos de violencia

electoral," *Siglo XXI,* May 4, 2007; Lucy Barrios, "Llegó la hora de votar," *La Hora,* September 7, 2007. The British Broadcasting Corporation (BBC) also covered electoral violence in Guatemala closely. See, e.g., Martin Murphy, "Bullets Overshadow Guatemala Ballot," BBC News Online, September 8, 2007, http://news.bbc.co.uk/2/hi/americas/6982050.stm (accessed June 26, 2008); "Guatemala Campaign Deaths Mount," BBC News Online, August 14, 2007, http://news.bbc.co.uk/2/hi/americas/6945744.stm (accessed June 26, 2008); James Painter, "Crime Dominates Guatemala Campaign," BBC News Online, May 10, 2007, http://news.bbc.co.uk/2/hi/americas/6643935.stm (accessed June 26, 2008).

2. Painter, "Crime Dominates Guatemala Campaign."

3. Some make the argument that lawlessness is an extension of the crime—the inability to discern what is and what is not state violence permits a cover under which people may be killed by gangs or death squads.

4. See "Bienvenidos a Familia El Shaddai" (September 2, 2007) (El Shaddai Sunday bulletin).

5. See, e.g., Olga López, Coralia Orantes, and Jéssica Osorio, "Viva queda fuera de la contienda electoral," *Prensa Libre,* July 7, 2007; Jéssica Osorio, "Harold Caballeros: Estoy tranquilo, vamos bien," *Prensa Libre,* June 22, 2007; "Caballeros descarta participar," *Prensa Libre,* July 10, 2007; Jéssica Osorio and Wendy Ruano, "Viva, en riesgo de no participar en comicios," *Prensa Libre,* June 21, 2007.

6. Caballeros, "Pongamos en práctica nuestros valores."

7. Caballeros, "Hacia una visión de una nación Cristiana."

8. The consensus in the mainstream media and beyond was that George Bush's six-day tour through Latin America was made to remind the region that it is still important to the United States but that the trip failed to have any significant effect. See, e.g., Rory Carroll, Sibylla Brodzinsky, and Jo Tuckman, "Bush Leaves Latin America Empty-Handed," *Guardian,* March 14, 2007, www.guardian.co.uk/world/2007/mar/14/usa.colombia (accessed June 26, 2008).

BIBLIOGRAPHY

PRIMARY SOURCES

Audiocassettes by Dr. Harold Caballeros

December 18, 1991. Escogé Tú.
June 18, 2000. El padre: Un ser especial.
October 28, 2001. La batalla entre dos reinos.
December 12, 2002. El desarrollo de una nación Cristiana.
June 13, 2004. Hacia una visión de una nación Cristiana, el papel de la cultura.
February 12, 2006. Que nos hace a nosotros ser relevantes.
February 26, 2006. El concepto de paz Shalom.
March 9, 2008. Pongamos en práctica nuestros valores.

El Shaddai Sunday Bulletins

June 18, 2006. ¡Feliz Día Papá!
July 2, 2006. Fortaleciendo el vínculo del amor.
July 23, 2006, ¡No te puedes perder!
July 30, 2006. Concierto de exaltación.
September 17, 2006. ¡Inscríbete ya!
October 25, 2006. Profecía: La revista del Congreso Mundial 2006.
December 23, 2006. Jesús: La razón de la navidad.

February 4, 2007. Los pasos del hombre son ordenados por Dios.
September 2, 2007. Bienvenidos a Familia El Shaddai.

Magazines and Newspapers

Aguilar, Rita María, and Otto Ángel. 2007. Reportan 43 casos de violencia electoral. *Siglo XXI,* May 4.

Alvarado, Hugo. 2008. Harold Caballeros: "Hay que expulsarlos." *Prensa Libre,* June 18.

Alvarado, Hugo, and Ana Lucía Blas. 2008. Feminicidios tienen nuevo investigador. *Prensa Libre,* March 7.

Ángel, Otto N. 2007. Candidatos conocerán CICIG. *Siglo XXI,* February 2.

Arias, Roberto. 2007. Candidatos y la mujer guatemalteca. *La Hora,* November 17.

Barrios, Lucy. 2007. Llegó la hora de votar. *La Hora,* September 7.

BBC News Online. 2007. Guatemala Campaign Deaths Mount. August 14, http://news.bbc.co.uk/2/hi/americas/6945744.stm (accessed June 26, 2008).

Carroll, Rory, Sibylla Brodzinsky, and Jo Tuckman. 2007. Bush Leaves Latin America Empty-Handed. *Guardian,* March 14, www.guardian.co.uk/world/2007/mar/14/usa.colombia (accessed June 26, 2008).

Daniel, Frank Jack, and Mica Rosenberg. 2007. Guatemala's Colom to Attack Drug Gangs. Reuters, November 6.

Economist. 2006. Christianity Reborn. December 19.

Fernández, Dina. 2006. Kaibiles en el Congo. *Prensa Libre,* January 30.

García, Óscar, and Mynor Cabrera. 2007. Matan a dos candidatos. *Siglo XXI,* July 5.

Grady, Lee. 2004. Small Nation, Big Faith. *Charisma,* January.

Grupo Seguridad y Justicia. 2004. Atemorizados por inseguridad. *Prensa Libre,* July 14.

Hernandez, Herbert, and Brendan Kolbay. 2008. Guatemala to Open Army Files to Probe War Crimes. Reuters, February 25.

Lavado, Joaquín Salvador. 2005. Quino. *Siglo XXI,* August 31.

López, Edgar. 2007. Menchú y Pérez atienden a indígenas. *Siglo XXI,* August 9.

López, Olga. 2005. Crearán policía comunitaria. *Prensa Libre,* March 16.

López, Olga, Coralia Orantes, and Jéssica Osorio. 2007. Viva queda fuera de la contienda electoral. *Prensa Libre,* July 7.

Los Angeles Times. 1906. Weird Babel of Tongues. April 18.

Mendoza, Alberto. 2007. Guatemala: Army Losing Fight against Crime. Inter Press Service, September 27.

Molina, Acisclo Valladares. 2005. Policía Comunitaria, seguridad y municipio. *El Periodico,* July 7.

Monzón, Marielos. 2007. Detrás de la mano dura. *Prensa Libre,* October 23.

Murphy, Martin. 2007. Bullets Overshadow Guatemala Ballot. BBC News Online, September 8, http://news.bbc.co.uk/2/hi/americas/6982050.stm (accessed June 26, 2008).

Osorio, Jéssica. 2007. Harold Caballeros: Estoy tranquilo, vamos bien. *Prensa Libre,* June 22.

Osorio, Jéssica, and Wendy Ruano. 2007. Viva, en riesgo de no participar en comicios. *Prensa Libre,* June 21.

Painter, James. 2007. Crime Dominates Guatemala Campaign. BBC News Online, May 10, http://news.bbc.co.uk/2/hi/americas/6643935.stm (accessed June 26, 2008).

Palencia, Gema. 2007. Diecisiete candidatos intensifican campaña. *Prensa Libre,* June 18.

Paredes, Jennyffer. 2006. Q67.33 millones cobra OIM en comisiones. *Prensa Libre,* September 11.

Pérez, Rodrigo, and Otto Ángel. 2007. Temen violencia pero no llegaría a "alto perfil." *Siglo XXI,* May 31.

Pollak, Sarah. 2005. Guatemala: The Miracle of Almolonga. *Christian World News,* June 10, www.cbn.com/cbnnews/CWN/061005Guatemala.aspx (accessed June 23, 2008).

Prensa Libre. 2007a. Caballeros descarta participar. July 10.

———. 2007b. Violencia contra los candidatos. August 9.

———. 2007c. Violencia política preocupa a CIDH. September 1.

Ramírez, Alberto. 2004. Tránsito, bajo el control edil. *Prensa Libre,* October 28.

Reuters. 2001. Guatemala Tax Protests Turn Violent. August 2.

Reynoso, Conié, and Gema Palencia. 2007. Discurso y canción de mano dura. *Prensa Libre,* October 21.

Riley, Naomi Schaefer. 2006. Can the Spirit Move You to Join the Middle Class? *Wall Street Journal,* October 13.

Rodríguez, Luisa F. 2007. Candidatos con fuertes dispositivos de seguridad. *Prensa Libre,* August 16.

Rodríguez, Luisa F., and Jéssica Osorio. 2007. Candidatos discuten planes de trabajo en cuatro áreas. *Prensa Libre,* August 9.

Rodríguez, M., and O. Figueroa. 2007. Mano dura contra mano aguada. *Prensa Libre,* June 4.

Sandoval, Julieta. 2007. Ofreció "mano dura" con sus propios funcionarios. *Prensa Libre,* May 27.

Seijo, Lorena. 2007. Policía será más accesible. *Prensa Libre,* October 9.

———. 2008. Ciudadanos angustiados por violencia y falta de recursos. *Prensa Libre,* June 15.

Tottens, Michael J. 2003. In Guatemala City. *Middle East Journal,* November 25, www.michaeltotten.com/archives/2003/11/in-guatemala-city.php.

Vargas, Juan Callejas. 2007. Elecciones y valores morales: Es un deber ciudadano construir ciudadanía. *Prensa Libre,* August 9.

Villaseñor, Claudia Méndez. 2005. Sitiados por la violencia. *Prensa Libre,* February 21.

Pamphlets and Speeches

Arzú, Álvaro. 2008. "Tú eres la ciudad" (public speech), January 12.

Cindy Jacobs Ministries. "Prophecy for the Philippines," by Cindy Jacobs, www.youtube.com/watch?v=49ZoRiz3VEY (accessed June 23, 2008).

El Shaddai. 2002. Reseña histórica (pamphlet).

———. 2006. *Profecía: La revista del Congreso Mundial 2006* (souvenir pamphlet).

GuateAmala. 2006a. *El cambio de GUATE empieza con vos* (pamphlet).

———. 2006b. *Cultura de la ciudadanía* (pamphlet).

———. 2006c. *Cultura de la vida: Forum 2006* (pamphlet).

———. 2006d. *Cultura de los sueños* (pamphlet).

———. 2006e. *Declaración de propósitos* (pamphlet).

———2006f. *¿Quiénes somos?* (pamphlet).

Guatemala City Municipal Government. N.d. *Tú eres la ciudad* (pamphlet).

———. 2006. *Soy la revolución* (pamphlet), August 4.

Oremos Online, www.oremos.net (accessed February 15, 2006).

Moral Manuals

Arthur, Kay, David Lawson, and B. J. Lawson. 2001. *How Do You Know God's Your Father?* Colorado Springs: Waterbrook Press.

———. 2003. *How to Make Choices You Won't Regret.* Colorado Springs: Waterbrook Press.

Caballeros, Harold. 1993. Defeating the Enemy with the Help of Spiritual Mapping. In *Breaking Strongholds in Your City.* Edited by P. Wagner. Ventura, Calif.: Regal Books, 123–146.

———. 2001. *Victorious Warfare: Discovering Your Rightful Place in God's Kingdom.* Nashville: Thomas Nelson.

Hormachea, Davíd. 2003. *¿Padre o progenitor?* Bogotá: Centros de Literatura Cristiana de Colombia.

Omartian, Stormie. 2005a. *El poder de los padres que oran: Libro de oraciones.* Translated by N. Pineda. Miami: Editorial Unilit.

———. 2005b. *Padres que oran: Un guía completa para saber si sólo engendró hijos naturalmente o los está criando sabiamente.* Miami: Editorial Unilit.

Pilon de Pacheco, Marta. 1998. *Intercessory Prayer: Weapon of God: A Handbook on How to Intercede.* Guatemala City: Intercessors of Guatemala.

Sjöberg, Kjell. 1993. Spiritual Mapping for Prophetic Prayer Actions. In *Breaking Strongholds in Your City*. Edited by P. Wagner. Ventura, Calif.: Regal Books, 97–122.

Valderrama, Gonzalo, ed. 2004a. *Carácter: Los verdaderos colores del carácter.* Bogotá: La Red Internacional.

———. 2004b. *Visión: Los verdaderos colores del carácter.* Colombia: La Red Internacional.

SECONDARY SOURCES

Abu-Lughod, Lila. 1991. Writing against Culture. In *Recapturing Ethnography: Working in the Present.* Edited by R. Fox. Santa Fe: School of American Research Press.

Adcock, Frank. 1957. *The Greek and Macedonian Art of War.* Berkeley: University of California Press.

Althoff, Andrea. 2005. Religion im Wandel: Einflüsse von Ethnizität auf die religiöse Ordnung am Beispiel Guatemalas. Ph.D. diss., Martin-Luther-Universität Halle-Wittenberg.

Althusser, Louis. 1998. Ideology and Ideological State Apparatuses. In *Literary Theory: An Anthology.* Edited by J. Rivkin and M. Ryan. Malden, Mass.: Blackwell.

Amnesty International. 1982. *Guatemala: Massive Extrajudicial Executions in Rural Areas under the Government of General Efraín Ríos Montt.* London: Amnesty International.

———. 2006. Guatemala: No Protection, No Justice: Killings of Women in Guatemala. *Amnesty International: Working to Protect Human Rights Worldwide* 34 (19).

Anderson, Benedict. 1991. *Imagined Communities: Reflections on the Origin and Spread of Nationalism.* London: Verso.

Apostolidis, Paul. 2000. *Stations of the Cross: Adorno and Christian Right Radio.* Durham: Duke University Press.

Appadurai, Arjun. 1988. Putting Hierarchy in Its Place. *Cultural Anthropology* 3 (1): 36–49.

———. 2001. Grassroots Globalization and the Research Imagination. In *Globalization.* Edited by A. Appadurai. Durham: Duke University Press.

Aquinas, Thomas. 1974. *Summa Theologica.* Indianapolis: Bobbs-Merrill.

Arana, Ana. 2005. How the Street Gangs Took Central America. *Foreign Affairs* 84 (3): 98–110.

Arendt, Hannah. 1958. *The Human Condition.* Chicago: University of Chicago Press.

———. 1978. *The Life of the Mind.* New York: Harcourt Brace.

Arriola, Arturo Taracena, and Jean Piel, eds. 1995. *Identidades nacionales y estado moderno en Centroamérica.* San José: Editorial de la Universidad de Costa Rica.

Asad, Talal. 2003. *Formations of the Secular: Christianity, Islam, Modernity.* Stanford: Stanford University Press.

Augustine of Hippo. 1961. *Confessions.* Translated by R. S. Pine-Coffin. New York: Penguin Classics.

———. 1993. *City of God.* Translated by M. Dods. New York: Modern Library.

Austin, John. 1975. *How to Do Things with Words.* Cambridge: Harvard University Press.

Austin-Broos, Diane. 1997. *Jamaica Genesis: Religion and the Politics of Moral Orders.* Chicago: University of Chicago Press.

AVANCSO. 2003. *El proceso de crecimiento metropolitano de la Ciudad de Guatemala.* Guatemala: Asociación para el Avance de las Ciencias Sociales.

Badiou, Alain. 2005. *Being and Event.* Translated by O. Feltham. London: Continuum.

Bakhtin, Mikhail. 1981. Discourse in the Novel. In *Dialogic Imagination: Four Essays by M. M. Bakhtin.* Edited by M. Holquist. Austin: University of Texas Press.

Barrett, David, and Todd Johnson. 2004. Annual Statistical Table on Global Mission. *International Bulletin of Missionary Research* 28 (1): 24–25.

Barrett, David, George Thomas Kurian, and Todd M. Johnson. 2001. *World Christian Encyclopedia.* New York: Oxford University Press.

Barry, Andrew, Thomas Osborne, and Nikolas Rose, eds. 1996. *Foucault and Political Reason: Liberalism, Neo-Liberalism, and Rationalities of Government.* Chicago: University of Chicago Press.

Bartkowski, John P. 2004. *The Promise Keepers: Servants, Soldiers, and Godly Men.* New Brunswick: Rutgers University Press.

Bastian, Jean-Pierre. 1993. The Metamorphosis of Latin American Protestant Groups: A Sociohistorical Perspective. *Latin American Research Review* 28 (2): 33–61.

Bastos, Santiago. 2000. *Poderes y quereres: Historias de género y familia en los sectores populares de la Ciudad de Guatemala.* Guatemala City: Facultad Latinoamericana de Ciencias Sociales.

Bastos, Santiago, and Manuela Camus. 1995. *Los Mayas de la capital: Un estudio sobre identidad étnica y mundo urbano.* Guatemala City: Facultad Latinoamericana de Ciencias Sociales.

———. 1997. *Sombras de una batalla: Los desplazados por la violencia en la Ciudad de Guatemala.* Guatemala City: Facultad Latinoamericana de Ciencias Sociales.

———. 1998. *La exclusión y el desafío: Estudios sobre segregación étnica y empleo en Ciudad de Guatemala.* Guatemala City: Facultad Latinoamericana de Ciencias Sociales.

Bebbington, David William. 1989. *Evangelicalism in Modern Britain: A History from the 1730s to the 1980s.* Boston: Unwin Hyman.

Bellah, Robert. 1992. *The Broken Covenant: American Civil Religion in Time of Trial.* Chicago: University of Chicago Press.

Benson, Peter, and Kevin Lewis O'Neill. 2007. Facing Risk: Levinas, Ethnography, and Ethics. *Anthropology of Consciousness* 18 (2): 29–55.

Benveniste, Emile. 1971. *Problems in General Linguistics.* Translated by M. E. Meek. Coral Gables: University of Miami Press.

Berger, Peter. 1986. *The Capitalist Revolution: Fifty Propositions about Prosperity, Equality, and Liberty.* New York: Basic Books.

———. 1990. Foreword. In *Tongues of Fire: The Explosion of Protestantism in Latin America.* Edited by D. Martin. Oxford: Basil Blackwell.

Béteille, Andre. 1986. Individualism and Equality. *Current Anthropology* 27 (2): 121–134.

Blakenhorn, David. 1995. *Fatherless America: Confronting Our Most Urgent Social Problem.* New York: Basic Books.

Boellstorff, Tom. 2005. *The Gay Archipelago: Sexuality and Nation in Indonesia.* Princeton: Princeton University Press.

Bornstein, Erica. 2001. Child Sponsorship, Evangelism, and Belonging in the Work of World Vision Zimbabwe. *American Ethnologist* 28 (3): 595–622.

———. 2005. *The Spirit of Development: Protestant NGOs, Morality, and Economics in Zimbabwe.* Stanford: Stanford University Press.

Bottomore, Tom. 1992. Citizenship and Social Class, Forty Years On. In *Citizenship and Social Class.* edited by T. H. Marshall and T. Bottomore. Chicago: Pluto Press.

Bourdieu, Pierre. 1984. *Distinction: A Social Critique of the Judgement of Taste.* Translated by Richard Nice. Cambridge: Harvard University Press.

Brakke, David. 2006. *Demons and the Making of the Monk: Spiritual Combat in Early Christianity.* Cambridge: Harvard University Press.

Bremer, Francis J. 2003. *John Winthrop: America's Forgotten Founding Father.* Oxford: Oxford University Press.

Brown, Peter. 1989. *The Body and Society: Men, Women and Sexual Renunciation in Early Christianity.* London: Faber and Faber.

Bruce, Steve. 1993. Religion and Rational Choice: a Critique of Economic Explanations of Religious Behavior. *Sociology of Religion* 54 (2): 193–205.

Brusco, Elizabeth E. 1995. *The Reformation of Machismo: Evangelical Conversion and Gender in Colombia.* Austin: University of Texas Press.

Bunyan, John. [1678] 2003. *The Pilgrim's Progress.* Oxford: Oxford University Press.

Burchell, Graham. 1993. Liberal Government and Techniques of the Self. *Economy and Society* 22 (3): 267–282.

Burchell, Graham, Colin Gordon, and Peter Miller, eds. 1991. *The Foucault Effect: Studies in Governmentality: With Two Lectures by and an Interview with Michel Foucault* Chicago: University of Chicago Press.

Burdick, John. 1993. *Looking for God in Brazil: The Progressive Catholic Church in Urban Brazil's Religious Arena.* Berkeley: University of California Press.

———. 1998. *Blessed Anastacia: Women, Race, and Popular Christianity in Brazil.* New York: Routledge.

Butler, Judith. 1997. *The Psychic Life of Power.* Stanford: Stanford University Press.

———. 1999. *Gender Trouble: Feminism and the Subversion of Identity.* New York: Routledge.

Caldeira, Teresa. 2001. *City of Walls: Crime, Segregation, and Citizenship in São Paulo.* Berkeley: University of California Press.

———. 2002. The Paradox of Police Violence in Democratic Brazil. *Ethnography* 3 (3): 235–263.

Caldeira, Teresa, and James Holston. 1999. Democracy and Violence in Brazil. *Journal for Comparative Study of Society and History* 41 (4): 691–729.

Camus, Manuela. 2002. *Ser indígena en Ciudad de Guatemala.* Guatemala City: Facultad Latinoamericana de Ciencias Sociales.

Canadian Red Cross. 2006. Facts and Figures: Guatemala 2005, www.redcross .ca/article.asp?id=020507&tid=001 (accessed July 19, 2007).

Cannell, Fenella. 2005. The Christianity of Anthropology. *Journal of the Royal Anthropological Institute* 11 (2): 335–356.

———. 2006. Introduction: The Anthropology of Christianity. In *The Anthropology of Christianity.* Edited by F. Cannell. Durham: Duke University Press.

Carmack, Robert M., ed. 1988. *Harvest of Violence: The Maya Indians and the Guatemalan Crisis.* Norman: University of Oklahoma Press.

Carr, David, and Jan Steutel, eds. 1999. *Virtue Ethics and Moral Education.* New York: Routledge.

Cary, Phillip. 2003. *Augustine's Invention of the Inner Self: The Legacy of a Christian Platonist.* New York: Oxford University Press.

Castel, Robert. 1994. "Problematization" as a Mode of Reading History. In *Foucault and the Writing of History.* Edited by J. Goldstein. Oxford: Blackwell.

Castillo, Augusto Gordillo. 1995. Historia urbana de la Ciudad de Guatemala en 1935: Una approximación al comercio. In *Memoria del segundo encuentro nacional de historiadores del 4 al 6 de diciembre de 1995 de Guatemala.* Guatemala City: Universidad del Valle de Guatemala.

Cattelino, Jessica R. 2004. The Difference That Citizenship Makes: Civilian Crime Prevention on the Lower East Side. *PoLAR: Political and Legal Anthropology Review* 27 (1): 114–137.

CEH. 1999. *Memoria del silencio. Guatemala: Comisión para el Esclarecimiento Histórico.* Guatemala City: Comisión para el Esclarecimiento Histórico.

CERD. 2006. *Civil Society Report, Guatemala: The Perspective of Indigenous Peoples on the Application of the International Convention on the Elimination of*

All Forms of Racial Discrimination. Guatemala City: United Nations Committee on the Elimination of Racial Discrimination.

Cerwonka, Allaine, and Liisa H. Malkki. 2007. *Improvising Theory: Process and Temporality in Ethnographic Fieldwork.* Chicago: University of Chicago Press.

Chakrabarty, Dipesh. 2000. *Provincializing Europe: Postcolonial Thought and Historical Difference.* Princeton: Princeton University Press.

Chase-Dunn, Christopher, Susanne Jonas, and Nelson Amaro, eds. 2001. *Globalization on the Ground: Postbellum Guatemalan Democracy and Development.* Lanham, Md.: Rowman and Littlefield.

Chinchilla, Laura. 2004. El caso del municipio de Villa Nueva, Guatemala. In *Calles más seguras: Estudios de policía comunitaria en América Latina.* Edited by H. Frühling. Washington, D.C.: Inter-American Development Bank.

CIEN. 2006. *Economía informal: Superando las barreras de un estado excluyente.* Guatemala City: Centro de Investigaciones Económicas Nacionales.

Clarke, Paul Barry. 1994a. The Christian Citizen. In *Citizenship.* Edited by P. B. Clarke. London: Pluto Press.

———. 1994b. The Inward Turn. In *Citizenship.* Edited by P. B. Clarke. London: Pluto Press.

Claussen, Dane S., ed. 2000. *The Promise Keepers: Essays on Masculinity and Christianity.* Jefferson, N.C.: McFarland.

Clifford, James, and George Marcus, eds. 1986. *Writing Culture: The Poetics and Politics of Ethnography.* Berkeley: University of California Press.

Coleman, John A., ed. 2007. *Christian Political Ethics.* Princeton: Princeton University Press.

Coleman, Simon. 2000. *The Globalisation of Charismatic Christianity: Spreading the Gospel of Prosperity.* Cambridge: Cambridge University Press.

Collier, Richard. 2001. A Hard Time to Be a Father? Reassessing the Relationship between Law, Policy, and Family. *Journal of Law and Society* 28 (4): 520–545.

Comaroff, Jean. 1985. *Body of Power, Spirit of Resistance: The Culture and History of a South African People.* Chicago: University of Chicago Press.

Comaroff, John, and Jean Comaroff. 1987. The Madman and the Migrant: Work and Labor in the Historical Consciousness of a South African People. *American Ethnologist* 14 (2): 191–209.

Conrad, Joseph. 1995. "Youth" / *Heart of Darkness* / "The End of the Tether." New York: Penguin Classics.

Corten, André. 1997. The Growth of the Literature on Afro-American, Latin American and African Pentecostalism. *Journal of Contemporary Religion* 12 (3): 311–330.

Corten, André, and Ruth Marshall-Fratani, eds. 2001. *Between Babel and Pentecost: Transnational Pentecostalism in Africa and Latin America.* Bloomington: Indiana University Press.

Coser, Lewis. 1971. *Masters of Sociological Thought: Ideas in Historical and Social Context.* New York: Harcourt Brace Jovanovich.

Costello, Patrick. 1997. Historical Background. In *Negotiating Rights: The Guatemalan Peace Process.* Edited by J. Armon, R. Sieder, and R. Wilson. London: Conciliation Resources.

Cott, Nancy. 2000. *Public Vows: A History of Marriage and the Nation.* Cambridge: Harvard University Press.

Cox, Harvey. 1995. *Fire from Heaven: The Rise of Pentecostal Spirituality and the Reshaping of Religion in the 21st Century.* Reading, Mass.: Addison-Wesley.

Critchley, Simon. 2004. *Very Little . . . Almost Nothing.* 2nd ed. New York: Verso.

———. 2007. *Infinitely Demanding: Ethics of Commitment, Politics of Resistance.* New York: Verso.

Cruikshank, Barbara. 1996. Revolution Within: Self-Government and Self-Esteem. In *Foucault and Political Reason: Liberalism, Neo-Liberalism, and Rationalities of Government.* Edited by A. Barry, T. Osborne, and N. Rose. Chicago: University of Chicago Press.

———. 1999. *The Will to Empower: Democratic Citizens and Other Subjects.* Ithaca: Cornell University Press.

Csordas, Thomas. 1992. Religion and the World System: The Pentecostal Ethic and the Spirit of Monopoly Capital. *Dialectical Anthropology* 17 (1): 3–24.

———. 1994. *The Sacred Self: A Cultural Phenomenology of Charismatic Healing.* Berkeley: University of California Press.

Cuneo, Michael. 2001. *American Exorcism: Expelling Demons in the Land of Plenty.* New York: Doubleday.

Dardón, Byron. 2007. Ingresan más de US$3 mil millones. *Prensa Libre,* January 10.

Davis, Mike. 1990. *City of Quartz: Excavating the Future in Los Angeles.* New York: Verso.

Dean, Mitchell. 1996. Foucault, Government and the Enfolding of Authority. In *Foucault and Political Reason: Liberalism, Neo-Liberalism, and Rationalities of Government.* Edited by A. Barry, T. Osborne, and N. Rose. Chicago: University of Chicago Press.

———. 1999. *Governmentality: Power and Rule in Modern Society.* London: Sage.

Deleuze, Gilles. 1992. Postscripts on the Societies of Control. *October* 59:3–7.

Dennis, Norman, and George Erdos. 1993. *Families without Fatherhood.* London: Institute of Economic Affairs.

Diamond, Sara. 1998. *Not by Politics Alone: The Enduring Influence of the Christian Right.* New York: Guilford Press.

Diaz, Steffan Igor Ayora. 2007. Translocalidad y la antropología de los procesos globales: Saber y poder en Chiapas y Yucatán. *Journal of Latin American and Caribbean Anthropology* 12 (1): 134–163.

Dickins de Girón, Avery. 2006. Connecting Rural Economies and Postwar Violence: The Security Guard Industry. Paper presented at the American Anthropological Association annual meeting, San Jose, Calif.

Donzelot, Jacques. 1979. *The Policing of Families.* Translated by R. Hurley. New York: Pantheon Books.

———. 1996. L'avenir du social. *Esprit* 219:58–81.

Dostoyevsky, Fyodor. [1880] 1957. *The Brothers Karamazov.* New York: Dell.

Douglas, Mary. 1966. *Purity and Danger: An Analysis of Concepts of Pollution and Taboo.* New York: Praeger.

Dowd, Nancy. 2000. *Redefining Fatherhood.* New York: New York University Press.

Dreyfus, Herbert. 1984. Beyond Hermeneutics: Interpretation in Later Heidegger and Recent Foucault. In *Hermeneutics: Questions and Prospects.* Edited by G. Shapiro. Amherst: University of Massachusetts Press.

Dumont, Louis. 1980. *Homo Hierarchicus: The Caste System and Its Implications.* Translated by G. Weidenfeld. Chicago: University Of Chicago Press.

Dwyer, Kevin. 1982. *Moroccan Dialogues: Anthropology in Question.* Baltimore: Johns Hopkins University Press.

Elisha, Omri. 2008. Moral Ambitions of Grace: The Paradox of Compassion and Accountability in Evangelical Faith-Based Activism. *Cultural Anthropology* 23 (1): 154–189.

Elwell, Frank. 2006. *Macrosociology: Four Modern Theorists.* Boulder: Paradigm.

Engelke, Matthew. 2002. The Problem of Belief: Evans-Pritchard and Victor Turner on "The Inner Life." *Anthropology Today* 18 (6): 3–8.

———. 2004. Text and Performance in an African Church: The Book, "Live and Direct." *American Ethnologist* 31 (1): 76–91.

———. 2007. *The Problem of Presence: Beyond Scripture in an African Church.* Berkeley: University of California Press.

Engelke, Matthew, and Matt Tomlinson, eds. 2006. *The Limits of Meaning: Case Studies in the Anthropology of Christianity.* Oxford: Berghahn Books.

England, Kim. 1993. Suburban Pink Collar Ghettos: The Spatial Entrapment of Women? *Annals of the Association of American Geographers* 83 (2): 225–242.

Englund, Harri. 2003. Christian Independency and Global Membership: Pentecostal Extraversions in Malawi. *Journal of Religion in Africa* 32 (1): 83–111.

Erasmus, Desiderius. 1964. *The Essential Erasmus.* New York: New American Library.

ERIC, IDESO, IDIES, and IUDOP. 2001. *Maras y pandillas en Centroamérica,* vol. 1. San Salvador: UCA Editores.

———. 2004a. *Maras y pandillas en Centroamérica: Pandillas y capital social,* vol. 2. San Salvador: UCA Editores.

———. 2004b. *Maras y pandillas en Centroamérica: Políticas juveniles y rehabilitación,* vol. 3. Managua: UCA Editores.

Falla, Ricardo. 1992. *Masacres de la selva: Ixcán, Guatemala, 1975–1982.* Guatemala City: Editorial Universitaria.

Ferguson, James. 1992. The Country and the City on the Copperbelt. *Cultural Anthropology* 7 (1): 80–92.

———. 2006. *Global Shadows: Africa in the Neoliberal World Order.* Durham: Duke University Press.

Ferguson, James, and Akhil Gupta. 2002. Spatializing States: Toward an Ethnography of Neoliberal Governmentality. *American Ethnologist* 29 (4): 981–1002.

Finke, Roger. 1990. Religious Deregulation: Origins and Consequences. *Journal of Church and State* 32 (3): 609–626.

Fischer, Edward F. 2002. *Cultural Logics and Global Economies: Maya Identity in Thought and Practice.* Austin: University of Texas Press.

———. 2004. Beyond Victimization: Maya Movements in Postwar Guatemala. In *The Struggle for Indigenous Rights in Latin America.* Edited by N. G. Postero and L. Zamosc. Brighton: Sussex Academic Press.

Fischer, Edward F., and Peter Benson. 2005. Something Better: Hegemony, Resistance and Desire in Guatemalan Export Agriculture. *Social Analysis* 49 (1): 3–20.

Fischer, Edward F., and R. McKenna Brown, eds. 1996. *Maya Cultural Activism in Guatemala.* Austin: University of Texas Press.

Foucault, Michel. 1971. *The Order of Things: An Archaeology of the Human Sciences.* New York: Pantheon Books.

———. 1973. *The Birth of the Clinic: An Archaeology of Medical Perception.* Translated by A. M. Sheridan Smith. New York: Pantheon Books.

———. 1977. *Discipline and Punish: The Birth of the Prison.* Translated by Alan Sheridan. New York: Pantheon Books.

———. 1978. *The History of Sexuality: An Introduction.* Translated by R. Hurley. New York: Pantheon Books.

———. 1985. *The Use of Pleasure: The History of Sexuality, Volume Two.* Translated by R. Hurley. New York: Vintage Books.

———. 1986. *The Care of the Self: The History of Sexuality, Volume Three.* New York: Vintage Books.

———. 1988. The Concern for Truth: An interview by Francis Ewald. In *Politics, Philosophy, Culture: Interviews and Other Writings, 1977–1984.* Edited by L. D. Kritzman. New York: Routledge.

———. 1991. Governmentality. In *The Foucault Effect: Studies in Governmentality: With Two Lectures by and an Interview with Michel Foucault.* Edited by G. Burchell, C. Gordon, and P. Miller. Chicago: University of Chicago Press.

———. 1993. About the Beginning of the Hermeneutics of the Self: Two Lectures at Dartmouth. *Political Theory* 21 (2): 198–227.

———. 1994. Sexuality and Solitude. In *Ethics: Subjectivity and Truth*. Edited by P. Rabinow. New York: New Press.

———. 1997. Technologies of the Self. In *Ethics: Subjectivity and Truth. Essential Works of Foucault, 1954–1984*. Vol. 1. Edited by P. Rabinow. New York: New Press.

———. 1999. *Religion and Culture*. Edited by J. R. Carrette. New York: Routledge.

———. 2001. *L'hermeneutique du sujet: Cours au Collège de France, 1981–1982*. Paris: Gallimard Seuil.

Franco, Jean. 2002. *The Decline and Fall of the Lettered City: Latin America in the Cold War*. Cambridge: Harvard University Press.

———. 2007. Rape: A Weapon of War. *Social Text* 25 (2): 23–28.

Freedom House. 2008. *Freedom in the World*. Washington, D.C.: Freedom House.

Freston, Paul. 1998. Evangelicalism and Globalization: General Observations and Some Latin American Dimensions. In *A Global Faith: Essays on Evangelicalism and Globalization*. Edited by M. Hutchinson and O. Kalu. Sydney: Centre for the Study of Australian Christianity.

———. 2001. *Evangelicals and Politics in Asia, Africa and Latin America*. Cambridge: Cambridge University Press.

———, ed. 2008. *Evangelical Christianity and Democracy in Latin America*. New York: Oxford University Press.

Friedman, Thomas L. 2005. *The World Is Flat: A Brief History of the Twenty-first Century*. New York: Farrar, Straus and Giroux.

Frisby, David, and Mike Featherstone. 1997. *Simmel on Culture: Selected Writings*. London: Sage.

Frühling, Hugo, ed. 2004. *Calles más seguras: Estudios de policía comunitaria en América Latina*. Bogotá: Alfaomega Grupo Editor.

———. 2007. The Impact of International Models of Policing in Latin America: The Case of Community Policing. *Police Practice and Research* 8 (2): 125–144.

Fuentes, Carlos Iván. 2008. The Applicability of International Humanitarian Law to Situations of Urban Violence: Are Cities Turning into War Zones? Working paper, Social Science Research Network, Centre for Human Rights and Legal Pluralism, McGill University.

Fyke, Joel, and Maureen Meye. 2008. No todo lo que es oro brilla / No todo lo que brilla es oro. *Foreign Affairs en Español* 8 (1): 25–31.

García, María Cristina Fernández. 2004. Lynching in Guatemala: Legacy of War and Impunity. Report prepared for Weatherhead Center for International Affairs, Harvard University.

García Canclini, Nestor. 1989. *Culturas híbridas: Estrategias para entrar y salir de la modernidad*. Mexico City: Grijalbo.

García-Ruiz, Jesús. 2004. Le Néopentecôtisme au Guatemala: Entre privatisa-tion, marché et réseaux. *Critique Internationale* 22:81–94.

Garrard-Burnett, Virginia. 1997. Liberalism, Protestantism, and Indigenous Resistance in Guatemala, 1870–1920. *Latin American Perspectives* 24 (2): 35–55.

———. 1998. *Protestantism in Guatemala: Living in the New Jerusalem.* Austin: University of Texas Press.

Garriott, William, and Kevin Lewis O'Neill. 2008. Who Is a Christian? Further Notes towards an Anthropology of Christianity. *Anthropological Theory* 8 (4).

Geertz, Clifford. 2005. Shifting Aims, Moving Targets: On the Anthropology of Religion. *Journal of the Royal Anthropological Institute* 11 (1): 1–15.

Gellert, Gisela. 1995. *Ciudad de Guatemala: Factores determinantes en su desar-rollo urbano (desde la fundación hasta la actualidad).* Guatemala City: Facultad Latinoamericana de Ciencias Sociales.

Gellert, Gisela, and Silvia Irene Palma C. 1999. *Precaridad urbana, desarrollo comunitario y mujeres en el área metropolitana de Guatemala, debate 46.* Guatemala City: Facultad Latinoamericana de Ciencias Sociales.

Gellert, Gisela, and J. C. Pinto Soria. 1990. *Ciudad de Guatemala: Dos estudios sobre su evolución urbana (1524–1950).* Guatemala City: Universidad de San Carlos de Guatemala.

Gifford, Paul. 1998. *African Christianity: Its Public Role.* Bloomington: Indiana University Press.

Gill, Anthony. 2002. Religion and Democracy in South America: Challenges and Opportunities. In *Religion and Politics in Comparative Perspective: The One, the Few, the Many.* Edited by T. G. Jelen and C. Wilcox. New York: Cambridge University Press.

Glendon, Mary Ann. 1991. *Rights Talk: The Impoverishment of Political Discourse.* New York: Free Press.

Goffman, Erving. 1969. *The Presentation of the Self in Everyday Life.* Harmondsworth: Penguin.

Goldman, Michael. 2005. *Imperial Nature: The World Bank and Struggles for Social Justice in the Age of Globalization.* New Haven: Yale University Press.

Gordon, Colin. 1991. Governmental Rationality: An Introduction. In *The Foucault Effect: Studies in Governmentality.* Edited by G. Burchell, C. Gordon, and P. Miller. Chicago: University of Chicago Press.

Graham, Steve. 2001. *Splintering Urbanism: Networked Infrastructures, Technological Mobilities and the Urban Condition.* New York: Routledge.

Grandin, Greg. 2000. *The Blood of Guatemala: A History of Race and Nation.* Durham: Duke University Press.

———. 2004. *The Last Colonial Massacre: Latin America in the Cold War.* Chicago: University of Chicago Press.

Greeley, Andrew. 2000. *The Catholic Imagination.* Berkeley: University of California Press.

Green, Linda. 1994. Fear as a Way of Life. *American Ethnologist* 9 (2): 227–256.

——. 1999. *Fear as a Way of Life: Mayan Widows in Rural Guatemala.* New York: Columbia University Press.

Grossmann, Roger. 2002. Interpreting the Development of the Evangelical Church in Guatemala. D.Min. diss., Southeastern Baptist Theological Seminary.

Guadeloupe, Francio. 2008. *Chanting Down the New Jerusalem: Calypso, Christianity, and Capitalism in the Caribbean.* Berkeley: University of California Press.

Gutiérrez, Gustavo. [1973] 1988. *A Theology of Liberation: History, Politics, and Salvation.* Translated by C. Inda and J. Eagleson. Maryknoll, N.Y.: Orbis Books.

Gutmann, Matthew C. 1996. *The Meanings of Macho: Being a Man in Mexico City.* Berkeley: University of California Press.

——, ed. 2003. *Changing Men and Masculinities in Latin America.* Durham: Duke University Press.

Gutterman, David S. 2005. *Prophetic Politics: Christian Social Movements and American Democracy.* Ithaca: Cornell University Press.

Gwynne, Robert N., and Cristóbal Kay, eds. 1999. *Latin America Transformed: Globalization and Modernity.* New York: Oxford University Press.

Hale, Charles R. 2006. *Más que un Indio: Racial Ambivalence and Neoliberal Multiculturalism in Guatemala.* Santa Fe: School of American Research Press.

Hall, Timothy. 1994. *Contested Boundaries: Itinerancy and the Reshaping of the Colonial American Religious World.* Durham: Duke University Press.

Hallum, Anne Motley. 2002. Looking for Hope in Central America: The Pentecostal Movement. In *Religion and Politics in Comparative Perspective.* Edited by T. Gerard, J. Wilcox, and C. Wilcox. Cambridge: Cambridge University Press.

Handy, Jim. 2002. Democratizing What? Some Reflections on Nation, State, Ethnicity, Modernity, Community, and Democracy in Guatemala. *Canadian Journal of Latin American and Caribbean Studies* 27 (53): 35–71.

Hannerz, Ulf. 1992. The Global Ecumene as a Network of Networks. In *Conceptualising Society.* Edited by A. Kuper. London: Routledge.

——. 1996. *Transnational Connections: Culture, People, Places.* London: Routledge.

Harding, Susan. 1991. Representing Fundamentalism: The Problem of the Repugnant Cultural Other. *Social Research* 58 (2): 373–393.

——. 2000. *The Book of Jerry Falwell: Fundamentalist Language and Politics.* Princeton: Princeton University Press.

Hardisty, Jean. 1999. *Mobilizing Resentment: Conservative Resurgence from the John Birch Society to the Promise Keepers.* Boston: Beacon Press.

Harrington, Daniel, and James Keenan. 2002. *Jesus and Virtue Ethics: Building Bridges between New Testament Studies and Moral Theology.* Lanham, Md.: Rowman and Littlefield.

Hartman, Esther Angela. 1951. Imaginative Literature as a Projective Technique: A Study of Bibliotherapy. Ph.D. diss., Stanford University.

Hartog, Hendrik. 2000. *Man and Wife in America*. Cambridge: Harvard University Press.

Headland, Thomas N., Kenneth L. Pike, and Marvin Harris, eds. 1990. *Emics and Etics: The Insider/Outsider Debate*. Newbury Park: Sage Publications.

Hegel, Georg Wilhelm Friedrich. 1954. *The Philosophy of Hegel*. Translated by C. Friedrich. New York: Modern Library.

Heidegger, Martin. [1949] 1977. *The Question concerning Technology and Other Essays*. Translated by W. Lovitt. New York: Harper and Row.

Hindess, Barry. 1993. Citizenship in the Modern West. In *Citizenship and Social Theory*. Edited by B. Turner. London: Sage.

———. 1996. Liberalism, Socialism, and Democracy: Variations on a Governmental Theme. In *Foucault and Political Reason: Liberalism, Neo-Liberalism, and Rationalities of Government*. Edited by A. Barry, T. Osborne, and N. Rose. Chicago: University of Chicago Press.

Houtum, Henk van, and Anke Struver. 2002. Borders, Strangers, Doors and Bridges. *Space & Polity* 6 (2): 141–146.

Iannaccone, Laurence. 1990. Religious Practice: A Human Capital Approach. *Journal for the Scientific Study of Religion* 29 (3): 297–314.

IDEA. 1998. *Democracy in Guatemala: The Mission for the Entire Nation*. Stockholm: International Institute for Democracy and Electoral Assistance.

Jenkins, Philip. 2002. *The Next Christendom: The Coming of Global Christianity*. New York: Oxford University Press.

Jonas, Susanne. 1991. *The Battle for Guatemala: Rebels, Death Squads, and U.S. Power*. Boulder: Westview Press.

Joyce, Patrick. 2003. *The Rule of Freedom: Liberalism and the Modern City*. London: Verso.

Jung, Karl. [1933] 2005. *Modern Man in Search of a Soul*. Translated by W. S. Dell and C. F. Baynes. New York: Routledge.

Karsten, Lia. 2003. Family Gentrifiers: Challenging the City as a Place Simultaneously to Build a Career and Raise Children. *Urban Studies* 40 (1): 2573–2585.

Kay, Cristóbal. 1989. *Latin American Theories of Development and Underdevelopment*. London: Routledge.

Keane, Webb. 2006. Anxious Transcendence. In *Anthropology of Christianity*. Edited by F. Cannell. Durham: Duke University Press.

———. 2007. *Christian Moderns: Freedom and Fetish in the Mission Encounter*. Berkeley: University of California Press.

Knott, Sarah. 2004. Sensibility and the American War for Independence. *American Historical Review* 109 (1): 19–40.

Kofman, Eleanore. 1995. Citizenship for Some but Not for Others: Spaces of Citizenship in Contemporary Europe. *Political Geography* 4 (2): 121–137.

Kundera, Milan. [1984] 2004. *The Unbearable Lightness of Being: Twentieth Anniversary Edition*. New York: Harper and Row.

Kymlicka, Will, and Will Norman. 1994. Return of the Citizen: A Survey of Recent Work on Citizenship Theory. *Ethics* 104 (2): 352–381.

Lake, Kirsopp, ed. 1912. Epistle to Diognetus, in *The Apostolic Fathers*. New York: Putnam.

Lambert, Frank. 1994. *"Pedlar in Divinity": George Whitefield and the Transatlantic Revivals, 1737–1770*. Princeton: Princeton University Press.

Latinobarómetro. 2007. *Informe Latinobarómetro 2007: Bancos de datos en línea*. Santiago: Corporación Latinobarómetro.

Latour, Bruno. 1999. *Pandora's Hope: Essays on the Reality of Science Studies*. Cambridge: Harvard University Press.

LCMS. 1968. *Christian Citizenship: A Report of the Commission on Theology and Church Relations of the Lutheran Church*. St. Louis: Lutheran Church—Missouri Synod.

Lefebvre, Henri. 1991. *The Production of Space*. New York: Wiley-Blackwell.

Lemke, Thomas. 2001. "The Birth of Bio-politics"—Michel Foucault's Lecture at the Collège de France on Neo-liberal Governmentality. *Economy & Society* 30 (2): 190–207.

Levenson-Estrada, Deborah. 1994. *Trade Unionists against Terror: Guatemala City, 1954–1985*. Chapel Hill: University of North Carolina Press

Levinas, Emmanuel. 1969. *Totality and Infinity: An Essay on Exteriority*. Translated by A. Lingis. Pittsburgh: Duquesne University Press.

———. 1978. *Existence and Existents*. The Hague: Nijhoff.

———. 1985. *Ethics and Infinity: Conversations with Philippe Nemo*. Translated by R. A. Cohen. Pittsburgh: Duquesne University Press.

Levine, Daniel H. 1995. Protestants and Catholics in Latin America: A Family Portrait. In *Fundamentalisms Comprehended*. Edited by M. E. Marty and S. Appleby. Chicago: University of Chicago Press.

Llorente, Laura. 2004. La experiencia de la policía comunitaria de Bogotá: Contexto y balance. In *Calles más seguras. Estudios de policía comunitaria en América Latina*. Edited by H. Frühling. Washington, D.C.: Banco Interamericano de Desarrollo.

Locke, John. 1801. *An Essay concerning Human Understanding: With Thoughts on the Conduct of the Understanding*. Edinburgh: Mundell and Son.

Lofton, Kathryn. 2008a. Evangelicalism. In *Encyclopedia of the Modern World*. Edited by P. N. Stearns. Oxford: Oxford University Press.

———. 2008b. Saving Soap: An Allegory of Modern Religion. Address given at Yale University, April 15.

Lonely Planet. 2001. *Guatemala*. Victoria, Australia: Lonely Planet Publications.

Low, Setha M. 2001. The Edge and the Center: Gated Communities and the Discourse of Urban Fear. *American Anthropologist* 103 (1): 45–58.

Lumsdaine, David Halloran. 2008. *Evangelical Christianity and Democracy in Asia.* New York: Oxford University Press.

Luther, Martin. 1961. *Martin Luther: Selections from His Writings.* Edited by J. Dillenberger. Garden City, N.Y.: Doubleday.

Lutz, Catherine A., and Jane L. Collins. 1993. *Reading National Geographic.* Chicago: University of Chicago Press.

Mahmood, Saba. 2005. *Politics of Piety: The Islamic Revival and the Feminist Subject.* Princeton: Princeton University Press.

Malinowski, Bronislaw. 1922. *Argonauts of the Western Pacific.* London: G. Routledge and Sons.

———. 1972. The Role of Magic and Religion. In *Reader in Comparative Religion: An Anthropological Approach* edited by W. A. Lessa and E. Z. Vogt. New York: Harper and Row.

Malkki, Liisa. 1992. National Geographic: The Rooting of Peoples and the Territorialization of National Identity among Scholars and Refugees. *Cultural Anthropology* 7 (1): 24–44.

———. 1994. Citizens of Humanity: Internationalism and the Imagined Community of Nations. *Diaspora: A Journal of Transnational Studies* 3 (1): 41–68.

———. 1997. Children, Futures, and the Domestication of Hope. Paper presented at the meeting Histories of the Future, University of California Humanities Research Institute Residential Research Group, Irvine.

Mann, Michael. 1987. Ruling Class Strategies and Citizenship. *Sociology* 21 (3): 339–354.

Manning, Frank. 1980. Pentecostalism: Christianity and Reputation. In *Perspectives on Pentecostalism: Case Studies from the Caribbean and Latin America.* Edited by S. Glazer. Lanham, Md.: University Press of America.

Manz, Beatriz. 1988. *Refugees of a Hidden War: The Aftermath of Counterinsurgency in Guatemala.* Albany: State University of New York Press.

Marostica, Matthew. 1998. Religion and Global Affairs: Religious Activation and Democracy in Latin America. *SAIS Review* 18 (2): 45–51.

Marshall, T. H. 1950. *Citizenship and Social Class and Other Essays.* Cambridge: Cambridge University Press.

Martin, David. 1990. *Tongues of Fire: The Explosion of Protestantism in Latin America.* Oxford: Basil Blackwell.

———. 2002. *Pentecostalism: The World Their Parish.* Oxford: Blackwell.

Martini, Pablo Rodas. 2000. *Ante la titubeante política tributaria: El reto es trazar lineamientos de largo plazo.* Guatemala City: Facultad Latinoamericana de Ciencias Sociales.

Massa, Mark. 1999. *Catholics and American Culture: Fulton Sheen, Dorothy Day, and the Notre Dame Football Team.* New York: Crossroad.

Massey, Douglas S., Jorge Durand, and Nolan J. Malone. 2004. *Beyond Smoke and Mirrors: Mexican Immigration in an Age of Economic Integration*. New York: Russell Sage Foundation.

Mauss, Marcel. 1979. Body Technique. In *Sociology and Psychology*. Translated by B. Brewster. London: Routledge and K. Paul.

———. 1990. *The Gift: The Form and Reason for Exchange in Archaic Societies*. Translated by W. D. Halls. New York: W. W. Norton.

McClain, Linda. 2002. The Place of Marriage in Democracy's Formative Project. *Good Society* 11 (3): 50–56.

McCleary, Rachel M. 1997. Guatemala's Postwar Prospects. *Journal of Democracy* 8 (2): 129–143.

McCreery, David, ed. 1994. *Rural Guatemala, 1760–1940*. Stanford: Stanford University Press.

McGrath, Alister, and Darren Marks, eds. 2004. *Blackwell Companion to Protestantism*. Malden, Mass.: Blackwell.

Menaldo, Rolando Escobar, and Ana Maritza Morales. 2000. *Relación estado-contribuyente*. Guatemala City: Facultad Latinoamericana de Ciencias Sociales.

Metz, Brent. 2008. Postcard from Guatemala: The Abduction of a Ladina Girl. *Anthropology News* 49 (1): 28–29.

Metzger, Bruce M., and Roland E. Murphy, eds. 1991. *The New Oxford Annotated Bible, with the Apocryphal/Deuterocanonical Books*. New York: Oxford University Press.

Meyer, Birgit, and Peter Geschiere, eds. 1999. *Globalization and Identity: Dialectics of Flow and Closure*. Oxford: Blackwell.

Miller, Donald. 1997. *Reinventing American Protestantism: Christianity in the New Millennium*. Berkeley: University of California Press.

———. 2007. *Global Pentecostalism: The New Face of Social Engagement*. Berkeley: University of California Press.

Miller, Perry. 1956. *Errand into the Wilderness*. Cambridge: Harvard University Press.

Miller, Peter. 1990. On the Interrelations between Accounting and the State. *Accounting, Organizations and Society* 15 (4): 315–338.

MINUGUA. 2002. *Los linchamientos: Un flagelo que persiste*. Guatemala City: Misión de Verificación de las Naciones Unidas en Guatemala.

Mitchell, Timothy. 2002. *Rule of Experts: Egypt, Techno-Politics, Modernity*. Berkeley: University of California Press.

Miyazaki, Hirokazu. 2006. Economy of Dreams: Hope in Global Capitalism and Its Critiques. *Cultural Anthropology* 21 (2): 147–172.

Moltmann, Jürgen. 1996. *The Coming of God: Christian Eschatology*. Translated by M. Kohl. Minneapolis: Fortress Press.

Morán Mérida, Amanda. 1997. *Condiciones de vida y tenencia de la tierra en asentamientos precarios de la Ciudad de Guatemala*. Guatemala City: Centro de Estudios Urbanos y Regionales, Universidad de San Carlos.

Morgan, Patricia. 1995. *Farewell to the Family? Public Policy and Family Breakdown in Britain and the USA.* London: Institute of Economic Affairs.

Morris, Brian. 1994. *Anthropology of the Self: The Individual In Cultural Perspective.* London: Pluto Press.

Murphy, Edward. 2004. Developing Sustainable Peripheries: The Limits of Citizenship in Guatemala City. *Latin American Perspectives* 31 (6): 48–68.

Nelson, Diane. 1999. *A Finger in the Wound: Body Politics in Quincentennial Guatemala.* Berkeley: University of California Press.

———. 2003. The More You Kill the More You Will Live: The Maya, "Race," and Biopolitical Hopes for Peace in Guatemala. In *Race, Nature, and the Politics of Difference.* Edited by D. Moore, J. Kosek, and A. Pandian. Durham: Duke University Press.

Nimatuj, Irma Alicia Velásquez. 2002. *La pequeña burgesia indígena comercial de Guatemala.* Guatemala City: Asociación para el Avance de las Ciencias Sociales en Guatemala.

Nock, Steven. 1998. *Marriage and Men's Lives.* Oxford: Oxford University Press.

O'Donnell, Mary Ellen. 2006. Cultural Catholics in America: Narrative, Authority and Identity since Vatican II. Ph.D. diss., University of North Carolina, Chapel Hill.

Offit, Thomas A. 2008. *Conquistadores de la Calle: Child Street Labor in Guatemala City.* Austin: University of Texas Press.

Oglesby, Elizabeth. 2004. Corporate Citizenship? Elites, Labor, and the Geographies of Work in Guatemala. *Environment and Planning D: Society and Space* 22: 553–572.

Okin, Susan. 1992. Women, Equality and Citizenship. *Queen's Quarterly* 99: 56–71.

Olcese, Orlando, Ramón Moreno, and Francisco Ibarra. 1977. *The Guatemala Earthquake of 1976: A Review of Its Effects and of the Contribution of the United Nations Family.* Guatemala City: United Nations Development Program.

Olson, Ernest. 2001. Signs of Conversion, Spirit of Commitment: The Pentecostal Church in the Kingdom of Tonga. *Journal of Ritual Studies* 15 (2): 13–26.

O'Malley, Pat. 1992. Risk, Power, and Crime Prevention. *Economy & Society* 21 (3): 252–275.

———. 1996. Risk and Responsibility. In *Foucault and Political Reason: Liberalism, Neo-Liberalism, and Rationalities of Government.* Edited by A. Barry, T. Osborne, and N. Rose. Chicago: University of Chicago Press.

———. 2004. *Risk, Uncertainty and Government.* London: Macmillan Education.

O'Neill, Bruce. 2009. The Political Agency of Cityscapes: Spatializing Governance in Ceauşescu's Bucharest. *Journal of Social Archeology* 9 (2): 92–109.

O'Neill, Kevin Lewis. 2005. Writing Guatemala's Genocide: Christianity and Truth and Reconciliation Commissions. *Journal for Genocide Research* 7 (3): 310–331.

————. 2007. Armed Citizens and the Stories They Tell: The National Rifle Association, Masculinity, and Rhetoric. *Journal of Men and Masculinities* 9 (4): 457–475.

————. 2009. But Our Citizenship Is in Heaven: A Proposal for the Study of Christian Citizenship in the Global South. *Citizenship Studies* 15 (3): forthcoming.

Orellana Gonzáles, René Arturo. 1978. *Guatemala: Migraciones internas de poblacíon, 1950–1973.* Guatemala City: Universidad de San Carlos.

Orsi, Robert. 1985. *The Madonna of 115th Street: Faith and Community in Italian Harlem, 1880–1950.* New Haven: Yale University Press.

————. 1996. *Thank You, St. Jude: Women's Devotions to the Patron Saint of Hopeless Causes.* New Haven: Yale University Press.

————. 2005. *The Religious Worlds People Make and the Scholars Who Study Them.* Princeton: Princeton University Press.

Ortega Gaytá, Jorge Antonio. 2003. *Los Kaibiles.* Guatemala City: Centro Editorial y de Documentación para la Historia Militar.

Paley, Julia. 2001. *Marketing Democracy: Power and Social Movements in Post-Dictatorship Chile.* Berkeley: University of California Press.

Parsons, Talcott. 1963. Christianity and Modern Industrial Society. In *Sociological Theory, Values, and Sociocultural Change: Essays in honor of Pitirim A. Sorokin.* Edited by E. A. Tiryakian. New York: Free Press.

————. 1971. *The System of Modern Societies.* Englewood Cliffs: Prentice-Hall.

Peace Accords. 2006. *Guatemala acuerdos de paz para todos.* Guatemala City: Editorial Piedra Santa.

Pedersen, David. 2008. Brief Event: The Value of Getting to Value in the Era of "Globalization." *Anthropological Theory* 8 (1): 57–77.

Peirce, Charles. 1955. Logic as Semiotic: The Theory of Sign. In *Philosophical Writings of Peirce.* Edited by J. Buchler. New York: Dover.

Petersen, Kurt. 1992. *The Maquiladora Revolution in Guatemala.* New Haven: Orville H. Schell, Jr., Center for International Human Rights at Yale Law School.

Pew Forum. 2006. *Spirit and Power: A 10-Nation Survey of Pentecostals by the Pew Forum on Religion and Public Life.* Washington, D.C.: Pew Forum on Religion and Public Life.

————. 2008. *Historical Overview of Pentecostalism in Guatemala.* Washington, D.C.: Pew Forum on Religion and Public Life.

Pinillos, Ileana Contreras. 1977. Desarrollo histórico urbanístico de la Zona 1 de la Ciudad de Guatemala de 1776 a 1976. Ph.D. diss., Universidad de San Carlos de Guatemala.

Poewe, Karla, ed. 1994. *Charismatic Christianity as a Global Culture.* Columbia: University of South Carolina Press.

Pope, Stephen, ed. 2002. *The Ethics of Aquinas.* Washington, D.C.: Georgetown University Press.

Portes, Alejandro, and Bryan R. Roberts. 2004. The Free Market City: Latin American Urbanization in the Years of Neoliberal Adjustment. Report for the Center for the Study of Urbanization and Internal Migration in Developing Countries. Austin: Population Research Center, University of Texas at Austin.

Postero, Nancy Grey. 2004. Articulations and Fragmentations: Indigenous Politics in Bolivia. In *The Struggle for Indigenous Rights in Latin America*. Edited by N. G. Postero and L. Zamosc. Brighton: Sussex Academic Press.

———. 2007. *Now We Are Citizens: Indigenous Politics in Postmulticultural Bolivia.* Stanford: Stanford University Press.

Pratt, Mary Louise. 1991. Arts of the Contact Zone. *Profession* 91:33–40.

Prechtel, Martín. 1998. *Secrets of the Talking Jaguar: Memoirs from the Living Heart of a Mayan Village.* New York: Penguin Putnam.

Putnam, Robert. 2000. *Bowling Alone: The Collapse and Revival of American Community.* New York: Simon and Schuster.

Rand, Ayn. 1957. *Atlas Shrugged.* New York: Random House.

Ranger, Terence O. 2008. *Evangelical Christianity and Democracy in Africa.* New York: Oxford University Press.

Rantanen, Terhi. 2005. Cosmopolitanization—Now! An Interview with Ulrich Beck. *Global Media and Communication* 1 (3): 247–263.

Remarque, Erich Maria. 1929. *All Quiet on the Western Front.* Translated by A. W. Wheen. Boston: Little, Brown.

REMHI. 1998. *Guatemala, nunca más. Proyecto interdiocesano de recuperación de la memoria histórica.* 4 vols. Guatemala City: Oficina de Derechos Humanos Arzobispado de Guatemala.

Robbins, Joel. 1998. On Reading "World News": Apocalyptic Narrative, Negative Nationalism, and Transnational Christianity in a Papua New Guinea Society. *Social Analysis* 42:103–130.

———. 2001. Introduction: Global Religions, Pacific Island Transformations. *Journal of Ritual Studies* 15 (2): 7–12.

———. 2003. What Is a Christian? Notes toward an Anthropology of Christianity. *Religion* 33 (3): 191–199.

———2004a. *Becoming Sinners: Christianity and Moral Torment in a Papua New Guinea Society.* Berkeley: University of California Press.

———. 2004b. The Globalization of Pentecostal and Charismatic Christianity. *Annual Review of Anthropology* 33: 117–143.

Roberts, Bryan R. 1973. *Organizing Strangers: Poor Families in Guatemala City.* Austin: University of Texas Press.

Romano, David Gilman. 2004. When the Games Began: Sport, Religion and Politics Converged in Ancient Olympia. *Archaeology Odyssey* 7 (4): 12–21.

Rosaldo, Renato. 1989. *Culture and Truth: The Remaking of Social Analysis.* Boston: Beacon Press.

————. 1994. Cultural Citizenship and Educational Democracy. *Cultural Anthropology* 9 (3): 402–411.

Rose, Nikolas. 1987. Beyond the Public/Private Division: Law, Power and the Family. *Journal of Law and Society* 14 (1): 61–75.

————. 1990. *Governing the Soul: The Shaping of the Private Self.* London: Routledge.

————. 1996a. *Inventing Our Selves: Psychology, Power, and Personhood.* Cambridge: Cambridge University Press.

————. 1996b. Governing "Advanced" Liberal Democracies. In *Foucault and Political Reason: Liberalism, Neo-Liberalism and Rationalities of Government.* Edited by A. Barry, T. Osborne, and N. Rose. Chicago: University of Chicago Press.

————. 1999. *Power of Freedom: Reframing Social Thought.* Cambridge: Cambridge University Press.

————. 2007. *The Politics of Life Itself: Biomedicine, Power, and Subjectivity in the Twenty-First Century.* Princeton: Princeton University Press.

Rose, Nikolas, and Peter Miller. 1992. Political Power beyond the State: Problematics of Government. *British Journal of Sociology* 43 (2): 173–205.

Rose, Nikolas, and Mariana Valverde. 1998. Governed by Law? *Social and Legal Studies* 7 (4): 541–553.

Said, Edward. 1978. *Orientalism.* New York: Pantheon Books.

Sanford, Victoria. 2003a. *Buried Secrets: Truth and Human Rights in Guatemala.* New York: Palgrave Macmillan.

————. 2003b. *Violencia y genocidio en Guatemala.* Guatemala City: F&G Editores.

————. 2008. Femicide in Guatemala. *ReVista* 7 (2): 21–22.

Sassen, Sasski. 2001. *The Global City: New York, London, Tokyo.* Princeton: Princeton University Press.

Scheper–Hughes, Nancy. 1995. Primacy of the Ethical: Propositions for a Militant Anthropology. *Current Anthropology* 36 (3): 409–420.

Schirmer, Jennifer. 1998. *The Guatemalan Military Project: A Violence Called Democracy.* Philadelphia: University of Pennsylvania Press.

Schlesinger, Stephen E., and Stephen Kinzer. 1999. *Bitter Fruit: The Story of the American Coup in Guatemala.* Cambridge: Harvard University David Rockefeller Center for Latin American Studies.

Seligson, Mitchell, and Minora A. Azpuru. 2004. *La cultura política de la democracia en Guatemala.* Guatemala City: Asociación de Investigación y Estudios Sociales.

Shah, Timothy Samuel. 2004. The Bible and the Ballot Box: Evangelicals and Democracy in the Global South. *SAIS Review* 24 (2): 117–132.

Sherman, Amy. 1997. *The Soul of Development: Biblical Christianity and Economic Transformation in Guatemala.* Oxford: Oxford University Press.

Sieder, Rachel. 1999. Rethinking Democratisation and Citizenship: Legal Pluralism and Institutional Reform in Guatemala. *Citizenship Studies* 3 (1): 103–118.

Sierra, Oscar, Hans Siebers, and Luis Samandu. 1990. *Guatemala: Retos de la Iglesia Católica en una sociedad en crisis.* San José: DEI.

Silverstein, Michael, and Greg Urban. 1996. The Natural History of Discourse. In *Natural Histories of Discourse.* Edited by M. Silverstein and G. Urban. Chicago: University of Chicago Press.

Simmel, Georg. [1909] 1997. Bridge and Door. In *Rethinking Architecture: A Reader in Cultural Theory.* Edited by N. Leach. London: Routledge.

Simpson, Alan. 1978. The Covenanted Community. In *Religion in American History: Interpretative Essays.* Edited by J. M. Mulder and J. F. Wilson. Englewood Cliffs: Prentice-Hall.

Smilde, David. 1998. "Letting God Govern": Supernatural Agency in the Venezuelan Pentecostal Approach to Social Change. *Sociology of Religion* 59 (3): 287–303.

———. 2007. *Reason to Believe: Cultural Agency in Latin American Evangelicalism.* Berkeley: University of California Press.

Smith, Andrea. 2008. *Native Americans and the Christian Right: The Gendered Politics of Unlikely Alliances.* Durham: Duke University Press.

Smith, Carol A. 1984. El desarollo de la primacia urbana en Guatemala. *Mesoamerica* 8: 195–278.

———, ed. 1990. *Guatemalan Indians and the State, 1540 to 1988.* Austin: University of Texas Press.

Smith, Gerald Birney. 1919. Making Christianity Safe for Democracy: IV, Christianity and Political Democracy. *Biblical World* 53 (4): 408–423.

Smith, Jonathan Z. 1978. *Map Is Not Territory: Studies in the History of Religions.* Leiden: Brill.

Smith, Michael Peter. 2001. *Transnational Urbanism: Locating Globalization.* Malden, Mass.: Blackwell.

Snyder, Rachel Claire. 1999. *Citizen-Soldiers and Manly Warriors: Military Service and Gender in the Republican Tradition.* Lanham, Md.: Rowman and Littlefield.

———. 2003. The Citizen-Soldier Tradition and Gender Integration of the U.S. Military. *Armed Forces & Society* 29 (2): 185–204.

Soja, Edward. 2000. *Postmetropolis: Critical Studies of Cities and Regions.* Oxford: Blackwell.

Sridhar, Archana. 2007. Tax Reform and Promoting a Culture of Philanthropy: Guatemala's Third Sector in an Era of Peace. *Fordham International Law Journal* 31 (1): 186–229.

Steigenga, Tim. 1999. Guatemala. In *Religious Freedom and Evangelization in Latin America: The Challenge of Religious Pluralism.* Edited by P. Sigmund. Maryknoll, N.Y.: Orbis Books.

Stoll, David, ed. 1990. *Is Latin America Turning Protestant? The Politics of Evangelical Growth*. Berkeley: University of California Press.

———. 1993. *Between Two Armies in the Ixil Towns of Guatemala*. New York: Columbia University Press.

———. 1994. "Jesus Is Lord of Guatemala": Evangelical Reform in a Death-Squad State. In *Accounting for Fundamentalisms: The Dynamic Character of Movements*. Edited by M. E. Marty and S. Appleby. Chicago: University of Chicago Press.

Stout, Harry S. 1991. *The Divine Dramatist: George Whitefield and the Rise of Modern Evangelicalism*. Grand Rapids: Wm. B. Eerdmans.

Strauss, Barry. 2003. Reflections on the Citizen-Soldier. *Parameter* Summer: 66–77.

Sullivan-González, Douglass. 1998. *Piety, Power, and Politics: Religion and Nation Formation in Guatemala, 1821–1871*. Pittsburgh: University of Pittsburgh Press.

Sutherland, Anne. 1998. *The Making of Belize: Globalization in the Margins*. Westport, Conn.: Bergin and Garvey.

Swartz, David. 1997. *Culture and Power: The Sociology of Pierre Bourdieu*. Chicago: University of Chicago Press.

Taussig, Michael. 1987. *Shamanism, Colonialism, and the Wild Man: A Study in Terror and Healing*. Chicago: University of Chicago Press.

Thomas, Kedron. 2006. The 1976 Earthquake in Guatemala. *ReVista* 6 (2): 8–9.

Thomas, Kedron, and Peter Benson. 2008. Dangers of Insecurity in Postwar Guatemala: Gangs, Electoral Politics, and Structural Violence. *ReVista* 7 (2): 39–41.

Thomas, Philip. 2002. The River, the Road, and the Rural-Urban Divide: A Postcolonial Moral Geography from Southeast Madagascar. *American Ethnologist* 29 (2): 366–391.

Thompson, Leonard. 1985. *The Political Mythology of Apartheid*. New Haven: Yale University Press.

Thumma, Scott, and Dave Travis. 2007. *Beyond Megachurch Myths: What We Can Learn from America's Largest Churches*. San Francisco: Jossey-Bass.

Tocqueville, Alexis de. [1835–1840] 2004. *Democracy in America*. New York: Penguin Putnam.

Tomlinson, Matt. 2009. *In God's Image: The Metaculture of Fijian Christianity*. Berkeley: University of California Press.

Trouillot, Michel-Rolph. 1991. Anthropology and the Savage Slot: The Poetics and Politics of Otherness. In *Recapturing Anthropology: Working in the Present*. Edited by R. Fox. Santa Fe: School of American Research Press.

Turner, Bryan. 1986. *Citizenship and Capitalism: The Debate over Reformism*. London: Allen and Unwin.

———. 1990. Outline of a Theory of Citizenship. *Sociology* 24 (2): 189–217.

———. 1993. Contemporary Problems in the Theory of Citizenship. In *Citizenship and Social Theory*. Edited by B. Turner. London: Sage.

Tyler, Stephen. 1991. Post-Modern Ethnography. In *Writing Cultures: The Poetics and Politics of Ethnography.* Edited by J. Clifford and G. Marcus. Berkeley: University of California Press.

UNDP. 2004a. La democracia en América Latina: Hacia una democracia de ciudadanas y ciudadanos. New York: United Nations Development Programme.

———. 2004b. *Democracy in Latin America: Towards a Citizens' Democracy.* New York: United Nations Development Programme.

UNFPA. 1999. *6 Billion: A Time for Choices.* New York: United Nations Population Fund.

United Nations. 2006. *Department of Economic and Social Affairs, Population Division, World Urbanization Prospects: The 2005 Revision.* Washington, D.C.: United Nations.

USAID. 2001. *Guatemala Tax and Investment Policy Reform Program: Fiscal Reform in Support of Trade Liberalization.* Washington, D.C.: United States Agency for International Development.

———. 2005. *Reflections on Community-Based Policing Programming in Guatemala.* Washington, D.C.: United States Agency for International Development.

———. 2006. *Central America and Mexico Gang Assessment.* Washington, D.C.: Bureau For Latin American and Caribbean Affairs, Office Of Regional Sustainable Development.

U.S. State Department. 2006. Background Note: Guatemala, Electronic Document, www.state.gov/r/pa/ei/bgn/2045.htm (accessed March 5, 2009).

Valdez, José Fernando. 2000. *La viabilidad de un pacto fiscal en Guatemala: Para los empresarios y la sociedad civil.* Guatemala City: Facultad Latinoamericana de Ciencias Sociales.

Valverde, Mariana. 1998. *Diseases of the Will: Alcohol and the Dilemmas of Freedom.* Cambridge: Cambridge University Press.

Véliz, Rodrigo J. 2006. Nuevas formas de "privatizar" lo público: Los vendedores informales del centro y la municipalidad, www.albedrio.org/htm/documentos/vendedoresRJV001.pdf.

Verdery, Katherine. 1998. Transnationalism, Nationalism, Citizenship, and Property. *American Ethnologist* 25 (2): 291–306.

Vintges, Karen. 2001. Must We Burn Foucault? Ethics as Art of Living: Simone de Beauvoir and Michel Foucault. *Continental Philosophy Review* 34 (2): 165–181.

Wacker, Grant. 1984. The Functions of Faith in Primitive Pentecostalism. *Harvard Theological Review* 77 (3/4): 353–375.

———. 2001. *Heaven Below: Early Pentecostals and American Culture.* Cambridge: Harvard University Press.

Walzer, Michael. 1989. Citizenship. In *Political Innovation and Conceptual Change.* Edited by T. Bell, J. Far, and R. L. Hanson. Cambridge: Cambridge University Press.

————. 1992. The Civil Society Argument. In *Dimensions of Radical Democracy: Pluralism, Citizenship and Community.* Edited by C. Mouffe. London: Routledge.

Warren, Kay. 1998. *Indigenous Movements and Their Critics: Pan-Maya Activism in Guatemala.* Princeton: Princeton University Press.

Weber, Max. [1905] 2002. *The Protestant Ethic and the Spirit of Capitalism.* Los Angeles: Roxbury Publishing.

————. [1921] 1958. *The City.* Glencoe, Ill.: Free Press.

Webre, Stephen. 1989. *La sociedad colonial en Guatemala: Estudios regionales y locales.* Antigua, Guatemala: Centro de Investigaciones Regionales de Mesoamérica.

————. 1990. Water and Society in a Spanish American City: Santiago de Guatemala, 1555–1773. *Hispanic American Historical Review* 70 (1): 57–84.

West, Cornel. 2004. Democracy Matters. Address delivered at the Aurora Forum, Stanford University, September 30.

Wilcox, W. Bradford. 2004. *Soft Patriarchs, New Men: How Christianity Shapes Fathers and Husbands.* Chicago: University of Chicago Press.

Williams, Marilyn Thornton. 1991. *Washing "The Great Unwashed": Public Baths in Urban America, 1840–1920.* Columbus: Ohio State University Press.

Williams, Raymond. 1973. *The Country and the City.* Oxford: Oxford University Press.

Williams, Rhys H., ed. 2001. *Promise Keepers and the New Masculinity: Private Lives and Public Morality.* Lanham, Md.: Lexington Books.

Winthrop, John. 1838. A Modell of Christian Charity. In *Collections of the Massachusetts Historical Society,* vol. 3. Boston: Massachusetts Historical Society.

World Bank. 2000. *World Development Report, 2000/2001: Attacking Poverty.* New York: Oxford University Press.

World Health Organization. 2002. *World Report on Violence and Health.* Washington, D.C.: World Health Organization.

Yanagisako, Sylvia, and Carol Delaney, eds. 1995. *Naturalizing Power: Essays in Feminist Cultural Analysis.* New York: Routledge.

Young, Iris Marion. 1990. *Justice and the Politics of Difference.* Princeton: Princeton University Press.

————. 1996. Communication and the Other: Beyond Deliberative Democracy. In *Democracy and Difference.* Edited by S. Benhabib. Princeton: Princeton University Press.

Zamosc, Leon. 2004. The Indian Movement in Ecuador: From Politics of Influence to Politics of Power. In *The Struggle for Indigenous Rights in Latin America.* Edited by N. G. Postero and L. Zamosc. Brighton: Sussex Academic Press.

Zinn, Howard. 1980. *A People's History of the United States: 1492–Present.* New York: Harper and Row.

INDEX

Abraham, 7, 122

Adam, 27, 71–722

Africa, xxii, 7, 9, 10, 52, 158, 174, 177, 180, 210, 236n1

agency, 35, 93, 114, 223n11, 236n33

Agreement on the Identity and Rights of Indigenous Peoples, 19

alcoholism, 68, 71, 110, 112, 118, 137, 155, 186

All Quiet on the Western Front, 87, 89, 112, 113

Almolonga, 180, 186, 187, 189

Alta Verapaz, 178

alterity, 144, 149

Althoff, Andrea, 219n11

Althusser, Louis, 33, 56–57

ambivalence, xv, 30, 84, 90, 92, 169

Amnesty International, 12, 21, 37

Anderson, Benedict, 7, 240n8

Anglicanism, 160, 184, 241n14

Antigua, 147

apocalypse, 54, 66, 142, 194

Appadurai, Arjun, 16; 157

Aquinas, Thomas, 28–29, 61, 225n2

Arbenz, Jacobo, 17

Arendt, Hannah, 27, 84

Arévalo, Juan José, 148

Argentina, 172, 175, 179, 189

Aristotle, 61, 225n2

Armenia, 175

Arriola, Arturo Taracena, 220n23

Arthur, Kay, 74, 76

Aruba, 173

Arzú, Álvaro, 40–43

Asia, xxii, 9, 10, 16, 174, 180, 236n1

aspirational document, 34

Asturias, Miguel Angel, 150

Atlanta, 188, 191

Atlas Shrugged, 205

attitude, xxv, 45–51, 55, 57–59, 62, 70, 72, 74, 81, 85, 129, 213, 236

audiocassettes, xx, 16, 66, 67, 69, 70, 73, 191, 217n15

Augustine, 28–29, 52, 60, 71, 72, 227n12

Austin, John, 73, 228n26

Australia, 180

Aycinena, Juan José de, 7

Azusa Street Revival, 9

Babel, Tower of, 7

Badiou, Alain, 202

Baja Verapaz, 178

intimacy, 24, 62, 73, 130, 132, 136, 137, 205
Iran, 180
Iraq, 180, 206
Islam, 189, 217
Israel, 7–8, 170, 171, 180, 184, 239n1
Italy, 174, 180
Izabal, 178

Jacobs, Cindy, 179, 188, 191
Jalapa, 178
Japan, 180
Jenkins, Philip, 240n4
Jericho, 2
Jordan, 180
Joyce, Patrick, xxiv, 224n11, 228n24
Juarez, Mexico, 21
Jung, Carl, 60
Jutiapa, 178

Kaibiles, 87–88, 91, 93, 110
Kansas, 9, 180
Keane, Webb, xxvii
Keenan, James, 226n3
Kenya, 175
kinship, 217n17, 222n5
Kundera, Milan, 6, 212–213, 219n7
Kunneman, Brenda, 188
Kunneman, Hank, 188, 191
Kuwait, 180

ladino, xviii, 10, 17, 19, 20, 31, 32, 149–151, 217n11
Latinobarómetro, 37, 38
Latour, Bruno, 211
Levenson-Estrada, Deborah, xxiii
Levinas, Emmanuel, 168, 232n28, 239n26
liberalism, 148, 161, 163, 203, 206, 228n24, 236n33
liberation theology, 24
The Life of the Mind, 84
literary turn, xxvi
Locke, John, 65, 227n12
Lofton, Kathryn, 238n19, 238n20
loneliness, 113
Los Angeles Times, 9
Luther, Martin, 62, 226n3
Lutheran Church, 221n33
Lutz, Catherine A., 236n3

Lux, Otila, 47
lynching, 22, 237n11

Machiavelli, 230n4
magic, 161, 163, 206, 231n14
Mahmood, Saba, 217n13, 236n33
Malinowski, Bronislaw, 222n5, 231n14
Malkki, Liisa, 155, 239n3
Mann, Michael, 217n17, 220n19
mano dura, 92
Manos de Amor, 143–147
maquiladora, 26
Martin, David, 174, 218
Maryland, 188
masculinity, 117, 119, 231n21, 235n31
Massachusetts Bay Colony, 241n13
massacre, 18, 88, 91, 92
Massey, Douglas, 235n28
Mauss, Marcel, 165
Maya, 17–20, 32, 34, 91, 96–101, 147–152, 159–165
McCreery, David, 220n23
Medellín, 20
mega-church, definition of, 216n5
Metz, Brent, 237n11
Mexican-American border, 59, 133
Mexico, 92, 172–176, 179, 189, 193–197, 235n28
Miami, 52, 158, 192
Michigan, 188
Microsoft, 175, 240n7
middle-class, xviii–xx, 2, 65, 120, 126, 134, 141, 145, 157
Middle East, 180, 189, 210, 224
Miller, Donald, 175
Miller, Perry, 207, 208, 241n14
Miller, Peter, xxiv
Mississippi, 180
Mitchell, Timothy, 220n20
Modern Man in Search of a Soul, 60
Molina, Otto Perez, 92
Moltmann, Jürgen, 239n1
Montículo de la Culbera, 98
Montt, Efraín Ríos, 12, 13, 24, 25
moral geography, 144, 166, 167, 236n2
morality, 3, 77, 126, 155, 186, 218n2, 232n1
moral manual, 52, 60, 61, 76, 77, 79, 81, 86
moral weight, 5–6, 15, 34–40

Moses, 7, 142
motherhood, 117, 122, 137, 139, 140, 161
Mozambique, 172, 175, 180, 187, 190, 206
multicultural, 5
multinational corporations, 4, 118, 212, 214
Municipal Citizen Security Council
municipal government, 64

Nebraska, 188
Nelson, Diane, 20, 149, 220n26
Nemo, Philippe, 232n28
neoliberalism, 36, 37, 58, 236n1
neo-Pentecostalism, definition of, 10–11
Newton, Isaac, 211
New York, 130, 180, 191
New Zealand, 179, 180, 181
Nicaragua, 97, 175, 177, 179
Nietzsche, Friedrich, 6, 203, 213, 219n7
Nigeria, 175
Noah, 7
North Korea, 180

Offit, Thomas, xxiii
O'Malley, Pat, xxiv
The Order of Things, xxiv
Oremos, 102–106, 111
organized crime, 4, 20, 39, 85, 155, 199
Orientalism, 164
Orsi, Robert, 4
Oslo Accord, 18

Pacheco, Marta Pilon de, 8.
Pakistan, 180
Paley, Julia, 4, 11, 44, 223n11
Panama, 13, 179
panopticon, 32, 65, 72, 74, 150, 227n11
Paraguay, 180
participation, paradox of, 4, 223n11
pastoral, xxiv
Paul, 71, 88
Peace Accords, 1996, 18–19, 31, 34, 36,
    39–41, 62, 89–92, 199, 210, 211
Pedersen, David, 215
Peirce, Charles, 222n4
Pentecostalism, definition of, 9–10
Pérez, Samuel, 50
Peru, 173, 175, 179
Petén, 99, 105, 152, 178

Pew Project, 175, 219n11
Piel, Jean, 220n23
Plato, 61, 225n2, 228n15
Poland, 175
policing, 22, 61–65, 73, 85–86, 226n7
population, 115, 118, 232n1
Portugal, 173, 180
Pratt, Mary Louise, 99
Prechtel, Martín, 150
preferential option for the poor, 10
priest, 23
private security, 21, 22, 62, 84, 151, 226n5
private sphere, 15, 220n18
privatization, 36, 37, 144
problematization, 117, 120, 122, 233n6
progenitor, 126, 127
El Progreso, 178
Promise Keepers, 119, 233n5
prosperity, 10, 35, 186
Protestant, 8–13, 22–25, 160–163, 182–183
prudentialism, 124, 234n15
The Psychic Life of Power, 56
public sphere, 3, 15, 218n4, 220n18, 230n4
Puerto Rico, 179, 188
Puritans, 7, 184–185, 207–208, 241n14
purity, 160, 190, 241n14
Putnam, Robert, 90

Quetzalcoatl, 100
Quetzaltenango, 24, 152, 159
Quiché, 178
Qur'an, 142

radio, 10, 12, 32, 152, 173, 208
Rand, Ayn, 206, 212
Recuperación de la Memoria Histórica, 91,
    210
Red Cross, 37
Reformation, 207–208, 226n3, 235n31
Remarque, Erich Maria, 87, 89, 112, 113
REMHI. See Recuperación de la Memoria
    Histórica
remittances, 36, 131
responsibility, 5–6, 15, 34–40, 102, 168,
    232n28, 239n26
Retalhuleu, 152, 178
Revelation, Book of, 89
revolution, 33, 47, 55, 56, 114, 150, 179

Río San José, 156
Robbins, Joel, xxii, xxvii, 219n11
Roberts, Bryan, xxiii
Roman Catholicism, xxi, xxvii, xxviii,
　7–12, 23, 78, 91, 121, 161, 168, 183, 184,
　210
Rose, Nikolas, 50, 75, 125, 220n19, 223n11,
　228n5, 229n31
Russia, 174, 175, 180, 182

Sacatepéquez, 178
Said, Edward, 164
salvation, national, 2, 66, 78, 181, 182, 192
sanctification, 62
Sanford, Victoria, 21, 40
San Marcos, 152, 178, 199
Santa Maria, 52, 158
Santa Rosa, 178
Satan, 10, 24, 25, 88–89, 95–96, 102–103,
　113, 135, 218n6
satellite church, 10, 152, 170, 173, 176, 186,
　193, 208
Schirmer, Jennifer, 91, 210
science, 161, 163
scorched-earth, 18
secular, 31, 89, 204, 210
security, private, 21, 22, 62, 84, 151, 226n5
self-help, 61, 62, 126, 129
self-regulating subjects, xv
September 11, 2001, 210
Serrano, Jorge, 12–13
The 700 Club, 12
Sieder, Rachel, 220n23
Simmel, Georg, 146
Singapore, 175
Smilde, David, 221n30
Smith, Carol A., 220n23
Smith, Jonathan Z., 161, 238n21
Snyder, Rachel Claire, 230n4
Social Darwinism, 161
Sololá, 178
South Africa, 11, 175, 176
South Korea, 11, 25, 26, 110, 172, 175–177,
　180, 187, 190
Soy la Revolución, 33, 55, 183
Spain, 7, 17, 147, 148, 173, 174
speaking in tongues, 9, 10, 94, 105, 127, 183
spiritual cartography, 88

spiritual mapping, 99, 100, 108
spiritual warfare, 88–90, 93–96
Stevens, Wallace, 203
stewardship, xxii
structural adjustment, xxiv
subjectivity, 14, 15, 49, 216n4
Suchitepequez, 178
Swartz, David, 216n9
Switzerland, 179

Taussig, Michael, 238n23
tax, 34–36, 93, 108, 167, 208, 212,
　224n14–15
technology, 50, 52, 75, 117, 123–125, 128,
　234n12–13
television, 10, 12, 32, 40, 152, 173
testimony, 10, 77, 89, 98
Texas, 9, 130, 180, 188
Titonicapán, 178
Thailand, 175
theology, 29, 61, 87, 183, 184, 205, 217n17
Theroux, Paul, 150
Tocqueville, Alexis de, 11, 101, 210, 220n18
Toronto, 180
Totonicapán, 152, 159
Tower of Babel, 7
traje, 149, 156, 157, 159
transnational governmentality, 16
transnationalism, 16, 171–176, 178, 181, 191,
　192
Tucurú, 159
Tu Eres la Ciudad, 33, 40–46, 53, 57, 58
Tufts University, xix
Turkey, 175
Turner, Bryan, 217n17
Turner, Victor, xxvii

Ubico, Jorge, 148
Uganda, 175
uncanny, 192
undocumented, 39, 131, 151, 220n21, 235n28
UNICEF, 37
United Fruit Company, 17
United Nations, 8, 18, 22, 35, 91, 210
United Nations Development Programme,
　35, 211
United States Conference of Catholic
　Bishops, 240n11

Text:	11.25/13.5 Adobe Garamond
Display:	Adobe Garamond
Compositor:	International Typesetting and Composition
Printer & Binder:	Sheridan Books, Inc.